Praise for John Chaffee's
THE THINKER'S WAY

"*The Thinker's Way* is not a self-help book. This is what you must read *before* you read a self-help book. Indeed, this is a book that you must read before you make too many more bad decisions. John Chaffee has written the thinking person's book on thinking. This work has depth *and* breadth, yet remains accessible and readable from the first page to the last."

— NELSON DeMILLE,
author of *Plum Island* and *The General's Daughter*

"Just a thought: Plato may have had it right when he said, 'The life which is unexamined is not worth living.' At least that's what John Chaffee believes. He just penned a beautifully insightful book called *The Thinker's Way*. His premise: Thinking is so crucial for any kind of rich life, even though it goes against the grain of a society that moves so quickly there is hardly time to think. Slow down enough to read this one."

— JAMIE TALAN,
New York Newsday

"If you thought you were done with personal growth materials — wait! John Chaffee is right; we are in a world of nonthinkers. Read *The Thinker's Way*, and you'll discover new thinking skills that will help you interpret life, make choices and become more creative in every aspect of your life."

— DONNA PAZ,
The Reader's Edge

"What a subversive, radical idea — that we can use our faculties of thinking and reasoning to improve our lives.... In an era of mindless 'step' books, John Chaffee identifies the true steps to living a mindful life. He shows in a clear and compelling way how we can combat irrationality and make wiser judgments — and, most of all, why we should want to."

— CAROL TAVRIS, Ph.D.,
author of *The Mismeasure of Woman*

"Superb.... Beginning with the provocative assertion that 'we have become a society of nonthinkers,' Chaffee sets out to replicate for a trade audience the academic course in critical thinking he created for the City University of New York.... The book provides an excellent course in critical thinking and logical reasoning."

— *Publishers Weekly*

"When did you last examine an issue in depth? ... *The Thinker's Way* not only helps you analyze yourself and improve your ability to think critically, but it addresses how important it is to take the time to examine information, despite today's glut of technology, news, and constant stimulation."

— COURTNEY PULITZER,
The CyberScene

"'It is never too late to be what you might have been' is the wonderful quotation from George Eliot that opens this work. Chaffee follows this help with topics such as living creatively, solving problems, and developing enlightened values. Chaffee includes many Thinking Activities and encourages readers to keep a 'thinking journal.' ... The author, a philosophy professor, shows how to use better reasoning to enhance our lives."

— MARK GUYER,
Library Journal

THE THINKER'S WAY

THE THINKER'S WAY

8 Steps to a Richer Life

John Chaffee, Ph.D.

BACK BAY BOOKS
LITTLE, BROWN

LITTLE, BROWN AND COMPANY

Boston   New York   London

Originally published in hardcover by Little, Brown and Company, 1998
First Back Bay paperback edition, 2000

"Violent End of the Man Called Malcolm," Life magazine, © 1965 by
Time Inc. Reprinted with permission.

Library of Congress Cataloging-in-Publication Data
Chaffee, John.
The thinker's way : 8 steps to a richer life / John Chaffee. —
1st ed.
p.   cm.
ISBN 0-316-13317-5 (hc)/0-316-13333-7 (pb)
1. Critical thinking. 2. Self-actualization (Psychology)
3. Quality of life. I. Title.
BF441.C356   1998
158.1 — DC21   98–18513

10 9 8 7 6 5 4 3 2 1

MV—NY

For Heide

CONTENTS

How to Use This Book

The Thinker's Way is a practical, self-paced guide to a better life; to attaining fulfillment of your potential as a human being. It has the power to enrich every area of your life by showing you how to make full use of your thinking abilities. Can this approach really work for you? Absolutely! Just as it has worked for the many thousands of people who have taken Critical Thinking courses based on my textbooks during the past twenty years. Improving your thinking abilities is the key to achieving success in your career, making intelligent decisions in your personal life, nurturing healthy relationships with friends and family, raising thinking children, revitalizing your life with creative energy, communicating clearly and effectively — in short, providing you the tools to become the extraordinary person you always dreamed you would be.

How can you best make use of *The Thinker's Way* in order to achieve optimal results? Here are some suggestions.

Explore the Table of Contents

THE TABLE of contents introduces all of the important ideas and topics in the book, and it shows you how the book is organized. Use it like a map, developing an understanding of the overall scope of the book as well as individual topics that may be of special interest to you. As you think your way through the book, return to the table of contents often to orient yourself and decide where you want to travel next in the life of your mind.

Focus on the Topics of Most Interest to You

THE CHAPTERS in the book are designed to work together but they also work independently. You don't have to begin on page 1 and read straight through to page 409. Instead, identify the topics that most interest you and begin with them. It makes sense to begin with chapter 1, because it serves as a general introduction to the book. And chapters 2, 3, and 4 are important because they introduce the fundamental principles of thinking that form the core of this approach. Later chapters apply these principles to many different situations: solving problems, communication, relationships, values, controversial issues, creating a life philosophy. The important thing is for you to *think critically* about the sections that are most relevant to you. For example:

- Do you feel your life has become boring and predictable, lacking vitality and creative energy? You may want to begin with Step 2, "Live Creatively," to learn how to identify and express your creative talents.
- Would you like to enhance the romantic relationships in your life? Then turn to page 370 in Step 8, "Think Through Relationships," for practical approaches to nurturing healthy relationships.
- Is there a complex and disturbing problem you are trying to solve? Step 4, "Solve Problems Effectively," will provide a powerful method to guide your thinking and choices.
- Do you feel trapped in patterns that limit your possibilities? The insights in Step 3, "Choose Freely," will help you expand your horizons by identifying new possibilities.
- Are you concerned about raising thoughtful and responsible children? The section "Nurture Thinking Children" on page 379 will show you how to stimulate and guide a child's natural curiosity.
- Do you have difficulty expressing your ideas clearly and persuasively to others? Step 5, "Communicate Successfully," will show you how to become an expert communicator.

In short, customize this book to your own needs and interests. *The Thinker's Way* was created to be a flexible tool, not a rigid set of instructions. Thinking critically about how you use it will produce the quickest and most satisfying results.

Keep a Thinking Notebook

CAN YOU REALLY learn to think better from a book? Yes, provided that you take a participatory approach. You need to be *actively* involved in the experience — thinking, articulating your ideas, evaluating the quality of your reasoning, refining and improving your thinking process. This is why *The Thinker's Way* is built around Thinking Activities, opportunities for you to *apply* the ideas you are reading about to situations in your daily life. As the Greek dramatist Sophocles observed, *"Knowledge must come through action."* Expressing your thinking in a Thinking Notebook is a crucial part of your thinking development. The process of writing stimulates your mind, helps shape your thinking, and enlarges your understanding of yourself and the world. Writing also creates a permanent record — a "snapshot" — of your thinking process that you can refer to and use as a foundation upon which to build more insightful and powerful thinking skills. A specific description of the Thinking Notebook is included on page 20.

Visit *The Thinker's Way* Web site: www.thinkersway.com

THIS WEB SITE contains Thinking Activities that you can use to exercise your mind's "muscle" and apply your critical thinking abilities to current events. New Thinking Activities and other features are added on a regular basis, and you will have the opportunity to share your thinking with others by submitting your responses.

Join "A Thinking World" at www.thinkingworld.com

"A THINKING WORLD" is an online community dedicated to developing a more thoughtful, reflective, and empathetic world in which every person will thrive. An online newsletter, "Creating a Thinking World," will give members the opportunity to share their thinking about important issues as well as productive thinking experiences they have had. Members will also have the ability to communicate with others of shared interests on such topics as becoming more creative, educating thinking people, and developing a morally enlightened world.

Create a Thinking Community of Your Own

WHILE A GREAT deal of thinking can be done on your own, fully developing your thinking abilities involves other people. There is no substitute for the intellectual stimulation of discussing ideas with others. It gives you the opportunity to articulate your ideas and to learn from the thinking of others. In addition to improving your communication skills, it broadens your understanding and also encourages you to be a thinker in an unthinking world. Find people who share your interest in ideas and set aside specific times to discuss particular themes or topics. There are many opportunities for keeping your mind toned with other people: for example, reading groups, writing groups, seminars, and courses.

Commit Yourself to the Life of the Mind

THE PHILOSOPHER Bertrand Russell observed, *"Thought is great and swift and free, the light of the world, and the chief glory of Man."* Just as a vigorous physical workout makes you feel euphoric and energized by releasing endomorphins, exercising your mind has a similar effect. Humans are designed to think, and when we do it well, it brings a profound satisfaction. Thinking deeply is the way we discover ourselves and create a life worth living. Commit yourself to *thinking critically, living creatively,* and *choosing freely.*

Contact the Author

I WELCOME your communication by e-mail (JCthink@aol.com) or standard mail (LaGuardia College, 31-10 Thomson Avenue, Long Island City, NY 11101). I appreciate hearing about which aspects of *The Thinker's Way* you have found most useful, and I welcome questions regarding the themes of the book.

ACKNOWLEDGMENTS

ACCORDING TO MARK TWAIN, "Really great people make you feel that you, too, can become great." *The Thinker's Way* was made possible by the contributions of a number of "great" people. If there is a Platonic ideal for literary agent, then my agent, Heide Lange, fulfills this ideal to perfection. She more than anyone is responsible for helping to shape the central ideas of this book and for finding the perfect publisher to make it a reality. Her astute insight, professional expertise, contagious enthusiasm, and devotion to the book made all the difference.

The Platonic ideal for publisher would have to include Little, Brown and Company as a shining example. Jennifer Josephy, my editor, believed in the promise of this book when it was only a concept, and then nurtured its creation with incisive suggestions and unwavering support. Terry Adams brought a fresh vision and creative energy to the Back Bay edition and I am grateful for his talented contributions. Sarah Crichton, my publisher, embraced the spirit of the book from the beginning and served as its champion with wise guidance and bold initiatives throughout its development. Larry Kirshbaum is the kind of publishing chairman that every author hopes for, a penetrating thinker whose creative energy inspires the same in everyone around him. Linda Biagi intuited the essence of this book immediately, and was able to communicate its message with irresistible enthusiasm and compelling insight. Beth Davey contributed her remarkable talents and personal verve to sharing the book's ideas with many different people, and Heather Rizzo brought a dynamic commitment to her role as publicist. Josh Marwell was invaluable in focusing and communicating the book's themes, while Carl Lennerz and Sairey Luterman devised original marketing approaches for reaching a broad audience. The entire project benefited from the artistic vision of Michael Kaye and Amy Goldfarb, who brought great creativity to the design of the cover and supporting materials. Emily Fromm addressed numerous responsibilities in a thoroughly professional fashion, and Emily Salkin made valuable contributions to this edition. The manuscript also benefited from the thoughtful copyediting of Mike Mattil.

"A friend may be reckoned the masterpiece of Nature," Ralph Waldo Emerson wrote, and I have been fortunate indeed to have many friends who have enriched my professional work over the years. Richard Lieberman has been a source of personal support and wise guidance; Gil Muller has provided insightful counsel on demand; and Janet Lieberman's creative spirit has been an ongoing source of inspiration. I am also indebted to the many faculty, staff, and administrators at La-Guardia College who have contributed to the success of the Critical Thinking program, and to the many thousands of students who have served as its reason for being. Alison Bernstein at the Ford Foundation has been a friend and long-time supporter of my work. I am also indebted to the National Endowment for the Humanities, the Annenberg Foundation, and the Corporation for Public Broadcasting, for their generous support over the years. Among the valued friends who have made specific contributions to my work are Charles and Gloria Mandelstam, Carol Goldberg, and Ken and Lois Lippmann. My friends at Sanford J. Greenburger Associates have been consistently generous in sharing their expertise and heartfelt support.

I want to thank my family, whose extraordinary "greatness" has inspired me in writing *The Thinker's Way* and whose love has infused my own life with richness and purpose. Our lives together have made clear the wisdom of Leo Tolstoy's observation that "the reason of life is for each of us to simply grow in love." My parents, Charlotte and Hubert, surrounded me with devoted love for all of their lives, a love that will always sustain me. My siblings, Judi and David, have contributed loving and sustained family relationships. In addition to being the central joy of my life, my children, Jessie and Joshua, were integral to the creation of this book. They have taught me many important lessons about life and about myself that have been expressed in these pages. Moreover, they were thoughtful reviewers of the manuscript, making wise suggestions that clarified and enhanced what I was trying to express. And finally, I want to thank my wife, Heide. She was the original catalyst for *The Thinker's Way*, and guided its growth through every stage. She devoted herself to bringing out the best thinking of which I was capable, and our shared work on this book reflects the intertwining of our lives together and the love that has knitted us and our family together. "Our hours in love have wings," a poet wrote, and for me this flight has been a lifetime.

THE THINKER'S WAY

TRANSFORM YOURSELF
THROUGH THINKING

It is never too late to be what you might have been.
— GEORGE ELIOT

YOU ARE AN ARTIST, creating your life portrait, and your paints and brushstrokes are the choices you make each day. How do you feel about the portrait you have created so far? Have you defined yourself as the person you always wanted to be, or are you a "work in progress"? Are you achieving your full potential as a human being, "actively exercising your soul's powers" — the ancient Greek definition of happiness *(eudaemonia)*? Or do you feel frustrated, incomplete, unfulfilled, and uncertain how to capture the meaning that you most desire in your life? Have you discovered your purpose in life, the mission that only you can fulfill? Or do you feel rootless, unsure about the direction your life should take? Do you possess a clear philosophy of life that acts as a guiding beacon, illuminating the whole of your life and showing you the path to wisdom and personal fulfillment?

Most of us rarely even stop to ask these questions, and when we do, the answers we struggle for are often unsatisfying, sometimes deeply disturbing. But as George Eliot reminds us, it's not too late for you to become that person you had imagined you would be, to create a vibrant life full of sparkling possibilities and rich in meaning. To do so, you must take the first step in this process: *You need to make a conscious decision to commit yourself to a journey of self-examination and self-transformation.* If your commitment is genuine, and you choose to use your courage and determination to work through the 8 Steps outlined in this book, then you will indeed improve your life in lasting, significant ways. When you complete this journey, you will feel that you are an individual with a mission, not randomly placed on earth, and you will have the personal tools you need to fulfill your mission. You will come to feel in control of your life, effectively steering a course that *you* are mapping, not traveling along roads others have designated for you.

The key to your journey will be learning to make the fullest use of the extraordinary power of your thinking process. It is your thinking process that will enable you to become the person you want to be, to create a life that is rewarding, fulfilling, and successful. Everybody "thinks" — *Homo sapiens* means "thinking man" — but most people don't "think" very well. The purpose of this book is to help you reach your full thinking potential. This kind of transformational process is possible because the thinking process is such an integral part of who we are. When we expand our thinking, we expand who we are as human beings: the perspective from which we view the world, and the concepts and values we use to guide our choices. By exploring your thinking process and using it in carefully designed activities, you can develop it into a powerful, sophisticated tool that will enrich all dimensions of your life. Developing the capacity to examine and refine your thinking process — to "think critically" — initiates a process that transforms the way you view yourself and conduct your business in the world. You will learn to live your life thoughtfully, insightfully, creatively — *The Thinker's Way*.

The Search for a Meaningful Life

Man's search for meaning is the primary motivation in his life. This meaning is unique and specific in that it must and can be fulfilled by him alone; only then does it achieve a significance which will satisfy his own *will* to meaning.

THIS INSIGHT by the psychiatrist and concentration camp survivor Victor Frankl penetrates to the soul of who we are. A well-known Viennese psychiatrist in the 1930s, Dr. Frankl and his family were arrested by the Nazis, and he spent three years in the Auschwitz concentration camp. Every member of his family, including his parents, siblings, and his pregnant wife, was killed. He himself miraculously survived, enduring the most unimaginably abusive and degrading conditions. Following his liberation by Allied troops, he wrote *Man's Search for Meaning*, an enduring and influential work, which he began on scraps of paper during his internment. Since its publication in 1945, it has become an extraordinary bestseller, read by millions of people in twenty languages. Its success reflects the profound hunger for meaning that people are experiencing, trying to answer a question that, in the author's words, *"burns under their fingernails."* This hunger expresses the pervasive meaning*lessness* of our age, the *"existential vacuum"* in which many people exist.

Dr. Frankl discovered that even under the most inhumane of conditions, one can live a life of purpose and meaning. But for the majority of prisoners at Auschwitz, a meaningful life did not seem possible. Immersed in a world that no longer recognized the value of human life and human dignity, that robbed them of their will and made them objects to be exterminated, most inmates suffered a loss of their values. If a prisoner did not struggle against this spiritual destruction with a determined effort to save his self-respect, he lost his feeling of being an individual, a being with a mind, with inner freedom, and with personal value. His existence descended to the level of animal life, plunging him into a depression so deep that he became incapable of action. No entreaties, no blows, no threats would have any effect on his apathetic paralysis, and he soon died, underscoring the Russian novelist Fyodor Dostoyevsky's observation: *"Without a firm idea of himself and the purpose of his life, man cannot live, and would sooner destroy himself than remain on earth, even if he was surrounded with bread."*

Dr. Frankl found that the meaning of *his* life in this situation was to try to help his fellow prisoners restore their psychological health. He had to find ways for them to look forward to the future: a loved one waiting for their return, a talent to be used, or perhaps work yet to be completed. These were the threads he tried to weave back into the patterns

of meaning in these devastated lives. His efforts led him to the following epiphany:

> We had to learn ourselves, and furthermore we had to teach
> the despairing men, that it did not matter what we expected
> from life, but rather *what life expected from us*. We needed to
> stop asking about the meaning of life but instead to think of
> ourselves as those who were being questioned by life, daily and
> hourly. Our answer must consist not in talk and medication,
> but in right action and in right conduct. Life ultimately means
> taking the responsibility to find the right answer to its prob-
> lems and to fulfill the tasks which it constantly sets for each
> individual.

We each long for a life of significance, to feel that in some important
way our life has made a unique contribution to the world and to the
lives of others. We each strive to create our self as a person of unusual
quality, someone who is admired by others as extraordinary. We hope
for lives characterized by accomplishments and lasting relationships
that will distinguish us as memorable individuals both during and after
our time on earth. Unfortunately, we often don't achieve these lofty
goals. In order to discover the meaning of our lives, we need to understand "who" we are. And we live in an age in which many people are
not sure "who" they are or whether in fact their lives have *any* significant meaning whatsoever.

When we are asked questions such as "Who are you?" or "What is
the meaning of your life?" we often lack any idea of how to respond. But
an even more revealing symptom of our confusion and alienation is the
fact that we rarely even pose these questions, to ourselves or to others.
We are too busy "living" to wonder *why* we are living or who is doing
the living. But can we afford to be too busy to find meaning in our lives?
Our lives depend on our answer to this question. Not our biological lives
necessarily, but the life of our *spirit*. We so often cruise along on
autopilot — days slipping into weeks, weeks merging into years, years

coalescing into a life — without confronting these important questions. If we are to become human in the fullest sense, achieving our distinctive potentials and living a life of significance, we must first have what the theologian Paul Tillich characterized as *"the courage to be."*

There is a terrible price to pay for this loss of wonder and lack of meaning, for it corrodes any life, eating it away from the inside until only a shell remains. Albert Camus, novelist and writer on existential themes, expressed it this way: *"To lose one's life is a little thing and I shall have the courage to do so if it is necessary; but to see the meaning of this life dissipated, to see our reason for existing disappear, that is what is unbearable. One cannot live without meaning."*

Many people are in fact living with a diminished sense of meaning, and they struggle to fill the void within them by frantically pursuing power, money, pleasure, thrills, mind-altered states, or the latest psychic fad. Yet these compulsive cravings only serve to reveal the *lack* of purpose in their lives, poor substitutes for a life built around authentic purpose and genuine meaning. Dr. Frankl provided an eloquent analysis of the desperate situation in which we find ourselves:

> Modern men and women are caught in an *existential vacuum,* the total and ultimate meaninglessness of their lives. They lack the awareness of a meaning worth living for. They are haunted by the experience of their inner emptiness, a void within themselves. The existential vacuum is a widespread phenomenon of the 20th century. . . . No instinct tells them what they have to do, and no tradition tells them what they ought to do; soon they will not know what they want to do.

"THE UNEXAMINED LIFE IS NOT WORTH LIVING"

The Greek philosopher Socrates made this provocative observation nearly 2500 years ago, and it is even more relevant today. In many respects, we have become a society of nonthinkers and as a consequence, people often express bewilderment when trying to understand the

complex forces shaping their lives, and frustration at their inability to
exert meaningful control over these forces. Consider how often we have
heard people say things like:

> Everything in my life is moving so quickly — I just can't seem
> to keep up. There are so many forces that are pushing and
> pulling me in different directions. Most of the time I feel that
> I'm just reacting to situations, jumping from crisis to crisis, not
> steering an independent course for myself. What choice do I
> have?

> I seem to spend a lot of time pretending to be someone I'm
> not. I lack confidence in my ideas, my perceptions, and my-
> self. I'm worried people won't like the "real me," and so I try
> to present an image that I think they will respond to. Who is
> the "real me"? What values should govern my life? These are
> essential questions, but I don't have time to think about what
> kind of person I want to be.

Socrates' message was that when we live our lives unreflectively, simply reacting to life's situations and not trying to explore its deeper meanings, then our lives have diminished value. When unreflective, we are
not making use of the distinctive human capacity to think deeply about
important issues and develop thoughtful conclusions about ourselves
and our world. We skate on the surface of life, meeting our endless responsibilities, bombarded with overwhelming amounts of information,
and seeming to be in perpetual motion. We simply don't have the time
or inclination to plumb the depths of ourselves, reflect on the meaning
of our existence, shape the direction of our lives, and create ourselves
as unique and worthy individuals.

The fact that you are reading this book suggests that you recognize
the importance of enriching your life by improving the quality of your
thinking abilities — a worthy goal indeed. And the truth is that your destiny is in your hands: You can shape yourself into the person you want
to be, and you can construct an effective and fulfilling life. In order to

do so you will have to *think critically*, *live creatively*, and *choose freely*. You will need to articulate the portrait of the person you want to become, use your creative imagination to invest your portrait with colors and textures, and then commit yourself to making the choices necessary to become this person in reality. Creating this portrait will be challenging work, but it is well worth the effort. Your portrait will be your contribution to the world, your legacy to present and future generations.

This book was written as a guide in your quest to create an enlightened self-portrait. It is intended to give you the conceptual tools to craft a life thrilling in its challenges and rich in its fulfillment. It is *not* intended to direct you to a specific life-portrait. That is your responsibility: to explore, to learn, to evaluate, to *think critically* — and then to create yourself in the image you have envisioned. The size of your canvas, the quality of your portrait, will expand in direct proportion to your imagination.

"Man is asked to make of himself what he is supposed to become to fulfill his destiny," Paul Tillich wrote. But how do we discover our destiny, the unique meaning of our lives? If our minds are clear and our spirits enlightened, life makes evident what is required of us.

As you follow your own path through the 8 Steps of this book, you will delve deep within yourself, laying bare the bedrock of truth that forms the core of your identity. Your journey will be a process of self-exploration and discovery, answering profound questions about your life and illuminating the mysteries of your existence. And in the course of your travels, as your mind clears and your spirit becomes enlightened, the meaning that life holds out to you will become visible — you will only have to seize it.

Enlightened Thinking Is the Key to a Successful Life

OVER THE past two decades I have worked with thousands of people to help them become more informed and enlightened thinkers — the key to living a life that is creative, professionally successful, and personally fulfilling. During my years of college teaching,

I have discovered that many of my students — representing a broad social, economic, ethnic, and age spectrum — have repeatedly expressed concerns about their inability to control the forces that shape their lives; they are insecure about their ability to think clearly and independently; and they are frustrated by the challenge of creating lives of purpose and significance. In response to this, I created a course entitled Critical Thinking, designed to help people develop crucial thinking abilities and enlightened self-awareness in a practical, systematic, and lasting way. This course has been enormously successful in achieving its objectives. It has been taught to more than 25,000 people at my college, and courses based on my textbook, *Thinking Critically*, have been taken by more than half a million people in every part of the country.

The Thinker's Way reflects all that I have learned about how to improve our thinking process in order to enrich our lives. It is designed to provide the knowledge, guidance, and practice needed to elevate our thinking abilities to an optimal level.

As a natural result of improving your thinking abilities, *The Thinker's Way* will help you enrich the quality of your life and who you are as a human being. In our present culture, a great deal of time, money, and effort is spent seeking to improve our health, condition our bodies, and better our personal appearance. Too often neglected is the most important ingredient: the core of who we are, our ability to think and reflect, to understand our past and create our futures. And while there are many self-help books and programs designed to teach us strategies for improving our lives, these approaches will always have limited success if they don't address the need to *think clearly*, which in turn empowers us to think for ourselves. This is the essence of independent thought. In the absence of insightful thinking and genuine choice, "how-to" techniques will simply be empty exercises with little lasting impact. Self-help books and programs are too often cosmetic approaches to human transformation, promising to change deeply rooted behaviors and attitudes with simplistic techniques.

We must restructure the way that we *think* in order to reshape the way we *are*. Each of us strives for a life of purpose. Such lives are within our grasp, but to achieve them we must harness the power of our minds.

The many people I have taught over the years have yearned for such lives, and I suspect that the concerns they have expressed will be familiar to you. Their success in meeting these challenges with a critical thinking approach to their lives is compelling testimony to the strength of the human spirit and the power of the human mind.

CREATING A MEANINGFUL LIFE

Ah, but a man's reach should exceed his grasp,
Or what's a heaven for?
— ROBERT BROWNING

> Throughout my life, I always had the confidence that I would achieve something unique, monumental, lasting — an achievement that the world would notice and acclaim. Somehow it hasn't worked out that way. I have certainly achieved many of my goals. I have a relatively secure job, a loving family, and a cherished collection of friends. But there is something missing. I just don't feel that I have put my personal stamp on the world, contributed something to others that is valuable and expresses my unique vision of the world. How can I do this?

It's probably safe to say that virtually everyone has goals that they have been unable to achieve, dreams they have not been able to realize. Perhaps it's finding the "right" person to spend your life with, attaining a high level of self-confidence, discovering the appropriate career, or reaching financial stability. In many cases, these goals could have been achieved had you used the full potential of your thinking abilities. For example, the passage above could have been written by me a number of years ago. Although I had earned a Ph.D. in philosophy, I had not been able to find a full-time teaching position in the city where I lived and, after a year of humiliating interviews and insincere promises, I had given up looking. I was working at a job that was secure but largely unfullfilling. I told myself that I could achieve a meaningful life outside my job — through family, friendships, travel, cultural activities, and other diversions. In truth, I was kidding myself. My life was comfortable, but unremarkable. I had even reached the point of no longer believing that I *was* capable of making some unique contribution to the lives of other people. There was an emptiness at the center of my life, which instead of diminishing was growing larger. I knew that as long as I clung to my secure job as if it were a life preserver, there was little chance that I would re-create myself. As I began to sense the desperateness of my situation, I finally took to heart the words of the Roman philosopher Seneca: *"It is not because things are difficult that we do not dare; it is because we do not dare that they are difficult."* And so I quit, letting go of my secure but unrewarding position to seek unexplored opportunities, a path that led me — ultimately — to my life's work.

The first thing I had to do to transform myself and salvage my life was to establish a goal. I decided that really I wanted to be an educator and began teaching part-time, developing after several years a course I called Critical Thinking. Instead of beginning with the ideas of the great thinkers and then trying to show students how these ideas applied to their lives, the course began with *students'* ideas and helped them enlarge their understanding until it encompassed the insights of the great thinkers. The course was also designed to help them develop sophisticated thinking and language abilities in a systematic and lasting way. And finally, the course created an environment for students to think for themselves and share their thinking with others. This approach was immediately and dramatically successful, the first step in my professional quest.

Meanwhile, I supplemented my limited income by becoming a (self-taught) furniture-maker, but my central commitment was to my teaching career. It was like walking down a fog-shrouded path. As I reached one short-range goal, I could see a little more of the path ahead of me and the next goal I wanted to achieve. I had no way of seeing the whole path, or where it would lead, but I had the confidence that I was doing the right thing, moving in the right direction.

As I traveled on my journey, I became more aware of the unique challenge and opportunity that life was presenting to me: to help people become more thoughtful, more successful, more fulfilled. I had discovered a central part of the meaning of my life by looking deep within myself, a universal human process of self-discovery described by Elisabeth Kubler-Ross when she wrote, *"Learn to get in touch with the silence within yourself and know that everything in this life has a purpose."*

A Thinking World

I AM SOMETIMES asked by people, "Aren't you concerned about what would happen if *everyone* became a critical thinker?" Let's imagine such a world. It would be a world in which everyone would be thoughtful. They would not act rashly or speak foolishly without thinking. They would be reflective, carefully considering different points of view and thinking deeply about important issues. People would listen to what you had to say and treat your views with respect, and if they disagreed with your point of view, they would explain why by providing intelligent reasons. At work, your boss would provide you with personal support and opportunities to take initiative, guiding you when you made mistakes, encouraging you to excel, and awarding you full credit for your accomplishments. Your relationships with family members would always be loving and honest, as you worked together harmoniously for common purposes. Your relationship with your romantic partner would be intimate and supportive, expressing deep commitment and emotional honesty. Parents would nurture their children with unconditional love and raise them to have respect for the needs of others. People of all ages would display enlightened values, empathizing with the needs of others and trying to help those less fortunate. Lying, cheating, stealing, personal violence: None of these would exist, replaced instead by kindness, generosity, consideration, goodwill. This would be a world filled with open-minded people who welcomed diverse ideas, customs, and personal differences. Racism, sexism, ageism, all forms of discrimination would be things of the past as all people would be treated with tolerance and consideration.

On a social level, all people would see themselves as members of the same community, with a responsibility for the well-being of all members, not just themselves. Everyone would work together to create a better life for all. Wise and principled political leaders would be elected by a thoughtful citizenry, and they would govern with insight, honesty, and compassion. Children would be educated in a system that encouraged their individual talents and respected their unique value. Television shows would be designed to stimulate thinking and expand understanding, as well as entertain. People on talk shows would express thoughtful, articulate opinions, never stooping to superficial analyses or personal insults. On the road, people would drive with safety and consideration, never letting their anger or desire to get ahead take hold of them at the expense of others. When people did make mistakes, they would always accept responsibility, never trying to blame others. Those who violated the law would be tried by juries who were astute thinkers, weighing the evidence judiciously and reaching fair-minded and well-supported verdicts.

On a personal level, you would be confident of your place in society, taken seriously by others who respected your special qualities. People would treat you with consideration, and you would reciprocate, with feelings of goodwill overwhelming any doubts or suspicions. You would think the best of people, and they would respond in kind. You would live your life under what philosophers used to call "the aspect of eternity," reflecting on the purpose of your existence and your connections to humanity and the universe. When working with others, your productive discussions would always move toward the most logical and informed conclusions. You would be able to navigate intelligently through the daily avalanche of information, separating the useful from the irrelevant. You would have a deep understanding of complex social issues, and would enjoy exploring their nuances through constructive conversations. You would live your life creatively, expressing yourself freely without fear of social condemnation. Your life would be vibrant, filled with satisfying relationships and accomplishments in which you would take great pride. You would enjoy the admiration of others as you steered a purposeful course that reflected your profound self-understanding. You would feel secure, strong, loved, happy, and fulfilled.

What would a world populated with critical thinkers be like? It would be a sublime world, the kind of world you would love to live in, the kind of world you would want for your children. It would be a world in which all people were able to achieve their personal potential, echoing the words of the writer Henry Miller:

> We are all part of things,
> We are all part of creation, all kings, all poets, all musicians,
> We have only to open up, to discover what is already there.

WHY PEOPLE DON'T THINK

It's painfully obvious that we don't live in the "thinking world" just described, and we suffer the consequences of this every day of our lives. Rather than cultivating the habit of thoughtfulness, people are chronically thought*less*. They often act rashly and speak foolishly, advancing ignorant opinions with supreme confidence. They frequently don't listen to what you have to say, instead focusing on their own ideas. At work, bosses typically give too little credit and too much blame, failing to respect adequately you or your ideas. Family relationships tend to be competitive and contentious, and romantic relationships often turn into a viper's tangle of resentment and suspicion or impersonal disaffection. Many parents have difficulty raising their children well, depriving them of sufficient love, attention, or guidance.

We live in a world full of closed-minded and dogmatic people, convinced they are always right. Our society has suffered a decline in values, an environment in which telling the truth, acting honestly, and treating people decently have been sacrificed in the name of the bottom line or "success." Discriminatory attitudes toward virtually every group are commonplace, and are rivaled only by people trying to gain advantage by casting themselves as victims. Our society has become increasingly factionalized, led by pandering and often corrupt politicians who magnify these divisions for their own purposes. Children are forced to endure an educational system that is often more concerned with the transfer of information than with genuine learning, a system that emphasizes conformity over personal development. We are inundated with mindless television shows, virulent hate-talk on the radio, music played too loud to let yourself think. We are forced to deal daily with people who are irrational, disorganized, confused, and inarticulate. In many respects we are experiencing the answer to the question: *"What happens when people live in an* un*thinking way?"*

What has gone so terribly wrong? If living in a thinking world is so clearly superior in every way to living in a nonthinking world, why have we created this thoughtless disaster? If thinking effectively is so important for achieving success and happiness in every aspect of our lives, why do most people make no concerted effort to improve their thinking? According to the philosopher Bertrand Russell, *"Most people would rather die than think — in fact they do!"* Think of how many times you've asked yourself in anger or amazement, "What is that person thinking?" Usually they aren't thinking at all, in any clear or meaningful sense. People seem to have lost sight of the fact that *thinking* is not dangerous. *Nonthinking* is dangerous: it endangers us, our lives, our welfare, our ability to become the people we have the potential to be. That's why I believe this course of study for becoming an enlightened thinker is so urgent, and why I want others to take this course as well.

Pervasive unthinkingness has a number of sources. People don't work on strengthening their thinking abilities because they simply don't know how to. Recent research and new technology have given us a greater understanding of how the mind works, and we are now in a position to translate this knowledge into strategies for helping people learn to think in more advanced ways, the goal of *The Thinker's Way*. For example, one recent study concluded that people's thinking and language abilities are directly correlated with how often they were spoken to during their first year of life, stimulating the development of neurological pathways. Another study found that the incidence of Alzheimer's is directly related to the complexity of the language syntax used earlier in life. Research cited by Marie Winn demonstrates that watching television at the expense of reading discourages active thinking; diminishes the imagination; inhibits the ability to think abstractly and perform complex symbolic transformations; damages the ability to concentrate; and can become addictive by causing brain changes analogous to drug-induced states.

Many people are intimidated by the thinking process, believing it to be a quasi-mystical ability awarded at birth, over which we have little control. This view couldn't be further from the truth. Thinking is not a process reserved for a few divinely blessed people, it's for everyone. It is an ability that can be improved through knowledge and guided practice. There is a structure to the way our minds operate, and by understanding that structure, we can improve our thinking abilities in all of life's situations.

Thinking clearly and deeply is hard work, particularly when you are learning how to do it. Many people are attracted to the seductive aspect of simplistic analyses and superficial perspectives because they can avoid mental exertion, not realizing that "lazy thinking" leads to low-quality conclusions. In addition, the thinking process is complex and elusive, and the relentless pace at which we typically live our lives works against thoughtful reflection. Psychologist David Perkins observes, *"Our thinking tends to be hazy, hasty, narrow or sprawling — casual terms for impulsive. Just like anything else, thinking skills require upkeep. If they aren't nourished, they'll fade away."*

Many people seem to be living with a consciousness that is ahistorical, ignoring the wisdom of the people who came before us and who can help inform our current thinking. We've stopped looking to wise men and women — past or present — to inspire and challenge us. We do so at our own peril, expressed in the philosopher George Santayana's much-repeated warning, *"Those who cannot remember the past are condemned to repeat it."*

The advent of the "information age" and the "information superhighway" has created unintended threats to our thinking well-being.

Today we are drowning in data, pelted by newspaper and magazine stories, 24–hour television news, E-mail, junk mail and faxes. Cellular phones, car phones and beepers insure that we are always on call, while ubiquitous television sets — in bars, sports arenas, airports and airplanes — insure that we never lack visual distraction. The average American spends 60 percent of the office day processing documents.

So writes David Shenk in his book *Data Smog*. Data smog is bad for our mental and emotional health, promoting stress, memory overload, compulsive behavior, and attention-deficit disorder. Its overstimulation also forces people to resort to hyperbole and histrionics to get attention — the "Madonna/Dennis Rodman effect" — which makes clear thinking and thoughtful reflection next to impossible. Television programmers, movie producers, performers, and spokespersons have "turned up the heat" so much that they have overwhelmed moderation and intelligence in our society, reduced our attention span, and made us numb to anything that doesn't lurch out and grab us by the throat.

Don't people learn to be critical thinkers in school? Not necessarily. Although we should have learned these crucial thinking abilities through education and general socialization, this is often not the case. Books like *The Closing of the American Mind* by Allan Bloom and *Cultural Literacy* by E. D. Hirsch popularized what educators were experiencing firsthand: the failure of schools to graduate sophisticated thinkers. Our educational system emphasizes acquiring often unrelated "bits" of information, like shopping at an "information supermarket," instead of developing a coherent framework of knowledge. *But information is not knowledge:* It doesn't become knowledge until the human mind acts on it and transforms it. The following aphorism sums up our ironic predicament in our "data-smogged" world: *"We're drowning in information, but we're starved for knowledge."*

This is what it means to become a critical thinker: to possess the wisdom to make intelligent judgments about the use of human knowledge in the context of daily life. Simply possessing information doesn't make us intelligent, if we don't know how to *analyze, organize, evaluate,* and *apply* the information for purposeful ends. That's why we need to improve the source of knowledge, our own thinking process, in order to become fully educated. The failure of society as a whole, and education in particular, to produce sufficiently mature thinkers should provoke alarm throughout our culture.

People are the products of many different influences in their lives. Some of these influences encourage us to become independent critical and creative thinkers, while others encourage us to become just the opposite. But whatever your history and current state, you are still evolving as a person and as a thinker. You have the ability to re-create yourself and shape your future through the choices you make, molding yourself to be the person you always wanted to be: thoughtful, informed, articulate, insightful, creative.

Reflect on your own thinking history and the influences that shaped the development of your mind.

- *Education:* Which teachers and educational experiences stimulated you to think and express your own independent ideas? Which expected you to learn the "correct answers" and not question what you were learning? Many people believe that education often *discourages* critical thinking, a view reflected in Neil Postman's observation, *"People enter schools as question-marks and they leave as periods."*
- *Parents:* In what ways did your parents encourage you to make independent decisions, express your individuality, and choose what you thought was right for yourself? To what extent did your parents expect to be obeyed without question, make important decisions for you, and resist providing you with responsibilities?
- *Peers:* To what extent did (and do) your friends support your ideas and personal choices even when they did not agree with them? To what extent did your friends pressure you to conform to the group norms, discouraging you when you deviated?

> • **Employers:** Which employers encouraged you to think inde-
> pendently and make creative decisions? Which employers gave
> you detailed instructions for performing every task, and dis-
> couraged you from suggesting improved ways of doing things?

Improving Your Thinking Abilities

THINKING IS AN ABILITY that we can all improve, since few of us
use our thinking abilities to the fullest extent possible. In this regard,
thinking is like many other human abilities. For instance, if we examine the people who are at the top of their careers — surgeons, professional athletes, accomplished musicians, CEOs — we find that one
thing they have in common is their desire to improve their abilities,
even though they are more proficient than the vast majority of people.
You must have that same commitment to excellence if you are to
achieve your thinking potential. By understanding how the thinking
process functions, you can learn to think better through systematic
study and guided practice.

The Thinker's Way is designed both to *stimulate* your thinking and to
guide you to think in more sophisticated, powerful ways. Throughout
the book you will be presented with Thinking Activities, opportunities
for you to think and then reflect on your thinking process in order to refine it. This is the only genuine way to improve your thinking abilities.
Although reading about effective thinking can provide useful background information, there is no substitute for actually doing it: working
your way through a thinking situation, making mistakes, and gradually
improving your performance with thoughtful reflection and informed
guidance. It is a learning process analogous to mastering any complex
skill, from driving a car to analyzing a spreadsheet or being a nurturing
parent. It is what the Greek dramatist Sophocles had in mind when he
wrote, *"Knowledge must come through action."* In other words, the only
way to become a better thinker is to *think.*

Can you really learn to think from a book? Yes, provided that you take an interactive, participatory approach. It is not possible to simply read your way to becoming a critical thinker. You need to be *actively* involved in the experience — thinking, articulating your ideas, evaluating the quality of your reasoning, refining and improving your thinking process. You will be expressing your ideas in your Thinking Notebook, a thinking tool that you will keep. Your Thinking Notebook will enable you to infuse the ideas in this book into your own life, applying them to your own personal situation. Be as honest as you can with yourself, and though you should try to express your thinking as clearly as possible, don't worry about style — it's for yourself. Thinking, writing, reflecting — these processes all work together to create the habit of thoughtfulness in you, a pattern of thinking that, once it gets established, will grow exponentially. High-level creative and critical thinking of this sort is an extraordinary gift that stirs our consciousness, liberates us from mundane concerns, expands our vision, and moves us forward, enriching our lives in countless ways. As Bertrand Russell eloquently wrote: *"Thought is great and swift and free, the light of the world, and the chief glory of man."*

You may be wondering that since thinking is a mental activity, why is it necessary to record your thoughts in writing? The answer is that writing is a vehicle for creating and communicating your ideas, a catalyst for your intellectual development. The intimate, interactive relationships that connect language, thinking, and writing have been remarked on by many people, including the writers Annie Dillard *("I don't know what I think until I see myself write")* and Elie Wiesel *("I write to understand as much as to be understood")*. The process of writing stimulates your mind, helps shape your thinking, and enlarges your understanding of the world. Just as significantly, writing creates a permanent record — a "snapshot" — of your thinking process at a specific point in time. You can return to your thinking snapshot as often as you wish, evaluate its logic and coherence, and use it as a foundation upon which to build a more insightful understanding. Your notebook can be of your choosing, and, of course, using a computer works just as well and has a number of additional advantages.

Whatever the notebook form, the key to success is developing the discipline and commitment to engage in the process, thinking deeply and expressing your ideas as clearly and specifically as possible. Once you have established this pattern of thinking and writing, you will find that it will become integrated into your life in a natural and profound way, leading you to deeper insights, creative ideas, and enriched meaning. Make your Thinking Notebook an intimate part of your daily life, keep it with you, let it remind you to think well. Your Thinking Notebook should provide a stimulating, liberating experience and help you formulate and externalize your thinking; the goal is not to write polished prose or to evaluate the worthiness of your ideas. So think hard, but enjoy yourself!

My experience with the thousands of people I have taught supports my guarantee that if you commit yourself to the course of study outlined in *The Thinker's Way*, your life will be transformed in every area. With powerful creative and critical thinking abilities at your disposal, people will seek out your advice and admire your insights; your relationships with loved ones will be more satisfying; you will have a clear sense of direction, your mission in life; and you will have the confidence that you can shape yourself into the person you always wanted to be.

You may have read other personal development books, motivated by your good-faith desire to improve yourself and the quality of your life. And though you gained insight and useful strategies for specific areas of your life, you may have been disappointed to find that they resulted in little lasting impact. *The Thinker's Way* will enable you take what you have learned from these other books and then *transcend* them, because in addition to providing a practical framework for living more effectively, this book also enables you to tap into the central core of who you are — a thinking, reflecting, creating, willing individual.

The 8 Steps of *The Thinker's Way*

YOUR THINKING PROCESS operates most effectively when it has an idea of where it's headed. As you read, think, and work through *The Thinker's Way*, you can imagine yourself embarking on a journey to enlightened thinking and an enhanced life. The 8 Steps of the book represent guideposts to help direct your travels. Although each person has to discover — and create — his or her own path, these guideposts are universal and apply to everyone. You cannot achieve your full potential as a thinker or as a person if you do not successfully complete each of these 8 Steps. Of course, working your way through each of these Steps is not a one-time experience: you will find that you must return to each of these Steps as you live your life and attain higher levels of understanding. Each time you return to the themes of a particular Step, you will do so at a deeper and more profound level, integrating the insights into your life with heightened meaning. It's a spiraling process similar to understanding a complex idea like "romantic love." The "puppy-love" of your youth is gradually transformed into deeper, richer, and more complex feelings toward others, although the core emotion of responding to another person in a loving way remains constant throughout.

In addition, you will find that the principles and insights of the various Steps all work together to create your enlightenment and personal transformation, like different instruments in an orchestra producing a majestic symphony. So although there is a logic to the sequence in which the 8 Steps are presented, you will find that you are continually using abilities developed in one Step to help you succeed in other Steps. For example, you need to apply the insights and methods involved in the initial Steps:

Think Critically	(Step 1)
Live Creatively	(Step 2)
Choose Freely	(Step 3)

in order to successfully

Solve Problems Effectively	(Step 4)
Communicate Effectively	(Step 5)
Analyze Complex Issues	(Step 6)
Develop Enlightened Values	(Step 7)
Think Through Relationships	(Step 8)

As you gradually master and refine the thinking abilities and insights in each of the Steps, you will discover that they are synergistic, strengthening and enhancing one another as you deploy them in an integrated way. Their combined power will enable you to transform yourself and create a life philosophy.

Three Transforming Principles

THE ABILITY to Think Critically (Step 1), Live Creatively (Step 2), and Choose Freely (Step 3) are the three life-principles of human transformation upon which this book is based. These three principles are interlocking pieces of the puzzle of your life. Working together as a unified force, these principles can illuminate your existence: answering questions, clarifying confusion, creating meaning, and providing fulfillment.

- *Think Critically*: When used properly, your thinking process acts like a powerful beacon of light, illuminating the depths of your personality and the breadth of your experience. Clear thinking is a tool that helps you disentangle the often confused jumble of thoughts and feelings that compose much of waking consciousness. By becoming a more powerful "critical thinker," you are acquiring the abilities you need to achieve your goals, solve problems, and make intelligent decisions. Critical thinkers are people who have developed thoughtful and well-founded beliefs to guide their choices in every area of their lives. In order to develop the strongest and most accurate beliefs possible, you need to become aware of your own biases, explore situations from many different perspectives, and develop sound reasons to support your points of view.
- *Live Creatively*: Creativity is a powerful life-force that can infuse your life with meaning. Working in partnership with critical thinking, creative thinking helps you transform your life into a rich tapestry of productivity and success. When you approach your life

with a mindful sense of discovery and invention, you can continually create yourself in ways limited only by your imagination. A creative lens changes everything for the better: Problems become opportunities for growth, mundane routines become challenges for inventive approaches, relationships become intriguing adventures. When you give free rein to your creative impulses, every aspect of your life takes on a special glow. You are able to break out of unthinking habitual responses and live fully in every minute, responding naturally and spontaneously. It sounds magical and it is.

- *Choose Freely*: People can only transform themselves if they *choose* to take different paths in their lives, but only if their choices are *truly free*. To exercise genuine freedom, you must have the insight to understand all of your options and the wisdom to make *informed* choices. When you fully accept your freedom, you redefine your daily life and your future in a new light. By working to neutralize the constraints on your autonomy and guide your life in positive directions, you see alternatives that were not previously visible, concealed by the limitations of your vision. Your future becomes open, a field of rich possibilities that you can explore and choose among. A life that is free is one that is vital and exciting, suffused with unexpected opportunities and the personal fulfillment that comes from a life well lived.

Your "self" is in its essence a dynamic life-force, capable of *thinking critically, living creatively,* and *choosing freely*. These three essential dimensions of your "self" exist optimally when they work together in harmonious unity. When working together, these three basic elements create a person who is intelligent, creative, and determined — the ingredients for success in any endeavor. But consider the disastrous consequences of subtracting any of these elements from the dynamic equation. If you lack the ability to *think critically*, you can't function very well in most challenging careers because you will have difficulty in thinking clearly, solving complex problems, and making intelligent decisions. What's more, whatever creative ideas you come up with will be rootless, lacking an intelligible framework or practical strategies for implementing them. You will be an impractical dreamer, condemned to a life of frustrated underachieving. Without insight into yourself, your freedom will be imprisoned, since you won't be able to see your choices clearly or liberate yourself from the influences that are constraining you.

If you lack the ability to *live creatively*, then your thinking abilities may enable you to perform in a solid, workmanlike fashion, but your work will lack imagination, you will be fearful of trying out original approaches because of the risk of failure, and your personality will be missing the spontaneous sparkle that people admire and are drawn to. You will in time become a competent but unimaginative "worker-bee," performing your duties with predictable adequacy, but never rising to the lofty heights of which you are capable. Your choices will be as limited as your imagination, and your habitual choices of the safe and secure paths will eventually create a very small canvas for your personal portrait.

If you lack the ability to *choose freely*, then your abilities to think critically or creatively cannot save you from a life of disappointment. Though you may be able to analyze clearly and understand, you will lack the will to make the difficult choices and stay the course when you encounter obstacles and adversities. And though you may develop unique and valuable ideas, your inability to focus your energies and make things happen will doom these ideas to anonymity. If you lack the *will* to create yourself as a strong individual of character and integrity, the people you encounter will come to view you as a shallow-rooted reed that bends with the wind of superficial trends, not someone deserving of authority and responsibility.

Think of what you aspire to: a life of purpose and meaning, the respect and devotion of those around you, success and fulfillment in your chosen endeavors, and a secure sense of who you are, with the courage and vision to accomplish great things. These aspirations are within your grasp, but only if you develop *all* of these fundamental dimensions of yourself to their fullest potential: to *think critically*, *live creatively*, and *choose freely* — to live your life *The Thinker's Way*.

THINKING ACTIVITY

Setting Goals for Your Journey: The Thinker's Way

Beginning your journey to more powerful thinking abilities and enlightened awareness means first establishing your goals. Research studies have shown that high-achieving people are able to envision a detailed, three-dimensional picture of their future on which their goals and aspirations are clearly inscribed. In addition, they are able to construct a mental plan that includes the steps they will have to take and strategies to employ for overcoming the obstacles they are likely to encounter. Such realistic and compelling concepts of the future guide their progress and enable them to make sacrifices in the present to achieve goals they envisioned for themselves. You can initiate this process by identifying the thinking goals you would like to achieve in working through *The Thinker's Way*. For example:

- *I would like to clarify my core beliefs about things like my values, moral issues, and spiritual concerns, and place these beliefs on a firm foundation.*
- *I would like to become better at solving complicated problems, particularly when other people are involved.*
- *I would like to identify the essential goals for my life and then develop a realistic plan to achieve them.*
- *I would like to feel that I am more in control of my life, that I can figure out what's going on and make intelligent choices that reflect the person I want to become.*
- *I would like to enrich the relationships in my life with those people with whom I am closest: to become more emotionally open and enjoy a genuine intimacy.*

STEP I

THINK CRITICALLY

Everybody "thinks" — it's just that some people think "better" than others: their thinking is more insightful, sophisticated, and profound. This chapter will show you how to become a more powerful "critical thinker," acquiring the abilities you need to achieve your goals, solve problems, and make intelligent decisions. Critical thinkers are people who have developed thoughtful and well-founded beliefs that guide their choices in every area of their lives. In order to develop the strongest and most accurate beliefs possible, you need to become aware of your own biases, explore situations from many different perspectives, and develop sound reasons to support your points of view. These abilities are the tools you need to become more enlightened and reflective — a "critical thinker."

Thinking Critically: An Essential Life Skill

SEVERAL YEARS AGO Reggie Lewis, star basketball player for the Boston Celtics, was diagnosed with a heart condition. A team of renowned cardiologists was assembled to evaluate his condition, and they concluded that he would be risking his life if he continued his basketball career. Not satisfied with this devastating diagnosis, Lewis sought out the opinion of an equally famous cardiologist, who assured him that he could safely resume his NBA career. Which doctors should he believe? The pressure to continue playing was enormous. The hopes of his family, the team, and millions of his fans rested on his shoulders. Not surprisingly, he chose to believe the latter doctor and began his comeback. Several months later, while practicing in a gym, Lewis collapsed and died.

Reggie Lewis's death underscores the need to develop the thinking tools required to weigh conflicting information accurately, and the potentially tragic consequences of failing to do so. Mr. Lewis should have exercised great caution in rejecting the initial recommendations of such a distinguished team of experts who provided a convincing diagnosis with his best interests in mind. And he should have made a special effort to analyze his decision objectively, ignoring the pressure of others' expectations and disregarding his own fervent wish to play.

In the same way that you use road maps to guide you to your destination, your belief system constitutes the "map" you use to inform your decisions. If your mental map of the world is reasonably accurate, then it will provide reliable guidance in helping you figure things out and make intelligent decisions. On the other hand, if your mental map is *not* accurate, then the results are likely to be unfortunate and even disastrous. In the case of Reggie Lewis, the map he was using was fatally flawed, and the consequences were tragic.

Thankfully, most of our flawed maps don't lead to the dire consequences suffered by Reggie Lewis, although there are probably many times in your life when, you realize, you barely avoided a tragedy. As a critical thinker, when such a "near miss" occurs, it should sober you enough to ask the question "How can I create a more accurate map for myself?" Consider the controversial issue of whether women under fifty years of age should get annual mammograms in order to provide the earliest detection of breast cancer. While the benefits of mammograms for women *over* fifty are clearly established by research studies — chances of dying from breast cancer are reduced by 30 percent — the benefits for women *under* fifty are uncertain. In order to resolve this question, an expert panel was formed by the National Institutes of Health. They presented their findings in January of 1997, concluding that there was not sufficient evidence to recommend routine annual mammograms for women under fifty. Their advice: Women under fifty should "weigh the risks and benefits of the test and decide for themselves." This conclusion prompted an immediate outcry from other experts in the field, including the American Cancer Society and prominent radiologists. Which expert advice should women follow?

How do we arrive at the answers to such complex questions? We need to develop the thinking tools and strategies that will enable us to think for ourselves and arrive at intelligent conclusions. We can't simply rely on expert opinions, because those opinions are often in conflict and influenced by the experts' own biases.

Of course, the thinking dilemmas posed by experts who disagree are not limited to medical situations — we constantly confront conflicting opinions and advice: voluminous and often contradictory financial data; conflicting scientific analyses on environmental concerns like global warming and overpopulation; contrasting advice from psychologists on how to eradicate that troubling neurosis or nurture the mystery of intimacy. It's no wonder that we sometimes feel like announcing, "It's all too much — not even the experts agree. I give up!" It's important to recognize that while, indeed, we have more data available to us now, life has always been complicated and demanded a thoughtful approach. But if we can't accept the recommendations of experts without question, what should we do? How do we decide what to believe?

There *is* a way to develop an accurate set of beliefs that you can use to guide you through life's treacherous currents. You need to develop and apply the skills of critical thinking in order to arrive at informed, intelligent opinions in every area of life.

DEVELOPING INFORMED BELIEFS

I am an insightful, powerful, confident critical thinker.	I'm not as strong a thinker as I feel I could be.

5   4   3   2   1

How would you rate yourself on this scale? If it's more toward the right side than the left, you have plenty of company. One reason for this response is that we live in a complex, challenging world that is extremely demanding intellectually. Each day we are called on to solve difficult problems, analyze tangled issues, and sift through a tidal wave of information. We are expected to make intelligent decisions, negotiate our way through a jungle of relationships, and communicate our ideas clearly and persuasively. It's no wonder that we often feel overmatched, unable to marshal the thinking abilities needed to succeed in all of these demanding contexts. Here, for example, are a few of the issues that appear daily in the media and about which we ought to develop informed opinions:

On Cloning Humans, "Never" Turns Swiftly into "Why Not"

There has been an enormous change in attitudes in the few months since Dolly the lamb became the first animal cloned from a cell taken from an adult. Contrary to early fears of a Brave New World, scientists have become sanguine about the notion of cloning human beings. Some infertility centers are already conducting experiments with human eggs that lay the groundwork for cloning. Ultimately, scientists expect cloning to be combined with genetic enhancement, adding genes to give desired traits.

— NEW YORK TIMES, December 2, 1997

Arab-Americans Protest "Profiling" at Airports

When Dr. Hassan Abbass, a Veterans Affairs Department surgeon, and his wife arrived at the airport to leave for vacation last May 24, they were pulled aside and forced to submit to a careful search before boarding the plane. They became one of thousands of Americans of Middle Eastern heritage who have complained that a secretive and wide-scale "profiling" system sponsored by the Government and aimed at preventing air terrorism has caused them to be unfairly selected for extra scrutiny at airports. "Profiling" of this type is being used more frequently in many areas of law-enforcement, raising fundamental questions of how a free society balances security fears with civil liberties and the desire to avoid offensive stereotyping.

— NEW YORK TIMES, August 11, 1997

Developing informed beliefs about these and other issues is an ongoing challenge to our thinking abilities. In thinking about these and any other issues, we should ask ourselves two important questions:

- *What is my opinion about this issue?* Do you believe that human cloning should be pursued? What about whether "profiling" is a legitimate technique for improving public safety?
- *Is my opinion informed by evidence and reasons?* For each of the opinions that you have regarding these (and other) issues, can you answer the question "Why do you have that opinion?" with intelligent and compelling reasons?

The truth is that while opinions are easy to come by, *informed* opinions are much more difficult to find. To express an opinion you merely have to say, "Well, I think . . ." or "I believe . . ." People are more than willing to make such pronouncements on virtually any subject. But to express an informed opinion means that you have some idea of what you're talking about: You have *explored* the subject, *examined* different points of view, *evaluated* the supporting reasons and evidence, and *synthesized* your analysis into a cogent and compelling conclusion. If someone asks you, "Why do you believe that human cloning should be prohibited?" you can provide a clear, articulate explanation.

If you examine the people around you — and to a certain extent yourself — you will probably discover that they express many more *uninformed* opinions than informed opinions. How can you tell? Informed opinions announce themselves when people consistently say, "I think ―― *because* . . . ," supporting their opinions with thoughtful reasoning. Or when you ask, "*Why* do you think ――?" they respond with a clear analysis and explanation. In contrast, when people rarely follow

"I think——" with a supporting rationale, or are unable to respond to "Why do you think ——?" with a cogent analysis, then you are most likely in the company of mere *un*informed opinions.

But isn't everyone "entitled to his or her opinion"? Yes and no. Living in a democracy with broad free-speech protections, people are allowed to think and express virtually *any* opinion, no matter how illogical, uninformed, or foolish. But this does not mean that they are entitled to have their uninformed opinions taken seriously, or that their opinions should be given the same consideration as informed opinions! Still, this "celebration of ignorance" is having a destructive effect on our culture, according to journalist Michael Kinsley:

> It's not just that Americans are scandalously ignorant. It's that they seem to believe they have a democratic right to their ignorance. All over the country — at dinner tables, in focus groups, on call-in radio shows, and no doubt, occasionally on the floor of Congress — citizens are expressing outrage about how much we spend on foreign aid, without having the faintest idea what that amount is (1 percent). This is not a question of being misinformed. People are forming and expressing passionate views about foreign aid on the basis of no information at all. Or perhaps they think that the amount being spent on foreign aid is a matter of opinion, like everything else. Populism, in its latest manifestation, celebrates ignorant opinion and undifferentiated rage. As long as you're mad as hell and aren't going to take it anymore, no one will inquire very closely into what exactly "it" is and whether you really ought to feel that way.
>
> —THE NEW YORKER, 1994

Americans are certainly capable of forming thoughtful opinions about complex social and policy issues, but they need to think critically in order to do so, and they often seem to be under the impression that they need not bother. But as Kinsley points out, it is contemptuous, not respectful, to excuse people from all demands of intellectual rigor. We do them a disservice by supporting the delusion that their judgments are wise by definition, and we undermine their intelligence by simply accepting their opinions. We show respect for other people — and ourselves — by challenging them to think critically about their beliefs.

Beyond the everyday thinking challenges we encounter, there are deeper, more profound issues that people need to grapple with. In the first chapter we explored the implications of Socrates' admonition that "*The unexamined life is not worth living.*" Becoming a critical thinker begins with the process of *reflection*, making a concerted effort to examine your thinking process, to explore the underlying levels of your "self," and to answer the "big" questions that life poses. Critical thinkers have a reflective attitude toward life, automatically exploring and questioning meanings in their experience. They think about *moral* questions ("What is the morally right thing to do?"); *spiritual* questions ("How can I best develop my spiritual nature?); *humanistic* questions ("How can I best achieve my human potential?"); *existential* questions ("What is the meaning of life?"); and many others as well. These are essential questions, but they are overwhelmed by the demands of daily life.

Who Is a "Critical Thinker"?

TRADITIONALLY, WHEN people refer to a "critical thinker," they mean someone who has developed a knowledgeable understanding of our complex world, a thoughtful perspective on important ideas and timely issues, the capacity for penetrating insight and intelligent judgment, and sophisticated thinking and language abilities. These goals of advanced understanding have remained remarkably similar for several thousand years. In ancient Greece, most advanced students studied philosophy in order to achieve "wisdom" (in Greek, *philosophy* means "lover of wisdom").

The word *critical* comes from the Greek word for "critic" (*kritikos*), which means to question, to make sense of, to analyze. It is by questioning, making sense of, and analyzing that you examine your thinking and the thinking of others. These critical activities aid us in reaching the best possible conclusions and decisions. The word *critical* is also related to the word *criticize*, which means to question and evaluate. Unfortunately, the ability to criticize is often used destructively, to tear down someone else's thinking. Criticism, however, can also be *constructive* — analyzing for the purpose of developing a better understanding of what is going on. You need to engage in constructive criticism as you develop your ability to think critically.

Becoming a *critical thinker* is a total approach to the way we understand our world, and it involves an integrated set of thinking abilities and attitudes that include the following:

- *Carefully analyzing and evaluating your beliefs* in order to develop the most accurate beliefs possible.
- *Viewing situations from different perspectives* to develop an in-depth understanding.
- *Supporting viewpoints with reasons and evidence* to arrive at thoughtful, well-substantiated conclusions.
- *Thinking critically about our personal "lenses,"* which shape and influence the way we perceive the world.
- *Synthesizing information into informed conclusions* that we are willing to modify based on new insight.

The best way to develop a clear and concrete idea of the critical thinker you want to become is to think about people you have known who can serve as critical thinking models. In my personal life, I had a number of teachers who taught me what it means to be a critical thinker through the example of their lives. I considered them to be brilliant critical thinkers because of the power of their minds and the commitment of their souls. They had a vision: a perspective on life that they were always trying to enhance through relentless curiosity and open-minded exploration. They also modeled a generosity of spirit as they sought to inspire thinking in others.

But you don't have to look only in college classrooms to find critical thinkers. They appear throughout humanity. The Greek philosopher Socrates was in many ways the original critical thinker for whom we have a historical record, and the depth and clarity of his thinking is immortalized in the *Dialogues* recorded by Plato, his student. As a renowned teacher in his native city of Athens, he had created his own school and spent decades teaching young people how to analyze important issues through dialectical questioning, an approach which became known as the Socratic Method. At the age of seventy, Socrates was deemed a dangerous troublemaker by the ruling politicians. Based on his teachings, students were questioning the politicians' authority, asking embarrassing questions, and threatening their political careers. The politicians gave him an ultimatum: either leave the city where he had spent his entire life, never to return, or be put to death. Rather than leave his beloved Athens and the life he had created, Socrates chose death. Surrounded by his family and friends, he calmly drank a cup of poisonous hemlock-laced tea. He reasoned that leaving Athens would violate the intellectual integrity upon which he had built his life and which he had taught his students. Instead of sacrificing his beliefs, he ended his life, concluding with the words *"Now it is time for us to part, I to die and you to live. Only God knows which is better."*

Today especially, we all need to become philosophers, to develop a philosophical framework. Critical thinking is a modern reworking of a philosophical perspective. Who would *you* identify as expert critical thinkers? To qualify, the people you identify should have lively, energetic minds that generally display the following qualities:

- **Open-minded:** In discussions they listen carefully to every viewpoint, evaluating each perspective carefully and fairly.
- **Knowledgeable:** When they offer an opinion, it's always based on facts or evidence. On the other hand, if they lack knowledge of the subject, they acknowledge this.
- **Mentally active:** They take initiative and actively use their intelligence to confront problems and meet challenges, instead of simply responding passively to events.

- **Curious:** They explore situations with probing questions that penetrate beneath the surface of issues, instead of being satisfied with superficial explanations.
- **Independent thinkers:** They are not afraid to disagree with the group opinion. They develop well-supported beliefs through thoughtful analysis, instead of uncritically "borrowing" the beliefs of others or simply going along with the crowd.
- **Skilled discussants:** They are able to discuss ideas in an organized and intelligent way. Even when the issues are controversial, they listen carefully to opposing viewpoints and respond thoughtfully.
- **Insightful:** They are able to get to the heart of the issue or problem. While others may be distracted by details, they are able to zero in on the essence, seeing the "forest" as well as the "trees."
- **Self-aware:** They are aware of their own biases and are quick to point them out and take them into consideration when analyzing a situation.
- **Creative:** They can break out of established patterns of thinking and approach situations from innovative directions.
- **Passionate:** They have a passion for understanding and are always striving to see issues and problems with more clarity.

THINKING ACTIVITY

Who Is a Critical Thinker?

Think about people you know whom you admire as expert thinkers and list some of the qualities these people exhibit that you believe qualify them as "critical thinkers." For each critical thinking quality, write down a brief example involving the person. Identifying such people helps us visualize the kind of people we'd like to emulate. As you think your way through this book, you will be creating a *portrait* of the kind of critical thinker you are striving to become, a *blueprint* you can use to direct your development and chart your progress.

Stages of Knowing

THE ROAD to becoming a critical thinker is a challenging journey that involves passing through different stages of knowing in order to achieve a sophisticated and effective understanding of the world. These stages characterize people's thinking and the way they understand their world, ranging from simple to complex. A critical thinker is a person who has progressed through all of the stages to achieve a sophisticated understanding of the nature of knowledge. This framework is based on the work of the Harvard psychologist Dr. William Perry (*Forms of Intellectual and Ethical Development in the College Years: A Scheme*), who used in-depth research to create a developmental model of human thought. I use a condensed three-stage version of Perry's framework:

> Stage 1: The Garden of Eden
> Stage 2: Anything Goes
> Stage 3: Thinking Critically

An individual may be at different stages simultaneously, depending on the subject or area of experience; for example, you might be at an advanced stage in one area of your life (your career) but at a less sophisticated stage in another area (your romantic relationships or conception of morality). In general, however, people tend to operate predominantly within one stage in most areas of their lives.

STAGE 1: THE GARDEN OF EDEN

People in the Garden of Eden stage of thinking tend to see the world in black and white, right and wrong. How do they determine what is right, what to believe? The "authorities" *tell* them. Just as in the biblical Garden of Eden, knowledge is absolute and unchanging, but it is in the sole possession of the authorities. Ordinary people can never determine the truth for themselves, they must rely on the experts. If someone disagrees with what they have been told by their authorities, then that person must be wrong. There is no possibility of compromise or negotiation.

Who are the authorities? The first authorities we encounter are usually our parents. When parents are rooted in this stage of thinking, they expect children to do as they're told, not to disagree, not to question. They are the authorities, and the role of children is to benefit from their years of experience, their store of knowledge, and their position of authority. Similarly, when children enter a school system built on the foundation of Stage 1 thinking (as most school systems are), they are likely to be told: "We have the questions and the answers — your role is to learn them, not ask questions of your own," an approach that runs counter to children's natural curiosity.

People who have been raised in a Stage 1 environment often become Stage 1 thinkers themselves when they mature. As parents, supervisors, and even friends, they are authoritarian and dogmatic. They believe they know what is right, based on what authorities have told them, and they are convinced that anyone who disagrees with them must be wrong. Organizations ranging from the armed services to "top-down-managed" companies are based on authoritarian principles, and they are often populated by Stage 1 thinkers.

People in this Garden of Eden stage of thinking become dissatisfied with it when they come to realize that they can't simply rely on authorities to tell them what to think and believe because *authorities disagree with each other* in virtually every arena, be the authorities doctors, religious leaders, economists, psychologists, educators, scientists, lawyers, parents, and many others besides. We explored this disturbing phenomenon earlier in the chapter, and it poses a mortal threat to Stage 1 thinking. If the authorities disagree with each other, then how do we figure out what (and whom) to believe? Stage 1 thinkers try to deal with this contradiction by maintaining that *my* authorities know more than *your* authorities. But if we are willing to think clearly and honestly, this explanation simply doesn't hold up: we have to explain *why* we choose to believe one authority over another. And as soon as that happens, we have transcended Stage 1 thinking. Just as Adam and Eve could not go back to blind, uncritical acceptance of authority once they had tasted the fruit of the Tree of the Knowledge of Good and Evil, so it is nearly impossible to return to Stage 1 after recognizing its oversimplifying inadequacies.

Why are some people able to go beyond Stage 1 thinking while others remain more or less stuck there throughout their lives? Part of the answer lies in how diverse their environment is. When people live in predominantly homogeneous environments, surrounded by people who think and believe the same way, it is much easier to maintain the artificially uniform worldview of the Garden of Eden thinking.

However, when people are exposed to diverse experiences that challenge them with competing perspectives, it is much more difficult to maintain the unquestioned faith in authoritarian dictates of Stage 1 thinking. For example, in my Philosophy of Religion classes, the final term project is for students to visit five different places of religious worship selected from a list of thirty I provide, ranging from Zen Buddhist to Pentecostal, Catholic to Southern Baptist, Jewish to Hindu. They are expected to involve themselves in the services to the extent that it is appropriate, and then write a report analyzing their experiences and applying the course concepts. Students invariably report that this project transformed their thinking, stimulating them to view religion in a richer, more complex light. It gives them the opportunity to see other people who were just as serious and devout as themselves engage in very different religious practices.

However, simply providing people with diverse experiences does not guarantee that they will be stimulated to question and transcend the limiting confines of Stage 1 thinking. We need to have the *emotional willingness* to open ourselves to new possibilities and the *intellectual ability* to see issues from different perspectives. Very often people are so emotionally entangled in their point of view that they are simply unwilling to question its truth, and so the power of their emotional needs inhibits the potential illumination of their reasoning abilities. Additionally, many people have not developed the flexibility of thinking needed to extricate themselves from their own point of view and look at issues from different perspectives. To become a Stage 2 thinker, both of these conditions must be met: the emotional willingness *and* the cognitive ability to be open-minded.

STAGE 2: ANYTHING GOES

Once one has rejected the dogmatic, authoritarian framework of Stage 1, the temptation in Stage 2 is to go to the opposite extreme and believe that *anything goes.* The reasoning goes something like this: If authorities are not infallible and we can't trust their expertise, then no one point of view is ultimately any better than any other. You have your opinion, I have my opinion, and there is no way to determine which is better. In Stage 1 the authorities could resolve such disputes, but if their opinion is on the same level as yours and mine, then there is no rational way to resolve differences.

In the tradition of philosophy, such a view is known as *relativism:* The truth is relative to any individual or situation, and there is no standard we can use to decide which beliefs make most sense. Take the example of fashion. You may believe that an attractive presentation includes loose-fitting clothing in muted colors, a natural hairstyle, and a minimum of makeup and jewelry. Someone else might prefer tight-fitting black clothing, gelled hair, tattoos, and body piercings. In Stage 2 thinking, there's no way to evaluate these or any other fashion preferences: They are simply "matters of taste." And, in fact, if you examine past photographs of yourself and what you considered to be "attractive" years ago, this relativistic point of view probably makes some sense.

Although we may be drawn to this seemingly open-minded attitude — *anything goes* — the reality is that we are often not so tolerant. We *do* believe that some appearances are more aesthetically pleasing than others. But there is an even more serious threat to Stage 2 thinking. Imagine the following scenario: As you are strolling down the street, you suddenly feel a gun pushed against your back accompanied by a demand for all your valuables. You protest, arguing with this would-be mugger that he has no right to your possessions. "On the contrary," your philosophically inclined mugger responds. "I believe that 'might makes right,' and since I have a weapon, I am entitled to your valuables. You have your beliefs, I have my beliefs, and as a Stage 2 thinker, there's no way for you to prove me wrong!" Preposterous? Nevertheless, this is the logical conclusion of an Anything Goes view of things. If we truly believe this, than we cannot condemn *any* belief or action, no matter how heinous, and we cannot praise *any* belief or action, no matter how laudatory.

When we think things through, it's obvious that the Stage 2 Anything Goes level of thinking simply doesn't work because it leads to absurd conclusions that run counter to our deeply felt conviction that some beliefs *are* better than other beliefs. So while Stage 2 may represent a slight advance over Stage 1 in sophistication and complexity, it's clear to a reflective and discerning eye that a further advance to Stage 3 is necessary.

STAGE 3: THINKING CRITICALLY

The two opposite perspectives of Stages 1 and 2 find their synthesis in Stage 3: Thinking Critically. When people achieve this level of understanding they recognize that some viewpoints *are* better than other viewpoints, not simply because authorities say so, but because *there are compelling reasons to support these viewpoints*. At the same time, people in this stage are open-minded toward other viewpoints, especially those that disagree with theirs. They recognize that there are often a number of legitimate perspectives on complex issues, and they accept the validity of these perspectives to the extent that they are supported by persuasive reasons and evidence.

Consider a more complicated issue, like abortion. A Stage 3 thinker approaches this as she approaches all issues: trying to understand all of the different viewpoints on the issue, to evaluate the reasons that support each of these viewpoints, and then to come to her own thoughtful conclusion. When asked, she can explain the rationale for her viewpoint, but she also respects differing viewpoints that are supported by legitimate reasons, even though she feels her viewpoint makes more sense. In addition, a Stage 3 thinker maintains an open mind, always willing to consider new evidence that might convince her to modify or even change her position.

A Stage 3 thinker recognizes that the world is a complex, ambiguous, and evolving place, and that our thinking has to be deep, open-minded, and flexible if we are to understand it and make intelligent decisions. But while people in the Thinking Critically stage are actively open to different perspectives, they also *commit* themselves to definite points of view, and are confident in explaining the reasons and evidence that have led them to their conclusions. Be aware that being open-minded is not the same thing as being intellectually wishy-washy. *In addition* to having clearly defined views, critical thinkers are always willing to listen to people who disagree with them, and, in fact, actively seek out opposing viewpoints, because they know that this is the only way to achieve the clearest, most insightful, most firmly grounded understanding. They also recognize that their views may evolve over time as they learn more.

Becoming a Stage 3 thinker is certainly a worthy goal, and it is the only way to adequately answer Socrates' challenge to examine our lives thoughtfully and honestly. But to live a life of reflection and action, of open-mindedness and commitment, of purpose and fulfillment, is not a simple endeavor. It requires the full development of our intellectual abilities and positive traits of character, a lifelong journey.

THINKING ACTIVITY

What Stage of Knowing Am I In?

We all know people who illustrate each of these three Stages of Knowing. Think about the people in your life — professionally and personally — and identify which stage you think they mainly fall into.

Consider carefully *your* beliefs in each of the following areas and evaluate in which of the three Stages of Knowing you predominantly think.

- professional area of expertise
- science
- moral issues
- religion
- human nature
- social relationships
- child-rearing
- aesthetics (beauty)

For example: *My beliefs in the area of child-rearing tend to be Stage 1. I have never really examined the way I was brought up, and I have raised my children pretty much the same way, without question.*

Or, *My beliefs in my area of expertise, medicine, are Stage 3. When confronted with a set of symptoms, I consider all of the possible diagnoses, carefully evaluate the relevant evidence, and then reach an informed conclusion that is open to modification as new information is developed.*

Analyze and Evaluate Your Beliefs

THE PATH to becoming a consistent Stage 3 or critical thinker begins with evaluating the process you use to form beliefs and reach conclusions about the world. Some of your beliefs are deep and profound, with far-reaching implications, such as your belief (or disbelief) in a Supreme Being, or opinion on whether the Golden Rule should govern people's actions. Other of your beliefs are less significant, such as whether vitamin supplements improve your health, or if having children wear school uniforms is beneficial. Your total collection of beliefs constitutes your Philosophy of Life, the guiding beacon you use to chart the course of your personal existence. That philosophy — and the confidence that comes from consciously building a firm foundation for it — is reflected in both the small details and the most profound aspects of your behavior.

Critical thinkers are people who have learned how to develop informed, well-founded beliefs. That's why they tend to be more successful in life. As you become a more accomplished critical thinker, you will develop beliefs that will enhance the quality of your life; beliefs that are clearly conceived, thoughtfully expressed, and solidly supported. This is the first step to constructing an enlightened philosophy, painting a portrait of yourself that you can present to the world with pride and satisfaction.

Everybody has a collection of beliefs that they use to guide their actions. What differentiates people is the *quality* of their beliefs, the strength of the reasons and evidence that support their beliefs. As a critical thinker, you should be striving to develop the most accurate beliefs possible, beliefs constructed through a process of thoughtful reflection and analysis. For example, think about the following belief expressed by one of my former students. How does he form and re-form his belief? Do you think he arrives at a reasonable conclusion? Do you agree with his belief? Why or why not?

It is time for me to tell my grandfather's story. After watching his mind deteriorate slowly over five years, and after seven months of prayerful reflection and planning, my grandfather quietly, with great dignity and grace, ended his life. He had my support and the help of a compassionate physician who prescribed sleeping pills for him. For more than forty years my grandfather was my closest confidant, guide, and friend. The only thing he ever asked of me, and the most difficult decision I ever had to make, was to help him in planning his suicide. I sought guidance in prayer and from friends before agreeing to help him.

He had worked as a volunteer at the local hospital in our county and was intimately aware of the end stages of Alzheimer's disease.

He told me that every time he walked out of the local hospital he prayed that it would not happen to him. But on some level he realized that he probably had it even then. The neurologist who diagnosed him told him that there was no treatment, and sent him to a psychiatrist.

He had endured twelve years of widowhood alone, maintaining staunchly that he would never move in with his children, despite repeated invitations. His pride and his close connection to many friends prevented him from coming until the Alzheimer's had so exhausted him that he could no longer live alone. The disease was also interfering with his relationships. By the time he came to live with us, six months before he died, he was unable to pursue any of his interests. Getting up was a chore. He could no longer read because he didn't know what the words meant; he forgot words and was embarrassed to speak at length. He could no longer distinguish the denominations of money. On several occasions he could not remember my father's name. He no longer wanted to shower, woke up every day confused, became incontinent at night, and began to hallucinate during the day. He developed gout and angina in addition to the arthritis and glaucoma, which were chronic but under control. His hearing was also impaired, and this increased his difficulty in communicating.

In witnessing the deterioration of my grandfather's body and the agony he was experiencing, I made the decision to assist him in the planning of his death. To this day I have no regrets with that decision. I strongly believe that life itself is precious and that we should do all we can to prolong our lives. But this was an exception because of all the pain and agony my grandfather was enduring along with all of us who loved him. I pray that if one day I am in a similar situation, I will have someone to support me and my beliefs.

Here is a brief survey of some beliefs that may contribute to your "Philosophy of Life." Without writing a full essay, answer the statements in the following Thinking Activity and note briefly how comfortable you would feel at this point in justifying your answers, as well as the paths you pursued to arrive at them. Would your "map" be clear and detailed? Or would it be winding, full of detours, and difficult for others to follow? Remember that these questions don't have a simple "right" or "wrong" answer.

THINKING ACTIVITY

Surveying Your Beliefs

Answer the following questions, based on what you believe to be true.

1. Is there a God?
2. Should research on the cloning of humans continue?
3. Should women have the legal right to have an abortion?
4. Are events on earth influenced by the positions of the planets and stars as expressed in astrology?
5. Is the death penalty justified for some convicted murderers?
6. Should health care workers and potential patients be tested for the AIDS virus, and if positive, be identified to each other?
7. Should the government provide public assistance to citizens who cannot support themselves and their families?
8. Should affirmative action programs be created to compensate for long-standing discrimination?
9. Have aliens visited Earth in some form?
10. Should parents be permitted to refuse conventional medical care for their children if their religious beliefs prohibit it?
11. Should certain "recreational" drugs, such as marijuana, be legalized?

12. Should people with terminal illnesses be permitted to end their lives with medical assistance, such as that provided by Dr. Jack Kevorkian?

Your responses to these questions reveal aspects of the way your mind works: your values, formative experiences, and reasoning processes. How did you arrive at these conclusions? Your views on these and other issues undoubtedly had their beginnings with your family, especially your parents. After we reach adulthood, our thinking continues to be shaped by personal experiences and the influence of others in our lives. And we are particularly susceptible to the sophisticated manipulation of the media.

As a result of our ongoing experiences, our minds — and our thinking abilities — ideally continue to mature. Instead of simply accepting the views of others, we gradually develop the ability to examine this thinking and to decide whether it makes sense to us and whether we should accept it. As we think through such ideas, we should use this standard to make our decision: *Are there good reasons or evidence that support this thinking?* If there are good reasons, we can actively decide to adopt these ideas. If they do not hold up to scrutiny, we can modify or reject them. This approach enables us, over time, to move from Stage 1 thinking to Stage 2, Anything Goes, and ultimately to Stage 3, Thinking Critically.

Of course, we do not always examine our own thinking or the thinking of others so carefully. In fact, we often continue to believe the same ideas we were raised with, without ever examining and deciding for ourselves what to think. And sometimes we blindly reject the beliefs we have been brought up with, without really examining the reasons why. In addition, we often pick up unexamined beliefs as we go along. Here is a sampling of beliefs that have been "borrowed" from others, lacking the deep understanding that comes through personal investigation.

- I was reading that the economy is in danger of overheating and the Federal Reserve should therefore raise interest rates. I agree, but don't ask me why.
- I hear that he is a duplicitous person, so I don't trust him.
- Last night on the news there was vivid film footage of a protest over budget cuts in social services. It was clear from the pictures and the reporter's presentation that these people are mainly trouble-makers and freeloaders.
- I read several reviews of that controversial book about race relations. The authors obviously don't know what they're talking about.

How do you know when you have examined and adopted ideas yourself instead of simply borrowing them from others? Think about your responses to the questions you answered in the previous Thinking Activity. To what extent do you feel that your beliefs were instilled by your parents or other influential people in your life? The fact is, it's sometimes hard to disentangle which threads of the fabric of our beliefs come from others and which originate from ourselves. The key point is that whatever the history of your beliefs, it's time for you to create your own distinctive portrait, to decide which colors and forms represent who *you* are. One clear indication of having thought through your ideas is being able to explain *why* you believe them — what reasons led you to these conclusions.

THINKING CRITICALLY ABOUT YOUR BELIEFS

Critical thinkers continually evaluate their beliefs by applying *intellectual standards* in order to assess their strength and accuracy. Uncritical thinkers generally adopt beliefs without thoughtful scrutiny or rigorous evaluation, letting these beliefs drift into their thinking for all sorts of superficial and illogical reasons.

The most effective way for you to test the strength and accuracy of your beliefs is to evaluate evidence that supports them. There are four categories of evidence: authorities, written references, factual evidence, and personal experience.

Not all evidence is equally strong or accurate. Here's an obvious example: Before the fifteenth century the common belief that the earth was flat was supported by the following evidence:

- *Authorities*: Educational and religious authorities taught people the earth was flat.
- *Written references*: The written opinions of scientific experts supported belief in a flat earth.
- *Factual evidence*: No person had ever circumnavigated the earth.
- *Personal experience*: From a physical vantage point, the earth *looks* flat.

So we see that our ability to apply this structure for evaluating our beliefs does not always ensure a correct conclusion or an invincible belief. Many considerations go into evaluating the strength and accuracy of evidence, and we will be exploring these areas in this chapter and future chapters. Here are the basic questions that critical thinkers automatically consider when evaluating evidence.

The Thinker's Way to Evaluate Evidence

- *Authorities*: Are the authorities knowledgeable in this area? Are they reliable? Have they ever given inaccurate information? Do other authorities disagree?
- *Written references*: What are the credentials of the authors? Are there others who disagree with their opinions? On what evidence do the authors base their opinions?
- *Factual evidence*: What is the source and foundation of the evidence? Can the evidence be interpreted differently? Does the evidence support the conclusion?

- *Personal experience:* What were the circumstances under which the experience took place? Were distortions or mistakes in perception possible? Have other people had either similar or conflicting experiences? Are there other explanations for the experience?

Now you may be thinking, "Will I be called upon to apply this structure — these thinking tools — to every situation?" It may be overly optimistic to expect that we can take time out to step back and evaluate all our situations this way, especially because we already feel so overly burdened and overextended. However, it is precisely because of this that we need to put on the brakes or risk losing ourselves in the frenetically accelerated flow of today's culture. What you are learning from these and further exercises is a way of approaching both small and large questions differently from the way you did before. By recognizing the need to impose these intellectual standards, this way of thinking will eventually become habitual.

THINKING ACTIVITY

Evaluating Your Beliefs

- Select several of your responses to the belief survey (pages 47–48) and explain the reasons, evidence, and experiences that led you to your conclusions. Be as specific as you can in expressing your thinking.
- After you have recorded your evidence, use The Thinker's Way to Evaluate Evidence to assess its accuracy and strength.
  Example: I believe that aliens have visited Earth in some form.
  Explanation: I have read a great deal about eyewitness sightings

and evidence of a government cover-up, and I have met people who believe they have seen UFOs.

Reasons/Evidence:

a. *Authorities:* Many reputable people have seen UFOs and had personal encounters with aliens. The government has documented these in secret files, which include the UFO crash at Roswell, New Mexico, in 1947. The government attempts at concealment and cover-up have been transparent.

b. *References:* There are many books supporting alien visitations and alien abductions.

c. *Factual evidence:* There are many photographs of UFOs and eyewitness accounts from people who have seen alien spacecraft. There have also been accounts of alien abductions. In addition, there is also a movie, *Alien Autopsy*, that purportedly shows an alien being dissected.

d. *Personal experience:* I have personally spoken to several people who are convinced that they saw things in the sky that looked like flying saucers.

Let's examine the process of critical evaluation by thinking through a sample belief: *"I believe that aliens have visited Earth in some form."* Interestingly, a recent Gallup Poll found that 42 percent of American college graduates believe that flying saucers have visited Earth in some form, and the popularity of shows like *The X-Files* has highlighted people's fascination with this subject.

• *Authorities:* Many reputable people have seen UFOs and had personal encounters with aliens. The government has documented these in secret files, which include the UFO crash at Roswell, NM in 1947. The government attempts at concealment and cover-up have been transparent.

Thinking Critically about Authorities: While there are many individuals who have testified to the existence of alien encounters over the years, virtually all scientific authorities have been extremely skeptical.

They emphasize that all of the "evidence" is unsubstantiated, controversial, indirect, and murky — the markings of pseudoscientific fantasies. If aliens and UFOs exist, why haven't they announced their presence in an incontrovertible fashion? Some of the most intriguing evidence comes in the form of the government's belated and somewhat bizarre explanations for UFO sightings and the alleged Roswell incident. On June 25, 1997, the United States Air Force announced that the mysterious happenings in the New Mexico desert in the late 1940s and 1950s were in fact experiments involving crash dummies and weather balloons. Six weeks later, on August 3, 1997, the CIA "admitted" that the U.S. government lied about alleged UFO sightings in the 1950s and 1960s in order to protect classified information regarding top-secret spy planes, the U-2 and SR-71. What's the reason for the government's sudden attempts after all these years to explain these mysteries? And why does there appear to be contradictory testimony from different parts of the government? Why do the government explanations seem almost as fanciful and far-fetched as the UFO stories?

• **References:** There are many books supporting alien visitations and abductions.

   Thinking Critically about References: Although many books regarding UFOs have been written, few have been considered serious works, since they involve more unsubstantiated speculation than evidence. Recently, Philip J. Corso, who served on the National Security Council under President Dwight D. Eisenhower, contended in his book, The Day After Roswell (1997), that he personally directed an army project that transferred to the military various types of technology recovered from the alien ship that crashed in the desert. To date, efforts to prove or disprove his account have been inconclusive. After reviewing written accounts and interviewing people claiming to be alien abductees, Dr. John Mack, a psychiatry professor at Harvard Medical School, came to the conclusion that many of these reports are true. Though he was harshly criticized by his colleagues, Dr. Mack became instantly popular on the UFO circuit, and he recently convened a conference at which two hundred mental health professionals gathered to discuss alien abductions.

• *Factual Evidence:* There are many photographs of UFOs and eye-witness accounts from people who have seen alien spacecraft. There have also been accounts of alien abductions. In addition, there is also a movie, *Alien Autopsy,* that purportedly shows an alien being dissected.

Thinking Critically about Factual Evidence: There have been innumerable UFO sightings, many of which can be explained by the presence of aircraft in the vicinity, meteors, or some other physical event. However, there is a core of sightings, sometimes by large groups of reputable people, that have not been satisfactorily explained. There are a number of photographs of "flying saucers" taken at a considerable distance, and though provocative in their possibilities, they are inconclusive. Most reports of alien abductions have been considered by the scientific establishment to be hoaxes or the result of mental illness or hallucinations — at least until Dr. Mack's analysis, noted above. Medical experts and moviemakers have derided Alien Autopsy *as a crude hoax, although a small number of people knowledgeable about physiology and moviemaking techniques find it persuasive. There is no documented history of where the film came from, a fact that undermines its credibility.*

• *Personal Experience:* I have personally spoken to several people who are convinced that they saw things in the sky that looked like flying saucers.

Thinking Critically about Personal Experience: The perceptions of eyewitness testimony are notoriously unreliable. People consistently mistake and misinterpret what they experience, and often see what they want to see. In evaluating the testimony of experience, it's essential to establish independent confirmation.

Viewing Situations from Different Perspectives

WHILE IT IS important to think for yourself, others may have good ideas from which you can learn and benefit. A critical thinker is a person who is willing to listen to and examine carefully other views and new ideas. In addition to your viewpoint, there may be *other* viewpoints that are equally important and need to be taken into consideration if you are to develop a more complete understanding of the situation.

As children, we understand the world from only our own point of view. As we grow, we come into contact with people with different viewpoints; we begin to realize that our viewpoint is often inadequate, that we are frequently mistaken, and that our perspective is only one of many. If we are going to learn and fully develop, we must try to understand and appreciate the viewpoints of others.

For most of the important issues and problems in our lives, one viewpoint is simply not adequate to give a full and satisfactory understanding. To increase and deepen your knowledge, you must seek other perspectives on the situations you are trying to understand. You can sometimes accomplish this by using your imagination to visualize other viewpoints. Usually, however, you need actively to seek (and *listen* to) the viewpoints of others. It is often very difficult for people to see things from points of view other than their own, and if we are not careful we can make the very serious mistake of thinking that the way we see things is the way things really are.

As well as identifying with perspectives other than your own, you also have to work to understand the *reasons* that support these alternate viewpoints. This approach deepens your understanding of the issues and also stimulates you to evaluate your beliefs. The following Thinking Activity gives you an opportunity to describe a belief that you have and to view the same issue from a contrasting perspective. You may find that it is difficult to adopt this unfamiliar point of view, but strive to make as strong a case for it as you can. This is how you increase your thinking power — by working on your areas of weakness as well as refining your areas of strength.

THINKING ACTIVITY

Seeing Two Sides of an Issue

- Describe a belief of yours that you feel very strongly about and explain the reasons and evidence that led you to this belief. You can use one of the issues included in the Thinking Activity on pages 47–48, or a different one.
- Next, describe a point of view that is opposite from your belief. Identify some of the reasons and evidence that might cause someone to hold this belief.
- Evaluate the evidence on both sides of the issues by using The Thinker's Way to Evaluate Evidence.

In completing this activity you probably found supporting a belief you agreed with to be a straightforward process, while defending the opposite position — one with which you disagreed — was difficult. That's because we normally *don't* try very hard to see opposing points of view. Instead, we concentrate on our own beliefs and the reasons that support them. In many cases we have spent years collecting evidence and developing reasons to support our beliefs on issues like abortion, gay rights, interracial adoption, and countless others. We read articles that agree with our points of view, and seek the opinions of people with similar perspectives so that we can reinforce each other's scripts. And since we gravitate to people with similar views, we are only rarely required to justify our positions. At the same time, most people avoid exploring conflicting perspectives on these same beliefs. And when we do engage in debates with people holding conflicting views, it's usually with the aim of proving the other person wrong, not increasing our understanding of all sides of the issue.

Being open to new ideas and different viewpoints means being flexible enough to change or modify your ideas in the light of new information or better insight. Each of us has a tendency to cling to familiar beliefs. If we are going to continue to grow and develop as thinkers, however, we have to be willing to change or modify our viewpoints when evidence suggests that we should. The fact is, all of us have grown up with certain prejudices, of which fear and suspicion of people different from ourselves is the most obvious. However, as we mature and our experience increases, we may find that the evidence of our experience conflicts with the views we have been raised with. As critical thinkers, we have to be *open* to receiving this new evidence and *flexible* enough to change and modify our ideas on the basis of it. This means having the courage to doubt, which, as Voltaire believed, is preferable to clinging tenaciously to a false certainty: *"It is only charlatans who are certain; doubt is not a very agreeable state, but certainty is a ridiculous one."*

By actively trying to put yourself in other people's shoes, you are developing one of the key human virtues: *empathy.* Empathy is a key element of thinking critically, and is a prominent part of many world religions, embodied in moral tenets like the Golden Rule. For a critical thinker, deciding on the morally right thing to do requires that you mentally and emotionally place yourself in the position of other people who might be affected by your actions and then make your decision based on what will be best for their interests as well as your interests. This does not mean abandoning your own views or automatically sacrificing your own interests. It simply means that as you work toward creating a fulfilling life for yourself, you take other people's interests into consideration.

Unfortunately, there are strong cultural forces that are working *against* becoming open-minded, as David Shenk details in his book *Data Smog.* Although mass communication was supposed to transform the world into a "global village," the village is becoming increasingly factionalized as people are forced to retreat into their own special interests by the overwhelming volume of information available. More and more, we see specialized magazines and advertising targeted at specific audiences, and the expansion of the Internet is accelerating this fragmenting into self-contained subcultures.

Like niche radio and cable TV, the Net encourages a cultural splintering that can render physical communities much less relevant and free people from having to climb outside their own biases, assumptions, inherited ways of thought. This is perhaps best evidenced by the ominous emergence of so-called *smart agents* which automatically filter out information deemed irrelevant to the customer. With smart agents, there is no stumbling across unexpected subject matter, and there are fewer exchanges with people with different interests and opinions. As a result, both the idea and practice of pluralism suffer.

Why People Have Different Perspectives

AS REVEALED in the many discussions you have with other people, you have a unique perspective on the world. How did your perspective develop? It is a result of your past experiences and your distinctive personality. Everything in your history has gone into forming the distinctive "lenses" through which you see and experience the world. Your lenses shape and influence your perceptions, the beliefs that you form, and the actions that you take. The problem is that most of us tend to forget that we are viewing the world through our own unique lenses, and instead assume that we are experiencing the world clearly and objectively. That's why we get into so many disagreements with people: We think that we are arguing over what is actually at issue, when in many cases we are really just expressing the differences in our perceiving lenses.

For example, think back on heated discussions you have had over recent jury decisions (O. J. Simpson, Louise Woodward), politics (Bill and Hillary Clinton, Jesse Helms), social policy (immigration quotas, affirmative action), criminal justice (appropriate sentences for juveniles who commit violent crimes), child-rearing (physical discipline, drinking age), and many others as well. In most cases, you and the other discussants were viewing these issues through lenses that *predisposed* you to think and feel a certain way. That's why lawyers and prosecutors conduct such in-depth research into the thoughts and values of potential jurors — they are trying to uncover the lenses that will influence the way the jurors approach the case: shaping, influencing, biasing, distorting.

As a critical thinker, you need to become aware of the nature of your own "lenses" to help eliminate any bias or distortion they may be causing. You also want to become aware of the "lenses" of others so that you can better understand why they view things differently from you. We color the people and events in our world in our own personal fashion, projecting onto them what we are feeling and thinking. It's somewhat like the coloring books we all grew up with. Although we may be in general agreement regarding the basic outlines of a situation, the colors we use to complete the picture are typically our own. In most instances this process of "coloring the world" and "reading in meaning" is *unconscious* — we assume that our "picture" is an accurate representation of the world.

To complicate the situation, our own limitations in perceiving are not the only ones that can cause us problems. Other people often purposely create perceptions and misperceptions. An advertiser who wants to sell a product may try to communicate the impression that your life will be changed if you use that product. Or a person who wants to discredit someone else may spread untrue rumors about her, in order to influence others' perceptions of her.

The Thinker's Way to Clarify Perceptions

The only way you can correct the mistakes, distortions, and incompleteness of your perceptions is to become aware of this normally unconscious process by which you create and understand your world. Once aware, you can think critically about what is going on and then correct your mistakes and distortions, creating a clearer and more informed idea of what is taking place. Perception alone cannot be totally relied on, and if you remain unaware of how it operates and of your active role in it, then you will be unable to exert any control over it. And in that case, you will be convinced that the way *you* see the world is the way the world is, even when your perceptions are mistaken, distorted, or incomplete. Here are the thinking tools from your Mental Tool Bag that you should use to correct your perceiving lenses:

> ### The Thinker's Way to Clarify Perceptions
>
> - Ask questions about what you are perceiving: Are my perceptions accurate and complete? What are other possible interpretations of this situation? What evidence supports these various perspectives?
> - Become aware of the personal factors your lenses bring to your perceptions.
> - Discuss your perceptions with others.
> - Seek independent proof regarding your perceptions.

Each of us brings to every situation a whole collection of expectations, interests, fears, and hopes that can influence what we are perceiving. Consider the following situations:

- Your supervisor at work asks you to evaluate the performance of a coworker who is being considered for a promotion. You don't like this other worker because he acts arrogant and selfish. How do you evaluate his performance?
- Your child is not placed on the starting team at school. What do you think of the coach's decision?

In both of these cases, you can imagine that your perceptions might be influenced by certain hopes, fears, or prejudices that you brought to the situation, causing your observations to become distorted or inaccurate. Although you usually cannot eliminate the personal feelings that are influencing your perceptions, you can become aware of them and try to compensate for their bias. For instance, if you are asked to evaluate a group of people, one of whom is a good friend, you should try to keep these personal feelings in mind in order to make your evaluation as accurate as possible.

One of your first tasks should involve trying to discover any independent proof or evidence regarding the viewpoint. When evidence is available in the form of records, photographs, videotapes, or experimental results, this will certainly help you evaluate the accuracy of your perceptions. For example, in the situation above in which you were asked to evaluate a disliked coworker, some of the independent forms of evidence you could look for in trying to verify your perceptions might include:

- past performance evaluations of the person;
- creating an organized evaluation chart and then filling it in as accurately and objectively as you can;
- constructing a series of objective questions and then asking other workers to evaluate the person, using your questions as a guide;
- describing in detail the reasons why you don't like this person, and then highlighting the areas that are relevant to the performance of his job.

OVERCOMING STEREOTYPES

Thinking critically about your perceptions means trying to avoid developing impulsive or superficial perceptions that you are unwilling to change. We must be thoughtful in approaching the world and open to modifying our views in the light of new information or better insight. Consider the following perceptions:

- Women are very emotional.
- Politicians are corrupt.
- Teenagers are wild and irresponsible.
- People in large cities behave rudely.

These types of general perceptions are known as *stereotypes* because they express a belief about an entire group of people without recognizing the individual differences among members of the group. For instance, it is probably accurate to say that there are some politicians who are corrupt, but this is not the same thing as saying that all, or even most, politicians are corrupt. Stereotypes affect your perception of the world because they encourage you to form an inaccurate and superficial idea of a whole group of people ("All men are insensitive"). When you meet someone who falls into this group, you automatically perceive that person as having these stereotyped qualities ("This person is a man so he must be insensitive"). Even if you find that this person does not fit your stereotyped perception ("This man is not insensitive"), this sort of superficial labeling does not encourage you to change your perception of the group as a whole. Instead, it encourages you to overlook the conflicting information in favor of your stereotyped perception ("All men are insensitive — except this one"). On the other hand, when you are perceiving in a thoughtful fashion, you try to see what a person is like as an individual, instead of trying to fit him or her into a preexisting category.

By viewing the world through the limiting blinders of stereotypes, we can do a lot of harm as we judge people prematurely or impose destructive preconceptions on them. Instead of viewing them as complex, three-dimensional individuals, we view them as simplistic cardboard cutouts who lack distinctive qualities. If, instead, we train ourselves to look beyond the monochromatic world of stereotypes, we are able to see a world that is full of vibrant colors and textures, a world of depth and dimension.

THINKING ACTIVITY

Stereotyping

- Describe an incident in which you were perceived as a stereotype because of your age, ethnic or religious background, employment, accent, or place of residence.
- Describe how it felt to be stereotyped in this way.
- Explain what you think are the best ways to overcome stereotypes such as these.

BELIEVING, KNOWING, AND TRUTH

The beliefs you develop in living your life help you explain why the world is the way it is, and they guide you in making decisions. But all beliefs are not equal. Some beliefs are certain ("I believe that someday I will die") because they are supported by compelling reasons. Other beliefs are less certain ("I believe that life exists on other planets") because the support is not as solid. As you form and revise your beliefs, based on your experiences and your reflection on these experiences, it is important to make them as accurate as possible. The more accurate they are, the better you are able to understand what is taking place and to predict what will occur in the future.

The beliefs you form vary tremendously in accuracy. The idea of *knowing* is one of the ways humans have developed to distinguish beliefs supported by strong reasons or evidence from beliefs for which there is less support. Other beliefs are disproved by evidence to the contrary (such as the belief that the earth is flat). This distinction between "believing" and "knowing" can be illustrated by replacing the word *believe* with the word *know* in statements. For example:

1. I *know* that I will die.
2. I *know* that there is life on other planets.
3. I *know* that working hard will lead me to a happy life.
4. I *know* that the earth is flat.

The only statement in which most people would agree it clearly makes sense to use the word *know* is the first one, because there is conclusive evidence that this belief is accurate. In the case of sentence 2, we might say that, although life on other planets is a possibility, there does not seem to be *conclusive* evidence at present (*The X-Files* notwithstanding) that supports this view. In the case of sentence 3, we might say that, although for some people working hard leads to a happy life, this is not always the case. Sentence 4 expresses a belief that we "know" is not true.

THINKING ACTIVITY

Evaluating the Accuracy of Your Beliefs

Indicate whether you think that each of the beliefs listed below is

completely accurate ("I know this is the case");
generally accurate but not completely accurate ("This is often but not always the case");
definitely not accurate ("I know that this is not the case").

After determining the *degree of accuracy* in this way, explain why you have selected your answer.

- I believe that "fate" plays an important role in determining life's events.
- I believe that your personality is mostly inherited from your parents.
- I believe that your astrological sign determines some of your basic personality.
- I believe that people have the freedom to change themselves and their circumstances if they really want to.

Now write some of your most important beliefs on the following subjects and evaluate them in the same way:

- love
- physical health
- happiness
- personal development

When someone indicates that he or she thinks a belief is completely accurate by saying, "I *know*," your response is often "*How* do you know?" If the person cannot give you a satisfactory answer to this question, you are likely to say something like, "If you can't explain how you know it, then you don't *really* know it — you're just saying it." In other words, when you say that "you know" something, you mean at least two different things.

1. I think this belief is completely accurate.
2. I can explain to you the reasons or evidence that support this belief.

If either of these standards is not met, we would usually say that the person does not really "know." We work at evaluating the accuracy of our beliefs by examining the reasons or evidence that support them (known as the *justification* for the beliefs). Your beliefs can be thought of as forming a continuum based on their accuracy and justification. As you learn more about the world and yourself, you try to form beliefs that are increasingly accurate and justified.

Determining the accuracy and justification of your beliefs is a challenging business. The key point is that, as a critical thinker, you should continually try to form and revise your beliefs so that you can understand the world in increasingly effective ways. Even when you find that you maintain certain beliefs over a long period of time, you should discover that your explorations result in a deeper and fuller understanding of these beliefs. In evaluating your beliefs, it is helpful to use certain *criteria* to evaluate how true they are, summarized in The Thinker's Way to Evaluate Beliefs.

The Thinker's Way to Evaluate Beliefs

- How effectively does the belief *explain what is taking place?*
- To what extent is the belief *consistent with other beliefs* about the world?
- How effectively does the belief help you *predict what will happen* in the future?
- To what extent is the belief *supported by sound reasons and compelling evidence derived from reliable sources?*

"*The truth will set you free.*" *Truth* and *knowledge* are terms that we use regularly in our conversations with others. For the most part, people in our culture are socialized to believe that knowledge and truth are absolute and unchanging, and that we can discover what they are by asking the right people or looking up the appropriate reference. However, a critical thinker understands that knowledge and truth are goals we are striving to achieve, processes that we are all actively involved in as we construct our understanding of the world. Developing accurate *knowledge* and discovering the *truth* about the world is a lifelong process of exploration that requires vigilance and your full complement of critical thinking abilities. Though the search for "absolute knowledge" and "eternal truth" may be misconceived, we are able to become wiser, more insightful, and more knowledgeable about the world and the mysteries of life.

> I *tore myself away from the safe comfort of certainties*
> *through my love for truth; and truth rewarded me.*
> — SIMONE DE BEAUVOIR

How Effective a Critical Thinker Am I?

DESCRIBED BELOW are key thinking abilities and personal attributes that are correlated with thinking critically. Evaluate your position regarding each of these abilities and attributes, and use this self-evaluation to guide your efforts to become a critical thinker.

Make Critical Thinking a Priority

I live as though critical thinking is important in all areas of my life.	I don't always live as though critical thinking is a priority.

5   4   3   2   1

The process of becoming a more powerful, sophisticated critical thinker begins with deciding that you *want* to become this kind of person.

   Strategy: *Having completed your portrait of a "critical thinker" earlier in this chapter, review your portrait regularly so that you can plan your thinking goals and evaluate your progress. Becoming a critical thinker is a long-term process that involves explicit goals, sustained effort, and ongoing self-evaluation.*

Become a Stage 3 Thinker in Every Area of Life

I am a Stage 3 thinker in most areas of life.	I am a Stage 1 or Stage 2 thinker in most areas of life.

5   4   3   2   1

The three Stages of Knowing introduced in this chapter are a useful vehicle for assessing your overall development as a critical thinker. Stage 3, Thinking Critically, represents the most advanced intellectual level, as people realize that some views *are* better than others, and it is their responsibility to develop informed beliefs by thinking for themselves.

   Strategy: *Once you recognize your own responsibility in constructing your understanding of the world, you can make meaningful progress in improving your sophistication as a thinker. Establish the habit of examining a variety of perspectives, critically evaluate the supporting reasons, develop your own well-reasoned conclusions, and remain open-minded to new insight.*

Develop Well-Reasoned Beliefs

I strive to form the most well-reasoned beliefs possible.	I have not carefully examined many of my beliefs.

5   4   3   2   1

The beliefs of a critical thinker form a coherent philosophy, a dynamic system in which all of the beliefs are organically related. Since their beliefs are the result of thoughtful reflection, critical thinkers are able to explain the rationale for their views, and they are open to productive discussions with conflicting perspectives.

Strategy: *Develop the habit of critically examining your beliefs: What do I believe and why do I believe it? Where did these beliefs originate, and what are the reasons that support them? What are other viewpoints that I haven't considered? Are my beliefs consistent with one another? If not, why not?*

Support Your Beliefs with Thoughtful Reasons and Compelling Evidence

I always try to support my beliefs with reasons and evidence.	I often just accept my beliefs without supporting them.

5   4   3   2   1

Critical thinkers recognize that it is not sufficient to have beliefs, it is necessary to provide *support* for your beliefs with thoughtful reasons and compelling evidence.

Strategy: *Every time you say (or think) "I believe . . ." or "I think . . ." develop the habit of explaining why you believe or think what you do. Similarly, when others offer their opinions, ask them, "Why do you believe that?" This way you will be improving their critical thinking abilities as well as your own. Use The Thinker's Way to Evaluate Evidence on pages 50–51 to guide your thinking.*

Strive to Be Open-Minded

I am very open-minded and view situations from many different perspectives.	I see things mainly from my own point of view and I can be fairly dogmatic.

5   4   3   2   1

Critical thinkers actively try to get outside of their own viewpoints and see issues and situations from alternate perspectives, particularly those that disagree with them. This perspective-taking helps you develop the strongest beliefs and broadest knowledge, and it contributes to productive relationships with other people.

Strategy: Seek out perspectives different from yours, particularly those that disagree with you. Listen openly and respectfully to the arguments others are making and strive to reach thoughtful conclusions that takes all the perspectives into account.

Become Aware of Your Personal "Lenses"

I am acutely aware of how my personal "lenses" shape and color what I experience.	I usually think that the way I see things is the way things are.

5   4   3   2   1

All of us view the world through "lenses" that influence and "color" how we experience things, process information, and make decisions. Critical thinkers seek to become aware of their own personal lenses and the lenses of others so that they can understand the meanings people are projecting and discover the "truth."

Strategy: Become aware of your lenses by developing the habit of asking yourself: Are my perceptions accurate and complete? How are my biases influencing my perceptions? Are there other ways of viewing this situation that I am not acknowledging? Which ways of viewing the situation make the most sense? The Thinker's Way to Clarify Perceptions on pages 59–60 provides a useful guide.

Evaluate the Accuracy of Information and the Credibility of Sources

I carefully evaluate the information that I receive and the sources that provide it.

I usually accept what I read and hear without much critical analysis.

5 4 3 2 1

Intelligent beliefs are the product of active investigation and critical evaluation. Your responsibility as a critical thinker is to analyze each perspective carefully; evaluate the accuracy of the information and the credibility of the sources; take into account the bias that is an inescapable part of every viewpoint; and then reach your own thoughtful conclusions.

Strategy: *When you are evaluating the validity of information and potential beliefs, ask yourself the questions included in The Thinker's Way to Evaluate Beliefs on page 65.*

Emulate Your Critical Thinking Portrait

I am an insightful, powerful, and confident critical thinker.

I am not as strong a thinker as I could be.

5 4 3 2 1

This chapter has given you the opportunity to create a more detailed portrait of a critical thinker that can serve as your paradigm as you seek to elevate your intellectual abilities and enhance your reflective insight.

Strategy: *Describe your portrait of a critical thinker on an index card that you can easily refer to, identifying the specific qualities that you would like to develop. Compare yourself to your portrait on a regular basis, noting the progress that you have made as well as the areas that need more attention.*

SCORING GUIDE

Add up the numbers you circled for each of the self-evaluation items above and use the following Scoring Guide to evaluate your critical thinking abilities.

Point Total	Interpretation
32–40	very critical
24–31	moderately critical
16–23	somewhat critical
8–15	comparatively uncritical

In interpreting your results, be sure to keep in mind that:

- This evaluation is not an exact measure of your critical thinking abilities, but is rather intended as a general indicator of how critically you approach your life.
- Your score indicates how critically you are functioning at the present time, *not* your critical thinking *potential.* If you scored lower than you would like, it means that you are underutilizing your critical thinking abilities, and that you need to follow the suggestions in the chapter to realize your talents fully.

THINKING ACTIVITY

Becoming a Critical Thinker

Select areas of your life in which you would like to improve your abilities as a critical thinker. Keep a record in your Thinking Notebook detailing your efforts and their results. Be sure to allow yourself sufficient time to develop these complex abilities and attitudes, and don't get frustrated if you don't succeed at once or if you suffer setbacks. Cultivate the qualities of thinking critically that we have explored in this section:

- Make critical thinking a priority.
- Become a Stage 3 thinker in every area of life.
- Develop well-reasoned beliefs to guide your actions.
- Support your beliefs with thoughtful reasons and compelling evidence.
- Strive to be open-minded.
- Become aware of your personal "lenses."
- Evaluate the accuracy of information and the credibility of sources.
- Emulate your critical thinking portrait.

STEP 2

LIVE CREATIVELY

Creativity is a powerful life force that can infuse your life with meaning. This chapter will help you discover the creative talents that should work in partnership with critical thinking to transform your life into a rich tapestry of productivity and success. It will guide you to overcome the momentum of habit, the weight of reality, and the coercion of conformity in order to discover your creative spirit, your creative essence. By learning to approach your life with a mindful sense of discovery and invention, you can continually create yourself in ways limited only by your imagination.

"Each of Us Is a Different Kind of Artist"

THE FOLLOWING SITUATION is undoubtedly familiar: You are in the middle of a large group's contentious debate — your department at work, the parents' association at your children's school — that is trying to solve a complex, emotionally charged problem. The volatile discussion and increasing dissension are generating heat but no light, and an intelligent solution appears unattainable. And then suddenly, like a lamp penetrating the gloom of confused thinking, someone offers a completely unique idea, an inventive proposal that is elegant in its simplicity but profound in its ability to transcend the conflict and achieve a genuinely insightful solution. You look around the room, eager to identify this impressive individual, and you can sense that others are looking as well. "Who is that? Wow, I'd like to be that creative!" You've identified a role model . . . the kind of person you would like to associate with, the kind of person you would like to become. Some people are threatened by such a penetrating mind, but others are inspired and motivated by it. This is the power of creativity in action, a thinking potential that we all possess but too few develop and use.

The first day of my course Creative Thinking: Theory and Practice, I always ask my students if they think they are creative. The majority usually respond that they are *not*. One reason for this is that people often confuse being "creative" with being "artistic" — skilled at art, music, poetry, writing, drama, dance. Although artistic people are certainly creative, there are an infinite number of ways to be creative that are *not* ordinarily considered artistic. Being creative is a state of mind and a way of life that is relevant to every human activity. As the writer Eric Gill expresses it: *"The artist is not a different kind of person, but each one of us is a different kind of artist."*

Are you creative? Yes! In order to understand the ways you are, you need to examine your life in terms of what creativity really means. For example, think of all the activities you enjoy doing: engaging in a sport, raising children, solving problems on the job, cooking, dancing, writing, or decorating. Whenever you are investing your own unique ideas, you are being creative. When you develop a new recipe or dance in your own distinctive style, you are being creative, as you are when you stimulate original thinking in your children or make your friends laugh with your singular brand of humor. Living your life creatively means bringing your unique perspective and creative talents to all the dimensions of your life. Creativity is not an add-on, something extra that you have to find time for in your busy life. Instead, creativity is a better, richer, more productive approach to doing what you are already doing. It's braided seamlessly into your life, not a bow that's added on for decoration.

Thinking Critically and Living Creatively

AS IMPORTANT as it is to become a *critical* thinker, it is equally important to become a *creative* thinker in order to develop a life philosophy that truly reflects who you are, a thinking framework that you can rely on to guide you through difficult decisions and challenging problems. The *creative thinking* process produces ideas that are unique, useful, and worthy of further elaboration, while the *critical thinking* process is used to evaluate the worthiness of ideas and organize plans for implementing them. Creative thinking and critical thinking thus work as partners to produce effective thinking, enabling you to lead a fulfilling and successful life. Living your life creatively means bringing your creative talents and critical thinking abilities to all the dimensions of your life, as illustrated in the following passages.

> Raising a child well is a challenging job both physically and mentally, demanding an extensive amount of creativity. As a single parent, I try different techniques to encourage my child, thinking of new and exciting ways to keep her focused in her early stages of learning. For example, each month of the year and day of the week has a tale behind it, as I embroider the subjects with stories in order to enhance her learning. I play with her by pretending that I am the daughter and she is the mother, which helps me understand how she sees me as a mother and provides her with an opportunity to act out her feelings. I try to stimulate her creativity (and preserve my sanity) by involving her in the process of cooking, giving her the skin from peeled vegetables and a pot so she can make her own "soup." Using catalogs, we cut out pictures of furniture, rugs, and curtains, and she pastes them onto cartons to create her own interior decor: vibrant living rooms, plush bedrooms, colorful family rooms. Beautiful bathtub boats are crafted from aluminum paper; we "go bowling" with empty soda cans and a ball; and she stars in

"track meets" by running an obstacle course we set up. Creativity is an instinctive drive inside of me that is expressed in so many ways for her: I am a seamstress for Halloween, a counselor for emotional distress, a nurse for life's unavoidable mishaps, a party planner, a gourmet chef, an award-winning teacher, and especially a friend.

One of the most creative aspects of my life is my diet. I have been a vegetarian for the past five years, while the rest of my family has continued to eat meat. I had to overcome many obstacles to make this lifestyle work for me, including family dissension. The solution was simple: I had to learn how to cook creatively. I have come to realize that my diet is an ongoing learning process. I slowly evolved from a person who could cook food only if it came from a can, to someone who could make bread from scratch and grow yogurt cultures. I find learning new things about nutrition and cooking healthful foods very relaxing and rewarding. I like being alone in my house baking bread; there is something very comforting about the aroma. Most of all I like to experiment with different ways to prepare foods, because the ideas are my own. Even when an effort is less than successful, I find pleasure in the knowledge that I gained from the experience. I discovered recently, for example, that eggplant is terrible in soup! Making mistakes seems to be a natural way to increase creativity, and I now believe that people who say they don't like vegetables simply have not been properly introduced to them!

These passages illustrate how the harmonious meshing of creative and critical thinking can enrich your life. Instead of living life on a flat plain, with gray colors and undistinguished topography, you can use these twin forms of thinking as tools to create a textured and vibrantly colored environment. By thinking critically and creatively, you develop a whole new approach to living, establishing new patterns to express your distinctive individuality. And possessing these powerful forms of thought will give you greater confidence to achieve lofty goals and solve challenging problems. You see your life in a newer, fresher way, full of possibilities that were previously invisible. Initiating new thinking patterns in one area of your life carries over into every other area, whether it's devising a creative solution to a troubling problem or formulating thoughtful opinions about complicated issues. You feel more empowered, more enabled in approaching your life. By beginning with the concrete areas of your everyday existence — raising children, cooking, relationships, job responsibilities — you can extend outward to the larger aspects of your life, until the ripples encompass your entire universe.

THINKING ACTIVITY

Describing a Creative Area in Your Life

Describe a creative area of your life in which you are able to express your unique personality and talents. Be specific and give examples.

Analyze your creative area by answering the following questions:

- Why do you feel that this area is creative?
- How would you describe the experience of being engaged in this creative activity? Where do your creative ideas come from? How do they develop?
- What strategies do you use to increase your creativity? What obstacles block your creative efforts? How do you try to overcome these blocks?

What Is Creativity?

THE MYSTERIOUS and elusive nature of creativity has not prevented people from *trying* to define it. Here is a sampling of their efforts:

> *Creativity is the search for the elusive "Aha," that moment of insight when one sees the world, or a problem, or an idea, in a new way.*
>> —LESLEY DORMEN and PETER EDIDIN,
>> creativity researchers

> *Creativity is a marriage between ideas which were previously strangers to each other.*
>> —ARTHUR KOESTLER,
>> psychologist and writer

> *Creativity is the magical, unreasonable leap that imagination willingly makes, allowing new, original ideas to be born.*
>> —JEROME BRUNER,
>> psychologist

> *Creativity is "the firing of my soul."*
>> —WOLFGANG AMADEUS MOZART

> *The key to successful methods comes right out of the air. A real new thing like an idea, a beautiful melody, is pulled out of space.*
>> —THOMAS EDISON

One thing all of these observations have in common is that there is no recipe for creativity, no easy formula. And perhaps it is its elusiveness that makes creativity the gift it is. If rigid limitations or fixed boundaries were imposed, creativity could not exist. Neither is it simply an uncontrollable instinct. There are guidelines, but not unbreakable rules. Creativity remains something we cannot define, something just outside of our grasp, something we strive for. It takes us to the limits of our potential and, if harnessed properly, it can infuse our lives with extraordinary richness and excitement. There is a magical element to creativity — like reaching a hand into a dark hat and pulling out . . . an idea!

Without creativity humans would be no more than a species of primates living on seeds and uncooked meat. The novelty of "fire" and of the "wheel" saved Homo sapiens from living in caves and took them out of the Stone Age. The main use of the wheel up until A.D. 1000 was for horse-drawn chariots. Then someone had the idea of using it as a back-saver in the form of the water wheel, grinding grains with water power. Manuscripts were painstakingly hand-copied until the day Johannes Gutenberg attended a wine harvest, got happily drunk, and suddenly connected the design of the wine press to individual letter types, resulting in the creation of the printing press. The concept of inalienable individual rights for all people did not really exist before the seventeenth century, and ideas like "democracy" and "progress" are relatively recent innovations as well. Human history is replete with these flashes of creative illumination that make the dramatic leap from what is known to what is unknown. These and countless other creative breakthroughs have resulted in civilizations and cultures.

But creativity is not just grand inventions that have altered the course of civilizations; it is a force that should play a prominent role in our everyday lives as well. It is in this sense that creativity is an *approach* to living, which helps define how we view the world and make decisions. If our minds are open and our sensibilities receptive, creative inspiration can strike us at any time, in any place. Once we have identified a goal to reach or a problem to be solved, a lively mind starts to generate ideas. Most are not usable, but then there is that triumphant moment when inspiration illuminates our mind like a meteor streaking across the night sky.

Although we each have unlimited potential to live creatively, most people use only a small percentage of their creative gifts. In fact, research has found that people typically achieve their highest creative point as young children, after which there is a long, steady decline into unimaginative conformity. Why? Well, to begin with, young children are immersed in the excitement of exploration and discovery. They are eager to try out new things, act on their impulses, and make unusual connections between disparate ideas. They are not afraid to take risks in trying out untested solutions, and are not compelled to identify the socially acceptable "correct answer." Children are willing to play with ideas, creating improbable scenarios and imaginative ways of thinking. When I talk to my children and their friends, I am always impressed by the liveliness of their minds, as each idea that we talk about generates new concepts, unusual images, and fresh ways of thinking. I was recently explaining to my twelve-year-old son, Joshua, how critical thinking can clarify the confusing issues we confront. "It's like watching a 3-D movie without the glasses," he responded excitedly. "Everything is fuzzy and blurry until you put on the glasses, and then it all gets clear!" A rich image, which led us into a spirited analysis of thinking and perceiving.

All of this tends to change as we get older. The weight of "reality" begins to smother our imagination, and we increasingly focus our attention on the nuts and bolts of living, rather than playing with possibilities. The social pressure to conform to group expectations increases dramatically. Whether the group is our friends, family, or coworkers, there are clearly defined "rules" for dressing, behaving, speaking, and thinking. When we deviate from these rules, we risk social disapproval, rejection, or ridicule. Most groups have little tolerance for individuals who want to think independently and creatively. For example, think about a time in your life when you came up with a new idea or a unique approach to completing a task. Did some people react negatively to your creative idea? Did you suffer some harsh consequences for daring to deviate from the norm? If so, you are in good company.

Why do people resist the creative ideas of others? We can find part of the answer by looking at the intriguing metaphor of "crabs in a bucket." If you put one crab in a bucket it will eventually find a way to hook a claw over the edge and escape. However, if you place a number of crabs in a bucket, none will ever escape because as soon as one gets near the top, the others reach up and pull it back down. Of course, it is unlikely that the crabs are consciously thwarting the perceived success of one of their own, but it does seem to express very human behavior. When people distinguish themselves from the crowd, instead of wishing them well and helping them on their way, the crowd has a common tendency to reach out and pull them back. This lack of charity often results from envy, as members of the crowd may feel that the success of others reflects negatively on their own lack of accomplishments.

The social price that people pay for offering up new ideas is indisputable. In 1543 the Polish astronomer Nicolaus Copernicus published a book arguing that the sun, not the earth, was the center of the solar system. This ran counter to the theological beliefs of the time, and he paid with his life for this heresy. Sixty-eight years later, the Italian physicist and astronomer Galileo also challenged Church teaching by championing Copernicus's views. He was summoned to Rome, where he was interrogated before the Inquisition and forced to publicly renounce his beliefs. Twenty years later he published an autobiographical account of his persecution and was sentenced to house arrest for the remainder of his life — with the added indignity of reciting once a week the Seven Penitential Psalms. In Vienna during the 1800s, an alarming number of women were dying of blood poisoning soon after giving birth. Acting on the belief that "childbirth fever" was being transmitted by unsanitary medical procedures, the Hungarian physician I. P. Semmelweiss insisted that doctors wash their hands in chlorine water before entering the maternity wards, reducing the annual death rate from 459 to 45. The reward for his creative breakthrough? He was ostracized by the medical establishment and driven out of Vienna by the ridicule of his "colleagues."

In your own life, when you come up with something creative, be prepared to meet negativity and skepticism, a common reaction that reflects one of the more unfortunate qualities of human nature. But if you are able to maintain your initiative, you will find that your courage will be rewarded, for while the price of creativity may sometimes be high, the debilitating cost of conformity is always higher.

There are other obstacles to realizing your creative potentials. As we become older, we also become more reluctant to pursue untested courses of action, because we become increasingly afraid of failure. Pursuing creativity inevitably involves failure, because we are trying to break out of established patterns and go beyond traditional methods. The history of creative discoveries is littered with failures, a fact we tend to forget when we are debating whether we should risk an untested idea. Thomas Edison held thousands of patents for ideas that must have seemed promising at the time but that never amounted to anything. Yet his relatively small number of successful ideas changed the course of civilization. Even these successful ideas did not come easily. For instance, as he struggled in his quest to develop the incandescent light bulb, an associate asked him in exasperation, *"Why do you persist in this folly? You have failed more than nine thousand times."* Edison was astonished at the question, replying, *"I haven't even failed once; nine thousand times I've learned what doesn't work."*

THINKING ACTIVITY

Your Creative History

Think back on your own creative history and describe some of your creative ideas and experiences. How did people respond? Were you ever penalized for trying out new ideas? Did you ever suffer the wrath of the group for daring to be different and violating the group's unspoken rules? How have your past experiences influenced the current level of creativity in your life?

The Gift of Creativity in Your Life

WE BEGAN this book by exploring Socrates' challenge: *"The unexamined life is not worth living."* More than two thousand years later, the philosopher John Stuart Mill responded to this challenge by posing a provocative question: *"It is better to be a human being dissatisfied than a pig satisfied; better to be Socrates dissatisfied than a fool satisfied.*" In other words, given a choice, is it better to live a life that is modestly happy but unremarkable, an unreflective life in which you pursue security and predictability, never wondering if there are vistas beyond the narrowly inscribed boundaries of your existence? Or is it preferable to live a life dedicated to increased understanding and transforming experiences, seeking to plumb life's depths and wrestle with profound questions, even at the risk of confusion, frustration, and even failure?

For most people who have chosen to pursue contentment above exploration, it's difficult to see that there are other life paths that they might choose. In contrast, people who are continually trying to enrich their lives, probing life's mysteries, are life's adventurers, loath to settle for the limited confines of a secure but unreflective existence.

Most of us fall between these two extremes, struggling every day to meet life's basic requirements while integrating whatever new and pleasurable experiences we can. It's just that in the battle between routine and innovation, routine is typically the clear winner. The weight of reality, the inexorable power of habitual patterns, the paralyzing fear of risk and failure, the pervasive influence of social conformity and others' expectations — all these forces conspire to keep us rooted in rigid patterns of behavior and extinguish our creative flames. However, the consequences of surrendering to these forces are devastating.

A Latin proverb states: *"Faber quisque fortunae sua"* — *"Every human being is the architect of his own fortune."* You create yourself and your destiny through the many choices that you make each day, shaping your identity as a sculptor gradually forms the clay in her hands. These choices are guided by the millions of thoughts that cross your mind every day. To transform these thoughts into lively and innovative ideas, you need to let your creative impulses influence your thinking, freeing these inventive ideas to take flight and soar. The more creative thinking you do, the more ideas you produce and the more competent you become, resulting in the most satisfying sense of accomplishment.

The truth is that living a Socratic life of reflection and creativity actually *enhances* your chances for achieving genuine fulfillment rather than superficial contentment. Creativity gives your body and soul much-needed energy to live a full and satisfying life. Creative thinking contributes insight, intuition, inner strength, illumination, and imagination. Creative behavior gives you new opportunities for novel experiences enabling you to redefine your life's meaning. This continuous process of taking fresh steps by rethinking your past learning enables you to face new challenges and strengthen your coping abilities. People who are creative and imaginative tend to handle new situations with more confidence and willpower than those who adopt a more limited, conventional approach to life.

Creativity enriches life in many different ways, helping people achieve self-actualization, a harmonious balance in life. Creativity enables us to bring the outside world in and to let the inside world out. This idea ties directly into the Chinese philosophical concept of Taoism, which the psychologist C. G. Jung described as *"the method or conscious way by which to unite what is separated."* A mind that is harmoniously integrated has long been seen as the hallmark of a healthy personality. From Socrates to Sigmund Freud, great thinkers have consistently emphasized the need to achieve personal harmony, balance, and integration. According to the psychologist Abraham Maslow, *"Self actualization includes an ever-increasing move toward unity, integration, or synergy within the person."* Creativity is the life-force that has the power to help you weave all of these various individual threads of your personality into an exquisite tapestry, contributing to a harmonious balance that incorporates every dimension of your life.

Creativity is a way of life, an attitude toward living. It should not be seen as a chance phenomenon, a once-in-a-lifetime occurrence, but as an integral part of human nature, a gift that can be cultivated and used over a lifetime. Why do we create? Perhaps it is an urge to look into oneself and express to the world what lies within, the soul or Essence, and to say: *"I am," "I exist," "I am unique."* Humans have been creating since the dawn of time, from practical inventions to the artistic creativity of the cave paintings more than forty thousand years ago. The evidence is clear: we are naturally creative beings, and being creative is a life-affirming aspect of the human condition that exists in all people. The real question isn't "Why do we create?" it's "Why aren't we *more* creative?"

Creativity is fundamental to getting about in the world. You need your creative abilities! The world we live in has grown increasingly complex and fast-paced, and the best way to survive and thrive is to be skilled at adapting to its ongoing flux. Though they lived three thousand years apart, Heraclitus *("All is change")* and Bob Dylan *("You better start swimmin' or you'll sink like a stone / For the times they are a-changing")* both articulated this essential insight. Creativity helps you live life experimentally, escaping from fixed routines as you move progressively toward the future, instead of being regressively mired in the past. Every area of your life can be improved; creativity opens your awareness to new possibilities, enables you to imagine how new choices will play out, and provides the means to bring about these changes.

Creativity is therapeutic and relaxing, helping you let go of problems and escape from life's frustrations. In our daily lives we are constantly pressured to be on time, listen, do as we are told, conform, be successful — it's enough to make you crazy! Creativity allows you to escape into the caves of your imagination and leave the mad din of reality behind. In order to develop yourself as a deeply thoughtful and reflective individual, you need to spend some quality time with your own thoughts, alone. This is becoming increasingly difficult, as most of us live in a world that demands our attention nearly every waking moment. Creative activities provide you with a way to turn down the volume on this demanding world, an opportunity to absorb yourself in productive pursuits that block out the distracting noise going on around you and instead tune in to the quiet whispers of your deepest being.

Creativity enriches human relationships on a daily basis. Encountering people can generate an explosion of sparks, the product of two dynamic selves coming into contact. It's these interactive sparks of creativity that join us together as a group despite our differences. Fueled by the honesty of these creative forces, defenses down, these spontaneous combustions bring us closer together. Our responses to the world should seek to create wonder and perhaps beauty where none was found previously. Creativity, in its bloom, refuels life, putting understanding and emotion in a sometimes illogical and uncaring world.

THINKING ACTIVITY

Imagining a More Creative Life

Based on the preceding passages, evaluate the creativity in your life by using the following questions as a guide:

- To what extent do you feel that the various parts of your life and mind work together in harmony, displaying a creative synergy?
- To what extent do you feel free to express your distinctive personality in creative ways, uninhibited by others' expectations and internal doubts?
- To what extent does your life reflect the vivid colors of creative adaptation rather than the monochrome of fixed patterns and predictable actions?
- How frequently are you able to immerse yourself in creative activities, blot out the distractions around you, and hear the quiet voice of your creative essence?
- How frequently do you experience creative encounters with others that stimulate your thinking and enliven your emotions?

After reflecting on your responses to these questions, use the power of your imagination to visualize your life enriched by greater creativity. In what ways would your life be changed? What new accomplishments would you achieve? How would your relationships with others be improved? In what ways would your sense of self and potential for happiness be enhanced?

Learning to Understand and Trust the Creative Process

DISCOVERING YOUR creative talents requires that you understand how the creative process works, and then have confidence in the results it produces. When we were younger, life for most of us was more adventurous, as we sought out new experiences and saw ourselves in the process of dynamic growth. But in the same way that moist clay in the sculptor's hands can be shaped into many forms until it gradually hardens, so the spirited growth that we once enjoyed tends to slow down and calcify into rigid, predictable patterns as we grow older.

The first step in returning to the dynamic and creative growth of our earlier years is to become aware that our lives can be changed in this way. If we fail to see that there are possibilities for us that extend beyond our current existence, then no changes can occur. You can't pursue what you can't see, an insight captured by the author Oscar Wilde: *"The true mystery of the world is the visible, not the invisible."* The second step is reinvigorating your life by choosing to break habits, alter routines, and experiment with new experiences. As Bob Dylan wrote: *"He not busy being born is busy dying."*

There are no fixed procedures or formulas for generating creative ideas because creative ideas by definition go beyond established ways of thinking to the unknown and the innovative. In the words of the ancient Greek philosopher Heraclitus: *"You must expect the unexpected, because it cannot be found by search or trail."*

While there is no fixed path to creative ideas, there are activities we can pursue that make the birth of creative ideas possible. In this respect, generating creative ideas is similar to gardening. You need to prepare the soil; plant the seeds; ensure a proper supply of water, light, and food; and then be patient until the ideas begin to sprout. Here are some approaches for cultivating your creative garden:

- *Explore the creative situation thoroughly.*
- *Work with absorption.*

- *Prime the creative pump.*
- *Allow time for ideas to incubate.*
- *Seize ideas when they emerge and follow them through.*

EXPLORE THE CREATIVE SITUATION THOROUGHLY

Creative ideas don't occur in a vacuum. They emerge from a great deal of work, study, and practice. For example, if you want to come up with creative ideas in the kitchen, you need to become knowledgeable about the art of cooking by reading cookbooks, trying out new recipes, patronizing a variety of restaurants, and taking cooking classes. The more knowledgeable you are, the better prepared you are to create delicious and innovative dishes. Similarly, if you are trying to develop a creative perspective for a project at work, you need to immerse yourself in the subject, developing an in-depth understanding of the central concepts and issues. Think critically about the project: Research the subject, gather diverse perspectives through discussions with other people, reflect on your own experiences in this area. Carefully exploring the situation "prepares the soil" for your creative ideas.

For example, writing is an important creative area for me, and my first step is typically to immerse myself in the topic I will be writing about: taking notes from various sources, recording what I already know about the subject, getting other people's points of view. In this way, I "prepare my mind" — the first stage in the creative process.

This principle was strikingly illustrated in Alexander Fleming's discovery of penicillin, which appeared on the surface to be the result of a series of remarkable coincidences. Although he had been working for years on trying to discover ways to combat bacteriological infections, it wasn't until a drip of mucus from his nose accidentally fell into a petri dish containing a solution he had been working with that he made his first breakthrough. The mixture resulted in a fledgling antibiotic, but it was too weak for effective use. Seven long years later an errant spore drifted through his open window and settled on a dish of this same solution in his laboratory, creating an antibiotic that we now know as penicillin. *Eureka!* But this discovery wasn't just luck: Fleming had been searching for an effective antibiotic for fifteen years, and when these chance occurrences happened, he recognized their significance and seized them. Another eminent creative thinker, Louis Pasteur, summarized this type of creative breakthrough with the statement *"Fortune favors the prepared mind."*

WORK WITH ABSORPTION

With your background knowledge as a foundation, it's time to focus intensely on the task at hand. Set a specific time aside when you can work on your project or activity without interruption, absorbing yourself completely in the task. When people are engrossed in this stage of the creative process, they typically report that they are completely unaware of what is going on around them, often losing the sense of time passing. When your mind is working at this optimal level, it is firing on all cylinders, tapping into mental resources that are often underutilized — an indepth creative thinking that is truly "the mind's best work."

Too often people try to work in the midst of distractions — watching television, listening to the radio, carrying on conversations — resulting in diminished results. Most people require complete concentration in order to work at peak mental capacity. When I am working at home in the evenings and on weekends in the midst of the normal activity of my family, I sometimes have to resort to wearing bright orange noise-suppressing ear muffs designed for chain saw users. My appearance is certainly bizarre, but this solution permits me to "work with absorption." Think about your own experience: What is your typical creative environment like? Does it permit you to focus on your activity with uninterrupted concentration, or are you surrounded by potential distractions that prevent you from delving deeply into your mind?

Sometimes, of course, we work collaboratively with other people on a creative project, and when this occurs, it is important for *everyone* to work with absorption. It only takes one social anarchist to derail the group's thinking process.

As important as a conducive environment is for brightening your creative flame, your mental preparation is just as vital. This is what

Heraclitus likely meant when he spoke about expecting the unexpected, and what the Greek dramatist Sophocles had in mind when he wrote, *"Look and you will find it — what is unsought will go undetected."* You need to train your mind to focus intensely in order to operate at peak mental effectiveness, to sensitize yourself in order to detect subtle signals from your creative *Essence*, a term coined by Michael Ray and Rochelle Myers, the developers of a course in creativity at Stanford University's Graduate School of Business.

This is a useful way to conceptualize your creative self: that there lies within you an Essence, your uncontaminated self, your center, your true personality. This Essence is a basic, fundamental part of us all, and creative reflection is the key to understanding this real self, your mystical, spiritual self. Creativity involves living your life under the guidance of your Essence, the birthplace of your creative impulses. Your Essence is your psychic center, the area in which the conscious and unconscious dimensions of your mind mesh, enabling the production of unique creations to occur within yourself. In the psychologist Arthur Koestler's words: *"The creative mind is a continuum of layers between the conscious and subconscious. We, as archeologists, have to sometimes dig to find our creativity."*

Developing the ability to concentrate in this deep, absorbed way is thus essential for "preparing your mind," and it can be accomplished in a variety of ways:

- *Conditioning:* In the same way that we are conditioned to act reverentially when we enter a place of worship, you need to associate your selected learning environment with focus and concentration. For example, select a favorite location that you devote specifically to creative reflection. That way, when you go there, you will already initiate the creative process by getting into a focused frame of mind.

- *Habits of mind:* Your personality contains a great deal of habitual behavior: some positive, some negative, and much of it neutral. Learning to concentrate fully usually involves breaking habits that interfere with deep concentration, such as trying to do a number of things simultaneously or allocating limited chunks of time for ambitious tasks. At the same time, developing the ability to focus and concentrate also involves establishing *new* habits of mind: identifying an appropriate location, committing sufficient time, and engaging in serious, creative reflection. These new efforts may require some initial start-up energy, but these behaviors will soon become natural and spontaneous.

- **Meditation:** Your mind is typically filled with thoughts, feelings, memories, plans — all of which are vying for your attention. This mental "chattering" increases throughout the day as you are inundated with stimuli to which you react both mentally and emotionally. In order to concentrate on your creative task, you need to purge and clarify your mind. One effective way to achieve this state of "mind*ful*ness" (as opposed to "mind*less*ness") is the following simple meditation exercise.

Meditating for Mindfulness

When you begin your creative reflection or activity, take about five minutes to get into the proper frame of mind. Sit comfortably in your chair, close your eyes, and take turns at first clenching and then relaxing each part of your body, starting with the tips of your feet and moving upward to the top of your head. Work especially at releasing the tension that has built up in key areas. After relaxing your body, turn your attention to relaxing your mind. Visualize your mind as a container filled with thoughts and feelings, and gradually empty these until there is nothing left. Imagine that you are in a pitch-black room, so dark that you cannot see anything. Sink into that feeling of relaxed darkness, letting all of the worries and anxieties drift away. After a while, gradually bring yourself back to awareness, finally opening your eyes. Then focus all your attention and energy on your creative project.

PRIME THE CREATIVE PUMP

Creative thinking requires that you loosen up your mind: experiment, fool around with ideas, become mentally playful. The soul of creativity is looking at one thing and seeing another, making surprising connections between things, generating unusual possibilities. In order to orient yourself to creativity, you must free yourself from slipping into familiar patterns of thinking and preconceived ideas about the way things *should* be. You have to be able to break through your habitual ways of looking at things in order to see them in a new light. There are a number of strategies you can use to ignite your mind in order to escape the chains of conventional "wisdom."

- *Brainstorm Ideas:* Brainstorming, a method introduced by Alex Osborn in 1963, builds on the strengths of working with other people to generate unique ideas and solve problems creatively. In a typical brainstorming session, a group of people work together to generate as many ideas as possible in a specific period of time. As ideas are produced, they are not judged or evaluated, as this tends to inhibit the free flow of ideas and discourages people from making suggestions. Critical evaluation is deferred until a later stage. People are encouraged to build on the ideas of others, since the most creative ideas are often generated through a constructive interplay of various minds. You can also brainstorm on your own, utilizing your unconscious flow of ideas and your mind's natural power of association.

- *Create Mind Maps:* Mind Maps are a versatile tool that can be used to generate ideas and represent the various relationships between them. You begin your Mind Map by writing your main subject in the center of a page, and then recording all of the ideas that you can relate to this subject by using connecting lines. Let your mind run freely, following its normal activity of making associations. You should work as quickly as possible, and don't worry about the order or structure. Let the organization grow naturally, reflecting the way your mind naturally makes associations and organizes information.

Once completed, the organization can be easily revised on the basis of new information and your evolving understanding.

- *Keep a "Dream Journal"*: *"Dreams are the royal road to the unconscious,"* according to Sigmund Freud, and they are a fertile source for discovering creative ideas. In addition to including material from your daily life, dreams express the logic and emotions of your deeper mental processes, those parts of your mind closely related to your creative Essence. Dreams, with their emotional power, vivid images, and unusual (sometimes bizarre!) juxtapositions, can serve as a real catalyst for your creative thinking. However, dreams are easily forgotten, evaporating like dew in the morning sun. In order to capture your dream, keep a pad next to your bed and write down as much of the dream as you can remember. Other parts of the dream may occur to you throughout the day, and jot these additional details down as well. Underneath your dream description, try to decipher what you think the dream is about, but let its content stimulate your creative imagination as well.

ALLOW TIME FOR IDEAS TO INCUBATE

After absorbing yourself in the task, the next stage in the creative process is to *stop* working on the problem. Although your conscious mind has stopped actively working, the unconscious dimension of your mind continues working — processing, organizing, and ultimately generating innovative ideas and solutions. This process is known as *incubation* because it mirrors the process in which baby chicks gradually evolve inside the egg until the moment comes when they break through the shell. Your creative mind is at work while you are going about your business until the moment of *illumination*, when the incubating idea finally erupts to the surface of your conscious mind. People report that these illuminating moments — when their mental light bulbs go on — often occur when they are engaged in activities completely unrelated to the task.

One of the most famous cases was that of the Greek thinker

Archimedes, whose moment of illumination came while he was taking a bath, causing him to run naked through the streets of Athens shouting *"Eureka!"* ("I have found it!"). You undoubtedly experience such "Eureka!" moments, both large and small, on a daily basis. On a modest level, think about times when you couldn't remember a name or important detail despite your best efforts. If you stop concentrating directly on this problem and shift your attention to something else, you often find that the elusive item suddenly appears in your mind unannounced. It's as if you had programmed a request into your mental computer, which continued scanning and processing until the answer suddenly appeared on the screen.

Of course, if incubation is to take place, you have to allow sufficient time for it to occur. Recall the last time that you didn't allow enough time to prepare for a meeting or compose a report. Afterward, you probably became aware of innovative ideas and insightful strategies that you had omitted because you hadn't given your mind sufficient opportunity to perform its "best work." As a natural process, creativity can't be telescoped or truncated, any more than you can speed up the birth of a baby chick by increasing the heat light on the egg. If you crack it open too soon, you're going to get breakfast, not a fluffy pet. You need to respect the creative process by awarding it enough time to operate until the breakthrough occurs in that "moment of illumination."

At this point you may be wondering: Suppose the moment of illumination doesn't happen — what then? If you have taken all the steps to prepare your creative garden bed, the ideas *will* sprout, and the more you see this creative process in action, the greater your confidence will be. Think of a Eureka! moment that you have had in your life and describe it in your Thinking Notebook. It might have been a unique solution for solving a problem, an improved way of reaching a goal, or simply an original idea. If no examples spring immediately to mind, try doing what I did when I just wrote this section: use the Meditating for Mindfulness activity described above in order to let your creative Essence speak to you. Just relax and be patient: before long the ideas will start emerging into your awareness, as they did for me. The paradoxical thing about your creative Essence is that the more you try to force it to perform, the more invisible it becomes. Instead, you need to surrender your conscious control, and let it work its magic in its own way and time.

Seize Ideas When They Emerge and Follow Them Through

The creative flash of illumination, when it arrives, is exhilarating. However, this moment marks the beginning, not the end, of the creative process. Generating creative ideas is of little use unless you recognize them when they appear and then act on them. Too often people don't pay much attention to these ideas when they occur, or they dismiss them as too impractical. You have to have confidence in the ideas you create, even if they seem wacky or far-out. Many of the most valuable inventions in our history started as improbable ideas, ridiculed by the popular wisdom. The idea of Velcro, for instance, originated with burrs catching on the pants of the inventor as he was walking through a field, and Post-it notes resulted from the accidental invention of an adhesive that was weaker than normal. In 1928, W. E. Diemer, a fledgling accountant, began experimenting with recipes for a gum base in his spare time. He unwittingly created the first batch of bubblegum, making it pink because that was the only shade of food coloring on hand, and blowing the first of the billions of bubbles to follow.

After the birth of an idea is when creativity becomes hard work. Most people enjoy coming up with creative ideas and discussing them with others. But fewer are prepared to commit the time and effort needed to make these ideas a reality. Thomas Edison wasn't exaggerating when he declared: *"Genius is one percent inspiration and ninety-nine percent perspiration."* Meaningful creative accomplishments in any area generally require years of experience, practice, and refinement. Even when it appears that something was produced in an instant of creative brilliance, that instant is usually only the tip of the iceberg of toil and commitment. That's the reason why, when the renowned photographer Alfred Eisenstaedt was asked how long it took him to take an acclaimed photograph, he replied, "Thirty years." And even though Einstein came up with the theory of relativity at the tender age of twenty-six, the fact is that he had been working obsessively on the problem from the even more tender age of sixteen.

What all this means is that thinking effectively involves both thinking creatively *and* thinking critically. After you use your *creative thinking* abilities to generate innovative ideas, you then must employ your *critical thinking* abilities to evaluate and refine the ideas, and design a practical plan for implementing them. You then need the determination to carry out your plan, dealing with the difficulties you will inevitably encounter in bringing your ideas to fruition. While this chapter is specifically devoted to nurturing your creative talents, the other chapters will help you make these ideas a reality through the power of critical thinking. But whether you are thinking critically or creatively, you need to develop approaches for overcoming obstacles to your thinking, the subject of the next section.

THINKING ACTIVITY

Using the Creative Process

Identify a project or activity that you would like to approach creatively — a project at work, a relationship, a new activity — and consciously use the steps in the creative process. As you immerse yourself in the process, keep a record in your Thinking Notebook that describes your approach to each step and the results you achieve. This record can serve as a model for future applications of the creative process to other areas of your life.

- Explore the creative situation thoroughly.
- Work with absorption.
- Prime the creative pump.
- Allow time for ideas to incubate.
- Seize ideas when they emerge and follow them through.

Eliminating the "Voice of Judgment"

THE BIGGEST THREAT to your creativity lies within yourself, the negative *Voice of Judgment* (VOJ), a term coined by Michael Ray and Rochelle Myers. The VOJ can undermine your confidence in every area of your life, including your creative activities, with such statements as:

> *"This is a stupid idea and no one will like it."*
> *"Even if I could pull this idea off, it probably won't amount to much."*
> *"Although I was successful the last time I tried something like this, I was lucky and I won't be able to do it again."*

These statements, and countless others like them, make us doubt ourselves and the quality of our creative thinking. For example, when you worked on the previous Thinking Activity, did you experience doubts about your creative abilities or the value of your ideas? Such negative self-evaluations are commonplace, and they have a debilitating impact on your self-esteem. As you lose confidence, you become more timid, reluctant to follow through on ideas and present them to others. After a while, your cumulative insecurity discourages you from even generating ideas at all, and you can end up simply conforming to established ways of thinking and the expectations of others.

Where do these negative voices come from? Often, they originate in the negative judgments you experienced while growing up, destructive criticisms that become internalized as a part of yourself. In the same way that praising children helps make them feel confident and secure, consistently criticizing them does the opposite. Although parents, teachers, and acquaintances often don't intend these negative consequences with their critical judgments and lack of praise, the unfortunate result is still the same: a Voice of Judgment that keeps hammering away at the value of yourself, your ideas, and your creations. As a teacher, I see the VOJ evident when students present their creative projects to the class, with apologies such as: "This isn't very good and it probably doesn't make sense." Disclaimers such as these immediately convey a lack of confidence to others, but more important, they act to lower your own self-esteem. Listen carefully to your language, because the words you choose in communicating reveal who you are and shape your relationships with others.

How do you eliminate this unwelcome and destructive voice within yourself? There are a number of effective strategies you can use, although you should be aware that the fight, while worth the effort, will not be easy.

BECOME AWARE OF THE VOJ

You have probably been listening to the negative messages of the VOJ for so long that you may not even be aware of it. To conquer the VOJ, you need first to recognize when it speaks. In addition, it is helpful to analyze the negative messages, to try to figure out how and why they developed, and then to create strategies to overcome them. A good strategy is to keep a VOJ journal, described below.

THINKING ACTIVITY

Keeping a VOJ Journal

- Take a small notebook or pad with you one day and record every negative judgment that you make about yourself. At the end of the day, classify your judgments by category. For example: negative judgments about your physical appearance, your popularity with others, your ability, and so on. This may be upsetting and difficult to do, but remind yourself that focusing on these negative personal judgments is part of the process of ridding yourself of the VOJ.
- Analyze the judgments in each of the categories by trying to determine where they came from and how they developed.
- Use the strategies described in this VOJ section, and others of your own creation, to start fighting these judgments when they occur.

Restate the Judgment in a More Accurate or Constructive Way

Sometimes there is an element of truth in our self-judgments, but we have blown the reality out of proportion. For example, if you fail to make a sale or get a promotion, your VOJ may translate this as "I'm a failure." Or if you ask someone for a date and get turned down, your VOJ may conclude, "I'm undesirable and unlovable!" In these instances, you need to translate the reality accurately: "I wasn't successful this time — I wonder what went wrong?"; "How I can improve my performance in the future?"; or "This person turned me down for a date — I guess I'm not her type, or maybe she just doesn't know me well enough."

Get Tough with the VOJ

You can't be a wimp if you hope to overcome the VOJ. Instead, you have to be strong and determined, telling yourself as soon as the VOJ appears: *"I'm throwing you out and not letting you back in!"* This attack might feel peculiar at first, but it will soon become an automatic response when those negative judgments appear. Don't give in to the judgments, even a little bit, by saying "Well, maybe I'm just a little bit of a loser." Get rid of the VOJ entirely, and good riddance to it! Although honest and objective self-assessments are valuable tools for improving yourself, the VOJ is a negative and destructive force that never has your best interest at heart. I can't stress enough how important it is to fight this inner battle vigorously, as the inner critic is responsible for holding so many of us back from reaching our potentials.

Create Positive Voices and Visualizations

The best way to destroy the VOJ for good is to replace it with positive encouragement. As soon as you have stomped on the judgment "I'm a loser," you should replace it with "I'm an intelligent, valuable person with many positive qualities and talents." Similarly, you should make extensive use of positive visualization, as you "see" yourself performing well on the job; being entertaining and insightful with other people; and succeeding gloriously in the sport or dramatic production in which you are involved. The importance of positive visualization is attested to over and over by people ranging from professional athletes to CEOs. If you make the effort to create these positive voices and images, they will eventually become a natural part of your thinking. And since positive thinking leads to positive results, your efforts will become self-fulfilling prophecies.

Use Other People for Independent Confirmation

The negative judgments coming from the VOJ are usually irrational, but until they are exposed to the light for examination, they can be very powerful. Sharing your VOJ with others you trust is an effective strategy because they can provide an objective perspective that reveals to you the irrationality and destructiveness of these negative judgments. This sort of "reality testing" strips the judgments of their power, a process that is enhanced by the positive support of concerned friends.

Establish a Creative Environment

AN IMPORTANT PART of fostering creativity and eliminating the negative voices in your mind is to establish environments in which your creative resources can flourish. This means finding or developing physical environments conducive to creative expression as well as supportive social environments. Working with other people may sometimes be stimulating and energizing to your creative energies; other times you may require a private place where you can work without distraction. Different environments work for different people; you have to find the one best suited to your own creative process, and then make a special effort to do your work there. You may find that you need a spare, unadorned space in which to create, lacking any distracting comforts, or you may discover that you require a stimulating environment with colleagues or friends, crackling with ideas and lively conversation, to catalyze your creative power source.

There is a rhythm to the creative process. During certain stages, thoughtful research, absolute concentration, and individual reflection are required. But during other stages, we need the conceptual energy and emotional support provided by like-minded people, others who are interested in lighting the creative flame and stoking it into a blaze. We can use creative interactions with others to realize our own unique vision of the world more fully. While the final product should be uniquely our own in some personal way, this should not prevent us from benefiting from the ideas of others and translating their perspectives into our own thinking vocabulary and syntax. Of course, when individuals work collaboratively on a group project, authorship is shared among the participating partners.

As members of communities, we have a responsibility to stimulate and support the creative endeavors of others. As we develop our own creative resources, it is only fitting that we give back to those who have nurtured and supported our achievements. The strength of a community, as opposed to a collection of individuals, lies in the concerted efforts of its individual members to work together to enrich the lives of all.

Thus the people in your life who form your social environment play an influential role in encouraging or inhibiting your creative process. When you are surrounded by those who are positive and supportive, this increases your confidence and encourages you to take the risk to express your creative vision. They can stimulate your creativity by providing you with fresh ideas and new perspectives. By engaging in activities like brainstorming, they can work with you to generate ideas and then later help you figure out how to implement the most valuable ones. By way of illustration, many writers participate in small writers' groups in which they read and critique one another's work as a way of stimulating and refining their creative work.

But there is a darker side to social influences on your creativity. When the people around you tend to be negative, critical, or belittling, then the opposite happens: You can lose confidence and may be reluctant to express yourself creatively. Eventually, you are likely to internalize these negative judgments, incorporating them into your own VOJ. When this occurs, you have the choice of telling people that you will not tolerate this sort of destructive behavior or, if they can't improve their behavior, moving them out of your life. Of course, sometimes this is difficult or even impossible because you work with them or they are related to you. In these cases, you have to work at diminishing their negative influence and spending more time with those who support you.

Cultivate Your Creativity

ALTHOUGH IMAGINATION is the driving force of creativity, it is often degraded by the "practical," "down-to-earth" members of society. "You must be imagining things!" "It's only your imagination." We don't need *less* imagination, we need a great deal *more* of it. But like any faculty, you need to exercise your imagination in order to keep it robust and vital. Otherwise it becomes submerged under the tyranny of "the way things are." You must adopt a playful attitude, a willingness to fool around with ideas, with the understanding that many of these fanciful notions will not be relevant or practical. But some will, and these creative insights can lead to profound and wondrous discoveries. At the same time, cultivating a creative attitude stretches your imagination and makes your life vibrant and unique. *"The quality of the imagination is to flow,"* the writer Ralph Waldo Emerson observed. When you are living creatively, you aren't "going with the flow": You *are* the flow.

Having learned to trust the creative process, diminish the voice of negative judgment in your mind, establish a creative environment, and commit yourself to trusting your creative gifts, you are now in a position to live more creatively. How do you actually do this? Start small. Identify some habitual patterns in your life and break out of them. Choose new experiences whenever possible — for example, trying unfamiliar items on a menu or getting to know people outside of your circle of friends — and strive to develop fresh perspectives on things in your life. Resist falling back into the ruts you were previously in by remembering that living things are supposed to be continually growing, changing, and evolving, not acting in repetitive patterns like machines. Choosing to live creatively may be one of the most fulfilling decisions that you make, a choice that will enhance the quality of your life and your personal development as well.

As you change your external behaviors, continue also to refine your internal creative impulses. Work to develop your *informed intuition*, that ability to see things clearly in a direct flash of insight. Informed intuition is based on years of careful thought and reflection — that's what makes it informed rather than ill-advised. But when informed intuitions occur, you need to be receptive and have confidence in them, even if you lack sufficient evidence to "prove" them. For example, if you have a strong intuition about how to approach a problem creatively, go with your idea, even if it runs counter to a logical solution. That's the essence of intuition — you are able to leap over conscious calculations directly to the conclusion, because the deeper operation of your mind is able to discern a convincing pattern or compelling insight. In time, you will learn to identify and trust your informed intuitions, distinguishing them from ill-informed hunches.

As people age, they tend to become more tentative, progressing carefully as if they were on thin ice that they could break through at any moment. *"Taking a new step, uttering a new word is what people fear most,"* the novelist Fyodor Dostoyevsky observed. Yet new steps and new words are the only way for you to become the person you are truly destined to be. There is a sense in which you have a solemn obligation to overcome your fears and contribute your unique talents to the world, for if you don't, the shimmering possibilities you might have created will never find reality, as the dancer Martha Graham warns us:

> There is a vitality, a life force, an energy, a quickening that is translated through you into action, and because there is only one of you in all time, this expression is unique. And if you block it, it will never exist through any other medium and will be lost.

How Creative Am I?

DESCRIBED BELOW are key personal attributes that are correlated with living creatively. Evaluate your position regarding each of these attributes, and use this self-evaluation to guide your choices as you shape the creative person that you want to become.

Make Creativity a Priority

I believe that creativity is important.			I believe that creativity is overrated.

5   4   3   2   1

Research demonstrates that creative people typically consider creativity to be more important than things like wealth and power, and they take pleasure in being imaginative, curious, and creatively expressive. The author Kahlil Gibran wrote: *"For the self is a sea, boundless and measureless."* For many people, that sea remains largely undiscovered.

Strategy: *Make creativity a conscious priority in your life by putting reminders in prominent places (a mirror, the refrigerator door, next to your phone at the office), and by evaluating your daily progress in your Thinking Notebook at the conclusion of the day. Habit and conformity are powerful forces that must be consciously struggled against in order to reshape your life.*

Take Creative Risks

I am willing to take creative risks.			I tend to avoid taking creative risks.

5   4   3   2   1

According to the French proverb, *"Only he who does nothing makes a mistake."* Most people avoid mistakes like bats flee light, but it's difficult to be creative if you aren't willing to risk failure. By consistently taking what the Danish philosopher Søren Kierkegaard characterized as a *"leap of faith"* toward your creative potential, the luminosity of your successes will far outshine the momentary disappointment of experiments gone awry.

Strategy: Take some genuinely risky creative actions, and if failures occur, view them as badges of courage, symbols of your own self-confidence and independent thinking. Your failure is a healthy indication that you are sufficiently alive to keep learning and growing as a unique, valuable individual.

Nurture Your Imagination

I make time to use my imagination.

I don't make time to use my imagination.

5   4   3   2   1

In one of his most memorable statements, Albert Einstein asserted, *"Imagination is more important than knowledge."* Caught up in "reality," we fail to see what *might* exist, a terrible loss, for as the philosopher Jean-Jacques Rosseau observed, *"The world of reality has its limits; the world of imagination is boundless."*

Strategy: Practice using your imagination to alter reality — playing with possibilities, creating new scenarios. Indulge your fantasies, challenge conventional ways of doing and thinking, try to come up with many ideas when you are making decisions or solving problems. Don't censor ideas, no matter how outlandish. Record your results and evaluate your progress in your Thinking Notebook.

Strive for Independence

My actions reflect my own ideas.

My actions are influenced by the ideas of others.

5   4   3   2   1

The journey toward increased creativity travels the same path as the journey toward independent thinking and action. When we subordinate ourselves to others at the expense of our own thinking and personalities, we are being "other-directed," surrendering the control of our lives to external forces. To live creatively, we have to be "inner-directed," maintaining our own personal vision of the world and making confident choices based on what *we* think, a crucial life-project, as the author Robert Louis Stevenson observed, *"To know what you prefer instead of humbly saying Amen to what the world tells you you ought to prefer, is to have kept your soul alive."*

Strategy: *Record in your Thinking Notebook the ideas you express that are directed toward pleasing or impressing others. Also record the ideas that you did not express because you were concerned that others would not appreciate or approve of them. After a few days you should be able to discern "inner-directed" and "other-directed" patterns in your life. If you conclude that the scales are tipped toward "other-directed," start making the appropriate adjustments and evaluate your daily progress.*

Foster Mindfulness

I am usually "mindful": sensitive, aware, focused.	I am not as "mindful" — sensitive aware, focused — as I could be.

5   4   3   2 1

The Buddhists use the term *mindfulness* to describe an openness to the rich complexity of your world and the intuitive prompting of your mind. The goal is to increase your sensitivity to and awareness of the mystery and beauty of life. Internally, worry and mental striving create anxiety that clogs rather than stimulates the flow of ideas. Be gentle with yourself, harmonize rather than try to conquer, listen carefully for the creative messages coming from deep within you, and in the words of Albert Einstein, *"The solution will present itself quietly and say 'Here I am.'"*

Strategy: *Tune up your sensitivity to your world. Make a special effort each day to see and feel the rich sensations of your experience, instead of plowing through your days in your own insulated capsule. It's the difference between viewing the landscape through the window of a car and actually walking through the terrain, touching, feeling, smelling, listening. Begin by applying heightened sensitivity to one area of your experience —*

for example, the sensations of tastes, aromas, and textures of the food you are eating — and then gradually branch out to other areas. Record your progress in your Thinking Notebook.

Cultivate Curiosity, Avoid Judgment

I approach life with a questioning attitude.	I often make quick, final judgments about things in my life.

5   4   3   2   1

"I like it." "I don't like it." "She's nice." "He's a fool." The problem with automatic judgments like these is that they close minds, cutting off lines of inquiry and paths of exploration, the heart of creativity. Instead of responding to someone's creation with "I don't like it," asking instead "I wonder what ideas she is trying to express" stimulates you to reflect and opens you to the possibility of new ideas. By asking questions instead of passing judgments, you are discovering significant things about yourself and the world, and you are training your mind to think productively and creatively.

Strategy: *Try playing different roles in order to increase your curiosity. For example, when you are speaking to others, adopt the role of a psychologist in your mind: What are they really trying to say, and are there deeper motivations at work? Why am I responding the way that I am? When you are examining someone's work, adopt the role of an investigator: What is the goal of this project? What specific suggestions can I make for improving its effectiveness? Record particularly effective questions and the new insights you discover in your Thinking Notebook.*

Develop Creative Communities

I often involve others in my creative process.	I do most of my creative work in isolation.

5   4   3   2   1

While independent thinking is a crucial ingredient of creativity, most individuals also need the stimulation and diverse perspectives provided by others in order to achieve their full creative potentials. There is a chemistry, a synergy, that occurs between active minds that share focusing on a problem or just playing with possibilities.

Strategy: *Seek out individuals and groups that have similar interests and creative aims. Invest your time in working collaboratively to enhance the others' efforts. As a critical thinker, be open to views different from your own and be honest in your responses. Keep in mind that those that share their intellectual wealth end up far richer than those who try to hoard.*

SCORING GUIDE

Add up the numbers you circled for each of the self-evaluation items above and use the following Scoring Guide to evaluate your creativity.

Point Total	Interpretation
28–35	very creative
21–27	moderately creative
14–26	somewhat creative
7–13	comparatively uncreative

In interpreting your results, be sure to keep in mind that:

- This evaluation is not an exact measure of your creativity, but is rather intended as a general indicator of how creatively you approach yourself and your life.
- Your score indicates how creatively you are functioning at the present time, *not* your creative *potential*. If you scored lower than you would like, it means that you are underutilizing your creative abilities, and that you need to follow the suggestions in the chapter to realize your creative gifts fully.

Thinking Activity

Fostering Creativity in Your Life

Select areas of your life in which you would like to be more creative: in your job, an activity you enjoy, or your relationship with someone. Make a special effort to infuse a fresh perspective and new ideas into these areas, and keep a record in your Thinking Notebook detailing your efforts and their results. Be sure to allow yourself sufficient time to escape from habitual forms and establish new patterns of thinking, feeling, and behaving. Focus on your creative antennae as you "expect the unexpected," and seize on new ideas when they emerge from the depths of your creative resource. Cultivate the qualities of creativity that we explored in this section:

- Make creativity a priority.
- Take creative risks.
- Cultivate your imagination.
- Strive for independence.
- Foster mindfulness.
- Cultivate curiosity, avoid judgment.
- Develop creative communities.

Step 3

CHOOSE FREELY

You have the power to create yourself through the choices that you make, but only if your choices are truly free. To exercise genuine freedom you must possess the insight to understand all of your options and the wisdom to make informed choices. In many instances passive, illogical, and superficial thinking inhibits peoples' abilities to make intelligent choices and erodes their motivation to persevere when obstacles are encountered. This chapter is designed to provide you with the general framework for understanding the nature of free choice and the practical thinking strategies needed to translate this understanding into transformed behaviors and attitudes. You can redefine your daily life in a new light and enhance its value through free choices derived from thinking critically and creatively.

Condemned to Be Free

Man is condemned to be *free*. Condemned, because he did not create himself, yet is nevertheless at liberty, and from the moment that he is thrown into this world, he is responsible for everything he does.

THIS BOOK IS BASED on the conviction, articulated here by the philosopher Jean-Paul Sartre, that we create ourselves through the choices that we make, and that we are capable of choosing different courses of action. But often we get so caught up in routine, so mired in the day-to-day demands of reality and the pressures of conformity that we don't even *see* alternatives to our condition, much less act on them. Our complaints often far outnumber our shining moments, as we tend to focus on the forces and people that have thwarted our intentions:

> "If only that person hadn't sabotaged my career, I would have . . ."
> "If only I had a chance to meet the right person . . ."
> "If only I got the breaks now and then . . ."
> "If only I could get rid of my habitual tendency to ———, I would . . ."
> "If only other people were as dependable and caring as I am . . ."
> "If only I had been given the advantages of a different background . . ."
> "If only the world had not become so competitive . . ."
> "If only I was given the opportunity to show what I could do . . ."

These complaints, and the millions of others like them, bitterly betray William Ernest Hanley's notion that *"I am the master of my fate; I am the captain of my soul."* It is much more common for people to believe that fate mastered them and that they never had sufficient opportunity to live life "their way." Instead of feeling free, we often feel beleaguered, trying desperately to prevent our small dinghy from getting swamped in life's giant swells, rather than serenely charting a straight course in our sleek sailboat.

The end result is that when people think of "being free," they often conjure up a romantic notion of "getting away" from their concerns and responsibilities, imagining a world where anything is possible and there is plenty of money to pay for it. However appealing this fantasy may be, it is a misconceived and unrealistic notion of freedom. Genuine freedom consists of making thoughtful choices from among the available options, choices that reflect your genuine desires and deepest values, resisting the pressures to surrender your autonomy to external pressures *or* internal forces.

The most important and disturbing element of personal freedom is that it necessarily involves *personal responsibility*. And personal responsibility is the main reason why people are reluctant to embrace their freedom and in fact actively seek to "escape" from it. If you acknowledge that your choices are *free*, then you must accept that you are *responsible* for the outcome of your choices. When you are successful, it is easy to take full responsibility for your success. But when failure occurs, people tend to dive for cover, blaming others or forces outside their control. This is exactly what's going on in all the *"If only"* statements listed above and any others like them: People all express the belief that if only some outside force had not intervened, they would have achieved the goal they set for themselves. However, in many instances, these explanations are bogus and these efforts to escape from freedom are illegitimate. They represent weak and inauthentic attempts to deny freedom and responsibility.

Free Choice: The Mainspring of Human Action

EVERY DAY we are confronted with the mystery of human action. One person commits an armed robbery, killing a guard in the process. Another person is found to have embezzled large sums of money from the charitable organization that he directed. A firefighter risks his life to save the life of an infant trapped in a burning building. A peaceful protest gets out of control and turns into a violent and destructive altercation. A respected member of the community is accused of abusing the children on the teams that he coached. Two teenagers are accused of murdering their newborn infant and dumping the body in a garbage container. An eighty-four-year-old woman who spent her life cleaning the homes of others donates her life savings — $186,000 — to a local college with which she had no previous relationship. In each of these instances, and countless others, we struggle to understand "why" people acted the way they did. Our answers typically depend on our deepest beliefs about the nature of the human self. For example:

Human nature: *"I believe in human nature; people are born with certain basic instincts that influence and determine how they behave."* Based on this view, the actions described above, whether "good" or "evil," are no more than the natural expression of a *universal nature* that is genetically hardwired into every person. From this perspective, we should no more hold people responsible for their destructive actions than we would an animal in the wild that kills in order to survive. There is no possibility of free choice because our actions necessarily follow from our inborn nature, and we cannot do other than what we are. Whether you do good or ill in your life is really beyond your control, and you cannot alter your fundamental character.

The environment: *"I believe that people are shaped by their environment, conditioned by their experiences to be the kind of people they are."* From this vantage point, the actions described above are the direct products of the *life experiences* that the individuals had. If the environment in which a person developed was deprived or abusive, then these forces shaped a violent individual with little regard for the rights or lives of others. On the other hand, if a person was fortunate enough to grow up in a loving and nurturing environment in which kindness and empathy were considered paramount values, then this upbringing shaped who that person is. But once again, you cannot be held responsible for how you turned out because you didn't choose your environment; you were a passive agent molded by forces beyond your control. And, of course, you are incapable of making free choices. We should no more condemn the embezzler than we should reward the firefighter who risks his life, since each is merely the product of an environment that is ultimately responsible for the person's behavior.

Psychological forces: *"I believe that people are governed by psychological forces, many of them unconscious, that cause them to think, feel, and act in certain ways."* Based on this point of view, the actions described above are the direct result of deep psychological impulses that have been formed by people's earliest relationships and experiences. Although these people may think they are choosing to do the things they do, in reality they are puppets manipulated by unseen psychological strings. The same is true for you. So when the coach sexually abused the children on his teams, he was not actually choosing this reprehensible course of action, he was impelled by *psychological forces* over which he had no control. Similarly, your behavior results from psychological motivations, often repressed, that form the basic structure of your personality. Your feelings of freedom are illusory.

Social dynamics: *"I believe that we are social creatures that are greatly influenced by the people around us."* From this perspective, your behavior results in large measure from the forces exerted by those around you. The need to conform to the prevailing norms, to be accepted by the groups to which you belong, to please those who are close to you, to obey those in positions of authority — these and other social needs determine your behavior and define who you are as an individual. For example, the violent actions of the initially peaceful demonstrators can be understood only by examining the dynamics of *social interaction*. Since the group as a whole is to blame, responsibility is removed from the individuals. In the same way, individuals who act illegally (or immorally) within an organization often seek to be exonerated on the grounds that they were merely acting as cogs in the machine, not independent agents. An extreme version of this occurred after World War II at the Nuremberg trials, when many people accused of wartime atrocities explained that they were "only following orders."

THINKING ACTIVITY

Your Theory of Human Behavior

Think about some of the actions described at the beginning of this section. How would *you* explain why they acted in the ways that they did? Which of these theories make the most sense to you? Do you have your own theory to explain why people behave the way they do?

CREATING YOURSELF THROUGH FREE CHOICES

If we examine all of these beliefs regarding the nature of human beings, we can see that they have several significant things in common:

- These beliefs represent attempts to explain human behavior in terms of factors that *precede* the action: a universal human nature, past experiences, psychological forces, and social dynamics. In other words, all of these beliefs assume that the "essence" of a person, as defined by the factors identified above, comes before the human actions and in fact *causes* these actions to take place.

- As a result, all of these beliefs about the human self have the effect of *removing responsibility* from the individual for his actions. If what you did was the direct result of human nature, past experiences, psychological forces, or social dynamics — then *you cannot be held accountable*. You didn't have a choice, your behavior was outside your control.

- As a final consequence, these beliefs about the self *limit future possibilities*. If your thoughts, feelings, and actions are caused by forces beyond your control, then it is not in your power to change, to alter direction, to improve — any more than a puppet can decide to act independently and contrary to the wishes of the puppeteer.

From a framework rooted in human freedom, these traditional perspectives regarding the nature of people are dangerous and destructive. One of the most passionate and articulate modern exponents of individual freedom was Jean-Paul Sartre. His position is extreme — you are completely free. *You create yourself* entirely through the free choices that you make every day of your life. Though you may try to pretend otherwise, the reality is that you are the originator of your actions, the master of your fate and the captain of your soul, for better or for worse. You may choose to surrender control of your life to other individuals or organizations, but this is ultimately a free choice that you make and for which you are completely responsible. Let's revisit the examples identified above and analyze them from this perspective.

Free Choice: *"I believe that people are free to choose their courses of action, and that they should be held responsible for the choices they make."*

- The person who committed the armed robbery and murdered the guard *freely chose* to steal money and he is completely *responsible*. He was not compelled to act in this fashion: He could have chosen not to.
- The person who embezzled money from the charitable organization that he headed *freely chose* to betray his trusted position out of greed and should be held fully accountable.
- The heroic firefighter *freely chose* to overcome his natural fear of death and risk his life to save someone else's, and he should be awarded full credit for his heroism.
- The child abuser *freely chose* to surrender to his destructive sexual impulses and he deserves to be condemned and fully punished.
- The infant-murdering teenagers *freely chose* to deal with their fear of having an unwanted child by killing it and trying to hide the body (despite having many other alternatives available), and they should be held fully responsible for their choice.
- The philanthropic senior citizen *freely chose* to donate her money

to improve educational opportunities for underprivileged young people rather than spending the money on herself, and she deserves to be praised for her altruism.

Each of these people had other alternatives available to them, and they could have made different choices — but they didn't. And so they must be held responsible for the choices that they *did* make.

But surely, you might be thinking, I can't be held *completely* responsible for my life. After all, there are many factors outside my control, people and forces that create obstacles and undermine my efforts. And we are subject to pressures and influences from within ourselves: feelings of greed, fear of death, altruistic impulses, sexual compulsions, need for social acceptance, and so on. Still, it is up to us to choose freely *which* impulses, motivations, fears, desires we want to act in accordance with. In other words, it is up to you, your "self." You make the ultimate choice regarding who you want to become and the direction of your life. When you look in the mirror, the person that you see reflected is the person you have created. If you are pleased with who you are and the state of your life, then you have every right to feel proud. On the other hand, if you are dissatisfied with the person you have become and disappointed with the course of your life, then you have to look no further than yourself to determine who is responsible. You must have the courage to accept full responsibility for your situation, but it is within your power to change, to improve yourself and your life through the free choices that you are able to make.

Sartre characterizes humans as the one living creature whose "existence" precedes its Essence. In other words, *you* create your Essence (your self, soul, personality) through the free choices that you make in your daily "existence."

> Man first of all exists, encounters himself, surges up in the world — and defines himself afterwards. Man simply *is* — he is what he *wills* to be after that leap towards existence. Man is nothing else but that which he makes of himself.

This is exactly what distinguishes human consciousness from the rest of the animal kingdom: when confronted with a decision situation, we are able to think about the options available to us and then make a free choice based on our evaluation. And that makes us responsible for our actions, as Sartre makes clear, *"If existence is prior to essence, then man is responsible for what he is, it puts every person in possession of himself as he is, and places the entire responsibility for his existence squarely on his shoulders."*

In today's culture, personal freedom and responsibility are in danger of extinction, threatened by an array of psychological, sociological, and genetic explanations that have the cumulative effect of robbing people of their autonomy and dignity. It is refreshing and enlightening to view people through the lens of personal freedom, awarding them the power to make free choices for which they are responsible, rather then viewing them as victims of circumstance with little control over their destinies. George Bernard Shaw dismissed this "victimized" view of life when he had one of his characters state, *"I don't believe in circumstances. The people who get on in this world are the people who get up and look for the circumstances they want, and, if they can't find them, make them."*

BECAUSE YOU ARE FREE . . .

This discussion of freedom may seem abstract and theoretical to you, and you might be asking yourself: What difference do my beliefs about personal freedom make in my life? The truth is that along with your beliefs about morality and religion, there is perhaps no other belief that has a greater impact on your life. Here are a few examples.

Self-improvement: If you are a person who is constantly striving to improve yourself and the quality of your life, then it is essential that you possess the freedom to make different choices from those you have previously made. *Personal freedom is the lifeblood of human change.* By using your critical thinking abilities, you can identify appropriate goals and intelligent alternatives; by exercising your freedom, you can choose the goals and alternatives that best meet your needs and fulfill your ideals. On the other hand, an exclusive belief in one of the "nonfreedom" theories (human nature, environmental determinism, and so on) undermines and even eliminates the possibility of changing yourself. The die has been cast, and whatever the future has in store for you, you cannot influence it in any meaningful way.

Morality: Morality deals with the way we relate to people around us. Societies have developed moral ideals and prohibitions to help their citizens live together in a harmonious and productive fashion. As a result, most societies consider things like murder, robbery, cheating, stealing, and raping to be "wrong," and they have enacted laws and punishments to discourage antisocial behavior. On the other hand, most societies consider things like compassion, altruism, sharing in communal responsibilities, working for the good of everyone as well as yourself to be "right," and this sort of behavior is encouraged through teaching, exhortation, and example. But none of this makes any sense if you don't believe that people are free to choose among different alternatives. If you believe that people are *not free*, that their actions are caused by genes, past conditioning, or uncontrollable impulses, then they cannot be held responsible for what they do, and there is little point in trying to encourage them to act differently. *Without freedom, morality becomes irrelevant.* People act the way they are programmed or compelled to act, and that's all there is.

Religion: Most of the world's religions offer a path to an ultimate, spiritual transformation. And this spiritual transformation requires devotion and commitment to religious principles and practices so that people can achieve a higher spiritual state on earth and in life after death. But if an individual is *not free* to choose — or not to choose — a spiritual path, then most religions lose their logic and rationale. If your religious actions are completely conditioned by your upbringing or determined by other factors beyond your conscious control, then you can never achieve any spiritual enlightenment through your own efforts. And since enlightenment through self-choice is the main purpose of most religions, then they require that individuals have the ability to choose freely in determining their spiritual destiny. *In the absence of freedom, religion becomes irrelevant.*

Social improvement: It doesn't take a Nobel Prize winner to see that we live in an imperfect world, saturated with poverty, discrimination, crime, substance abuse, addictions, war and strife, political repression, environmental pollution, child and spousal abuse, and so on. Many people want to create a better world, but to do so requires the ability to change the present by freely choosing to alter the future. *But if freedom doesn't exist, then there is no point in even trying to solve social problems and improve society as a whole.* Without the possibility of free choice, these problems are destined to take their own course, and all we can do is watch as passive spectators. On the other hand, if freedom *does* exist, then it is our responsibility to envision a better future and to make choices that will help make this future a reality.

Raising children: Whether or not you believe people are capable of free choice can make a dramatic difference in how you approach raising your children. If you believe that people are the product of their circumstances, then you will emphasize external forms of motivation like rewards and punishments; and if you believe that personalities are genetically constructed, you may minimize your involvement in the natural unfolding of who they are. However, if you believe that your children are capable of making free, independent choices, then you will work to educate them regarding the responsibility they have for directing their lives and the importance of thinking critically about their alternatives. *With free choice as a framework, you will seek to help them become reflective and principled individuals* who make thoughtful decisions and accept the responsibility for their choices. In other words, you will want them to understand the nature of their freedom and to exercise its power wisely.

Crime and punishment: In recent years we have been subjected to a number of high-profile criminal trials, including those of Susan Smith, Jeffrey Dahmer, O. J. Simpson, Ted Bundy, the Menendez brothers, Louise Woodward, and Timothy McVeigh. Every trial attempts to answer two basic questions: Did the accused person commit the crime he (or she) is charged with? Did he know what he was doing and make a free choice to do it? If the first question is answered "yes," then the second question becomes pivotal in evaluating a person's guilt and responsibility. *But in order to hold people responsible for what they do, we have to believe that they are capable of making free choices.* If people's behavior is caused by other factors, then they couldn't help what they did and it makes no sense to hold them responsible, any more than we should hold a rabid raccoon or a trained pit bull personally responsible for their attacks. These types of defenses are becoming increasingly prevalent. It used to be that the "insanity defense" was reserved for the most obviously deranged criminal defendants. More recently, however, this type of defense has spread like a virus.

To sum up, whether or not you believe that people are capable of making free choices — independent of habit, past conditioning, genetic heritage, social pressure, psychological compulsions, and so on — will have a significant and far-reaching impact on the way you think and act toward yourself, others, and the world as a whole. The way you live your life is a direct reflection of your deepest-held beliefs, and your understanding of freedom is one of the cornerstones of your Philosophy of Life. Having a clear and accurate understanding about your freedom of choice will enable you to create yourself as the kind of person you want to be, and to inspire the best in others as well. The German poet Rilke wrote, *"We are always becoming the self that we are."* Your freedom gives you the power to discover and become your true, authentic self.

Using Your Freedom to Shape Your Life

CLEARLY, YOU ARE capable of making free choices. But how can you be sure? You are born with a *genetic heritage* that doesn't just determine your gender, race, and physical characteristics, but influences your personality as well. For example, studies of identical twins (thus possessing identical genetic "fingerprints") who were separated at birth and reared in different environments have revealed provocative (although complex) results. Years later, despite great differences in their experiences since birth, some twins have exhibited remarkable similarities: identical gestures and sense of humor; the same number (and even names) of children; similar careers and hobbies — all underscoring the influence of genetic factors.

We know that the *environment* also plays a significant role in shaping people's characters and personalities. Young children are indeed like sponges, absorbing all of the information and influences around them and incorporating these elements into their thinking and behavior. Our attitudes, values, beliefs, interests, ways of relating to others — these and many other qualities are influenced by family, friends, and culture. This is the process by which positive values like empathy and commitment get transmitted from generation to generation, and it is also how negative behaviors like racism and violence are perpetuated.

If our genetic heritage and environmental background are such powerful forces in molding who we are, how is it possible to think that we are capable of making free choices in any meaningful sense? The answer to this enigma was initially suggested in Step 1: Think Critically, which recognized that despite the early influences on our development, our mind — and our thinking — continues to mature. Not only do you have ongoing experiences but you *reflect* on these experiences and *learn* from them. Instead of simply accepting the views of others, you gradually develop the ability to *examine* this thinking and to *decide* whether it makes sense to you and whether you should accept it. So while there are many beliefs that you might share with your parents or the prevailing culture in which you were raised, there are likely many other areas of disagreement. Although your parents might believe that sex should begin with marriage or that the most important thing about a career is job security, you might have gradually developed very different perspectives on these issues.

The same is true of your personality. Although your genetic background and early experiences might have contributed to shaping the framework of your personality, it is up to you to *decide* what your future self will be. For example, your personality may incorporate many positive qualities from your parents but some that you dislike as well — such as a quick temper. But you can decide not to let this temper dominate your personality or be expressed inappropriately. With sufficient determination, you can be successful in controlling and redirecting this temper, though there may be occasional lapses. In other words, you can take a personality tendency formed early in your development and reshape it according to your own personal goals. In the same way, if your early history created qualities of insecurity, shyness, pessimism, insensitivity, passivity, or other qualities that you are unhappy about, realize that these traits do not represent a life sentence! You have it within your power to *remold* yourself, creating yourself to be the kind of person that you wish and choose to be. *This is the essence of freedom.* Free choice means dealing with an existing situation, selecting from a limited number of options, and working to reshape the present into the future.

Freedom does not, however, involve limitless and unconstrained options — this idea of freedom is a fantasy, not a realistic perspective. Freedom doesn't occur in a vacuum, it always involves concrete options and limited possibilities. In analyzing your personality, you may feel that you too often lack confidence and are beset with feelings of insecurity. In reviewing your personal history, you may discover that these feelings stem in part from the fact that your parents were excessively critical and did not provide the kind of personal support that leads to a solid sense of security and self-worth. You might discover other factors in your history that contributed to these feelings as well: painful disappointments like a divorce or a career rejection. All of these experiences will have influenced who you are, and these historical events cannot now be changed. But the significant question is: What are you going to do now? How are you going to respond to the results of these events as embodied in your current thinking and behavior? *This is where free choice enters in.* While you can't change what has previously happened, you can control *how you respond* to what happened. You can choose to let these historical influences continue to control your personality, like specters long dead reaching from the grave to influence and entangle the present and future. Or you can choose to move beyond these historical influences, to choose a different path for yourself that transcends their influence and liberates your future. Victor Frankl explains:

> Man is not fully conditioned and determined but rather determines himself whether he gives in to conditions or stands up to them. In other words, man is ultimately self-determining. Man does not simply exist but always decides what his existence will be, what he will become in the next moment. No matter what the circumstances we find ourselves, we always retain the last of human freedoms — the ability to choose one's attitude in a given set of circumstances.

Of course, change doesn't occur immediately. It took a long time for your personality to evolve into its present state, and it's going to take a while for you to reconceptualize and redirect it. It's like changing the course of a large ship: you need to turn the rudder to change course, but the past momentum of the ship makes the turn a gradual process, not a radical change of direction. The same is true with the human personality; meaningful change is a complex process, but by choosing to set the rudder on a new course and maintaining its position, *you will change*.

Escaping from Freedom

GIVEN THE POWER of freedom to create and transform people's lives, it would be logical to think that they would enthusiastically embrace their power to make free choices. Unfortunately, people are often not very logical. In fact, they often spend an extraordinary amount of time, thought, and energy actively trying to *deny* and *escape from* their freedom. Why?

The short answer is *responsibility*, summed up in the clever Chinese proverb *"Success has a thousand fathers, but failure is an orphan."* In other words, people are generally delighted to acknowledge their freedom when the results of their choices are successful, but shrink from responsibility when the result is failure.

This panicked flight from responsibility is evident in every area of life. Think about life at your workplace. The credit for success generally moves up the hierarchy, with people in the upper echelons congratulating themselves and enjoying the fruits of success. Although the people on the lower rungs might deserve the lion's share of the credit, their role is usually progressively diminished and eventually forgotten. In the case of failure, the process is exactly the reverse — blame tends to move down the hierarchy, ending up with the lowest possible fall guy. That's how Oliver North ended up shouldering the entire responsibility for the Iran-Contra scandal, as if this lowly colonel had been running his own private war completely unknown to his superiors.

There has been an increasing trend in our society to evade responsibility by becoming a *victim*. Becoming members of this "new culture of victimization" is attractive for many people because it confers on them the moral superiority of innocence and enables them to avoid taking responsibility for their own behavior — and offers the additional enticement of gaining financial awards through the legal system. One woman sued Disney World for the "emotional trauma" her daughter endured when she inadvertently saw Mickey Mouse without his costume head. After spilling a cup of McDonald's coffee on her lap while driving a car, another person brought suit for the "psychological scars" which resulted — and received an award of $650,000. People are grasping for their tickets to fame and fortune, without regard to whether their behavior is ethically "right."

Focusing attention on "deserving" victims such as battered wives, abused children, and casualties of crime is certainly commendable. But as the journalist John Taylor pointed out in his 1991 article "Don't Blame Me!" the trend toward universal "victimology" (a new academic discipline!) has snowballed out of control. Thus, lifelong smokers are blaming cigarette companies for their own choice to smoke; vicious criminals blame their actions on oppressive social forces; the parade of social misfits on the morbidly voyeuristic afternoon talk shows blame everything except themselves for their plight; even participants in "refrigerator races" have sued manufacturers because the warning labels did not specifically warn against the dangers of racing with the mammoth appliances strapped to your back! Fear of liability suits has resulted in the elimination of diving boards at public pools, the outlawing of sports like pole-vaulting at many schools, the exorbitant prices of equipment like football helmets, and the withdrawal of sponsors for Little League teams. Lawyers actively solicit and encourage such suits, buying police logs of accident and crime victims and acquiring access to the registries of handicapped children in order to locate potential victims. In perhaps the last word on victimology, a New York man was mutilated after jumping in front of a subway, and then sued the city because the train had not stopped in time to avoid hitting him. He received an award of $650,000.

All of this stems from the increasing sense of entitlement that people have developed: They have come to assume that they deserve to be personally fulfilled, financially prosperous, successful in their careers — and if they aren't, then they are being victimized by someone else who must be held accountable. They have become convinced that they are entitled not merely to the right to "life, liberty, and the pursuit of happiness," but to happiness itself. In fact, they have come to believe that they are entitled to a steadily increasing list of "rights" — but without the *responsibilities* that typically accompany these rights, as Roger Connor, director of the American Alliance for Rights and Responsibilities, explains:

> If you try to think where we went wrong, it was in delinking rights and responsibilities. People are fixated on their rights but have a shriveled sense of responsibility, so if they don't have what they want, they assume it must be someone else's fault.

Looking outside one's self for explanations of misfortune is understandably seductive, but this attitude is ultimately *dis*empowering, having the cumulative effect of stealing one's dignity, self-respect, and freedom. It is analogous to a pact with the devil, in which one's soul is progressively exchanged for the fleeting satisfaction of holding others responsible for the disappointments and mistakes in your life. But the converse is also true: fully accepting your personal responsibility is personally empowering, for you are seizing the freedom to shape your destiny through the choices that you make.

THINKING ACTIVITY

Escaping from Your Freedom

Reflect on the choices that you make in your life and respond to the following questions in your Thinking Notebook.

- Identify areas in your life in which you consistently *accept your freedom*. Provide several specific examples. For example, describe situations in which you have sufficient confidence in yourself to say "*I made a free choice and I am responsible for what happened.*"
- Identify areas in your life in which you seek to *escape from your freedom* and provide some examples. You can use your reluctance to fully accept responsibility for your choices (and their consequences) as a clue to "escape attempts." For example:

  - Do you find that you try to shift blame for mistakes in your job/career to other people or "circumstances beyond your control"?
  - In your relationships with friends, family, and lovers, do you find that you try to evade or diminish your responsibility when things go wrong?
  - Do you habitually defer to someone else's ideas and opinions, permitting them to influence your thinking and actions to an inappropriate extent?
  - Do you make rationalized excuses for your lack of progress in improving personal qualities in yourself?
  - Are you a member of any organizations or social groups that pressure you to submerge your critical thinking abilities and your ability to choose independently?

Increase Your Freedom by
Eliminating Constraints

FREEDOM CONSISTS of making thoughtful choices that reflect your authentic self: your genuine desires and deepest values. But there are many forces that threaten to limit your freedom and even repress it altogether. The limits to your freedom can either come from outside yourself — *external constraints* — or they can come from within yourself — *internal constraints*. While external factors may limit your freedom — for example, being incarcerated or working in a dead-end job — the more challenging limits are imposed by *yourself* through internal constraints. For instance, people don't generally procrastinate, smoke, suffer anxiety attacks, feel depressed, or engage in destructive relationships because someone is coercing them. Instead, they are victimizing themselves in ways that they are often unaware of.

In order to remove constraints, you first have to *become aware* that they exist. For example, if someone is manipulating you to think or feel a certain way, you can't begin to deal with the manipulation until you become aware that it exists. Similarly, you can't solve a personal problem like insecurity or emotional immaturity without first acknowledging that it *is* a problem, and then developing insight into the internal forces that are driving your behavior. Once you have achieved this deeper level of understanding, you are then in a position to *choose* a different path for yourself, using appropriate decision-making and problem-solving approaches. But there is a great deal of ignorance and confusion regarding the nature of free choice. Let's examine some of the major myths.

MYTH #1: FREEDOM MEANS SIMPLY MAKING A CHOICE

Many times we make choices that are not free because the choices are compelled by others. For example, if you are threatened with bodily harm by a mugger or an abusive spouse, your choices are made in response to these threats and are clearly not free. Similarly, if you are being subjected to unreasonable pressure on the job by someone who has the power to fire you, the choices that you make are obviously constrained by the circumstances. These kinds of limitations on your freedom are known as *external constraints*, because they are external influences that force you to choose under duress. While hostage taking, ransom demands, and blackmail threats are extreme examples of this sort of coercion, there are many incipient forms of it as well. The appeal to fear used by political leaders, the subtle manipulations of an acquaintance, the implied threat by a panhandler, the sexual harassment perpetrated by someone in authority — these and countless other instances are testimony to the prevalence of external constraints on your freedom.

The way to free yourself from external constraints is to *neutralize* or *remove* them, so that you can make choices that reflect your genuine desires. For example, if your choices are constrained by an abusive spouse or an unreasonable boss, you either have to change their coercive behavior or you have to remove yourself from the situation in order to achieve genuine freedom. If you believe that your choices are excessively limited by the geographical location in which you live, you might have to move in order to increase your possibilities.

MYTH #2: FREEDOM IS LIMITED TO CHOOSING FROM AVAILABLE OPTIONS

This second myth about freedom interferes with people's capacity to make free choices because it encourages them to accept passively the alternatives presented to them. However, the most vigorous exercise of freedom involves *actively creating* alternatives that may not be on the original menu of options. This talent involves both thinking critically — by taking active initiatives — and thinking creatively — by generating unique possibilities. For example, if you are presented with a project at work, you should not restrict yourself to considering the conventional alternatives for meeting the goals, but should instead actively seek improved possibilities. If you are enmeshed in a problem situation with someone else, you should not permit them to establish the alternatives from which to choose, but you should instead work to formulate new or modified ways of solving the problem. Too often people are content to sit back and let the situation define their choices instead of taking the initiative to shape the situation in their own way. Critical and creative thinkers view the world as a malleable environment that they have a responsibility to form and shape. This liberates them to exercise their freedom of choice to the fullest extent possible.

MYTH #3: FREEDOM MEANS SIMPLY "DOING WHAT YOU WANT"

"No man is free who is a slave to himself." This saying captures the insight that while you may believe that you are making a free choice because you are not the victim of visible *external constraints*, your choice may indeed be *un*free. How is this possible? Because your choice can be the result of *internal constraints*, irrational impulses that enslave you. Even though you may on one level be choosing what you "want," the "want" itself does not express your truest self, your deepest desires and values. Consider the following examples:

- You are addicted to cigarettes and have been unable to quit despite many attempts.
- You are consumed by jealousy and find yourself unable to break free of your obsession.
- You can't go to bed without checking all of the locks three times.
- Whenever you think about speaking in front of a group of people, you are paralyzed by anxiety, and you perform miserably.
- You have frequent and lasting episodes of depression from which you are unable to rouse yourself and that sap your interest in doing anything.

This is just a small sampling of common behaviors that are clearly "unfree," despite the fact that there are no external threats that are compelling people to make their choices. Instead, in these instances and countless others like them, the compulsions come from *within* the person, inhibiting him or her from making choices that originate from the *genuine* self. How can you tell if your choice originates from your genuine self or whether it is the result of an internal constraint? There is no simple answer. You have to think critically about your situation in order to understand it fully, but here are some questions to guide your reflective inquiry:

- Do you feel that you are making a *free, unconstrained choice* and that you could easily "do otherwise" if you wanted to? Or do you feel that your choice is in some sense beyond your conscious control, that you are "in the grip of" a force that does not reflect your genuine self, a compulsion that has in some way "taken possession" of you?
- Does your choice *add positive qualities* to your life: richness of experience, success, happiness? Or does your choice have negative results, which undermine many of the positive goals that you are striving for?
- If you are asked "why" you are making the choice, are you able to provide a persuasive, *rational explanation*? Or are you at a loss to explain why you are behaving this way, other than to say, "I can't help myself."

Let's apply these criteria to an example like smoking cigarettes.

- When people are addicted to cigarettes, they usually feel that they are *not* making a free, unconstrained choice to smoke because it is very difficult for them to stop smoking. Instead, they generally feel that they are *enslaved* by the habit, despite their numerous and determined attempts to quit.
- Smoking cigarettes adds many *negative elements* to a person's life, including health risks to himself and others near him, stained teeth, and bad breath. On the positive side, people cite reduced anxiety, suppressed appetite, and lessened social awkwardness.

But smoking only deals with the symptoms of these problems, not the causes. On balance, the bottom line on smoking is clearly negative.

- Most people who want to stop are *at a loss to explain why* they smoke, other than to say, "I can't help myself."

Using these criteria, habitual smoking clearly seems to be an example of an internal constraint. Of course, while smoking might not be your concern, it is likely that there are other elements of your life which are. While you might find it easy to advise, "Just say no!" to cigarettes, you might have great difficulty accepting this same simple advice when confronted with an urge for a chocolate eclair, a panicked feeling of insecurity, or a deep depression.

Some internal constraints originate from the expectations of others, which we have unconsciously "adopted" as our own. For example, someone in your life may demand exaggerated deference from you, and over time you may internalize this expectation to the point where you actually believe that you are freely choosing to exhibit this self-denying subjugation. But although you may have convinced yourself on a surface level, on a deeper level it is clear that you have *surrendered your psychological freedom* to the demands of someone else. That's one reason why people have difficulty in breaking out of abusive and destructive relationships: They don't view the relationships as abusive or destructive, and instead may believe that they have freely chosen to be where they are.

This same psychological pattern repeats itself throughout your social life. It is in people's nature to want to be loved, accepted, and respected by others; to fit in with the larger social whole; and secure the rewards that others can provide. But though you may try to convince yourself otherwise, your choices in response to these pressures and needs are often not truly free because the impetus for these actions does not originate with you, but rather from outside yourself. The key variable is the extent of your self-awareness. Free choice demands that you are consciously aware of social pressures and expectations and that you consciously choose how to respond to them. This crucial awareness is often lacking, and so our behavior is the result of external manipulation rather than self-originated choice. The psychologist Erich Fromm provides penetrating insight into this complex phenomenon in his seminal work, *Escape From Freedom:*

> Most people are convinced that as long as they are not overtly forced to do something by an outside power, their decisions are theirs, and that if they want something, it is they who want it. But this is one of the great illusions we have about ourselves. A great number of our decisions are not really our own but are suggested to us from the outside; we have succeeded in persuading ourselves that it is we who have made the decision, whereas we have actually conformed with expectations of others, driven by the fear of isolation and by more direct threats to our life, freedom, and comfort.

Even though you may believe that you are making a genuinely free choice, the reality may be that you are making a "pseudo-choice" in response to internal or external constraints. And because you are unaware of the influences that are acting upon your behavior, you are living the illusion of the puppet who does not see the strings controlling his every movement.

While everybody engages in some pseudo-thinking and pseudo-choosing, the crucial question is to what extent. If you are a person who reflects, reasons, and thinks critically about your beliefs and your choices, then you will be a predominantly *"inner-directed"* person, who is the author of the majority of your thinking and choosing. On the other hand, if you are a person who spends comparatively little time thinking critically about your beliefs and choices, then you will be a much more *"other-directed"* person, who is defined in terms of the expectations of others or inner demons over which you have little control. Genuine freedom requires the will and the capacity to reflect, reason, and think critically about our "self," and in the absence of these abilities, we are in danger of becoming a "pseudo-self."

It would be natural to think that since your freedom is so often limited by internal and external constraints, this diminishes your responsibility, since these seem to be factors beyond your control. However, this is not the case. *You are still responsible.* Why? Because the constraints you find yourself burdened with are typically the result of choices that you previously made. For example, although you may now feel under the spell of some drug or in an emotionally and/or physically abusive relationship, the fact is that your enslavement took place over time. You may now feel that you are trapped and can't even envision different possibilities. Yet your situation didn't happen overnight; it is the result of a long series of choices that you have made. It's similar to thread being slowly wrapped around your hands, binding them together. In the early stages, it is easy for you to break free, but if no action is taken, it gradually reaches the point at which you cannot extricate yourself without outside help. Still, it is within your power to choose to seek such assistance. And so you are responsible for what occurs.

But what about situations like recurring depression, phobias, emotional insecurity, and other paralyzing and debilitating psychological problems? Should people be held responsible for these circumstances as well? While we have "progressed" to medicating almost every symptom, especially in the psychological realm, we need to step back and view the role of *thinking* in these emotional disturbances, as we are often unwittingly complicit in perpetuating and even strengthening them through our thinking and choices. Of course, in the case of serious, chronic, long-term emotional disturbances, professional therapeutic help is essential. But in the case of the more common disturbances that keep us from fulfilling our human potential, we can often work our way out of the thickets of these kinds of difficulties if we *think clearly* and *choose freely*.

Thinking Activity

What Are the Limitations to Your Freedom?

Making full use of your freedom involves first eliminating the constraints that limit your freedom. Use this Thinking Activity to begin this "Search, Challenge, and Solve" operation, which will prepare you for increasing your freedom.

1. Identify some of the important *external constraints*, limitations on your options that are imposed by people or circumstances outside you. Are there people in your life who actively seek to limit your freedom? Are you locked into situations that present limited opportunities? After identifying some of the significant external constraints, identify ways to diminish their impact on your freedom by either modifying or eliminating them.

2. Evaluate the extent to which you are passively content to choose from a *limited selection of alternatives* that are presented to you. Identify several situations to begin actively creating your own possibilities.

3. Identify some of the important *internal constraints* in your life using the following criteria to identify behaviors which:
   - you feel are out of your conscious control;
   - add negative results to your life;
   - you cannot provide a rational explanation for.

A Practical Example: Freeing Yourself from Depression

BUT HOW DO these abstract ideas work in real life? Let's examine an example that everyone is familiar with, to one extent or another: *depression*. Think about the last time you were depressed. Did you feel listless, unmotivated, pessimistic about the future? Did you feel that this black mood was beyond your control to change, even though you tried? Research on severe depression reveals the following disturbing facts:

- It is ten times more prevalent today than it was fifty years ago.
- It assaults women twice as often as men.
- It now strikes a full decade earlier in life on average than it did a generation ago.

There are two traditional explanations for chronic depression:

1. It results from a *deep-seated psychological problem* reflecting unresolved childhood conflicts and unconscious anger directed inward that requires years of clinical therapy to analyze and improve. Naturally, this approach involves a significant expenditure of time and money, and there is no guarantee that even after all of this the problem will be solved.
2. It results from a *chemical imbalance in the brain* that requires the ingestion of antidepressant drugs like Prozac or Paxil. In fact, these chemical treatments are becoming increasingly prevalent not just for severe cases of depression but in the general population as well. More and more people are looking to the miracle of science to provide simple treatments to help them deal with complex psychological difficulties. If we can "cure" depression by simply popping pills, perhaps we can use the same psychopharmaceutical approach for any emotional difficulty.

If these are the only two possible explanations for depression, then where does that leave freedom? On the surface, depression seems to be such a pervasive and debilitating internal constraint that it is meaningless to talk about freedom to choose in any genuine way. How can people be held responsible for a situation that seems so clearly beyond their control? On the other hand, if it can be demonstrated that depression *is* often the result of choices people have made, and that they can diminish its presence in their lives by making different choices, then it will be clear that freedom and clear thinking are the keys to happiness and success in *all* areas of life.

THINKING ACTIVITY

Analyzing Your Depression

Think about the last time you felt depressed and describe the experience as specifically as you can. Was there an event or events that triggered the depression? How frequently do you get depressed and how long does the depression generally last? In what ways does your depression affect your motivation and behavior? How does it affect your relationships with others? How do you feel about the future and your power to control your life? What approaches did you use to diminish the depression? Were these successful? Why do you think the depression finally lifted?

The first thing to realize is that even when you are in the throes of a powerful constraint like deep depression, you still have choices to make. For example, when Nelson Mandela was imprisoned in a small cell for thirty years, it would have been easy for him to withdraw into depression and simply wait to die, and few of us would have blamed him. But despite the extraordinary limits on his freedom, he chose to exercise his ability to *choose freely* to the greatest extent possible, continuing an active role in coordinating the antiapartheid efforts in South Africa. Those efforts contributed to his ultimate release from prison and subsequently his election as president of the country that had imprisoned him all those years.

Similarly, when you are feeling extremely depressed, you can choose to surrender to your depression, letting it rob you of your desire to live a meaningful and productive life, or you can choose to fight it. What weapons do you have to attack this enemy that originates within yourself? You have the *power of your mind*, to think critically, reason clearly, and ultimately choose freely. This is precisely the conclusion that the psychologist Albert Ellis came to thirty years ago. Ellis developed a very direct and deceptively simple approach to human behavior. Maladjusted behavior and neurotic feelings are based on beliefs that are illogical and self-destructive; the behavior and feelings can be transformed in positive ways by *changing the way you think*. Although Ellis had been trained in traditional Freudian psychotherapy, which focuses on unconscious childhood traumas and long-term therapy, he came to the conclusion that virtually all serious emotional distress — like depression — and neurotic behavior are the result of "bad thinking." Thinking that is unclear, illogical, and misdirected creates psychological problems, and these problems can be alleviated by clarifying inappropriate thinking patterns. Ellis based this belief on research that found that individuals can alter patterns of thinking by choosing the way they think. Previously, it was thought that people's thinking was either "pushed" by internal psychological drives or "pulled" by external forces. But if people can control their thinking, Ellis concluded, then they can control how they feel and behave. Let's analyze an example.

Imagine that you are patiently waiting in line for a bus when suddenly someone gives you a hard shove from behind. How do you feel? If you think that someone has pushed you intentionally, you are likely to feel annoyed or even angry. Now imagine that when you turn around to see what happened, you see that the person who pushed you is wearing dark glasses and is using a cane to make his way around. How do you feel now? If you think that the person is blind, you may feel embarrassed about your initial anger, believing that you jumped to the wrong conclusion. Now imagine that after everyone gets on the bus, and you guide this person to a seat, he takes off his dark glasses and begins reading a newspaper. How do you feel now? Well, you get the idea. Our *emotional* reactions toward events in the world are directly dependent on how we *think* about things. When your thinking changes, your feelings change.

This was the basic insight upon which Dr. Ellis developed Rational-Emotive Psychotherapy (RT), an approach to improving the quality of people's lives, which is based on the following principles:

- Neurotic tendencies are often inborn or acquired at a young age, but these tendencies are sustained and perpetuated by the individual's *repeating to himself* early acquired neurotic beliefs.
- Since emotions are closely allied to and the products of human thinking, neurosis consists of *mistaken, illogical beliefs* that cause the person to feel and act in self-destructive ways.
- People can rid themselves of these self-destructive tendencies by *changing their warped patterns of thinking* and replacing them with *clear, intelligent patterns of thought.* This is accomplished by identifying the illogical beliefs that they repeat to themselves to create disordered emotions and self-defeating behavior, challenging and contradicting these beliefs, and then replacing them with appropriate beliefs that they act upon. The end goal is a basic reorientation in the person's philosophy of living that influences every aspect of his life.

Over the years, this Rational-Emotive approach has been validated as extremely effective in helping people deal with their personal problems, so let's apply this approach to the problem of depression we have been considering in order to see it in action. After developing a clear understanding of how the method works, you will be able to apply it to any area of your life in which you want to increase your freedom and happiness.

According to psychologists Martin Seligman and Aaron T. Beck, chronic depression is a disorder of conscious thought, the natural result of a pessimistic view of the world. When misfortune happens to a *pessimist,* as it does to everyone sooner or later, the pessimist responds in a way that is guaranteed to perpetuate her pessimism and risk a full-fledged depression: *"It's entirely my fault, it's going to last forever, it's going to undermine everything I do."* This reaction is automatic and habitual, reflecting a pattern of thinking that plays a central role in shaping the individual's life. When the same misfortune happens to an *optimist*, the optimist reacts in a way that diminishes the sense of frustration and helplessness: *"The fault was due mainly to circumstances, it's probably going away quickly anyway, and besides, there's much more in life."* This response is instrumental in helping the optimist avoid full-blown depression when adversity strikes.

The habitually negative responses of the pessimist reflect mistaken and illogical beliefs, which create many emotional problems, including depression. The way to alleviate these problems, according to psychologists like Ellis, Seligman, and Beck, is to replace these mistaken beliefs with accurate beliefs in order to establish new patterns of thinking and responding. For example, pessimists can learn to think — and feel — like optimists by changing their *explanatory style*, the manner in which they habitually explain to themselves why events happen. Your explanatory style reflects your basic beliefs about yourself and the world — it embodies your Philosophy of Life. Are you a deserving and worthy person, or without real significance? Can you improve yourself and enrich the quality of your life, or are you helpless to effect meaningful change? Your explanatory style, as Dr. Seligman notes, reflects *"the word in your heart,"* a no or yes. As you repeat messages to yourself, which reflect your explanatory style, day after day, year after year, you establish patterns of thinking and feeling that shape your personality.

For example, imagine that you just found out that you are going to lose your job in two weeks, and you have no prospects for new employment, a devastating psychological blow for anyone. But although the same event may befall both the pessimist and the optimist, they have very different responses, reflecting their contrasting explanatory styles. Let's compare:

Pessimist	Optimist
1. It's my fault. I just wasn't good enough. I deserved to be fired.	1. I was at least in part the victim of circumstance. I could have improved my deficiencies, but the company didn't appreciate my value.
2. I'll probably never get another job as good as this one.	2. I'll be able to find a better job, one that makes better use of my talents, and I'll continue to improve.
3. This will undermine every area of my life. Everything is ruined.	3. I have many other positive things going on in my life. I won't let this unfortunate event affect those other areas.

1. **Personalization:** As reflected in these statements, pessimists tend to blame misfortune *entirely on themselves*, resulting in low self-esteem; they conclude that they are worthless, talentless, and unlovable. Optimists, on the other hand, clearly see the role of *external circumstances* in their misfortune. They can objectively evaluate their own strengths and failings, and look positively to the future to improve themselves, resulting in greater self-esteem than those who chronically blame themselves. The situation is reversed when good things happen: Pessimists habitually give the lion's share of credit to external circumstances and people, while optimists tend to give themselves credit they deserve for success.

2. **Permanence:** As expressed in the statements above, pessimists tend to view misfortune as *permanent*, a series of negative events that will always occur to ruin their happiness. Optimists, in contrast, tend to view misfortune as *temporary*, viewing negative events as short-lived setbacks that they will overcome and triumph over. The positions are reversed for positive occurrences: Pessimists tend to view success and happiness as temporary, while optimists are confident that such success and happiness are a normal state.

3. *Pervasiveness:* Finally, pessimists, as reflected in the statements above, see unfortunate events as infecting *every area of their lives*, emblematic of a life of futility. Optimists, on the other hand, view negative events as *specific and isolated*, insulated from the other areas of their lives. Again, it's exactly the reverse for positive occurrences, as pessimists believe that their success is limited to that single event, while optimists view success as symbolic of the overall success of their lives.

There are compelling research results, presented by Dr. Seligman in his book *Learned Optimism*, that optimists are more successful than pessimists in every area of life: school, work, sports, health, and even longevity. As important as talent and motivation are in achieving success, optimism appears to be a third crucial ingredient. Changing the negative things that you say to yourself when dealing with adversity (the Voice of Judgment that we identified in the previous chapter) is the central skill of optimism, enabling you to learn a new set of cognitive skills and attitudes that reshapes your outlook on the world in productive ways. This new outlook will liberate you, giving you the power to make genuinely free choices that reflect your most authentic, truest self. And as you learn these positive thinking skills, you can also teach them to your children and others in your life.

An Approach for Thinking Positively

WE WILL BE USING a three-part approach to create this new, positive outlook on yourself and your life: *Search, Challenge,* and *Solve.* It is based on the empirically validated approaches of Ellis and Seligman, and reflects the basic principles of *The Thinker's Way.*

SEARCH OUT YOUR NEGATIVE JUDGMENTS

A pessimistic explanatory style consists of illogical beliefs and negative self-judgments that are habitual and automatic. You can't do anything to affect their debilitating influence until you become aware of their existence. To this end, identifying your chronic pessimistic judgments in a special section of your Thinking Notebook is a necessary starting point. Only then can these negative beliefs be eradicated and replaced by logical beliefs and positive self-judgments.

CHALLENGE THE LOGIC OF YOUR NEGATIVE JUDGMENTS

Once the enemy is recognized, you need forcefully to challenge it, using the critical thinking skills you have been developing in this book.

- What *evidence* is there for the negative judgments you are making to yourself and the beliefs upon which they are based?
- Are there *alternative perspectives* from which to view this situation?

SOLVE THE PROBLEM WITH A NEW WAY OF THINKING

Once you have challenged your negative reactions to difficulties in your life, you are in a position to replace them with positive, constructive explanations and answer the question "What practical solutions are there for this problem?" Simply repeating empty "feel good" platitudes will not help you reshape your thinking. Instead, you need to attack very specifically the pessimistic explanations that you are using to make sense of adversity, and then replace these negative characterizations with positive ones. Let's apply this Search, Challenge, and Solve method to some examples.

Search
1. **Missed Deadline:** I struck out again. I had a project to do and I didn't make the deadline. I just can't do anything right.
2. **Rejected for a Date:** I finally summoned the courage to ask this person out for a date and she rejected me. No wonder: I'm unattractive and uninteresting. Why would anyone want to go out with me? I'll never find anyone to share my life with.
3. **Yelling at Children:** I lost control and yelled at my children again. I'm just not a fit parent. The slightest disturbance sets me off and

I lose it. I know I'm taking out a lot of other frustrations on them, but I can't help myself. My life is a mess.

Challenge

1. **Missed Deadline**

   Evidence: While it's true that I didn't meet this deadline, it's also true that this project was assigned at the last minute and I had many other responsibilities. I did the best I could to meet all of my responsibilities, but there just wasn't time.

   Alternative perspectives: Another point of view might commend me for getting as much done as I did in the time allocated, instead of condemning me for what I didn't finish. However, since this instance *is* part of a pattern of consistently missing deadlines, this is a problem that needs to be analyzed.

2. **Rejected for a Date**

   Evidence: Although I sometimes feel unattractive, many people have told me that I'm quite attractive; I just have trouble believing them. Just because this person wasn't a good match for me is no reflection on my value. It's difficult to find someone to be compatible with, but if I keep looking, there's a good chance I will be successful.

   Alternative perspectives: Maybe this person really was busy for the night that I asked. She did say that she would like to get together another time. I have some fine qualities, and after we have a chance to spend some time together, we'll have a better sense of our compatibility.

3. **Yelling at Children**

   Evidence: It's true that I yelled at my children, but it only happens occasionally. Most of the time I have a good relationship with them, so I have to keep things in perspective. That doesn't mean that I shouldn't work to keep better control, but I shouldn't overreact to my yelling either.

   Alternative perspectives: Raising children is stressful, and I have a lot of additional pressures on me as well. Sometimes I just feel overwhelmed, and when my children misbehave, they become the targets of my pent-up tension.

Solve

1. ### Missed Deadline
   Solution: Since the problem involves the excessive amount of work being assigned, I need to discuss this with my supervisor and get her recommendations on establishing priorities in my work. But I shouldn't beat myself up over it; it's a common problem and I can overcome it with intelligent action. I'm going to keep reminding myself that I am a talented and conscientious worker, but I can't do the impossible. When I am assigned too many responsibilities in too little time, I need to work with my supervisor to establish clear priorities. And since I do occasionally have a tendency to procrastinate, I'm going to analyze and solve this problem.

2. ### Rejected for a Date
   Solution: I need to develop my confidence and keep taking chances in order to meet people and have a fulfilling social life. I'm going to keep reminding myself that I am an attractive and worthy person who would love to find a soul mate, and I'm sure I will eventually. In the meantime, I need to take the initiative in meeting new people. While many of these efforts may not work out, that's no reflection on my value.

3. ### Yelling at Children
   Solution: I need to get my life better organized so that I don't feel like I'm on a treadmill that's moving too fast. I also have to find more positive ways to control and release my tension. Finally, I need to develop more constructive ways to deal with my children when they misbehave. I need to keep reminding myself that I am a loving and concerned parent. I'm going to work at reducing the stress in my life, controlling my temper, and explaining to my children that I need their help in solving our common problems and meeting our goals.

THINKING ACTIVITY

Becoming a More Optimistic Person

Focus on a chronically pessimistic part of your personality and apply the method described in this section to help you create a more optimistic explanatory style and outlook on the world.

Search: Record your negative explanations in your Thinking Notebook over a period of several days. Use the constraints you identified in the Thinking Activity on page 135 to get you started. Look for patterns in your explanations and identify which mistaken category each illustrates: *personalization, permanence, pervasiveness.*

Challenge: Challenge the logic and accuracy of the explanations you have recorded by addressing these questions:

- *Evidence:* What evidence supports your explanation and does the evidence make sense?
- *Alternative perspectives:* Are there other, more positive, explanations? What evidence supports these explanations?

Solve: After analyzing your explanations, create solutions to your situation that reflect a more optimistic point of view. Eliminate your habitual explanations and transform your thinking (and feeling) by developing optimistic explanations. Write these down and use them on a consistent basis.

Choosing the Good Life

WHAT IS the ultimate purpose of your life? What is the Good Life that you are trying to achieve?

The psychologist Carl Rogers, who has given a great deal of thought to these issues, has concluded that the Good Life is

> not a fixed state like virtue, contentment, nirvana, or happiness;
> *not* a condition like being adjusted, fulfilled, actualized;
> *not* a psychological state like drive or tension reduction.

Instead, the Good Life is a *process* rather than a state of being, a *direction* rather than a destination. But what direction? According to Rogers, *"The direction which constitutes the Good Life is that which is selected by the total organism when there is psychological freedom to move in any direction."* In other words, the heart of the Good Life is creating yourself through genuinely free choices, once you have liberated yourself from external and internal constraints. When you are living such a life, you are able to fulfill your true potential in every area of your existence. You are able to be completely open to your experience, becoming more able to listen to yourself, to experience what is going on within yourself. You are more aware and accepting of feelings like fear, discouragement, and pain, but also more open to feelings of courage, tenderness, and awe. You are more able to live fully your experiences, instead of shutting them out through defensiveness and denial.

How do you know what choices you should make, what choices will best create the self you want to be and achieve your Good Life? As you achieve psychological freedom, your intuitions become increasingly trustworthy, since they reflect your deepest values, your genuine desires, your authentic self. It is when we are hobbled by constraints on ourselves that our intuitions are distorted and often self-destructive. As previously noted, you need to think clearly about yourself, to have an optimistic explanatory style that enables you to approach life in the most productive way possible. When you have achieved this clarity of vision and harmony of spirit, what "feels right" — the testimony of your reflective consciousness and common sense — is a competent and trustworthy guide to the choices you ought to make. The choices that emerge from this enlightened state will help you create a life that is enriching, exciting, challenging, stimulating, meaningful, and fulfilling. It will enable you to stretch and grow, to become more and more of your potentialities.

> *Freedom is nothing else but a chance to be better,*
> *whereas enslavement is a certainty of the worst.*
>
> —ALBERT CAMUS

How Free Am I?

DESCRIBED BELOW are key personal attributes that are correlated with choosing freely. Evaluate your position regarding each of these attributes, and use this self-evaluation to guide your choices as you shape the free person you want to become.

Make Freedom a Priority

I believe that personal freedom is of paramount significance.	I believe that personal freedom is less significant than meeting my needs.

5   4   3   2   1

Achieving greater freedom for yourself is based on placing a high value on personal freedom. If you are primarily focused on meeting your needs within the existing structure of your life, then maximizing your choices and enlarging the scope of your life may not be a top priority. If you feel dissatisfied with the status quo and long to increase your options and your ability to choose them, increasing your personal freedom will be a very important goal.

Strategy: *Complete a brief inventory of your life, identifying some of the areas you would like to change, as well as those you are basically satisfied with but would like to enrich. Think about the way increasing your personal freedom and making different choices can help you achieve these life goals.*

Accept Your Freedom and Responsibility

I willingly accept my freedom and my responsibility.

I often try to escape from my freedom and evade personal responsibility.

5   4   3   2   1

Your reaction to responsibility is an effective barometer of your attitude toward freedom. If you are comfortable with your personal responsibility, able openly to admit your mistakes as well as take pleasure in your successes, this is an indication that you accept your freedom. Similarly, if you take pride in your independence, welcoming the opportunity to make choices for which you are solely responsible, this also reveals a willing embracing of your freedom.

Strategy: *Create a "responsibility chart" that evaluates your acceptance of responsibility (and freedom) in various areas of your life. On one side of the page describe common activities in which you are engaged ("Decisions at work," "Conflicts with my partner") and on the other side list typical judgments that you make ("I am solely responsible for that mistaken analysis"; "You made me do that embarrassing thing and I can't forgive you"). After several days of record-keeping and reflection, you should begin to get an increasingly clear picture of the extent to which you accept (or reject) your personal freedom.*

Emphasize Your Ability to Create Yourself

I believe that I create myself through my free choices.	I believe that I am created by forces over which I have little control.

5   4   3   2   1

Although you may not be fully aware of it, you have your own psychological theory of human nature, which is expressed in how you view yourself and deal with other people. Do you believe that your personality is determined by your genetic history or the environmental circumstances that have shaped you? Or do you believe that people are able to transcend their histories and choose freely?

   Strategy: *Instead of explaining your (and others') behavior entirely in terms of genes and environmental conditioning, develop the habit of analyzing your behavior in terms of the choices you make. I have personally witnessed many people who have triumphed over daunting odds, and I have seen others who have failed miserably despite having every advantage in life. The key ingredient? An unshakable belief in the ability to choose one's destiny.*

Become Aware of Constraints on Your Freedom

I am aware of the constraints on my freedom.	I am generally unaware of the constraints on my freedom.

5   4   3   2   1

The key to unlocking your freedom is becoming aware of the external and internal forces that are influencing you. As long as you remain oblivious to external manipulations and internal compulsions, you are powerless to escape from their hold. However, by using your critical thinking abilities, you are able to identify these influences and then neutralize their effect.

Strategy: *In your Thinking Notebook, identify the external limitations (people or circumstances) on your freedom and think about ways to remove these constraints. Then identify — as best you can — the internal compulsions that are influencing you to act in ways at variance with your genuine desires. Use the indicators on page 131 to help in your identification. Then use the Search, Challenge, and Solve approach (pages 142–145) to diminish or eliminate their influence.*

Will Yourself to Break Free from Constraints

I am highly motivated to free myself from my constraints.	It is difficult for me to break free from my constraints.

5   4   3   2   1

What is the original source of human action? Why does one person combat adversity with tenacity, while another in similar circumstances seems weak-willed and lacking resolve? According to the philosopher Frederick Nietzsche, each individual's *"will to power"* is the ultimate source of personal identify and impetus to action. You must simply *will* yourself to action, and by exercising your will, it becomes stronger.

Strategy: *Make a special effort to become aware of your "will," focusing on the way you exercise it and the way your willpower increases with use. Begin with modest goals and will yourself to achieve them, not permitting doubt, fears, or inertia to deflect you. Then gradually expand the scope to include more ambitious challenges.*

Create New Options to Choose From

I usually try to create additional options to those presented.	I usually accept the options that are presented.

5   4   3   2   1

Active thinking, like passive thinking, is habit-forming. But once you develop the habit of looking beyond the information given, to transcend consistently the framework within which you are operating, you will be increasingly unwilling to be limited by the alternatives determined by others. Instead, you will seek to create new possibilities and actively shape situations to fit your needs.

Strategy: *When you find yourself in situations with different choices, make a conscious effort to identify alternatives that are different from those explicitly presented. You don't necessarily have to choose the new options you have created if they are not superior to others, but you do want to start developing the habit of using your imagination to look beyond the circumstances as presented.*

Become Aware of Your Explanatory Style

I am aware of my inner messages that I repeat to myself.	I have difficulty "hearing" the inner messages that I repeat to myself.

5   4   3   2   1

The process of thinking involves your *explanatory style*, an internal dialogue with yourself that shapes the way you think about your life, positively or negatively. Becoming aware of your inner messages is called *metacognition*, a heightened cognitive sensitivity. It's like developing a new sense, an "inner hearing," that enables you to tune in to these messages and modify them if necessary.

Strategy: *Using your Thinking Notebook to record your results, focus your attention on your inner dialogue, making note of the positive statements ("That was a very intelligent idea") and the negative statements ("How could I have made the same mistakes again? I'm hopeless"). After doing this for several days, classify the types and frequency of your statements and see what inferences you can make about the way you view yourself and your life.*

Replace Your Pessimistic Explanatory Style with an Optimistic Style

I am able to challenge my negative attitudes and replace them with positive ones.	It is difficult for me to change my negative attitudes into positive ones.

5   4   3   2   1

Once you have attuned your sense of inner hearing to the ongoing dialogue taking place, you can then begin to reshape this dialogue to better reflect the person you want to become.

Strategy: Those negative, pessimistic statements that keep appearing like unwanted viruses can be successfully challenged using the strategies described on page 142. Those statements that are positive and optimistic can be strengthened and expanded. You are developing an "inner freedom" by successfully choosing to shape the potent, personal dialogue that you may have been previously unaware of.

Work Purposefully to Achieve the Good Life for Yourself and Others

I have a clear idea of the Good Life that I want to create for myself.

I am confused about what the Good Life is and how to achieve it for myself.

5   4   3   2   1

The Good Life is different for each person, and there is no single path or formula for achieving it. It is the daily process of creating yourself in ways that express your deepest desires and highest values — your authentic self. Thinking critically and creatively provides you with the insight to clearly see the person you want to become, while choosing freely gives you the power actually to create the person you have envisioned.

Strategy: Describe your ideal Good Life in your Thinking Notebook. Make full use of your imagination and be specific regarding the details of the life you are envisioning for yourself. Compare this imagined Good Life with the life you have now. What different choices do you have to make in order to achieve your Good Life?

SCORING GUIDE

Add up the numbers you circled for each of the self-evaluation items above and use the following Scoring Guide to evaluate your personal freedom.

Point Total	Interpretation
36–45	very free
27–35	moderately free
18–26	somewhat free
9–17	comparatively unfree

In interpreting your results, be sure to keep in mind that:

- This evaluation is not an exact measure of your personal freedom, but is rather intended as a general indicator of how freely you approach yourself and your life.
- Your score indicates how freely you are functioning at the present time, *not* your *potential* to choose freely. If you scored lower than you would like, it means that you are underutilizing your capacity to be free, and that you need to follow the suggestions in this chapter to fully realize your freedom potential.

THINKING ACTIVITY

Increasing Your Freedom

Select areas of your life in which you would like to be more free: personal habits and behaviors, relationships with others, your career. Make a special effort to become aware of the constraints that are limiting your freedom and the internal messages that are shaping your thinking. Keep a record in your Thinking Notebook detailing your efforts and their results. Be sure to allow yourself sufficient time to escape from habitual forms and establish new patterns of thinking, feeling, and choosing. Cultivate the qualities of choosing freely that we explored in this section:

- Make freedom a priority.
- Accept your freedom and responsibility.
- Emphasize your ability to create yourself.
- Become aware of the constraints on your freedom.
- *Will* yourself to break free from constraints.
- Create new options to choose from.
- Become aware of your explanatory style.
- Replace your pessimistic explanatory style with an optimistic style.
- Work purposefully to achieve the Good Life for yourself and others.

STEP 4

SOLVE PROBLEMS EFFECTIVELY

Solving challenging problems effectively involves using an integrated set of thinking abilities. In this chapter, you will learn how to: identify the "real" problem, generate a diverse set of alternatives, evaluate these alternatives in terms of advantages and disadvantages, develop an intelligent solution with a specific plan of action, and monitor the results of this plan for possible modification. By applying this approach to a variety of problems in your personal life, you will learn to internalize this mode of thinking as a natural part of the way you approach problems and seek solutions.

What Kind of Problem-Solver Are You?

SOMETIMES OUR LIVES SEEM awash with problems, difficult, vexing situations that cause irritation and anxiety. Of course, there are many minor problems that we solve each day: negotiating a construction detour on the road, working through an unexpected difficulty at our job, helping an upset child deal with a disappointment. Relatively simple problems like these do not require a systematic or complex analysis. We can solve them with just a little effort and concentration. But the difficult and complicated problems in life require more attention.

The idea of "having a problem" certainly conjures up unpleasant associations for most people, but the truth is that solving problems is an integral and natural part of the process of living. It is the human ability to solve problems that accounts for our successful longevity on this planet. At the same time, it is our inability to solve problems that has resulted in senseless wars, unnecessary famine, and irrational persecution. You can undoubtedly discern this same duality in your own life: Your most satisfying accomplishments are likely the consequence of successful problem-solving, while your greatest disappointments probably resulted at least in part from your failure to solve some crucial problems. For example, think about some of the very difficult problems you have solved through dedication and intelligent action. How did your success make you feel? What were some of the positive results of your success? On the other hand, review some of the significant problems that you have been unable to solve. What were some of the negative consequences of your failed efforts? The psychiatrist and author M. Scott Peck sums up the centrality of problems in our lives:

> Problems call forth our courage and our wisdom; indeed, they create our courage and our wisdom. It is only because of problems that we grow mentally and spiritually. When we desire to encourage the growth of the human spirit, we challenge and encourage the human capacity to solve problems, just as in school we deliberately set problems for our children to solve.

Problems are the crucible that forges the strength of our characters. When you are tested by life, forced to overcome adversity and think your way through the most challenging situations, you will emerge a more intelligent, resourceful, and resilient person. However, if you lead a sheltered life that insulates you from life's trials, or if you flee situations at the first sign of trouble, then you will be weak and unable to cope with the eruptions and explosions that are bound to occur even in your carefully protected world. Adversity reveals for all to see the person you have become, the character you have created, as the Roman philosopher and poet Lucretius explained, *"So it is more useful to watch a man in times of peril, and in adversity to discern what kind of man he is; for then, at last, words of truth are drawn from the depths of his heart, and the mask is torn off, reality remains."*

The quality of your life can be traced in large measure to your competency as a problem-solver. The fact that some people are consistently superior problem-solvers is largely due to their ability to approach problems in an informed and organized way. Less competent problem-solvers just muddle through when it comes to meeting up with adversity, using hit-or-miss strategies that rarely provide the best results. How would you rate yourself as a problem-solver? Do you generally approach difficulties confidently, analyze them clearly, and reach productive solutions? Or do you find that you often get "lost" and confused in such situations, unable to understand the problem clearly and break out of mental ruts? Of course, you may find that you are very adept at solving problems in one area of your life — such as your job — and miserable at solving problems in other areas, such as your love life or your relationships with your children.

If you are less able to solve complex and challenging problems than you would like, don't despair! Being an expert problem-solver is not a genetic award, it is for the most part a learned skill that you can develop by practicing and applying the principles described in this chapter. You can learn to view problems as *challenges*, opportunities for growth instead of obstacles or burdens. You can become a person who attacks adversity with confidence and enthusiasm. This possibility may seem unlikely to you at this point, but I can assure you that, based on my experience teaching thousands of people for the past twenty years, becoming an expert problem-solver is well within your grasp.

An Organized Approach to Solving Problems

LET'S BEGIN by examining an exasperating problem that almost everyone can relate to — *procrastination*. In fact, when I ask groups of people how many have some difficulty with this problem, nearly everyone's hand is raised as soon as I utter that dreaded word, usually accompanied by rueful laughs and knowing smiles.

Procrastination: "I am a procrastinator. Whenever I have something important to do, especially if it's difficult or unpleasant, I tend to put it off. Though this chronic delaying bothers me, I try to suppress my concern and instead work on more trivial things. It doesn't matter how much time I allow for certain responsibilities, I always end up waiting till the last minute to really focus and get things done, or I overschedule too many things into the time available. I usually meet my deadlines, but not always, and I don't enjoy working under this kind of pressure. In many cases I know that I'm not producing my best work. To make matters worse, the feeling that I'm always behind is causing me to feel really stressed out and undermining my confidence. I've tried every kind of schedule and technique, but my best intentions simply don't last, and I end up slipping into my old habits. I must learn to get my priorities in order and act on them in an organized way so that I can lead a well-balanced and happier life."

Very often when we are faced with difficult problems like this, we simply do not know where to begin to try to solve them. Every issue is connected to many others. Frustrated by not knowing where to take the first step, we often give up trying to understand the problem. In many cases, we may simply do nothing, waiting for events to make the decision for us ("I'll wait and see what happens") or hoping that the problem will go away ("Maybe I'll improve"). Or we may take the attitude that "Nobody's perfect!" and "That's just the way I am." Acting impulsively, without thought or analysis, is another common response ("I'll quit all nonessential activities so I'll have more time"). And sometimes we ask for advice and then follow others' suggestions without seriously evaluating them ("Tell me what I should do — I'm tired of thinking about this").

None of these approaches is likely to succeed in the long run, and they will gradually reduce our confidence in dealing with complex problems. What we need is a versatile, powerful approach to solving problems that will enable us to analyze the most challenging problems effectively and reach intelligent and lasting solutions. The approach to problems presented in this chapter has been used successfully to solve thousands of the most difficult and diverse problems that people encounter in their everyday lives. It is a method that builds directly on Steps 1, 2, and 3 of this book: to be an expert problem-solver, you must *think critically, live creatively,* and *choose freely.* These are the tools of mind and traits of character you will need in order to take full advantage of the 7-Step method outlined below.

The Thinker's Way to Solve Problems

Step 1: Have I accepted the problem?
Step 2: What do I know about the problem?
Step 3: How can I define the problem?
Step 4: What are the alternatives?
Step 5: What are the advantages and/or disadvantages of each alternative?
Step 6: What is the solution?
Step 7: How well is the solution working?

Admittedly, human minds do not always work in such a logical, step-by-step fashion, but this is the best way to begin your analysis. When first learning a problem-solving method like this, it is generally wise not to skip steps, because each step deals with an important aspect of the problem. As you become more proficient in using the method, you will find that you can apply its concepts and strategies in an increasingly flexible and natural way, just as learning the basics of an activity like a new sport or dance gradually gives way to a more organic and integrated performance of the skills involved.

In the remainder of this chapter you will explore this versatile problem-solving approach by seeing it applied to a variety of complex, difficult problems, including the one described by the procrastinator above.

Most important, you will be encouraged to develop your own proficiency as a problem-solver by selecting a difficult, unsolved problem in your own life and applying this method to it, a step at a time. This is the best way to learn a thinking approach like this, by using it to analyze a frustrating situation that you really care about. As you experience the success of your efforts firsthand, the various steps will come alive and you will have an opportunity to witness the method in action. By developing insight into the way your mind operates when you are thinking effectively, you will be able to apply this improved understanding to challenging situations throughout your life, refining your problem-solving skills with each application.

Before the Analysis: "Do I Have a Problem?"

MOST OF US have little difficulty identifying problems we would like to solve. As you begin to think about some of the problems in your life, review some of the problem descriptions below from people I have worked with.

Losing weight: "My problem is the unwelcome weight that has attached itself to me. I was always in pretty good physical shape when I was younger, and if I gained a few extra pounds, they were easy to lose by adjusting my diet slightly or exercising a little more. As I've gotten older, however, it seems easier to add the weight and more difficult to take it off. I'm eating healthier than I ever have and getting just as much exercise, but the pounds just keep on coming. My clothes are tight, I'm feeling slow and heavy, and my self-esteem is suffering. How can I lose this excess poundage?"

Sarcasm: "Sarcasm is an important element of my personality and it serves many purposes for me. It's an emotional release valve to express my discontent with situations and people; it's a psychological defense to protect myself against unwanted criticism; and it's a way I can get attention and be amusing. However, my sarcasm can cause others to feel hurt, challenged, or invaded. I realize my sarcastic verbal assaults can be extremely hurtful. I do not want to relinquish my sarcasm completely, but I want to purge it of its destructive elements."

Smoking: "One problem in my life that has remained unsolved for about twelve years is my inability to stop smoking. I know it is dangerous for my health, and I tell my children that they should not smoke. They tell me that I should stop and I explain to them that it is very hard. I have tried to stop many times without success. The only times I was able to stop were during my two pregnancies, because I didn't want to endanger my children's health. But after their births I went back to smoking, although I realize that secondhand smoke can also pose a health hazard. I want to stop smoking because it's dangerous, but I also enjoy it. Why do I continue, knowing it can only damage myself and my children?"

Dealing with Down's syndrome: "My most prominent problem concerns my son Michael, who has Down's syndrome. He is fourteen years old, and he's affectionate, well behaved, and a pleasure most of the time. My problem is getting him to function in everyday life all by himself. He must learn how to talk so other people can understand him. He must learn how to go to stores and how to use money. He must learn how to travel, cook, clean house, take care of errands, and so on. Normally these things would come easily to a person, but not to Michael. I'm worried because if he doesn't learn how to survive alone, what will happen to him when I die? He will most likely wind up in a home for the mentally disabled, and this upsets me because I know he will not be happy under those conditions. Every day I work with him, but with limited success. I really find this problem difficult to handle."

THINKING ACTIVITY

What Problem Do I Want to Solve?

As these descriptions suggest, there are as many different problems as there are people who have them. Think about your own life. What are some of the most pressing problems that you would like to solve? Select one (or more) of these problems and describe it as specifically as you can. As this chapter progresses, you will be analyzing your problem using the steps and strategies of the 7-Step Problem-Solving Method. By the conclusion of your analysis, you should find that you have made substantial progress toward finding a solution. If you are having difficulty thinking of a problem, review the following list for ideas. Though the list may seem long, it's actually fairly short when compared with the many problems that life presents.

I am unable to maintain sufficient motivation and focus to reach my goals.

It's difficult for me to make a serious commitment to any thing or person in my life.

I can't seem to find the time to exercise, even though I need to.

My son has a problem with drugs and it's destroying the family.

I have a paralyzing fear of speaking in front of other people.

I can't establish a harmonious custody arrangement with my former husband.

I can't get over the death of my father.

My family does not approve of my fiancée because she is of a different race.

My mother constantly criticizes the way I am raising my child.

My husband and I are often at each other's throat.

People say I sometimes have an arrogant and annoying attitude.

I am unhappy in my job and I don't know what career would make me happy.

I have developed a mental block that is inhibiting my creative work.

I am having a difficulty getting along with my father, though we used to be close.

I frequently get depressed and don't feel like doing anything.

My children don't communicate to me what they are thinking or feeling.

I act overly possessive and controlling toward the people in my life.

I am an underachiever in most areas of my life.

I have difficulty in expressing my true feelings toward other people.

I have a problem with alcohol.

As a recent immigrant, I am having trouble adjusting to this new culture.

I have trouble saying no to people, and they take advantage of me.

I have poor eating habits, with a diet consisting mainly of junk food at irregular hours.

I am very impatient with people's shortcomings and stupidities.

I am so involved with my friends' problems that I don't have time for my own.

I tend to take people for granted, not expressing my appreciation of or love for them.

I am reluctant to express my opinions, especially when they disagree with others'.

I have chronic migraine headaches.

My son is exhibiting serious behavior problems in school.

I am addicted to candy, especially chocolate.

I have a very low opinion of myself, and create situations in which I am a victim.

My boss makes suggestive comments and inappropriate proposals to me.

I feel that I need to lose weight, though my friends don't agree.

I'm a compulsive shopper, spending money I don't have on things I don't need.

I can't get my mother to take her medication and stick to her diet.

I need to focus; my life is too chaotic and disorganized.

I am very shy; it's hard for me to meet people and I feel very lonely as a result.

It is very difficult for me to accept criticism, and I respond in a hostile way.

I can't stand the people that I work with.

I am too dependent on the approval of other people and am afraid simply to be myself.

A longtime friend wants to have a romantic relationship, but I don't.

I have poor communication with the other members of my family.

I am adopted and I can't stop thinking about my natural parents.

Instead of using my free time productively, I waste it.

I feel panicked in groups of people so I spend most of my time at home.

I am recently separated and am having trouble reorienting my life.

No matter how much money I earn, I seem to spend more.

I lack confidence and feel inadequate much of the time.

My children are pushing me over the edge and I end up screaming at them.

My ex-boyfriend has been stalking, harassing, and threatening me.

My boss and I don't see eye-to-eye and we clash on a regular basis.

I am unable to control my rage when I am mad at someone, and I always regret it.

I am having trouble dealing with my parents' getting older.

Step 1: Have I Accepted the Problem?

It seems like common sense: If you don't *acknowledge* that a problem exists, then there is no reason for you to solve it, and so you likely won't. But many people *don't* readily acknowledge their problems. They may feel that their problem reflects unfavorably on themselves. We all have *self-concepts*, images of ourselves that we carefully create and that often present an idealized version of who we are. We also have *social concepts*, images of ourselves that we present to other people. These social images that we create tend to be even more flattering than our self-concepts. When we acknowledge problems in our lives, we are threatening these positive and optimistic versions, admitting to ourselves and others that we are not perfect, that there are things that we would like to improve but can't, that we are a "work in progress."

Another reason people are reluctant to acknowledge a problem is that by formally recognizing you have a problem, you are implying that *you should do something about it.* But doing something about a problem often means hard work, discomfort, disruption of your accustomed ways of behaving, and other unpleasant effects. For example, once you admit that you have trouble meeting deadlines, it's clear that you should make the effort to overcome this problem. Or, if you are willing to state, "I have poor communication with my family members," then the implication is that you should take steps to improve the situation. By failing to acknowledge the problem, you thereby eliminate the need to take any action regarding it. Of course, the problem remains unsolved.

However, mere acknowledgment is not enough to solve a problem, either. Once you have identified a problem, you must *commit* yourself to trying to solve it. Successful problem-solvers are highly motivated and willing to persevere through the many challenges and frustrations of the problem-solving process. This is where your *freedom to choose* comes into play. Your free will is a force of great power, and once you decide that a goal is sufficiently important, you can marshal this willpower and choose to make it happen. Too often people are not prepared to make the total commitment necessary to solve a difficult problem like smoking, and so they are destined to fail.

For example, you may have had the experience of speaking at length to friends about problems they are having, helping them identify solutions, and then discovering to your dismay that they took absolutely no action. Often our minds are willing, but our wills are weak. Newton's law that *"A body at rest tends to stay at rest"* applies to human behavior as well. Inertia and habit are powerful forces, and it takes a strong and conscious act of will to overcome them. But the more you successfully exercise your free will, the stronger it becomes, as you gain confidence in your own power to shape the direction of your life, underscoring another of Newton's laws: *"A body in motion tends to stay in motion."* Success is habit-forming, and it's the kind of habit that we should all develop.

STRATEGIES FOR ACCEPTING MY PROBLEM

There is a profound difference between understanding this problem-solving method on an intellectual level and actually making it work in your life on a practical and emotional level. That's why, in addition to the descriptions of the various problem-solving steps and examples to illustrate them, *Strategies* have been included to help you apply these ideas to your life in a meaningful way.

Formalize Your Acceptance: When you formalize your acceptance of a problem, you are "going on record," either by preparing a signed declaration or by signing a "contract" with someone else. This formal commitment serves as an explicit statement of your original intentions and encourages you to "draw a line in the sand" and stick to your resolution — not allowing you to blur the line gradually until it no longer exists and you find yourself in the same predicament in which you began. Here are some examples from my workshops of several resolutions that helped individuals acknowledge their problems and commit themselves to solving them.

Procrastination: "I, ——, *hereby declare myself as an individual who procrastinates. It is with this realization that I will put forth an unrelenting effort to overcome this destructive habit. Even though procrastination has taught me to work under pressure and think on my feet, I want to leave this dead-end street that I'm on. I shall devote myself to becoming consistently punctual and timely. Whenever I receive a task that I must complete before a given time, I pledge to work on it as soon as I can so that I will avoid doing things at the last minute. Whenever I get the urge to fall back into my old habits, may the words of this declaration be a reminder of the promise that I made on this day. The above signature represents a solemn promise to myself to "do today what I thought I could do tomorrow."*

Smoking: "I, ——, *promise to stop smoking. Although I have certain problems that might give me the urge to smoke, I will try everything in my power not to have a breakdown if I feel the need for a cigarette. I will take long walks or talk to friends who can support me. I have come to the realization that smoking is a substitute that I use to escape my problems. I realize that the only person who can help me is myself, and that to stop this addiction I must be willing to take responsibility by confronting my problems. I love living too much to continue this addiction and end up with cancer or heart disease, and I love those close to me too much to endanger their health. I have people who love me who want me to stop smoking, and it is about time I take some action."*

List the Benefits: Making a detailed list of the benefits you will derive from successfully dealing with the problem is an excellent strategy for helping you accept your problem. It helps you clarify why you want to tackle the problem and motivates you to get started. A list makes explicit the way your life will be improved by solving your problem, and you can use it for encouragement when you encounter difficulties or lose momentum. Here is a sample list:

Procrastination: By solving my problem of procrastination I will achieve the following benefits:

- *a less stressful life because I won't be doing things at the last minute*
- *more free time because of improved time management*
- *the exhilarating feeling of having completed things on time*
- *a more confident and optimistic attitude toward life*
- *losing the reputation of being "the last one"*
- *diminishing the anxiety of "I waited too long" or "I won't be able to finish in time"*
- *the certainty that I had the power to beat this problem*
- *a more organized life and the feeling that I'm "in control"*
- *less guilt when I think about all that I have to do*
- *the opportunity to do my best work*

Create a "Worst-Case" Scenario: Some problems persist because you are able to ignore their possible implications. When you use this strategy, you remind yourself, as graphically as possible, of the potentially disastrous consequences of your actions. For example, using vivid color photographs and research conclusions, you can drive home the point to yourself that excessive smoking, drinking, or eating can lead to myriad health problems, social and psychological difficulties, and an early and untimely demise. Here's an example of a worst-case scenario:

Smoking: *"It is the year 2003. At the age of forty-four, just when my children are reaching independence and my life is once again my own, I am lying in a bed at Sloan-Kettering Hospital undergoing my third course of chemotherapy for lung cancer. My cancer is rapidly spreading, devastating both my body and spirit. My skin is burned from radiation treatments, my body weight has dwindled to eighty pounds, my hair is gone, and what's worse, I don't even care anymore. I can't walk, can barely speak, and every breath is an agonizing effort. My family is emotionally and financially exhausted and growing more and more resentful of me and my illness. I never did heed their warnings or the advice of my doctors over the years. This was not supposed to happen to me. I pray for death, but death eludes me. I linger for months and months. Technology keeps me alive but I am no longer in control. I have lost any quality of life as well as my dignity. The prime of my life has gone up in smoke."*

THINKING ACTIVITY

Accepting My Problem

Think about the problem that you decided to work on earlier in this chapter. There are probably powerful forces that have made it difficult to solve this problem. Has it been hard for you to acknowledge the problem? Have you experienced difficulty in committing yourself to solving it? If so, select several of the strategies described in this section (or create your own strategies) and then *use* the strategies to illuminate your recognition of the problem and strengthen your resolve in solving it.

- Formalize your acceptance.
- List the benefits.
- Create a "worst-case" scenario.

Record the results in your Thinking Notebook.

Step 2: What Do I Know about the Problem?

SOLVING A PROBLEM begins with developing information about the problem. How do you do this? You begin by putting down everything you know about the problem. Often we know more than we are consciously aware of, and the process of writing things down triggers this latent knowledge and brings it to the surface. In addition, there are several other strategies that you can employ to unearth important information, and these are described below.

STRATEGIES FOR FINDING OUT INFORMATION ABOUT MY PROBLEM

Ask — and Answer — Key Questions: By asking and trying to answer basic questions about your situation, you are establishing a sound foundation for the exploration of your problem.

Who are the people involved in this situation?

Who can help me solve it?

What are the various parts or dimensions of the problem?

What are my strengths and resources for solving this problem?

What additional information do I need to solve this problem?

Where can I find people or additional information to help me solve the problem?

When did the problem begin?

When should the problem be resolved?

How did the problem develop or come into being?

Why is solving this problem important to me?

Why is it difficult to solve?

What Is the History? Most serious problems do not appear suddenly; they develop gradually over time. In order to understand fully the present incarnation of your problem, it is helpful to identify its point of origin and trace its evolution. Just as pulling out a weed without extracting its roots fails to kill it, so trying to solve a problem without understanding its history often leads to results that are only temporary. Here is one person's example of tracing the history of his problem:

Sarcasm: I had to really dig deep within myself to discover why I was so sarcastic and raw. In some ways it hurt to dig so deep to find an answer. I went back to when I was a young child: extremely shy, timid, and reclusive. I preferred being alone, observing rather than participating. I felt I was an outsider, and compared to other children, I felt abnormal. At some point in my life, probably at about eight years old, I began to realize that sarcasm was one device I could use to get noticed. People deal with conflicts in various ways: They cry, become physically violent, or give up . . . I was sarcastic! It was the way I could feel in control of my life.

What's Preventing Me from Solving the Problem? If you have been trying without success to solve an important problem, it is likely that there are significant forces inhibiting your efforts. These inhibiting forces can take the form of habits that are difficult to break; positive reinforcement that you are receiving from the problem situation; fear of painful results if you try to solve the problem; or some external impediment. In your quest to gather information about your problem, it is useful to identify the obstacles that are preventing you from seeking a successful solution, as this should help you devise specific strategies for overcoming these obstacles. Here is an example of inhibiting forces that one person identified, along with the appropriate "antidote":

Smoking: Why I have been unable to stop smoking:
  Inhibition: *I have tried before to quit and failed.*
    Antidote: *Previous failures give me an edge. I already know what doesn't work.*
  Inhibition: *Smoking is my crutch. When I'm nervous or sad, I light up.*
    Antidote: *Perhaps keeping a journal of my feelings will help me deal with stress, sort out emotions, and serve as a substitute for smoking.*
  Inhibition: *I have been a smoker for a very long time.*
    Antidote: *My extensive experience should strengthen my determination to stop this self-destructive habit.*
  Inhibition: *It is a part of my daily rituals. I wake up to coffee and a cigarette.*
    Antidote: *Change my morning rituals — create new ones.*

THINKING ACTIVITY

Finding Information about My Problem

Focusing on the problem that you are working to solve in this chapter, write down all that you know about your problem situation. Then use the strategies described in this section to help you discover additional relevant information.

- Ask — and Answer — Key Questions
- What Is the History?
- What's Preventing Me from Solving the Problem?

Record your results in your Thinking Notebook.

Step 3: How Can I Define the Problem?

HAVING ACCEPTED your problem and developed some background information about it, the next step is to determine exactly what the central issues of the problem are. If you do not clearly understand what the heart of the problem really is, then your chances of solving it are considerably reduced. You may believe that the root of the problem is one thing, when it may actually turn out to be something quite different. For example, you may identify "anxiety attacks" (or depression, overeating, procrastination, and so on) as a problem you are experiencing, though it is likely that the anxiety is a *symptom* of the underlying *real problem*.

Another common difficulty in defining your problem accurately comes from thinking about the problem in terms that are too general. For instance, consider how these contrasting formulations might lead you in different directions in trying to solve the problems:

- "I'm a failure" vs. "I was unable to complete an important project."
- "Work is boring" vs. "I feel bored at this particular job."
- "I'm unlovable" vs. "This relationship didn't work out."

In each of these cases a very general conclusion (the first statement) has been replaced by a more specific characterization of the problem (the second statement).

STRATEGIES FOR DEFINING MY PROBLEM

What Results Am I Aiming for in This Situation? This strategy consists of identifying the specific results or objectives you are trying to achieve. Identifying the results is important because it provides a clear direction for your problem analysis and it establishes benchmarks that will let you know when you have succeeded. In the case of *procrastination*, for example, results would include meeting deadlines in a timely fashion; having an organized schedule that provides structure to your life; eliminating the anxiety and guilt that accompanies always leaving things to the last minute; replacing the urge to delay with a desire to be early. Once you achieve these objectives, you will know that your problem has been solved to your satisfaction.

Identify Component Problems: Larger problems are often composed of component problems. To define the larger problem, it is often necessary to identify and describe its subproblems. For example, poor performance on the job might be the result of a number of factors — ineffective work habits, inefficient time management, interpersonal difficulties with coworkers or supervisors, preoccupation with a personal problem, or health difficulties. Defining and dealing effectively with the larger problem means first dealing with the subproblems. Here are some examples of component problems comprising more complex problems:

Complex Problem: Procrastination
Component Problems:

- I sometimes lack motivation because I often don't enjoy what I'm doing.
- I have developed the habit of making excuses instead of taking responsibility.
- I give in to temptations that take me away from my primary responsibilities.
- My fear of failure and lack of confidence inhibit me from committing myself fully.
- I don't like being controlled by other people's deadlines, and so I rebel by delaying.

Complex Problem: Overeating
Component Problems:

- I dislike physical exercise.
- I am addicted to drinking beer, wine, soda.
- I use excess weight as a defense to repel others and as a form of sexual avoidance.

- I have low self-esteem and my overeating acts as a self-fulfilling prophecy: Since I look so unattractive, I can't be worth much.

Describe Perspectives on the Problem: Perspective-taking is a key ingredient of thinking critically, and it can help you zero in on defining the essence of your problem as well. For example, when you describe how various individuals might view a given problem, the essential ingredients of the problem may begin to emerge more clearly. It is a process analogous to the "triangulation" that takes place in navigation: by utilizing three or more fixed points of reference, you are able to establish your exact position with increasing certainty. Here is an example of using multiple perspectives to help define the essential problem:

Problem: Smoking
Perspectives:

- Children: My children have a very strong opinion about my smoking. They hate it! They wave their hands and hold their noses and make it perfectly clear that this is unacceptable to them.
- Husband: My husband, although a smoker himself, would love to see me quit and has always been supportive of any effort I have made to do so. Likewise, I am concerned for his health and well-being and hope to make this crusade a team effort.
- Mother: My mother blames herself for my addiction because she feels that she did not supervise me well enough.
- Friends: Most of my friends are nonsmokers and are always advising me to quit. Their advice is typical of a nonsmoker: "Just stop."
- Myself: I am beginning to see that my smoking grew out of an emotional need and continues to this day to be connected to my lack of skill in dealing with my emotions.

THINKING ACTIVITY

Defining My Problem

Concentrate on the problem that you have been analyzing in this chapter and try to define what the "real" problem is, clearly and specifically. Be aware that this may involve going beyond the surface symptoms to the deeper, underlying dynamics. Use the strategies we have explored in this section (or create your own strategies) to help in your analysis.

- What results am I aiming for in this situation?
- Identify component problems.
- Describe perspectives on the problem.

Record your results in your Thinking Notebook.

Step 4: What Are My Alternatives?

ONCE YOU HAVE defined your problem, you are now in a position to generate and evaluate possible courses of action that might help you solve it. Too often people jump ahead to identifying alternatives before properly defining the problem. But if their definition of the problem is not accurate, then the alternatives they identify will probably not be useful. For example, a family I knew had a fourth-grader, Philip, who was acting disruptively in school. The school officials jumped to the conclusion that the child was emotionally disturbed, and mandated that he undergo counseling and possible placement in a special education class. During routine testing, the psychologist discovered that Philip was reading at an eighth-grade level and had a seventh-grade-level math capability. This information suggested a redefinition of the problem — Philip was bored in class — and, as a result, presented different alternatives. Philip was transferred to a gifted and talented program at another school, where he thrived.

Of course, when you first start working on your problem, it may not be initially clear exactly what the "real" problem is. As with Philip, it may only become clear as you work through your problem analysis, gradually developing a more profound understanding of the heart of your problem. That's why, as a critical thinker, you remain open-minded and flexible as you think through a problem, always looking for new clues that will refine your definition of the problem and reorient your analysis. When *un*critical thinkers stubbornly stick to the original direction they established for themselves, they run the likely risk of ending up at a destination far removed from the problem they endeavored to solve.

After you're reasonably confident regarding your definition of the problem, it's time to identify alternatives for solving the problem.

Try to generate as many as ten alternatives. This is where creative thinking comes in. The first few alternatives are likely to be the obvious ones, while extending your thinking to produce additional possibilities is likely to result in some truly creative approaches. In this phase of problem-solving, it is essential that you focus your mental energies on generating possibilities, *not* evaluating them. Use your creative thinking abilities to the fullest, making new connections, coming up even with weird ideas, developing new paths, instead of walking down the well-worn avenues. You will have ample opportunity to evaluate your ideas critically in the next stages of the process, but for now let your mind run free, unfettered by doubts and critiques. Sometimes the most far-fetched ideas end up being transformed into the most elegant and effective solutions.

You can use several strategies to unleash your creative thinking abilities in order to generate innovative and effective approaches.

STRATEGIES FOR GENERATING ALTERNATIVES

Discuss the Problem with Other People: Discussing possible alternatives with others employs a number of critical and creative thinking abilities explored in earlier chapters, including seeing situations from different viewpoints and using your imagination to invent unique ideas. As critical thinkers we live — and solve problems — in a community, not simply by ourselves. Other people can often suggest alternatives that we haven't thought of, in part because they are outside the situation and thus have a more objective view, and in part because they naturally view the world differently than we do, based on their past experiences and personalities. Besides, there is also an emotionally cathartic effect that comes from sharing your problems with others, an unburdening that lightens your soul, renews your spirit, and helps you find a clear path out of your dilemma.

Brainstorm Ideas: Brainstorming, a method which we examined in Step 2: Live Creatively, builds on the strengths of working with others to generate ideas and solve problems. In a typical brainstorming session, a group of people work together to generate as many ideas as possible in a specific period of time. As ideas are produced, they are not judged or evaluated, as this tends to inhibit the free flow of ideas and discourages people from making suggestions. Evaluation is deferred until a later stage. Participants are encouraged to build upon the ideas of others, since the most creative ideas are often generated through the constructive interplay of diverse minds. A useful visual adjunct to brainstorming is creating Mind Maps, a process we also explored in Step 2: Live Creatively.

Don't Reinvent the Wheel!: Although we like to think of our problems as being unique, the truth is that many other people have wrestled with problems identical to or very similar to our own. What makes these problems unique is that they're happening to *us*. And since these problems are in some sense universal, professionally qualified (and unqualified) people have written books, created programs, developed videotapes, and initiated support groups. In short, there are many resources available that are as close as your nearest bookstore or newspaper. However, while these resources can be very helpful, and you should consider exploring them, it is important to remember that they are *resources*, not guaranteed solutions. *You* are the only person who can ultimately solve your problem, and you will need to exercise your abilities to *think critically, live creatively,* and *choose freely,* in order to accomplish this goal.

Using these three strategies, here are thirty-five alternatives that people in my workshops came up with to solve the problem of procrastination:

Problem: Procrastination

1. Organize a specific schedule to accomplish tasks — and stick to it!
2. Think of the consequences in the future and even exaggerate them. "If I don't stop procrastinating, I will be fired/have a nervous breakdown/lose my friends/get sick."
3. Set earlier deadlines for myself in order to be forced to finish tasks ahead of time.
4. Always start with the most difficult things, not the easiest.
5. Plan leisure activities for right after my work is done, as an incentive.
6. Force myself to do the work NOW.
7. Strictly limit time-wasters like television and gabbing on the phone.
8. Plan to do complex tasks a piece at a time, instead of all at once.
9. Don't think so much about it — just do it!
10. Treat meeting deadlines as a life-or-death situation.
11. Visualize a well-organized, in-control life where I meet all deadlines easily.
12. Work together with a friend who procrastinates so we can support each other.
13. Encourage nonprocrastinating friends and family to constantly remind me of my promise and my responsibilities.
14. Don't get defensive when #13 happens.
15. Develop more time-efficient ways to do things.
16. Establish my priorities and *stick to them.*

17. Remember that procrastination limits my chance for success and interferes with my relationships with friends.

18. Seek counseling to determine why I have this problem: Is it a fear of success? Fear of failure? Rebellion against authority?

19. Eliminate some nonessential activities in my life.

20. Write down how good it felt when I accomplished something on time.

21. Make daily lists of things to do and check them off as I do them.

22. Think before I do something: Is there something more urgent to be done?

23. Carry my declaration with me at all times to remind me of my pledge.

24. Use all spare time productively.

25. Start each task on the day that it is given.

26. Read articles and books on procrastination.

27. Post reminders of what must be done all over my home and office.

28. Think about how everyone appreciates a responsible person.

29. Learn to say no to people who ask for favors.

30. Set specific, rational, realistic goals.

31. Make a practice of *over*estimating the amount of time things will take.

32. Stop rebelling against authority and running away from responsibility.

33. See if I can find other ways to accomplish the things I don't enjoy doing (for example, having someone clean my house every two weeks).

34. Remember that doing something right away is much easier than procrastinating.

35. Interview people who have overcome this problem and find out how they did it.

THINKING ACTIVITY

Generating Alternatives for Solving My Problem

Having defined your problem, generate a list of alternatives for
solving your problem. Do not censor or evaluate any responses,
and let your mind work as creatively as possible. Try to come up
with at least ten alternatives — the more the better. Don't worry if
some of your alternatives seem similar or overlap. After thinking
of as many as you can, use the strategies in this section to add to
your list:

- Discuss the problem with other people.
- Brainstorm ideas.
- Don't reinvent the wheel!

Record results in your Thinking Notebook.

Step 5: What Are the Advantages and Disadvantages of Each Alternative?

ONCE YOU HAVE generated many possible alternatives for solving
your problem, the next step is to *evaluate* the viability and practicality
of your alternatives. Which ones will work best?

For example, one alternative to solve the problem of procrastination
was "Organize a specific schedule to accomplish tasks — and stick to it."

- The *advantage* of such an alternative is that if it works, you will
  have gone a long way toward solving your problem.
- But a potential *disadvantage* might be the legitimate concern of
  an inveterate procrastinator: "Why should this alternative work
  now when it's never worked before? I've made up countless schedules, and I simply end up ignoring them. And schedules can be

too rigid and inflexible: there are always unexpected occurrences that threaten to disrupt the best-laid plans."

In addition to identifying the advantages and disadvantages of each alternative, determine if there is *additional information* needed in order to consider the alternative fully. In other words, for each alternative there are probably questions that must be answered if you are to establish whether the alternative will work. You also need to know where you can *find* the information (sources). One useful way to identify the information you need is to ask yourself the question "What if I select this alternative?" ("Can I create a schedule that has flexibility built into it to allow for unexpected occurrences? Once made, will I be able to stick to the schedule in a lasting way?")

As we have seen, performing this sort of rigorous and detailed evaluation of *each* alternative is time-consuming and mentally taxing. Yet this ability is one of the qualities that distinguishes successful problem-solvers from unsuccessful ones. *"The devil is in the details"* is an expression that applies here. Powerful thinkers don't only think big thoughts — they also have the mental rigor and determination to focus on the *specifics*, approaching them with organization and thoroughness. And the more you get into the habit of using your mind in this way, the stronger your mental powers, and the more natural such a disciplined and vigorous use of your mind becomes.

Included below is a sampling of alternatives from some of the problems we have been exploring, along with an evaluation of *advantages*, *disadvantages*, and *further information needed*.

Sarcasm

Alternative #1: Remind myself of how much I despise sarcastic personalities, such as Howard Stern and Dennis Miller. These characters generally receive false respect because of their negative attitudes and I do not want to be seen as insulting and hurtful in the same way.

Advantages: Personalizing my behavior this way may help me see the unflattering way other people view me and discourage this sarcastic behavior.

Disadvantages: I may be unable to sustain the identification of myself with these larger-than-life people.

Information needed: Do I really believe that I share the same qualities with these extremely cynical and sarcastic people? Can I use them to help myself?

Alternative #2: "Unknown tape recorder." I will have my wife tape me secretly while I am involved in spontaneous conversation with her and/or others.

Advantages: This will give me an opportunity to hear exactly how frequent my negative sarcasm is and how it sounds.

Disadvantages: I may be extra careful around my wife, knowing that she might be taping me.

Information needed: Will my wife agree to participate? Can I act naturally around her? Will my behavior convince me that I sometimes go too far with my sarcasm?

Down's Syndrome Child

Alternative #1. Continue to try to meet Michael's needs at home.

Advantages: Michael will continue to be with me most of the time. He feels secure and seems to be happy. I can teach him homemaking skills as well as try to work with him in other areas.

Disadvantages: I'm not qualified to teach him language skills, nor do I always have the patience needed. Since he spends most of his time at home, this is a limited environment and there are many things and people he is not being exposed to. If something happens to me, he will not be prepared to adapt to a new situation.

Information needed: Are there important experiences Michael will be missing? Are there things he should be learning that I can't teach him?

Alternative #2. Have Michael attend a special-needs school.

Advantages: He may learn how to communicate outside the home and learn additional skills. He will find friends his age and develop social skills. If something happens to me, he will be better prepared to face the world.

Disadvantages: He may be fearful about going, and his sense of security may be undermined. He may experience social rejection from other kids, since people don't take to him unless they know him well.

Information needed: What programs are available? What are their curricula? Is the staff qualified and will the other children accept Michael? How much will it cost? Is state financing available?

THINKING ACTIVITY

Evaluating My Alternatives

Evaluate the alternatives you identified for the problem you are working on by specifying the advantages, disadvantages, and information needed for *each* alternative. Although you will have to use some mental exertion on this step, your energy will be well spent. Record the results in your Thinking Notebook.

Step 6: What Is the Solution?

THERE IS NO simple formula or recipe to tell you which alternatives to select. As you work through the different courses of action that are possible, you may find that you can rule some out immediately. For example, in the sample problem of procrastination, you may know with certainty that you don't want to cut out or limit any activities that you are currently involved in, because they are important to you. However, it may not be so simple to select which of the other alternatives you wish to pursue. How do you decide?

The decisions you make usually depend on what you believe to be most important to you. These beliefs are known as *values*, a topic explored in depth in Step 7: Develop Enlightened Values. Your values strongly influence your decisions by helping you set *priorities* in life — that is, deciding what aspects of your life are most important to you. For example, you might decide to change careers because doing something you find personally rewarding is more important than job security or a higher income. Unfortunately, your values are not always compatible. Although you may desire a career that is challenging, you may also want a job that is secure and well-paying. Very often the conflicts *between* your values constitute the problem, and in that case you need to decide which values are more important. This is often a complex calculation. For example, you may be willing to accept a low-paying, insecure job because it is a unique opportunity to learn a new field or work with an unusually creative individual. In another situation, you may decide to take a higher-paying job in which you are less interested for a period of time because you need to establish some financial stability. The point is that every situation is distinctive, and you need to *think critically* in order to arrive at the clearest understanding.

Once you have decided on the best alternative(s) to pursue, your next move is to *plan the steps* you will have to take to put it into action. As we have emphasized before, while thinking carefully is necessary, it is not enough if you hope to solve the problem: You need to *take action* and *implement* your plan. This is where many people stumble in the problem-solving process, paralyzed by inertia or fear. Sometimes, to overcome these blocks and inhibitions, you need to reexamine your original *Acceptance* of the problem, perhaps making use of some of the acceptance strategies that you used in that stage. Once you get started, the rewards of actively attacking your problem are often enough incentive to keep you focused and motivated.

STRATEGIES FOR SELECTING ALTERNATIVES

Compare Alternatives with Your Original Goals: Although each alternative may have certain advantages and disadvantages, not all advantages are equally desirable or potentially effective. For example, quitting your job to reduce your stress level would certainly solve some aspects of your stress problem, but its obvious disadvantages would likely rule out this solution for most people. Thus it makes sense to match up the various alternatives you generated with the "results" you identified in Step 3: What Is the Problem? Examine each of the alternatives and assess how well it will contribute to achieving the results you are aiming for in the situation. You may want to rank the alternatives in terms of their relative effectiveness.

Synthesize a New Alternative: After reviewing and evaluating the alternatives you generated, you may create a *new* alternative that combines the best qualities of several options while avoiding the disadvantages some of them have if chosen exclusively. For example, in the sample problem of procrastination, you might combine

- organizing a schedule;
- setting earlier deadlines;
- making daily lists that you check off;
- establishing priorities that you stick to.

Try Out Each Alternative in Your Imagination: Focus on each alternative (or combination of alternatives) and try to imagine as concretely as possible what it would be like if you actually selected it. Visualize what impact your choice would have on your problem and what the implications would be for your life as a whole. By trying it out in your imagination, you can sometimes avoid unpleasant results or unexpected consequences. As a variation of this strategy, you can sometimes test alternatives on a very limited basis in a practice situation. For example, if you are trying to overcome your fear of speaking in groups, you can practice various speaking techniques with your friends or family until you find an approach you are comfortable with.

THINKING ACTIVITY

Selecting Alternative(s) to Solve My Problem

Reflect thoughtfully on your values and the results you are aiming for in your problem situation and then select the alternative(s) that you think has the best chance of succeeding. Use the strategies included in this section if appropriate:

- Evaluate and compare alternatives.
- Synthesize a new alternative.
- Try out the alternative in your imagination.

Record your results in your Thinking Notebook.

Step 7: How Well Is My Solution Working?

AS YOU WORK toward reaching a reasonable and informed conclusion, you should not fall into the trap of thinking that there is only one "right" decision and that all is lost if you do not figure out what it is and carry it out. You should remind yourself that any analysis of problem situations, no matter how careful and systematic, is ultimately limited. You simply cannot anticipate or predict everything that is going to happen in the future. As a result, every decision you make is provisional, in the sense that your ongoing experience will inform you if your decisions are working or if they need to be changed and modified. This is precisely the attitude of the critical thinker — someone who is receptive to new ideas and experiences and flexible enough to change or modify beliefs based on new information.

How do you evaluate your success? In many cases the relative effectiveness of your efforts will be apparent. Your problem will either be solved or you will be clearly moving in a successful direction. Congratulations! Pop the cork, have a glass of champagne — and take your increased confidence to your next problem. In other cases, it will be helpful to pursue a more systematic evaluation. As a result of your review, you may discover that the alternative you selected is not feasible or is not leading to satisfactory results. At other times you may find that the alternative you selected is working out fairly well but still requires some adjustments as you continue to work toward your desired outcome. In fact, this is a typical situation that you should expect to occur. Even when things initially appear to be working reasonably well, an active thinker continues to ask questions such as "What might I have overlooked?" and "How could I have done this differently?"

Sometimes your proposed solutions may not work at all and may even result in unanticipated disasters. Don't be discouraged! Problem-solving is a process, and as a critical thinker it is essential that you retain the flexibility and optimism you need to be successful. The truth is that we often learn more from alternatives that *don't* work out than from those that do. Armed with this knowledge, you should return to your initial analysis and:

- Add your newly discovered knowledge to what you know about the problem.
- Refine your definition of the problem.
- Add any new alternatives or modify the original ones based on your experience and new knowledge.
- Try a new alternative(s).

Often, difficult problems require a number of attempts until we conquer them. And all the time we are striving toward this goal, we are also developing the qualities of persistence, commitment, and confidence that are required for success in virtually every area of life.

Here are some strategies that you can use to help you evaluate the results of your problem-solving efforts and to make the appropriate modifications.

Strategies for Evaluating Your Solution

Write an Evaluation: Writing out an evaluation encourages you to examine the situation with an organization and thoroughness that isn't usually found by just reviewing things in your mind. The essence of evaluation is comparing the results of your efforts with the initial goals you were trying to achieve. To what extent did your solution meet your initial goals? Are there goals that are not likely to be met? Asking these and other questions will help you clarify the success of your efforts, and provide a foundation for future decisions.

Get Other Perspectives: As you have seen throughout the problem-solving process, getting the opinions of others is a productive strategy at virtually every stage, and this is certainly true for evaluation. Other people can often provide perspectives that are both different and more objective than yours. To receive specific, practical feedback from others, you need to ask specific, practical questions that will elicit this information. General questions ("What do you think of this?") typically result in overly general, unhelpful responses ("It sounds okay to me"). Be focused in soliciting feedback, and remember: You *do* have the right to ask people to be *constructive* in their comments, providing suggestions for improvement rather than only expressing what they think is wrong.

Included below are a number of evaluations completed by people working on the problems we have been examining:

Procrastination: "I have organized, thought out, and started to utilize the ideas that I have developed and they have all helped. In particular, I have created a time-task schedule so that I can see before me exactly what has to be done and how much time it should take to do it. The best part is when a task is finished and I can cross it out — that is the true feeling of conquest. I have also decided to take initiative. Having gone through all of the rationalizations, excuses, and guilt associated with this problem, I will now accept responsibility and take matters into my own hands. I am confident in my power to change the situations around me and am now motivated by my emotional strength to carry out the changes. Fear, instability, threats, and uncertainty have kept me hostage for too long. Once I traced the history of the problem, I could see that there are different, more productive ways of dealing with situations. I have decided to move on and do it now. During the last two weeks I have managed to finish several projects that have been haunting me for years. I have introduced organization and punctuality into my life, and it feels great! I now feel that I am controlling my life instead of being controlled by outside forces. Solving this problem has given me insight into how to go about solving other problems, and this kind of thinking has become a part of me. I now see that regardless of the past, I can always change the future as long as I am determined. I've stopped procrastinating; now I do things the moment I think of them, which has added more spontaneity to my life . . . I love it. Every day is a learning process. Now, on to my next problem!"

Smoking: "I chose the date of May 24, two weeks ago, to begin my stop-smoking efforts. I chose this date for symbolic reasons as it was on this day thirteen years ago that my father died of heart disease as a direct result of a lifetime of smoking. During this time I have been keeping a journal and working on my self-esteem. I am smoking my cigarettes only halfway down, limiting myself to five per day, and smoking them only in the bathroom or outside the house to avoid exposing my family to secondhand smoke. I have created a specific reduction schedule and so far I am right on target. I am also trying to convince my husband to attempt stopping again, and I have asked my friends and family to support and encourage me. I am visualizing my tragic scenario and these disgusting black lungs on a daily basis. I am also working on a chart that keeps track of the cigarettes I am smoking and, more important, the reasons why I am smoking: physical craving, emotional need, mindless habit. As for now, I feel the time and attention I have devoted to my problem have provided me with valuable insight and an advantage that I did not have in previous efforts to stop smoking. I am beginning to feel healthier and I am gaining confidence and self-esteem with each passing day. I am confident that I will succeed, but if I have not reached my goals after three months, I will try hypnosis or enter a stop-smoking program."

Down's Syndrome Child: "My original goals were for Michael to improve his communication skills, to learn to survive outside the home, and to be happy and secure. I have concluded that I don't have the time or expertise to reach these goals and that he needs outside help. In the last week I have

- contacted the Committee on the Handicapped in my area to find out what programs are available;
- contacted a speech tutor to evaluate his future learning possibilities;
- spoken with other parents I have met who have children with Down's syndrome;
- spoken to my family and friends to enlist their support.

I have been very gratified by the helpfulness and support I have received from all of the people I have spoken with, and I am very confident that I am doing the right things. I feel much less alone in dealing with this almost overwhelming responsibility, and I feel more relaxed and optimistic than I have in years."

Sarcasm: "I evaluated the effectiveness of my alternatives with a method I developed entitled 'A week at the races,' based on a 1 – 10 point system.

- The contract: Generally, I have respect for legal documents but in this case I did not. There was no authority to bind me to it, and my wife, as a witness to the contract, easily forgave my weakness in breaking it. Score: 3
- Obnoxious, sarcastic personalities: Reminding myself of despised sarcastic personalities worked well. It was easy to do since they are always present in some form of the media. This method was being enforced every day by simply listening to Howard Stern on the radio and watching television. Score: 7

- Unknown tape recorder: I was not expecting this method to be the winner, but it was. My wife, over the course of the week, taped me four times. When we played the tape back I did not believe that it was me saying those things. Some of it was funny, but much of it was shocking. I was embarrassed at myself! It seemed that most of what I said consisted of sarcastic opinions, sarcastic insults, or sarcastic observations. It is difficult to change because we must first understand ourselves — that can take much 'undoing' and can also be unsettling. But I am now committed to purging negative sarcasm from my life before I'm seen by people as little more than a nasty little twerp. Score: 9"

Overeating: "I have implemented the solutions I reached and have lost approximately eight pounds. To make sure I stay on the right track, I have placed the binding contract that I signed in the Acceptance stage on my refrigerator, committing me to the diet reforms that I have selected. The intensive analysis of this problem has brought me to the point where I can see the problem for what it really is — i.e., low self-esteem — as opposed to complaining about the symptoms of that problem — i.e., the weight. I believe that I can get control of this problem because, although I care about overeating, I care even more about my feelings of self-worth. Understanding how overeating and low self-esteem are linked, I doubt I will be eating in excess in the future. And I think that building my self-esteem and strengthening my self-discipline not only will help me reach the immediate goal of losing weight, but will also help me become a better person and improve my future life."

(Note: When I saw this person a year later, he had lost an additional fifteen pounds and was in excellent spirits.)

THINKING ACTIVITY

Evaluating My Solution

After trying out the alternatives you selected and implemented, evaluate the relative success of your efforts. Write your evaluation in your Thinking Notebook, assessing to what extent your solution has helped you achieve your original goals. If you have been successful so far, explain why; if not, explain why not. Discuss what other things you can do to refine or improve the situation. You might want to ask other people familiar with your problem for their evaluation of your efforts to solve your problem. If you find that it is difficult for you to take action or follow through, return to the Acceptance stage and recommit yourself to solving the problem. If your alternative has not worked out at all, analyze what went wrong. Does this new information alter your definition of the problem? Are there new alternatives that occur to you? Develop a new plan of action and implement it. Don't get discouraged! Remind yourself that achieving meaningful goals in life almost always involves struggle and failure before ultimate triumph.

How Expert a Problem-Solver Am I?

DESCRIBED BELOW are key personal attributes that are correlated with being an expert problem-solver. Evaluate your position regarding each of these attributes, and use this self-evaluation to guide your choices as you shape the type of problem-solver that you want to become.

Make Problem-Solving a Priority

I actively work to identify and solve problems in my life.

I don't pay much attention to the problems in my life.

5   4   3   2   1

Accomplished problem-solvers willingly acknowledge the problems in their lives and attack them with enthusiasm, instead of trying to deny, avoid, or ignore them. It is pleasurable to use your thinking abilities to disentangle a complex problem, and rewarding to achieve productive solutions through your skillful efforts.

Strategy: Make a list of all of the problems in your life that you are currently facing, large and small. Place an asterisk next to those problems that you have been avoiding or ignoring, and think about why that has been the case. Move these problems to the top of your priority list, and begin taking steps to solve them today using the method developed in this chapter.

Develop a Confident Attitude

I am a confident, effective problem-solver.

I am confused and frustrated by the problems in my life.

5   4   3   2   1

Success breeds success. When you are successful at solving problems, it increases your confidence, which in turn emboldens you to approach other problems with initiative, thoughtfulness, and decisive action.

Strategy: If you find yourself confused and frustrated by the problems in your life, devote yourself to learning the problem-solving method described in this chapter. Begin by applying it to several manageable challenges and then, as your confidence grows, gradually move on to the most difficult problems you face.

Accept the Problem

I willingly acknowledge my problems and commit myself to solving them.

I often evade my problems and fail to follow through in solving them.

5   4   3   2   1

"Accepting" a problem means saying honestly, and without excuse, "Yes, I have a problem, and I am committed to do what it takes to solve it." It's amazing how resistant people are to making this simple, courageous statement.

Strategy: Using the list of problems that you developed in the first question, create a timetable for solving each one. If you find that you are having particular difficulty in acknowledging or committing yourself to one or another problem, review the strategies for Acceptance described on pages 167–169 to ignite your determination.

Gather Useful Information

I always research a problem thoroughly in trying to solve it.	I usually work with the information that I already have in solving problems.

5   4   3   2   1

Every problem exists in a context, and you need to understand the context fully in order to have the best chance of solving it. How did the problem develop? How are other people involved in the problem? What factors have prevented you from solving the problem? These and many other questions need to be addressed in order to "get inside" the problem and fully appreciate it in all of its intricacy and subtlety.

Strategy: Using the strategies described in Step 2, What Do I Know about the Problem? on pages 170–172, write a full "report" for each difficult problem that you work on. You will discover all of the information that you know and the information that you need to know in order to move ahead in solving the problem.

Define the Problem Clearly

I get to the "heart" of problems and define them clearly.	I often get confused trying to identify the "real" problem.

5   4   3   2   1

Many people end up going round and round on problems because they are unable to penetrate beneath the surface to the "real" problems. They skate on the surface, mistaking the *symptoms* for the problem itself. As a critical thinker, you should distrust the simplest explanation of a problem, always asking yourself "What are some underlying causes of the problem?" "What are some issues that I may be overlooking?" "Are there ways of looking at this that I haven't considered?"

Strategy: *By developing your abilities as a critical thinker, you will naturally learn to look beyond the superficial explanations to a more sophisticated understanding. You can also use the strategies described in Step 3, Defining the Problem, on pages 173–175, including specifying the results, identifying component problems, and viewing the problem from multiple perspectives.*

Generate Many Alternatives

I usually come up with many diverse alternatives for solving a problem.	I generally focus on just two or three alternatives in solving a problem.

5   4   3   2   1

Expert problem-solvers have lively, fertile minds that identify many different options for solving a problem. Rather than stopping at the obvious alternatives, they push themselves to think of many additional possibilities, using their creative talents to generate inventive and unique options. They also view other people as resources for helping them think of alternatives they might not have come up with on their own.

Strategy: *When analyzing a problem, set a goal of generating ten, fifteen, or twenty alternatives, forcing yourself to break out of fixed mental ruts and go beyond the obvious to identify unusual possibilities. The chapter on creativity, Step 3: Live Creatively, will help you unleash your creative potential in every area of life.*

Evaluate the Alternatives Thoughtfully

I evaluate alternatives in an
organized way.

I use my intuition to pick the
best alternative.

5   4   3   2   1

While *creative thinking* plays the main role in generating many diverse alternatives, your critical thinking abilities come into play in evaluating the viability of these alternatives: the advantages, the disadvantages, and what further information is needed. If you start evaluating too early, when you are still generating possibilities, you run the risk of shutting off the creative flow. However, having generated the potential alternatives, if you *fail* to evaluate them in a rigorous and organized way, then you have no basis on which to reach an informed solution. Intuitions are only reliable when they are based on a great deal of thoughtful reflection and analysis.

Strategy: *It is essential to evaluate these alternatives in a disciplined and organized way in order to reach an intelligent conclusion. This rigorous analysis is the mark of an expert problem-solver as much as the ability to create inventive possibilities. Use the framework described on pages 181–184 to evaluate your options before trying to reach a solution.*

Reach Intelligent Solutions

I am skilled at finding solutions
for my problems.

I consistently have difficulty
in reaching solutions.

5   4   3   2   1

While many people are perfectly willing to perform a thoughtful analysis of their problems, they often seem paralyzed when it comes time to synthesize their ideas and commit themselves to a course of action. Why? Perhaps they lack confidence in their own thinking abilities or are reluctant to take the risks that come with taking action. Whatever the reason, a chronic inability to forge a solution and commit yourself to a plan of action is a serious disability, virtually guaranteeing a life of frustration, regret, and unfulfilled dreams.

Strategy: *If you have difficulty in reaching solutions and taking action to implement your plan, treat this chronic inability as a problem and use the problem-solving method to analyze it*: What is the problem? *Is it lack of confidence, lack of clarity, or lack of will?* What are your alternatives? *And so on.*

Make Necessary Adjustments

I take a flexible approach to making adjustments and trying new alternatives.	I tend to stick with my original plans, even when they run into difficulties.

5   4   3   2   1

As important as it is to commit yourself to a solution with determination, it is equally important to keep an open and critical mind as you implement your ideas. In most cases your solution will need adjustments, which you should willingly make.

Strategy: *Commit yourself to your solutions wholeheartedly, but begin monitoring the results of your plan immediately. Make the necessary adjustments to adapt to unforeseen circumstances. If it becomes clear that your solution is not working, move quickly and decisively to implement a new solution, informed by what you have learned. Solving problems is a* process, *and the important thing is to keep moving forward in a positive direction, not stubbornly reenacting the Charge of the Light Brigade.*

SCORING GUIDE

Add up the numbers you circled for each of the self-evaluation items above and use the following Scoring Guide to evaluate your effectiveness as a problem-solver.

Point Total	Interpretation
36–45	very effective problem-solver
27–35	moderately effective problem-solver
18–26	somewhat effective problem-solver
9–17	comparatively ineffective problem-solver

In interpreting your results, be sure to keep in mind that your score indicates how effective a problem-solver you are at the present time, *not* your *potential* to become an expert problem-solver. If you scored lower than you would like, it means that you need to follow the suggestions in this chapter to increase your problem-solving abilities to the level you are capable of achieving.

THINKING ACTIVITY

Becoming an Expert Problem-Solver

No matter how accomplished you are as a problem-solver, you can enhance your abilities by *choosing* to pursue this aim. Your critical thinking abilities will give you the means to explore the problems in your experience with insight, and your personal dedication to improvement will provide you with the ongoing motivation. Remember that becoming an expert problem-solver is both a daily and a lifetime project. Nurture your continued growth in every area of your life by cultivating the qualities that we explored in this section:

- Make problem-solving a priority.
- Develop a confident attitude.
- Accept the problem.
- Gather useful information.
- Define the problem clearly.
- Generate many alternatives.
- Evaluate the alternatives thoughtfully.
- Reach intelligent solutions.
- Make necessary adjustments.

STEP 5

COMMUNICATE SUCCESSFULLY

Communicating effectively is essential for developing your mind, nurturing healthy relationships, and achieving success. This chapter will improve your communication skills by helping you think clearly and express yourself precisely. You will learn how to engage in productive discussions, communicate well in diverse social settings, work collaboratively in groups, exercise influential leadership, and speak publicly without fear. All of these language and thinking skills are within your grasp and they will enhance every dimension of your life.

HAVING COMPLETED THE first 4 Steps in this book, you will have noticed that as you've improved your thinking abilities, your ability to communicate has improved remarkably as well. Language, whether spoken or written, is a window into your mind: Clear communication expresses clear thinking, while muddled communication reflects muddled thinking. When we admiringly refer to people as having "lively minds," we have usually formed this impression based on their speaking and writing. We say they are *articulate*. In relating a story, they "put you there" by using details and a rich variety of adjectives and adverbs. If they are explaining an idea, their analysis is well organized and specific.

Effective communication is crucial for success in every area of life, personally and professionally. Consider the following situations:

- When explaining your ideas to others, you encounter difficulty communicating what you are thinking clearly and precisely.
- You are engaged in a discussion regarding an emotional issue with someone who disagrees with you, but what started out as a reasonable exchange of ideas quickly degenerates into a shouting match of insults and accusations.
- You have been asked to speak in front of a large group of people, a prospect that is causing you paralyzing fear and heart-palpitating anxiety.
- You attempt to persuade people at work to accept your analysis about an important decision, but find you have difficulty articulating your ideas clearly and presenting cogent arguments.
- You find that you sometimes experience miscommunications with people of different cultures, ages, sexual orientations, or backgrounds.
- You are reluctant to participate in group discussions, and rarely attempt to take a leadership role.

Communication is a process by which ideas and feelings are expressed and then understood. The meaning that someone expresses may be intentional or unintentional, and it may involve verbal or nonverbal forms of expression. For example, saying something verbally ("I love you") expresses meaning based on the spoken words, but that meaning is enriched and embroidered by the tone of voice and physical gestures that accompany the words. On the other side of the communication process, the understanding of the receiving person (or people) is often altered by their own perceiving lenses. In short, the process of communication is enormously subtle and complex, mirroring the complexity of language and the human personality.

Developing these sophisticated communication abilities is a challenging task: You must master the intricate vocabulary of both verbal language and body language, and you must develop the higher-order thinking abilities that make effective communication possible. In addition, you must learn to attune yourself to your audience, forming a direct connection that enables you to gauge their responses to your expression and using this feedback to adjust your message for greater clarity.

Language and Thought

LANGUAGE IS a tool that is powered by patterns of thinking. With its power to represent your thoughts, feelings, and experiences symbolically, language is the most important tool your thinking process has. Although research shows that thinking and language are two distinct processes, they are so closely related that they are often difficult to separate or distinguish.

Language's link with thinking makes language so powerful a tool that we not only rely on it as a vehicle for communicating, we also use language to provide a *structure* for thinking. Language relates one idea to the others so that their combinations, many and varied, can be reported with strength and vitality, creating meaning that no one idea could convey alone. Used expertly, language *expresses* your thinking in a way that clearly evokes the images, feelings, and ideas that you as a speaker and writer want to present. It also *communicates* your thinking in such a way that others can comprehend your meaning and, in turn, make appropriate inferences and judgments and thereby expand their own thinking.

The key to effective thinking and communicating, however, lies in using language *clearly* and *precisely*, a vital requirement if other people are going to be able to understand the thoughts you are trying to convey. In most cases, when you are thinking clearly, you are able to express your ideas clearly in language. If you are *not* able to develop a clear idea of what you are thinking, then you have great difficulty in expressing your thinking in language. When this happens, you may say something like this:

"I know what I want to say, but I just can't find the right words."

Of course, when this happens, you usually *don't* "know" exactly what you want to say — if you did, you would say it!

This interactive relationship between thinking and language is particularly well explicated in George Orwell's essay "Politics and the English Language":

> A man may take to drink because he feels himself to be a failure, and then fail all the more completely because he drinks. It is rather the same thing that is happening to the English language. It becomes ugly and inaccurate because our thoughts are foolish, but the slovenliness of our language makes it easier for us to have foolish thoughts. The point is that the process is reversible. Modern English, especially written English, is full of bad habits which spread by imitation and which can be avoided if one is willing to take the necessary trouble. If one gets rid of these habits, one can think more clearly.

Just as the drunkard falls into a vicious circle that keeps getting worse, the same is true of the relation between language and thinking. When our use of language is "sloppy," it leads to thinking of the same sort. Of course, the reverse is also true: Clear and precise language leads to clear and precise thinking.

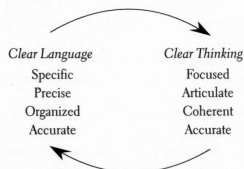

Clear Language   *Clear Thinking*
Specific   Focused
Precise   Articulate
Organized   Coherent
Accurate   Accurate

Vague Language, Unclear Thinking

ON JANUARY 29, 1990, an Avianca Airlines flight from Colombia, South America, to New York City crashed, killing seventy-three persons. The plane had run out of fuel before it could land, after circling Kennedy Airport for forty-five minutes, apparently the result of imprecise communication between the plane's pilot and the air traffic controllers. According to verbatim transcripts, the Avianca crew told regional controllers about forty-five minutes before the plane crashed that "we would run out of fuel" if the plane was redirected to Boston instead of being given priority to land at Kennedy, and that the plane could continue in its holding pattern for "about five minutes — that's all we can do" before the plane would have to land. However, the regional controllers who gave that message to the local controllers, who were to guide the plane on its final descent to Kennedy, did not tell them that there was a problem with fuel supplies on the jet. According to R. Steve Bell, president of the National Air Traffic Controllers Association, the Avianca pilots were to blame for this because "The Avianca pilot never declared a 'fuel emergency' or 'minimum fuel,' both of which would have triggered an emergency response by controllers. Stating that you are low on fuel does not imply an immediate problem." This was an instance in which unclear communication had tragic consequences.

Of course, unclear language doesn't usually lead to such grave results, but it does have a pervasively destructive effect on the clarity of thinking in individuals and society as a whole. For example, consider the *vague* — general, imprecise — words in the following sentences:

- I had a *nice* time yesterday.
- That is an *interesting* book.
- She is an *old* person.

In each of these cases, the italicized word is vague because it does not give a precise description of the thought, feeling, or experience that the writer or speaker is trying to communicate. Most words of general measurement — *short, tall, big, small, heavy, light,* and so on — are vague. The exact meanings of these words depend on the specific situation in which they are used and on the particular perspective of the person using them. For example, your use of the terms *middle-aged* or *old* is relative to your own age in the same way that whom you consider to be *wealthy* depends on your own financial status. When my grandmother was a robust seventy-nine years old, someone made the mistake of referring to her as being "old." "I'm not old!" she exclaimed angrily, and stormed out of the room.

Although the vagueness of general measurement terms can lead to confusion, other forms of vagueness, such as terms like *nice* and *interesting,* are more widespread and often more problematic. Vagueness of this sort permeates every level of human discourse, undermines clear thinking, and is extremely difficult to combat. To use language clearly and precisely, you must develop an understanding of the way language functions and commit yourself to breaking the entrenched habits of vague expression.

Read the following opinion of a movie and identify all the vague, general words that do not express a clear meaning.

> *Men in Black* is a really funny movie about some really unusual aliens and the people who hunt them down. The movie consists of the main characters trying to track down different aliens and save the world. Some of the scenes are nerveracking and others are hilarious, but all of them are very well done. The plot is very interesting and the main characters are excellent. I liked this movie a lot.

Because of the vague language in this passage, it expresses only general approval — it does not explain in exact or precise terms what the experience was like. Thus the writer of the passage is not successful in communicating the experience.

One useful strategy used by journalists for clarifying vague language is to ask and try to answer the following questions: *Who? What? When?*

Where? Why? How? Let's see how this strategy applies to the movie vaguely described above.

- *Who* were the people involved in the movie (characters portrayed, actors, director, producer)?
- *What* took place in the movie (events, plot development)?
- *When* do the events in the movie take place (historical situation)?
- *Where* does the movie take place (physical location, cultural setting)?
- *How* does the film portray its events? (How do the actors create their characters? How does the director use film techniques to accomplish his goals?)
- *Why* do I have this opinion of the film? (What are the reasons for my opinion?)

Even if we don't give an elaborate version of our thinking, we can still communicate effectively by using clear and precise language. For example, examine a review excerpt of *Men in Black* by the professional film critic Anthony Lane. Compare and contrast it with the earlier review.

> Written by Ed Solomon and directed by Barry Sonnenfeld, this picture is easy — indolent, confident, and shy of risks, but so relaxed that you can hardly be bothered to complain. The Men in question are Agent K (Tommy Lee Jones) and Agent J (Will Smith), who dress like the Blues Brothers and spend their days policing the activities of resident aliens. Most aliens, it appears, are law-abiding citizens, who like to keep all three noses clean, but there are a few rogue elements to be arrested and, when necessary, splattered. . . . No other director is so enthralled by black as a color and a mood, so eager to stretch its possibilities. The fetishistic gleam of the men's car is spectrums away from the flat black of their suits, or from the sharp shadows in which they hunt their quarry, or from the funereal fug so beloved of Morticia Addams. Against it you have the

blaring brightness of the men's headquarters and of the Guggenheim Museum, not to mention the daft white plastic pod in which Agent J is hunched when he first applies for the job. Thanks to a kind of double-jointed chronology, Sonnenfeld delivers a nineties take on a sixties idea of what the future — a nineties future, for instance — would be like.

— THE NEW YORKER, July 7, 1997

Strong language users have the gift of symbolizing their experiences so clearly that you can actually relive those experiences with them. You can identify with them, sharing the same thoughts, feelings, and perceptions that they had when they underwent (or imagined) the experience. Consider how effectively the following passage written by William Least Heat Moon communicates the thoughts, feelings, and experiences of the author. After losing his teaching job at a university and separating from his wife, he decided to explore America, driving around the country using back roads (represented on the maps by blue lines) rather than superhighways.

It was May Day, and the warm air filled with the scent of pine and blooming manzanita. To the west I heard water over rock as Hat Creek came down from the snows of Lassen. I took towel and soap and walked through a field of volcanic ejections and broken chunks of lava to the stream bouncing off boulders and slicing over bedrock; below one cascade, a pool the color of glacier ice circled the effervescence. On the bank at an upright stone with a basin-shaped concavity filled with rainwater, I bent to drink, then washed my face. Why not bathe from head to toe? I went down with rainwater and lathered up.

Now, I am not unacquainted with mountain streams; a plunge into Hat Creek would be an experiment in deep-cold thermodynamics. I knew that, so I jumped in with bravado. It didn't help. Light violently flashed in my head. The water was worse than I thought possible. I came out, eyes the size of biscuits, metabolism running amuck and setting fire to the icy flesh. I buffed dry. Then I began to feel good, the way the old Navajos must have felt after a traditional sweat bath and roll in the snow. I dressed and sat down to watch Hat Creek.

— WILLIAM LEAST HEAT-MOON, *BLUE HIGHWAYS*

Naturally, very few of us have the writing skills of William Least Heat Moon, but we can all become more articulate by using more detail, adjectives, adverbs, and metaphors in order to communicate a richer, more vital picture of our thoughts and experiences. In many instances we take a "lazy" approach to our communications, relying on clichés, vague terms, and expressions like "You know what I mean."

THINKING ACTIVITY

Describing an Experience

In your Thinking Notebook describe an experience you had recently, concentrating on expressing your ideas clearly and precisely. Use appropriate who, what, where, when, how, why questions to guide your writing. After completing your first draft, imagine yourself as your audience — will they be able to "relive" your experience by reading about it?

Virtually all of us use vague language extensively in our day-to-day conversations. In many cases, it is natural that your immediate reaction to an experience would be fairly general ("That's nice," "She's interesting," and so on). If you are truly concerned with sharp thinking and meaningful communication, however, you should follow up these initial general reactions with a more precise clarification of what you really mean.

- I think that she is a nice person *because* . . .
- I think that he is a good friend *because* . . .
- I think that this is an interesting career *because* . . .

Vagueness is always a matter of degree. In fact, you can think of your informative use of language as falling somewhere on a scale between extreme generality and extreme specificity. For example, the following statements move from the general to the specific.

General

Anna is a good friend.
She is always there when I need her.
She makes time to discuss what's on my mind.
Last Saturday she spent the afternoon helping me deal with a serious problem I was having.

Specific

Although different situations require varying degrees of specificity, you should work at becoming increasingly precise in your use of language. For example, examine your description of an experience from the previous Thinking Activity. Circle the general words and either replace them with more precise terms or elaborate them with specific descriptions and concrete examples.

Discussing Ideas in an Organized Way

LANGUAGE IS a social phenomenon. As children, we internalize language from our social surroundings and develop it through our relations with other people. At the same time, our thinking capacities expand as well. Other people help advance our thinking, and as we become more literate, our interactions with these people help shape our thinking. Relationships also act as important vehicles for fostering precise thinking and language use: We talk to others and are responded to; we write and then discover how others understand (or misunderstand) our ideas.

Too often, our conversations with other people about important topics are not productive exchanges and sometimes they even degenerate into name-calling, shouting matches, or worse. Consider the following dialogue.

> PERSON A: My best friend's father had a heart attack six months ago and he's been in a coma ever since, kept alive by a ventilator and feeding tube. The family is thinking about having these life supports withdrawn and letting him die. What do you think?
>
> PERSON B: Well, I think that "pulling the plug" like that is murder. Your friend's family don't want to be murderers, do they?
>
> PERSON A: How can you call them murderers? Withdrawing technological support in this kind of situation is euthanasia, not murder. After all, people have a right to die with dignity.
>
> PERSON B: Right to *kill*, you mean. Whether you try to dress it up as euthanasia, "mercy killing," or whatever, it's still killing another human being, and your friend and her family don't have the right to do that.
>
> PERSON A: Well, you don't have the right to tell them what to do — it's their loved one and their decision. Nobody should be forced to prolong someone's life beyond his natural time.
>
> PERSON B: Nobody has the right to commit murder — that's the law.
>
> PERSON A: But euthanasia isn't murder.
>
> PERSON B: Yes, it is.
>
> PERSON A: No, it isn't.
>
> PERSON B: Good-bye! I can't talk to anyone who defends murderers.
>
> PERSON A: And I can't talk to anyone who tells other people how to run their lives.

If we examine the dynamics of this dialogue, we can see that the two people here are not really:

- expressing their views clearly and supporting them with reasons and evidence;
- listening to each other and responding to the points being made;
- asking — and trying to answer — important questions;
- trying to increase their understanding rather than simply winning the argument.

In short, the people in this exchange are not *discussing* their views, they are simply *expressing* them and trying to influence the other person into agreeing. Contrast this first dialogue with the following one. Although it begins the same way, it quickly takes a much different direction.

> PERSON A: My best friend's father had a heart attack six months ago and he's been in a coma ever since, kept alive by a ventilator and feeding tube. The family is thinking about having these life supports withdrawn and letting him die. What do you think?
>
> PERSON B: Well, I think that "pulling the plug" like that is murder. Your friend's family don't want to be murderers, do they?
>
> PERSON A: Of course not! But why do you believe that euthanasia is the same thing as murder?
>
> PERSON B: Because murder is when we kill another human being, and when you engage in euthanasia, you are killing another human being.
>
> PERSON A: But is someone who is comatose, who has no chance of recovering consciousness, really a "human being" in the fullest sense? Simply because his body is still functioning due to life-support machines doesn't mean that he is "alive" in the normal sense. He can't speak, feel, think, remember, communicate — all of the things we associate with being alive. Don't you agree?

PERSON B: I think such a person is still alive. I don't see how we can differentiate ways of being "alive." Either your body is functioning or it isn't.

PERSON A: I can see why you would think that someone who is still functioning on their own should be maintained. If we ended a person's life under these circumstances, say with a lethal injection, that would be *active euthanasia.* But in my friend's father's case we're only talking about *passive euthanasia:* withholding or withdrawing medical treatment and allowing him to die naturally. After all, this is exactly what would have happened before the invention of sophisticated medical equipment to sustain life.

PERSON B: Let me think about that for a minute. I understand the distinction you are making between active and passive euthanasia, and I think it's a useful one. The problem is that we do have this medical technology, and that's what has created these modern ethical dilemmas, not just with euthanasia, but also with things like reproductive technologies and cloning. But I still believe that we don't have the right to end life prematurely — only God has that right.

PERSON A: But don't you think we're playing God by keeping people artificially alive beyond what nature intended?

PERSON B: The writer C. S. Lewis once said that the ultimate determination of these matters usually revolves around the question of whether we are the "landlord" or the "tenants" of our lives. If we are the landlords, then there is no limit to the autonomy that we can exercise with respect to our lives, including euthanasia. But if we are the tenants of our lives, we see life as an inalienable gift, as an endowment that we don't have the right to give back. From this perspective, we have no "right to die."

PERSON A: I see what you're saying. But what about the *quality* of my friend's father's life? Is the treatment he is receiving providing any *benefit* to him?

PERSON B: Are you suggesting that because he will never achieve a conscious state that his life is not worth living?

PERSON A: I think that we're making a quality-of-life decision whichever way we act. I knew my friend's father, and he was a very active, vital person who would never have wanted to be maintained on life support this way. I think it's ethically appropriate for his family to take everything they know about him into consideration and make a determination of what he would want if he could speak for himself.

PERSON B: Are you telling me that he would have *wanted* to die by starvation and dehydration? That's what's going to happen if you remove the feeding tube that is providing nutrition and hydration.

PERSON A: I don't think we can call it dying by "starvation" and "dehydration" as these words are typically used. When someone is in a persistent vegetative state, he is incapable of experiencing pain or suffering, like someone who is starving under normal circumstances. This is according to the American Academy of Neurology.

PERSON B: But just because there is no pain doesn't mean he is not objectively starving to death.

PERSON A: I think you're making a good point. But it still comes back to what the patient would have wanted, and the family are the people who are in the best position to make that determination. I'm not saying what they should do. I think that each case is unique and that it's an emotionally wrenching process for families going through it. They have to make the decisions most consistent with their value systems, religious beliefs, and their understanding of what the patient would have wanted.

PERSON B: I can certainly empathize with what you're saying. But I'm really concerned that if we make euthanasia legal that we will be creating opportunities for abuse. For example, a doctor whom I know told me about a case of a wealthy man who remained on life supports in a comatose state for months until he finally came out of it. He ultimately recovered entirely. But during all of this time his family members tried to get the hospital to withdraw the life supports, presumably so that they could inherit his money. My concern is that once we begin to tamper with trying to keep people alive at all costs, we're moving into dangerous territory. If we're not careful, we can end up blurring the distinction between reason and violence, placing at risk people whom society considers extraneous or not that important. After all, where there's life, there's hope.

PERSON A: Well, these issues are obviously more complicated that we first thought! I have to go now, but I'd like to continue our discussion. It's apparent that I have a lot more work to do before I can figure out what I believe.

Naturally, discussions are not always quite this organized and direct, although much of this dialogue is based on an actual debate that took place between two experts in medical ethics. Nevertheless, this second dialogue does provide a good model for what can take place when we carefully explore an issue or a situation with someone else. Let's take a closer look at the principles of effective discussions.

EXPRESSING VIEWS CLEARLY AND SUPPORTING THEM WITH REASONS AND EVIDENCE

Every meaningful exchange of ideas begins with a clear statement of what the participants believe. You need to "define your terms" in order to understand exactly what it is you are discussing. What do we mean by "euthanasia"? Are there different kinds of euthanasia? What category does the example they are discussing (Person A's friend's father) fit into? Notice that in the first dialogue the people never specify answers to any of these questions, dooming their exchange from the start. But in the second dialogue, all of these questions are answered as the participants systematically explore the different meanings of the concept of "euthanasia."

The Siamese twin of expressing your views clearly is providing persuasive support for your views: What are the *reasons* and *evidence* that have led you to your beliefs? In the first dialogue, the participants simply state their views without any effort to provide supporting reasons and evidence. As noted in Step 1: Think Critically, this approach to discussion reflects a rudimentary understanding of the nature of knowledge. A more sophisticated perspective recognizes that every viewpoint is only as viable as the quality of the supporting reasons and evidence. The participants in the second dialogue are careful always to provide supporting reasons and evidence, which can then be evaluated in terms of its truth and relevance.

LISTENING CAREFULLY AND RESPONDING TO THE POINTS BEING MADE

Carrying on a productive discussion is a shared responsibility, a complex give-and-take in which each partner must be attuned to subtle, nuanced moves of the other. In this context, listening is not a passive activity: it is an active, critical thinking activity. You need to try to understand the thought processes of the person to whom you are listening — to think empathetically within their viewpoint. This means that you have to:

- *Suspend judgment* as you make a genuine effort to appreciate the ideas being expressed. Premature evaluations like "This doesn't make sense" short-circuit the communication process. You need enough patience to let others express themselves fully.
- *Don't start formulating your response* until you have had a chance to understand all of what the other person is saying. Once you start developing your own response, you are only half-listening to what is being said.
- *Listen actively* as you evaluate the accuracy and relevance of the ideas being expressed and ask probing questions that clarify the points being made.

When people engage in effective discussion, they *respond directly* to the points being made instead of simply trying to make their own points.

In the second dialogue, Person A responds to Person B's view that "euthanasia is murder" with the question "But is someone who is comatose, who has no chance of recovering consciousness, really a 'human being' in the fullest sense?" When you respond directly to other people's views, and they to yours, you extend and deepen the explorations into the issues at hand. Although people involved in the discussion may not ultimately agree, they should develop a more insightful understanding of the important issues and a greater appreciation of other viewpoints. If you examine the sample dialogue again, you'll notice how each person keeps responding to what the other is saying, creating an ongoing interaction of ideas.

ASKING QUESTIONS

Asking questions is one of the driving forces in your discussions with others. You can explore a subject by raising important questions and, then, trying to answer them together. This questioning process gradually reveals the various reasons and evidence that support each of the different viewpoints. For example, although the two dialogues begin the same way, the second dialogue moves in a completely different direction from the first when Person A poses the question "But why do you believe that euthanasia is the same thing as murder?" Asking this question directs the discussion toward a mutual exploration of the issues and away from angry confrontation.

INCREASING UNDERSTANDING

When you discuss subjects with others, you often begin by disagreeing with them. In fact, this is one of the chief reasons that you have discussions. In an effective discussion, however, your main purpose should be to *develop your understanding* — not to prove yourself right at any cost. If you are determined to prove that you are right, then you are likely not to be open to the ideas of others and to viewpoints that differ from your own. This is the essence of being a critical thinker — striving to view issues from a variety of perspectives, particularly those that you disagree with. This is the only way to enlarge your vision and construct beliefs that are deeply rooted. There are people in the world who are intelligent, knowledgeable, and skilled in debate and argumentation, but when their main purpose is to prevail, to prove that their beliefs are right and others' are wrong, then they are not acting like critical thinkers. Thinking critically means being open-minded, respecting the views of others, and working together to achieve a mutually enhanced understanding. At the conclusion of the second dialogue, while the participants still have different viewpoints on the issue of euthanasia, they have begun a shared journey of exploration and discovery. They are beginning to make important distinctions and reach significant insights regarding this complex issue, and they are profiting from the experience, both intellectually and personally.

THINKING ACTIVITY

Writing a Dialogue

In the next day or two, listen in on other people's discussions (or arguments!) — or your own — and write or imagine a *new* script that reflects your heightened awareness of these principles of effective discussion:

- Expressing views clearly and supporting them with reasons and evidence
- Listening to each other and responding to the points being made
- Asking — and trying to answer — important questions
- Trying to increase understanding rather than simply winning the argument

This activity will give you the opportunity to bring your new learning — and thinking — from this book into the world, allowing life to happen and then applying these new concepts. And it will have the added bonus that people will notice the thoughtful tools you're bringing to your discussions.

You may be wondering whether it's really necessary to actually *do* these Thinking Activities: Isn't it sufficient to read and think about the points being made in order to become a better critical thinker? Unfortunately, there are no real shortcuts in this regard. The amount of effort that you invest in practicing these skills will pay great dividends when you attempt to use them in your life. Although reading alone can certainly prove to be enlightening, studies in developing thinking abilities underscore the need to engage actively in the thinking process through structured exercises. For example, watching Julia Child create exquisite pastries on television is certainly informative, but it is no substitute for the practical expertise that comes from being elbow-deep in flour in your kitchen.

Communicating in Social Contexts

THE BEDROCK of effective communication is shared language, both verbal and nonverbal. Whether by design or default, we spend most of our time with people of similar backgrounds and inclinations, and so you can assume a common meaning to your language and gestures. If you think about the groups you generally associate with — professional colleagues, friends, family members — you can detect a distinctive "language" that the members of each group share. However, on those occasions when we deal with people from very different backgrounds, we often misunderstand their language or gestures, and confusion can easily result. For example, an English woman might innocently advise her American date to "*knock her up*" at 8:00 o'clock, a request that he might find rather surprising. Similarly, the American penchant for shaking hands when first meeting someone is considered rude and offensive in some cultures. Successful communication with people from different backgrounds requires that you think critically — imagine yourself in their position and try to think within their frame of reference.

Even within our own culture we encounter many different ways of communicating, which vary depending on people's age, background, gender, geographical location, career, and other factors. Linguists have identified these different ways of communicating as *language styles*. Becoming a successful communicator depends on recognizing and adjusting to the specific language style of the person you are dealing with. Language is always used in context. That is, you always speak or write with a person or group of people in mind. You may converse with your friends, meet with your boss, or carry out a business transaction at the bank or supermarket. In each of these cases, you use the language style that is appropriate to the social situation. For example, think about how you usually greet the following people when you see them: a good friend, a parent, an employer, a waiter. Your particular greeting likely varies depending on the person, ranging from informal to formal in language style. Informal language styles abbreviate not only sentence structure but also the sounds that form words: "Hi'ya, Susan. How're ya doing?" Formal language styles use more complex sentence structures as well as complete words in terms of sound patterns: "Hello, Ms. Jones. How are you today?"

As a critical thinker, you need to recognize a social situation and then determine the language style to use. The connection between language and thought turns language into a powerful social force that separates you from as well as binds you to others. The language that you use and the way you use it serve as important clues to your social identity. For example, *dialect* identifies your geographical area or group; *slang* marks your age group and subculture; *jargon* often identifies your occupation; and *accent* typically suggests the place you grew up and your socioeconomic class. Social dimensions of language are important influences in shaping your response to others. Sometimes they can trigger stereotypes you hold about someone's social class, intelligence, personal attributes, and so on. The ability to *think critically* gives you the insight and the intellectual ability to distinguish people's language use from their individual qualities, to correct inaccurate beliefs about people, and to avoid stereotypical responses in the future. One arena in which two distinct language styles clash repeatedly is male/female communication, which we will explore in the next section.

Male/Female (Mis)Communication

"Men are so insensitive. My partner never wants to just sit down, look me in the eye, and spend some time having a real conversation about our thoughts, feelings, or even the day's events. He seems so impatient and just doesn't listen. Even when I'm upset or have a serious problem I'm working through, he tends to minimize it or suggests ways to solve it, instead of trying to understand what I'm experiencing."

"Why do women like to spend so much time talking, especially about the same things? My partner likes to take a subject and trample it to death, going over and over it. She seems more interested in wasting time talking about problems instead of figuring out how to solve them. And she can talk about the day's events until I'm falling asleep. She seems to think we're having a problem communicating, but things seem all right to me."

DO EITHER of these quotes strike responsive chords from your experience? If so, you are not alone. In her book *Divorce Talk*, the sociologist Catherine Kohler Riessman reports that most women when interviewed cited *lack of communication* as the main reason for their divorces, while only a few of the men identified this as a reason. With a current divorce rate approaching 50 percent, the issue of miscommunication between the sexes is damaging the relationships of millions of people. What's going on here? When we analyze the reasons for so much failed communication, it becomes clear that the essential difficulty can be traced to different concepts of language and its role in relationships. And these langauge differences reflect contrasting perspectives on the world. The bestselling books by John Gray and Deborah Tannen reflect the current interest in sociolinguistic variations between men and women. Dr. Gray provides a detailed and insightful map to the confusing terrain of male/female relationships in his enlightening book *Men Are from Mars, Women Are from Venus*:

. . . men and women differ in all areas of their lives. Not only do men and women communicate differently but they think, feel, perceive, react, respond, love, need, and appreciate differently. They almost seem to be from different planets, speaking different languages and needing different nourishment. This expanded understanding of our differences helps resolve much of the frustration in dealing with and trying to understand the opposite sex.

According to Dr. Tannen (*You Just Don't Understand*), instead of blaming one gender or the other for the communication problems, it makes more sense to view the difficulties as analogous to those arising in cross-cultural communication, like Dr. Gray's analogy of inhabitants from "Mars" and "Venus." Her research suggests that boys and girls are usually socialized differently, leading to very different patterns of communication, patterns that often don't work harmoniously with one another.

For women, as for girls, intimacy is the fabric of relationships, and talk is the thread from which it is woven. Little girls create and maintain friendships by exchanging secrets: similarly, women regard conversation as the cornerstone of friendship. So a woman expects her husband to be a new and improved version of a best friend. What is important is not the individual subjects that are discussed but the sense of closeness, a life shared, that emerges when people tell their thoughts, feelings, and impressions.

Bonds between boys can be as intense as girls', but they are based less on talking, more on doing things together. Since they don't assume talk is the cement that binds a relationship, men don't know what kind of talk women want, and they don't miss it when it isn't there. Boys' groups are larger, more inclusive, and more hierarchical, so boys must struggle to avoid the subordinate position in the group. This may play a role in women's complaints that men don't listen to them. Some men really don't like to listen, because being the listener makes them feel one-down, like a child listening to adults or an employee to a boss.

In short, men and women tend to develop, through their social experiences, contrasting views of how language functions in relationships, and these different language practices create a *dissonance* and *misalignment* in the mechanics of conversation. It's like trying to fit together puzzle pieces from two different puzzles: frustration and misunderstanding cannot help but result.

Here are some of the key areas of language conflict, according to Dr. Tannen, accompanied with critical thinking strategies for improving communication.

PHYSICAL MISALIGNMENT

When girls and women speak to each other, they invariably face each other and stay focused on the other's face. Boys and men, on the other hand, typically sit at angles to one another, their eyes moving around the room and only occasionally looking at those to whom they are speaking. This is true even when males are discussing serious subjects and are clearly engaged in the conversation. It's easy to see how these contrasting communication patterns might then create misunderstanding between men and women. Since the men are not looking directly at them, as they are accustomed, women may feel that the men are not "really listening." On the other hand, men may feel uncomfortable with the experience of having someone "staring" at them so intently as they are speaking.

Strategy: When each gender recognizes the physical inclinations of the other, this paves the way for understanding their misreading of the other's behavior. Women can better appreciate that men can be listening intently even if they're not looking at them directly, and men can better appreciate women's need for direct eye contact. With this shared recognition as a foundation, each side can begin altering in its conditioned behavior in order to improve communication.

TOPICAL MISALIGNMENT

Tannen's research reveals that girls and women tend to talk at length about one topic, analyzing it from different perspectives, reflecting, ruminating, considering, and reconsidering. Further, the subjects frequently concern stories about people they know, problems in relationships, and their emotional reactions to situations. In contrast, boys and men tend to touch on many different topics in their conversations, jumping from one subject to another, rarely exploring any one in great depth. Rather than focusing on personal relationships and emotional reactions, their conversation typically emphasizes events in the world, things they have done or experienced, interspersed with a great deal of joking and teasing. Women may feel that men are superficial in their interests and emotionally shallow. Men, on the other hand, may feel that women are too focused on analyzing relationships to the exclusion of other potential topics, and are excessively concerned with trying to understand and relive their emotional reactions.

Strategy: By recognizing the subject preferences of others, you can make a greater effort to appreciate and learn from their interests, instead of dismissing them out of hand. And by breaking out of your own communication patterns, you can improve your thinking and enrich your life.

FEEDBACK MISALIGNMENT

Another source of miscommunication between the genders is the discrepancy in listener feedback during a conversation. According to the linguist Lynette Hirschman, women make more listener-noise than men, with sounds like "mhm," "unhuh," and "yeah," to show "I'm with you." In contrast, men tend to give quiet attention to the person speaking. However, since women are used to steady feedback, they interpret this quiet attention as *lack* of attention, while men can find the steady listener noise from women to be annoying and distracting, particularly when it escalates to finishing their sentences and overlapping their speech.

Strategy: Recognizing these variant forms of listening increases your flexibility and adaptability. If people are providing active listening re-

sponses, you can appreciate their efforts to respond to what you are say-ing. At the same time, if they are listening quietly but intently, you can assume that they are focused on what you are saying and are waiting for the right time to respond.

PROBLEM-SOLVING MISALIGNMENT

Discussing personal problems is another area of missed signals and broken lines of communication. When women are sharing personal concerns, Tannen has observed, they are often seeking empathy and understanding: "I know what you're going through, I know it's difficult, but you'll get through it." Men tend to approach problems, even personal problems, more pragmatically: "You have a problem, let's figure out how you can solve it." As with other communication patterns, both approaches work well until they intersect with each other — then misunderstanding flourishes. Expecting an empathetic response to the problem they are sharing, women can be put off by men's "What's the problem and how can we solve it" approach. Similarly, men are often impatient with women's supportive empathy when they are looking for practical ways to improve the situation. Once again, good intentions founder on the shoals of miscommunication.

Strategy: It's important to recognize the need for both empathetic sup-port and constructive solutions. These different approaches to others' problems are not in competition, they are synergistic, and people benefit from both. Analysis and practical solutions should always be proposed within the context of sensitive understanding and support, and it is very useful for such empathetic support to be directed toward improving the situation.

ANALYSIS-STYLE MISALIGNMENT

Another area of communication breakdown occurs in discussing is-sues. For many women, when you state your point of view, you can rea-sonably expect your conversation partner to express agreement and support. Talk creates closeness and intimacy, and that's its primary pur-pose. Men have typically been socialized in much more competitive environments. When they express a view, they are not surprised when others disagree with them or present alternate perspectives: Debate and disagreement are essential ingredients in discussion, and language is often used as a vehicle to express competitive impulses. Mixing these two approaches is clearly a recipe for communication disaster. When women find their point of view being questioned and disagreed with, they feel betrayed, the victims of disloyalty. Men are likely to find this reaction bewildering.

Strategy: *While it's useful to feel the personal support of others, it's also productive to have your ideas tested and for you to explore many different perspectives on issues. In fact, this sort of multiperspective analysis is one of the key ingredients of thinking critically and expanding your mind. However, it's crucial to maintain a distinction between people and their views. While it is appropriate to challenge and question a person's views, it is not productive to attack them personally. Instead, debate and discussion of issues should always be done within a context of personal respect for the other person.*

THINKING ACTIVITY

Communicating with the Opposite Sex

The ideas in this section are *generalizations* about groups of people, in this case men and women. Generalizations are only expected to be true in "most" cases, not all, and they usually have exceptions. Think about your own experiences of communicating with the opposite sex. Do you think that the conclusions about the way men and women communicate match up with your experiences? If so, in what way? If not, what are the exceptions? Do you feel that *you* fit the profile described for your gender? Having thought about these issues, respond to the following questions in your Thinking Notebook.

- Think about difficulties you have had in communicating with the opposite sex. Do you discern any patterns to these problems that reflect the ideas in this section?
- Devise strategies for dealing with the communication problems you have encountered in the past with the opposite sex. You might adapt strategies described in this section or create your own. Since these miscommunications occur in social as well as business or work relationships, it's important to be aware of them and to implement your knowledge of this at work as well.

Working Collaboratively with Others

YOUR SUCCESS in life, personally and professionally, depends on how well you are able to work constructively with other people. The term *collaboration* refers to the social relationships that typically occur in group situations. Groups are usually defined as a collection of people who work together in order to achieve a common goal or goals. The members of a group interact and communicate, assume various roles within the group, and establish a group identity.

As with other human activities that we have considered, some people are more effective group members than others. Succeeding in groups involves a complex set of thinking and language abilities that many people have not systematically investigated or fully developed. You've undoubtedly noticed socially adept people: They effortlessly adapt to any group situation, engage in friendly conversation with many different individuals, work productively and harmoniously with others, influence the group's thinking with articulate and persuasive points, deal effectively with group tensions and egos, inspire members to work with commitment and creativity, and are able to keep everyone focused and moving in a coherent direction. As Daniel Goleman documents in his bestselling book *Emotional Intelligence*, these complex thinking, communication, and social skills are often more important for success in life than traditional ideas of intelligence or professional expertise. You have likely scratched your head in wonder at the success of people you have known who don't seem to be the most knowledgeable or intelligent, chalking their accomplishments up to "who they know." But "who you know," the relationships you have cultivated, and your skill at influencing people to work on your behalf are precisely the kinds of social and communication skills that you can (and need to!) develop through insight, practice, and thinking critically.

Working collaboratively has numerous advantages over working individually. To begin with, the group members bring diverse backgrounds and interests, which can generate a multiplicity of perspectives. And working with others actually creates ideas that none of the individuals would have come up with on their own. In addition, group members provide support and encouragement for one another, and each person can contribute his or her specialized skills. The sense of group identity inspires members to achieve lofty goals, a feeling of "teamwork" that brings out the best in each member. And since "many hands make light work," a group of people working together can accomplish impressive results in limited time if they are focused and well organized.

Naturally, working in groups has disadvantages as well. Since they involve many individuals with different and sometimes competing needs, groups often take more time to reach conclusions than individuals working alone. Additionally, you must be willing to sacrifice some personal autonomy in order to work with others, bringing a willingness to listen and compromise, if necessary, in order to achieve group goals. There is always a tension between the needs of the individuals and the needs of the group, and each group has to establish its own balance. Sometimes one or more group members want to dominate the group deliberations, trying to control and intimidate the other group members. Other times groups are plagued by a member who doesn't want to do his or her share. This is particularly damaging in small groups, where the contribution of each member is essential. And sometimes there are just personality incompatibilities, when you are expected to work with someone who drives you crazy.

One serious danger of groups is the phenomenon of *groupthink*, which occurs when the pressure to conform to the group's way of thinking overrides the realistic appraisal of alternative courses of action. The space shuttle *Challenger* disaster is a case in point. There were compelling reasons *not* to go ahead with the launch that spring morning in 1986: The temperatures were colder than launch guidelines permitted and there had been indications of fuel leakages through the crucial O-rings during previous flights. The low temperatures made the O-rings less pliable and thus vulnerable to potential leaks. NASA had even been warned repeatedly by at least one engineer member of the team regarding these dangers during the months leading up to the launch. However, this critical perspective, and others like it, were ignored and repressed because of the political pressures to launch the "first teacher in space," Christa McAuliffe. The overriding desire to have the launch take place on time created a "groupthink" momentum that distorted objective critical appraisal of the risks and suppressed dissenting views. Other prominent examples of the risks of groupthink include the failed Bay of Pigs invasion of Cuba in 1961 and the tragic U.S. involvement in the Vietnam War. Groupthink is also fueled by the fear of speaking out against a powerful member of the group — like the president or the head of NASA — and the repercussions that are likely to ensue from such perceived "disloyalty."

THINKING CRITICALLY ABOUT GROUPS

By understanding the social dynamics of groups, you can learn to enhance your participation and exert meaningful leadership. There are key abilities that you need to develop in order to work collaboratively with others.

Participate Actively: Every member has an important perspective to contribute and it is your responsibility to make your contributions. In many group situations it's tempting to let others do the heavy intellectual lifting and carry the brunt of the discussion, while you sit quietly as an interested bystander. But this is not how you develop your social skills, earn the respect of other group members, or influence the group's deliberations. And since you are equally responsible for the group's ultimate decisions, whether you are active or silent, you might as well contribute your perspective. If you feel intimidated at the prospect of speaking up, or feel that your ideas are less worthy than others', you need to recognize that these feelings are likely the result of the destructive self-talk analyzed in Step 3: Choose Freely. Use the strategies described in that chapter to create more positive inner messages. The first step is to realize that your feelings are probably irrational and have no basis in fact. My experience suggests that the people who are most concerned that "Everyone will think I'm stupid and laugh at me" are typically the most thoughtful and insightful contributors. In fact, it's often the most garrulous people who, lacking self-awareness, prattle on, filling the room with hot, unenlightened air. If you are anxious, you need to force yourself to take the first step. Start small, and as your irrational fantasies subside and your confidence grows, you can gradually increase your participation.

Employ the Qualities of Effective Discussion: Earlier in the chapter we analyzed the ingredients of an effective discussion and the communication abilities that you need to achieve this standard. Participating in a group requires similar skills to one-on-one discussion; it's just that you're dealing with more partners.

- *Express your views clearly* and always provide supporting reasons and evidence.
- *Listen carefully* to what others are saying, trying to understand their points and supporting reasons.
- *Respond directly* to the points being made instead of simply trying to make your own point.
- *Ask relevant questions* in order to explore fully the issue being discussed and then try to answer the questions.
- *Focus on increasing understanding* rather than trying to prove yourself right at any cost.

Treat All Group Members with Respect: This is a basic ground rule for collaborative success. Though you may be convinced that you are more knowledgeable than the other participants, it's important to let them express their views without cutting them off or expressing impatience. Creating and maintaining this *group process* is essential for healthy functioning, and there may be other occasions in which *you* are the less-knowledgeable person. There are also likely to be occasions in which other members won't agree with your analysis or conclusion, even though you are certain you are right. When this occurs, you need to work toward a compromise position, and if this fails, simply accept the fact that you've done all that you can to express your viewpoint and get it accepted.

Encourage Diverse Ideas from Others and Don't Judge the Ideas Prematurely: In addition to contributing your own ideas, you should encourage other group members to contribute their ideas as well. When people offer ideas, respond positively and constructively.

Evaluate Ideas Objectively, Not Personally: When the group evaluates ideas from its members, they should be evaluated using the skills of critical thinking: What is the issue or problem? How does this idea address it? What reasons or evidence support it? What are its risks or disadvantages? It's important for each member to realize that it is the ideas that are being evaluated, not the person who suggested the idea. One of the most common thinking mistakes is the ad hominem fallacy in which the person is attacked instead of his view being evaluated. Responding to a competing viewpoint with "I disagree for the following reasons . . ." instead of "You're an ignoramus" fosters informed communication rather than acrimony.

Analyze the Players, Power Distribution, and Relationships: Groups are like living, evolving organisms composed of individuals in complex, dynamic relationships with one another. In the same way that at a ballgame "you can't tell the players without a scorecard," functioning effectively in a group requires that you figure out who the "players" are, the nature of their relationships to each other, and how the decision-making power is distributed. Determining this information is particularly important in new groups with which you are unfamiliar, providing you with a "thinking context" within which you speak and respond.

EXERCISING GROUP LEADERSHIP

Although you may not think of yourself as a "leader," you should seriously consider choosing to develop your leadership potential in some of the groups of which you are a member. Taking a leadership role stimulates your personal growth and increases your confidence and self-esteem. People accord you a special respect and you have the opportunity to guide the direction of your group and help it achieve meaningful goals. You will also be developing the ability to inspire people and orchestrate their efforts toward productive aims, abilities that you can transfer to many social situations. The most accomplished leaders are able to influence the thinking and behavior of group members so that they willingly follow the path suggested to them. Leadership breeds success in every area of life and is best developed through practice and experience. Still, there are some useful insights to keep in mind as you pursue your leadership potential.

Keep the Group Focused and "On Task": Many groups end up wasting time because they cannot stay focused on the task at hand, or they are unable to bring their deliberations to closure. It's helpful to establish a *time frame*, which commits you to making a decision, and it's also useful to establish a *decision-making process* in case there are deep disagreements. This often requires a balancing act on your part, inviting people to participate actively and share their views on the one hand, and encouraging people to make relevant, succinct comments that propel the discussion forward on the other. In time you will develop an inventory of tactful phrases and the sense of timing to use them:

- "That's an interesting point: Perhaps you can explain how it relates to the issue at hand?"

- "I apologize for interrupting, but in the interest of time . . ."
- "Since we have to bring this matter to a close, are there any final comments that introduce points we haven't already considered?"

Leading a group is a little like herding sheep, in the sense that in order to keep the group moving forward, you have to maintain gentle pressure, round up strays, and never lose sight of the goal or schedule. Though there are times you may feel heavy-handed, if you remain courteous and respectful, most people will respond positively.

Assign the Group Responsibilities Equitably: It is important that all group members undertake substantive responsibilities, avoiding the divisions between the "workhorses" and the "freeloaders." Everyone has important talents and energy to contribute, and shared responsibility promotes positive group morale. This means that you need to develop the art of delegating responsibilities. Even when you feel that "It would be easier if I do it myself," it is vital for the group process that members feel they are being taken seriously and making important contributions. If you provide people with a clear agenda and recognize their contributions with explicit compliments, you will be pleasantly surprised at the quality of their work and their enthusiastic participation. Be generous with credit: It doesn't cost you anything but it buys a great deal of goodwill and positive morale.

Use Appropriate Decision-Making Approaches: It's important for each group to establish an appropriate decision-making process to ensure that you don't get mired in the muck of controversy and inertia. Before you reach the point of bringing deliberations to closure and designing plans of action, there is a general process to be followed:

Define the issue or problem: This is the first and in some ways most crucial goal to achieve. What exactly *is* the issue to be decided or the problem to be solved? Don't assume common agreement: Often people have different concepts, concerns, and agendas (sometimes "hidden agendas"), and it is essential to have the purpose of the discussion clarified explicitly before moving ahead.

Encourage creative ideas: As emphasized in Step 2: Live Creatively, innovative ideas often provide the most powerful solutions to problems or decisions. As a leader, you need to create a climate in which members feel sufficiently secure to risk volunteering unique possibilities. You should state this explicitly ("Let's make an effort to go beyond the obvious solutions"), reward people for taking risks ("That's a very creative idea I never considered"), and discourage others from being negative or judgmental ("It's not helpful to respond with 'That's a silly idea' or 'It will never work'; instead, try to improve on the proposed solution").

Insist on rigorous analysis and evaluation: Once a sufficient number of alternative solutions or choices have been generated and recorded, they need to be analyzed and evaluated in a forthright, objective way: advantages, disadvantages, anticipated consequences, likelihood of success, further information required, and so on. Remind people that "this is not personal." Once members recognize that this is a communal enterprise in which they all share both the credit and the blame, it will be easier for them to get beyond their egos and insecurities.

Bring things to closure in a timely fashion: At a certain point in the deliberative process it will be time to bring things to closure, either because you are running out of time or because the discussion has become repetitive. This is the moment when the group needs to decide on a specific course of action: an alternative to be pursued, a choice to be implemented, or a committee formed to gather more information. You will often encounter resistance to closure from some members. They may not feel that their views have received an adequate hearing, they may prefer talking to acting, or they may be procrastinators who have difficulty bringing anything to closure. In any case, this is the juncture when you need to exercise firm control and insist that the group make a decision. There are different decision-making models you can employ, and it's best if you decide *in advance* which the group will be using.

- If the group is small and people are in general agreement, you can use a *consensus* model in which everyone present simply agrees with a given course of action.

- If there are two competing ideas, a *majority* model can be used in which the alternative receiving the majority of the votes (more than half of those present) will be pursued. If there are significant unanswered questions, this vote can be deferred until a future meeting while further information is gathered.
- If there are a number of competing options, the group can decide with a *plurality* model. In this case, the option receiving the most votes will be chosen.

If the discussion has proceeded in an open and honest fashion, and people have agreed in advance to the decision-making model, then the members should be encouraged to act maturely and endorse the will of the group. This requires that people think *socially* instead of *individually*, and as the leader you can help them rise to this more enlightened level of awareness.

Deal Directly with Problem Members: Don't let problem members disrupt the group's functioning. If someone tries to dominate the discussion or impose his or her ideas, let that person know directly that such behavior is inappropriate. If a member is excessively negative and critical, encourage that person to participate in a more constructive way. For example, a number of years ago I was the president of a board of trustees for a land conservancy organization. Most of the trustees were hardworking and positive individuals, but there was one who was unrelentingly negative and critical of everything that I and the other trustees proposed. After several failed efforts to deal with the problem, I employed the following critical thinking strategy. To every negative comment from this person, I would respond: "You might be right in your criticism — what do you suggest as a better idea?" And every time the trustee asked why the organization wasn't doing one thing or another, I would respond: "That's an excellent suggestion — I'm putting you in charge of implementing this idea." It wasn't long before the disruptive negativity was stilled, and the board was able to work productively without this annoying distraction.

> ### THINKING ACTIVITY
>
> #### *Enhancing Your Group Participation*
>
> Reflect carefully on the various groups of which you are a member and your relationship to them. Identify the groups in which you can take a more active role as a participant and also as a leader. Use the strategies suggested in this section to enhance your group participation and develop your leadership skills. Keep a record of your progress in your Thinking Notebook.

Speaking Publicly

THERE ARE few things that strike greater fear in most human hearts than the prospect of speaking in front of a large group of people. Not surprisingly, one national study (*Goldring Research Report*, February 1993) found that public speaking is the number-one fear of Americans, beating out financial problems, heights, deep water, insects and bugs, loneliness, flying, and even death! Visions of being catatonically tongue-tied and publicly humiliated overwhelm any rational assessment of the situation and destroy one's confidence. And in one of life's cruel ironies, such anxiety often becomes a self-fulfilling prophecy: Fear leads to an insecure, mumbling, apologetic performance that simply reinforces your conviction that you were destined for public speaking failure. Yet the opposite scenario is just as possible: By learning to approach your public speaking confidently and competently, you can create a successful experience for yourself. But you first have to realize that such success is within your grasp.

Too frequently people fall into the trap of thinking that being an effective public speaker is a genetically inherited trait, a belief expressed in comments like "She's just a natural speaker in front of others," or "I hate public speaking — it's just the way I am." The truth is that public speaking is a set of skills that every person can develop and refine. Research shows that the quality of an oral presentation is directly tied to the amount of *preparation time*, the amount of *research*, the number of *rehearsals*, and the effort spent on preparing *speaking notes* and *visual aids*. No matter how uncomfortable you are speaking publicly, with the right preparation you can become an effective presenter. Who knows — in time, you might actually learn to enjoy speaking publicly! My first professional presentation was made to a grand total of three people. I was petrified. We sat in a small circle and I read a paper in a low monotone, rarely looking up at my "audience." Since that embarrassing beginning, I have worked hard to develop my skills and confidence as a speaker, and I now actually look forward to speaking: the larger the group the better. Amazing!

GETTING STARTED: FINDING A TOPIC

Finding a topic for an oral presentation involves the same approach and strategies explored in Step 2: Live Creatively, and earlier in this chapter. You need to immerse yourself in the subject; use techniques like brainstorming, Mind Mapping, and free writing, and then narrow your topic down to a specific, focused theme. In developing your theme, you need to think about what you want to accomplish with your presentation. Do you want to *inform* people about important facts or ideas? Do you want to *persuade* them to accept a belief, change a point of view, or take an action? Or do you hope to accomplish some combination of these two basic speaking purposes? In other words, it is useful to begin at the *conclusion* of your presentation by identifying the goals you hope to accomplish, and then work backward to construct your presentation so that it meets these goals. As Alice in *Alice in Wonderland* was told: *"If you have no idea where you are going, how will you know when you get there?"*

ORGANIZING YOUR PRESENTATION

Probably the greatest fear of people making oral presentations is that they will "get stuck" or lose their train of thought. If you have a clear map of the main ideas and their relationships either in your mind or in notes, the chances of this sort of "freeze-up" are considerably reduced. Oral presentations are typically divided into three general sections: an introduction, a main body, and a conclusion.

The Introduction: This communicates the main ideas that you are trying to express, but it also needs to engage the interest of your audience. Many speakers like to begin with a personal experience that relates to the theme about which they are speaking. This helps you make a personal connection to the audience, and engages their attention on that level. Other introductory approaches include using a vivid illustration, telling a humorous story, asking the audience to respond to a provocative question, or repeating a memorable quotation. In creating your introduction, think about what openings engage your attention when *you* are a member of the audience.

The Main Body: This consists of the development of your central ideas. In addition to clearly articulating your central points, you also need to *support* the points you are making with illustrations, examples, reasons, evidence, and the testimony of others. The exact organization of the main body depends on the subject of your presentation and the goals you want to accomplish. There are a number of thinking patterns that you can use to organize both written papers and oral presentations, and it is generally appropriate to use several at one time. For example, when I conduct workshops on critical thinking, I do the following:

- *Compare* and *contrast* the qualities of critical and uncritical thinkers.
- *Create analogies* between effective teaching and good coaching.
- *Analyze the causes* for the prevalence of uncritical thinking in our culture.
- *Define the problem* of how to teach people to think critically and discuss *solutions*.

- *Discuss research* that corroborates how traditional educational approaches often reinforce uncritical thinking.
- *Make predictions* about what will happen if we don't teach people to think critically.
- *Evaluate the effectiveness* of strategies for fostering critical and creative thinking.
- *Discuss arguments* for using a critical thinking framework to approach every area of life.

The Conclusion: The conclusion brings everything together, summarizing the main points and ending with a bang, known as "the clincher." Like your introduction, your clincher can be a personal experience, a humorous story, a vivid example, or a memorable quotation.

CREATING SUCCESSFUL PRESENTATIONS

Having a thoughtfully researched and clearly organized presentation is an essential element in achieving success in your public speaking, but there are other important factors as well.

Prepare Clear Notes and Become Thoroughly Familiar with Them: Although you may have written out your presentation in its entirety, *don't read it*. When you read from a prepared script, you run the danger of sounding unspontaneous and mechanical, and you will be making less eye contact with your audience. People enjoy being spoken *to*, which means that you should be looking directly at them and speaking dynamically, showing that you are actually thinking as you speak instead of simply reading previously prepared thoughts. In order to speak effectively without reading you need to rehearse your presentation until you are thoroughly familiar with it, and then develop clear notes that remind you of the main ideas. Don't worry if you can't find the exact words or perfect phrases contained in the written version of your text: the direct and personal contact you are making with your audience more than compensates for this.

Use Supplementary Visual Aids: Research shows that humans can only process and remember a relatively small portion of what they hear, considerably less than what they see or experience personally. As a result, visual enhancements like charts, diagrams, illustrations, photographs, excerpts from videos, and so on are very effective ways of supporting and reinforcing the ideas you are speaking about. They provide your audience with other points of reference that help them integrate your ideas into their own framework of understanding. Many people use overhead projectors to present this material, although I personally prefer using handouts that the audience can make notes on and keep for future reference.

Speak Confidently and Energetically: Although you may be screaming with panic and insecurity on the inside, it is essential that you put on a confident appearance. Acting confidently will actually make you *feel* more confident, and it will inspire the audience's confidence in you. Stand up straight and look directly at your audience; speak loudly, clearly, and not too fast; and act as if you're enjoying yourself. By acting as if you believe in yourself and your message, your audience is inclined to believe in you as well, which in turn bolsters your confidence and helps you believe in yourself even more.

Be physically dynamic. A great deal is communicated without language — "nonverbally" — through facial expressions, gestures, tone of voice, and body movements. Try to loosen up and move your body as you speak, investing energy and feeling into the words you are speaking, the ideas you are communicating. Practice in front of your friends or family members (as well as the mirror!), and ask for their feedback. Remember the advice of the famous orchestra conductor Arturo Toscanini: *"You don't do anything in a performance that you haven't done a thousand times in practice."*

Involve the Audience: Successful speakers pay attention to their audience and engage them in active participation as much as possible. Your audience sends out many signals to let you know what they're feeling and thinking. If they start to look bored or distracted, then it's time to shake things up. As you undoubtedly know from personal experience, it's easy to slip into a passive, unthinking frame of mind when listening to someone else speak. That's why if your presentation lasts for more than just a few minutes, you should find ways to engage the minds of your audience:

- Ask them to think about a question and then invite them to respond.
- Give them a brief writing assignment.
- Assign a brief project in which they speak to their neighbors.
- Engage them in an activity to get them out of their seats and moving around.
- Alternate your speaking with other presentation modes such as visual aids or video.

In other words, do whatever it takes to keep your audience actively engaged in the presentation. It will make the experience more entertaining for you as well.

Overcoming Public Speaking Anxiety

You can probably identify with the following situation: You have been asked (pressured?) to speak to a large group of people — a business presentation, a formal dinner, a political rally, a church service — and you are terrified. All you can think of is the spectacle of humiliating yourself in front of this group.

What can you do to combat the debilitating effects of "public speaking anxiety"? The problem-solving approach introduced in Step 4: Solve Problems Effectively provides a conceptual framework for analyzing and overcoming a problem such as this and countless others. Let's use a shortened version of it to address this problem.

What Is the Problem?

The "real" problem is not necessarily that you fear public speaking, per se. It may well have a deeper origin. Perhaps it stems from your dislike of being placed in a vulnerable position in front of people you don't know that well. Or perhaps it expresses your fear of appearing inept and foolish, as you imagine your tongue-tied presentation degenerating into a series of unintelligible croaks. In either case, your stress originates from the prospect of being placed in a situation in which you might lose control, with disastrous results. And it is this problem that is likely responsible for the stress symptoms that you are experiencing.

WHAT ARE THE ALTERNATIVES?

Alternative #1: Enhance the "Voice of Confidence" and Banish the "Voice of Panic."

Each of us has voices inside of our minds that speak to us with what psychologists describe as "self-talk." Often these voices are negative and destructive, undermining your self-esteem and shattering your self-confidence with messages such as "I am going to make a fool of myself." In order to influence these voices, you first need to become aware of them, and making daily entries in your Thinking Notebook is a good way to start. When the negative Voice of Judgment shows up, you need to get tough with it and banish it from your mind. At the same time, you need to make conscious efforts to send positive messages to yourself through your Voice of Confidence.

Alternative #2: Analyze the Reality of Your Anxiety-Provoking Situation as Objectively as Possible.

Much of the stress that you experience is needless in the sense it is not grounded in reality. For example, the anxiety you are feeling about your upcoming public speaking is fueled by fantasies of humiliating yourself. Yet these fantasies are just that — fantasies. The reality of the situation is that if you prepare carefully, your presentation at the very least will be adequate.

Alternative #3: Seek the Support of Other People.

Other people can provide reality checks to help you keep things in perspective, and they can also provide positive support in helping you deal with stressful situations. You shouldn't be reluctant to express your fears and anxieties to others, since they are probably experiencing similar feelings of their own and will welcome someone to talk to. This also underscores the importance of choosing friends who have caring and supportive attitudes toward others.

Alternative #4: Create a Plan of Action and Implement It.

Since stress is caused by circumstances that threaten your sense of control, you can reduce stress by working to take control of the situation that you are in. In order to do this, you have to create an intelligent plan of action designed to help you control the stressful situation. For example, by following the speech-making strategies that you have been exploring in this chapter, you have good reason to feel confident about your performance. By combining the public speaking strategies with the stress-reducing approaches explored in this section, you should find yourself dealing more effectively with stress, and this will bolster your confidence and sense of control.

Alternative #5: Promote Relaxation: Meditate.

As already discussed on page 91, meditation is a powerful tool for developing control over your thinking and emotions. It helps you to relax, focus, and concentrate, and enables you to let go of many of the irrational fears and anxieties that are crowding your consciousness.

Alternative #6: Use Positive Visualization.

Research has also found that positive visualization can contribute significantly to a successful performance. Imagine yourself speaking dynamically and effectively, to the thunderous applause of the audience. Think only of how things are going to go well, not letting yourself fall into the trap of focusing on potential disasters.

WHAT IS MY SOLUTION?

The alternatives identified above are sound starting points for crafting your own personal public speaking solution, and you should experiment with them and perhaps develop some additional ones of your own. Create a plan that integrates the most successful of these strategies, and then commit yourself to implementing your ideas. This is no time to feel queasy. When my then six-year-old daughter was working up the courage to sing a solo rendition of "The Greatest Love of All" in front of more than one hundred people at a company talent show, she turned to my wife and announced with fierce determination, "I'm not going to let the chicken get me!" And she didn't, performing flawlessly. This is good advice for all of us to keep in mind as we prepare for public speaking experiences: Don't let the chicken get you.

THINKING ACTIVITY

Planning a Public Speaking Presentation

The next time that you are asked or have the opportunity to volunteer to make a public presentation, use the strategies in this section to assist in your preparation and presentation.

- Develop an engaging theme.
- Organize your presentation.
- Prepare clear notes and use supplementary aids.
- Speak confidently and dynamically.
- Involve the audience.

In addition, use the strategies explored in this last section to overcome any public speaking "jitters" or "butterflies" that you may be experiencing.

How Effective a Communicator Am I?

DESCRIBED BELOW are key thinking abilities and personal attributes that are correlated with communicating effectively. Evaluate your position regarding each of these abilities and attributes, and use this self-evaluation to guide your efforts to become an expert communicator.

Make Communication a Priority

I *act* as if communication is   I treat communication very
extremely important.   casually.

5   4   3   2   1

Although few people are likely to go on record as believing that effective communication is not important, the paradoxical truth is that many people *act* as if they believed it, failing to take intelligent steps to improve their communication abilities.

   Strategy: *After you have completed the evaluation of your communication abilities in this section, identify in your Thinking Notebook goals you would like to achieve. Review your goals each day so that you can plan your communication initiatives and evaluate your progress.*

Connect Your Thinking and Language

I actively connect my thinking   I focus on my thinking and
and language.   language separately.

5   4   3   2   1

In most areas of life, becoming an expert thinker involves becoming an expert user of language, and vice versa. That's why it's important to express your thinking in *writing*, because the process of writing helps you generate ideas and clarify your thoughts. Similarly, *discussing* your thinking with others encourages you to articulate your ideas and test the quality of your beliefs. Even when you are thinking on your own, you should try to elaborate your thoughts fully, striving to give them form and clarity.

   Strategy: *Develop the habit of expressing yourself in writing. A good way is by keeping a Thinking Notebook as previously suggested. Think critically about the ideas you have expressed, evaluate them for clarity and value, and reflect on how you can improve your thinking. In your conversations with others, pay particular attention to the language you are*

*using to express your ideas, and work toward refining the quality of both
your thinking and language.*

Communicate Your Ideas Precisely and Coherently

I express my thoughts   I express my thoughts in
precisely and coherently.   vague and disorganized ways.

5 4 3 2 1

Precise and well-organized use of language contributes to clear and cogent thinking. It is much easier to communicate in vague and general
terms because that doesn't require the rigor and articulation of careful
thought. But this comes at a high cost, diluting the quality of our communication and our thinking.

 *Strategy: Work continually to refine the precision of both your lan-
guage and thinking. When you express yourself in writing, always treat
your initial effort as a first draft to be refined and improved, asking yourself, "Could I say this more clearly?" When speaking with others, try to
express exactly what you are thinking or feeling. Use examples and analogies to enrich your expression by developing the habit of saying "For example . . . ," "In other words . . . ," "It's analogous to . . ."*

Listen Carefully to Other Viewpoints

In discussions, I listen   I focus more on expressing
carefully to others.   my views than listening.

5 4 3 2 1

A meaningful exchange of ideas requires that each party listen carefully to the other, and try to appreciate fully that person's position.
This is the soul of thinking critically — striving to move outside of
your own limited perspectives and think empathetically within other
viewpoints.

Strategy: *When you discuss issues that you feel passionate about, focus on your role as a listener. Give the other people your complete attention and, instead of mentally evaluating or disagreeing with what they are saying, try to put yourself in their position in order to understand what they are proposing and why they think it. Make a conscious effort not to speak until they have expressed themselves fully, and defer your response until you have reached an in-depth understanding of their point of view.*

Respond Directly to the Views of Others

I respond directly to the views of others.	I focus on stating my views as strongly as possible and proving the other view wrong.

5   4   3   2   1

To sustain an effective discussion, listening is only half of the job. Once you have understood what the other person is saying, you have to respond in a productive way. Although it may be tempting for you to express what you believe, it is important to respond directly to what they are saying.

Strategy: *When you are discussing issues with others, make a special effort to respond directly to what they are saying in a way that encourages further discussion. Avoid responses that don't relate to their ideas or undercut their points, and instead ask questions like "Why do you believe . . . ?" or "Have you considered the point . . . ?" As all parties begin to establish a sense of trust, respect, and mutual commitment to increase understanding, this will encourage them to forsake their aggressive and defensive postures. Discussions should be mutual explorations, not war.*

Use the Appropriate Language Style

I adapt my language style to the social situation.	I am unaware of my use of language styles.

5   4   3   2   1

Every communication situation is like a problem to be solved, and the language style that you use will have a significant impact on your success. You must analyze whether your communication should be formal or informal, and whether it is appropriate to use slang or jargon.

Strategy: *Develop the habit of evaluating your communication situations from a critical thinking perspective, asking yourself: What are my communication goals? Which language styles will help me accomplish these goals? If I use slang or jargon, will my audience understand the terms? Monitor the effectiveness of your communication by asking: "Does my audience seem to understand what I am trying to express?*

Communicate Effectively with the Opposite Sex

I communicate well with the opposite sex.

I have difficulty communicating with the opposite sex.

5   4   3   2   1

Research by people like Deborah Tannen supports the belief that men and women have different communication styles. This doesn't mean that there won't be many exceptions to these generalizations, but these gender-based patterns are nevertheless useful in understanding the frequent *mis*communications between women and men. By becoming aware of these different styles, both sexes can better understand and communicate with each other.

Strategy: *Make a special effort to become aware of the communication styles of members of the opposite sex that you have dealings with, including different approaches to eye contact and posture, favored topics, feedback behavior, and approaches to solving problems and analyzing issues. In addition, discuss these communication differences with the other person so that he or she can make the same effort you are in building communication bridges.*

Learn to Work Collaboratively

I work extremely well with people in groups.	I have difficulty working in group situations.

5   4   3   2   1

Much of your success and fulfillment in life depends on being able to work together with others productively and harmoniously.

   Strategy: Use the guidelines discussed on pages 229–232 to plan and evaluate your participation in various groups of which you are a member. Remember that applying and refining these social skills takes time, but if you are conscientious you will see immediate results that will continue to develop.

Exercise Group Leadership

I am an effective leader in group situations.	I rarely display leadership in group situations.

5   4   3   2   1

Everyone has the potential to exercise leadership qualities in at least some group situations, and developing these qualities will enhance many areas of your life.

   Strategy: Begin by selecting one group in which you would like to improve your leadership participation. Take a proactive approach, employing the group skills identified on pages 232–235. You must seize the leadership role since it will rarely be awarded.

Become an Effective Public Speaker

I am a confident, effective public speaker.	I am very anxious when I speak in public.

5   4   3   2   1

If you rated yourself 1 or 2 on this scale, you are not alone! As noted, public speaking is public enemy number one as rated by Americans. Yet despite the terrifying anxieties evoked by the prospect of speaking before a group, this is a dragon that can be slain fairly easily by implementing the guidelines discussed earlier in the chapter.

Strategy: *Volunteer to speak publicly and use the guidelines on pages 236–241 to ensure your success. As you prepare and practice, think about the types of presentations that you most enjoy listening to, and then integrate those qualities into your event.*

SCORING GUIDE

Add up the numbers you circled for each of the self-evaluation items above and use the following Scoring Guide to evaluate your communication abilities.

Point Total	*Interpretation*
40–50	very effective communicator
30–39	moderately effective communicator
20–29	somewhat effective communicator
10–19	comparatively ineffective communicator

In interpreting your results, be sure to keep in mind that:

- This evaluation is not an exact measure of your communication abilities, but is rather intended as a general indicator of how insightfully you approach the communication process in your life.
- Your score indicates how you are functioning at the present time, *not* your communication *potential*. If you scored lower than you would like, it means that you are underutilizing your communication abilities, and that you need to follow the suggestions in this chapter to fully realize your talents.

THINKING ACTIVITY

Becoming a Successful Communicator

Select areas of your life in which you would like to improve your communication abilities and attempt to do so. Keep a record in your Thinking Notebook detailing your efforts and their results. Be sure to allow yourself sufficient time to develop these complex abilities and attitudes, and don't get frustrated if you don't succeed at once or if you suffer setbacks. Cultivate the qualities of effective communication that we have explored in this chapter:

- Make communication a priority.
- Connect your thinking and language.
- Communicate your ideas precisely and coherently.
- Listen carefully to other viewpoints.
- Respond directly to the views of others.
- Use the appropriate language style.
- Communicate effectively with the opposite sex.
- Learn to work collaboratively.
- Exercise group leadership.
- Become an effective public speaker.

ANALYZE COMPLEX ISSUES

Reason is the instrument that shapes your thinking into intelligible patterns, providing the means to understand the world and reveal the mysteries of the person you are and the person you are becoming. This chapter provides a clear blueprint of the fundamental forms of reasoning that you need to function as a sophisticated critical thinker: constructing and evaluating arguments; analyzing complex issues, understanding polls and surveys; reasoning through court cases; and critically evaluating information from news sources. You will learn how to use the power of reason to make successful decisions, provide insightful explanations, make accurate predictions, and construct persuasive arguments.

The Gift of Reason

Man has received direct from God only one instrument wherewith to know himself and to know his relation to the universe: that instrument is reason.

— LEO TOLSTOY

"KNOW THYSELF," Socrates advised, because self-knowledge is the keystone of your life: Lacking this foundation, a life becomes a charade, an accidental collection of roles and masks rather than a coherent, integrated self. The first page of this book initiated your journey of self-discovery and transformation, *The Thinker's Way*, and your reasoning ability has been your guiding light through each of the five Steps you have taken since. Reason is the instrument that has given form to your thinking, enabling you weave your ideas together into patterns of meaning, illuminating the mysteries of the person you are and your vision of the person you are becoming.

This chapter marks a new stage in your journey in two ways: it focuses the spotlight of analysis directly on the reasoning process, and it enlarges the scope of inquiry from yourself to the world of which you are a part. You've expended a great deal of effort strengthening and refining yourself as a thinker: Now it's time for you to take your newly developed thinking abilities out into the world. This chapter, Step 6, provides a blueprint for reasoning through the complex social issues that involve other people and penetrate every part of our lives. Step 7: Develop Enlightened Values extends this social exploration to the moral values that govern our relationships with others. And Step 8: Think Through Relationships provides the capstone to these three chapters by illuminating the nature of healthy relationships in general: friendship, intimate, and parent-child.

These three Steps represent a challenging part of your personal odyssey, but you have been developing all of the prerequisite skills you need through your work up to this point. You have every reason to be confident of your success, and you should move ahead with courage. *"If we would be guided by the light of reason, we must let our minds be bold,"* the jurist Louis Brandeis observed. Think critically. Live creatively. Choose freely. Reason boldly.

The Power of Reason

THE HUMAN MIND is an enormously powerful and versatile instrument for making sense out of the apparent chaos of the world, and the ability to *reason* is the soul of this process. What exactly *is* "reasoning"? The psychologist Jerome Bruner characterized it as the mind's ability to *"go beyond the information given"* to decide, explain, predict, or persuade. The quality of your reasoning process depends on how effectively you are able to go beyond the information given in order to make successful decisions, provide insightful explanations, make accurate predictions, and construct persuasive arguments.

Expert reasoners use all of the intellectual skills and critical attitudes you have been developing in this book including being mentally active, asking insightful questions, viewing issues from different perspectives, engaging in productive discussions, being thoughtfully reflective, thinking creatively, and developing informed reasons to support conclusions. It is this last quality, "developing informed reasons to support conclusions," that will be the focus of this chapter.

We live in a complex world filled with challenging and often perplexing issues that, as thoughtful individuals and informed citizens, we are expected to make sense of. The media informs us every day of issues related to AIDS, crime and punishment, euthanasia, immigration, genetic engineering, environmental pollution, racial conflict, reproductive technology, and many other things. Often these broad social issues intrude into our own personal lives, taking them from the level of abstract discussion into our immediate experience. For example, you may be the victim of a crime or serving on a jury and find yourself wrestling with the issues of good and evil, freedom and responsibility. Or you may be thinking about the moral issues of using the new reproductive technology to create a child of your own. At some point in your life you will likely be faced with a right-to-die decision involving someone close to you, forcing you to engage in the deep reflection that such a situation requires. As a critical thinker, your goal should be to reason your way to informed, intelligent opinions about these and other issues so that you can function as a responsible citizen as well as make appropriate decisions.

Another challenge to your reasoning abilities is the results of "scientific studies." Hardly a day goes by that there isn't a new study published regarding diet, AIDS, child-rearing, sleep, cancer, genetics, or innumerable other topics. In many instances, the conclusions of the studies suggest that people should behave a certain way, eat less of a certain kind of fat, be tested for hereditary illnesses, pursue a certain lifestyle, and so on. Yet in many cases these studies are limited in scope or contradict the findings of other studies. To interpret them properly, it is important to understand the reasoning upon which they are based: the design of such studies, what the results are actually saying, and how the study relates to others that have been done in the field.

The criminal justice system is also an area that requires advanced reasoning abilities. In our society, court cases have become the major venue for exploring issues of morality, freedom and responsibility, sanity and mental illness. But many people, including jurors, display a very unsophisticated approach to these complex issues, frequently basing their opinions on insufficient information that is irrelevant to the central issues involved. Often people can't understand why a jury reached a particular verdict, a mystery compounded when the jurors themselves are unable to articulate a coherent rationale for their verdict. This has fueled suspicion that many of the people selected for jury duty have not developed the reasoning abilities needed for a thoughtful and impartial consideration of the evidence. The issues have simply become too complex, the scientific evidence too technical, the skill of the defense attorneys and prosecutors too manipulative, the thinking abilities of the jurors too undeveloped, for the judicial system to work as it was intended.

Information from the media is another arena that requires the sophisticated reasoning abilities that most people lack. We are inundated with a continual flood of information from television, radio, newspapers, magazines, and the Internet. The sheer volume discourages us from using our reasoning abilities to evaluate consistently the *truth*, *objectivity*, and *credibility* of the information we are absorbing. Much of this information has the nutritional value of intellectual junk food, and we don't bother to distinguish the truth from the Twinkies — we simply ingest it whole. We expect to digest it "later," but later never comes because we're always on to our next meal. As thoughtful reasoners, we need to exercise specific habits of mind with respect to this information: to approach it with a healthy skepticism and the enlightenment that embodies the skills you have developed in this book. How do we differentiate between factual reports and unsubstantiated opinions? Between slanted and biased interpretations and objective accounts? Between manipulated findings and valid conclusions?

In this chapter, you will learn to reason analytically through all of these different thinking challenges. This will require commitment and effort on your part, but there is no other way. You can't expect to reason through complex issues with a simplistic way of thinking, any more than you could expect to create an artistic masterpiece with a box of crayons, or repair a jet engine with a hammer and a screwdriver. By becoming an expert reasoner, you are taking the next step on your journey, and in so doing you will be joining a select group of individuals. Three hundred years ago the Scottish poet William Drummond summed up what is the prevalent state of affairs today when he wrote, *"He who will not reason is a bigot; he who cannot is a fool; and he who dares not is a slave."* He who chooses to reason becomes a critical thinker, a person of insight and courage following *The Thinker's Way*.

The Thinker's Way to Analyzing Complex Issues

THE HEART of the reasoning process is the ability to reach conclusions that are not obvious from the information we have available — to "go beyond the information given." For instance, imagine that you are trying to *decide* whether to pursue a new job opportunity. As part of your reasoning process, you identify and evaluate the pros and cons of giving up your current job for a new position, and you ultimately reach a conclusion that you hope will turn out to be the "right" one for you. We might diagram your train of thought in this way:

- At my current position, opportunities for further advancement are limited.
- The new job will offer a number of possibilities for advancement.
- I will have the chance to gain knowledge and develop new skills.
- There's a certain amount of risk involved, but I have confidence in myself.
- *Therefore, I'm going to accept this new job.*

Your conclusion, the last line, expressed in italics, is based on the considerations that precede it, which are termed *reasons*. In order for you to reach an informed, intelligent conclusion, you have to do a skillful job of weighing all the reasons, pros and cons, and then figure out which decision will best meet your needs. If you are happy in your new job, then you have reasoned well. If not, then something went awry in your reasoning: Perhaps you lacked all of the information needed (e.g., you weren't told that many people resign or are fired because of the abrasive personality of the person in charge), or perhaps you failed to weigh the various reasons accurately (e.g., you miss the close relationships you had developed at your original job more than you expected). Part of reasoning well in this kind of situation is neutralizing "the grass is always greener" syndrome: the tendency to *undervalue* the positive elements of your current situation (while emphasizing the negative), and *overvalue* the possibilities of the new opportunity (while minimizing the negative). This reasoning insight applies to any decision that involves leaving the old for the new, whether it's a job, a relationship, or the place where you live.

Thus, we frequently use reasoning to *predict* what will happen in the future, leading the German philosopher Arthur Schopenhauer to observe, *"Reason deserves to be called a prophet; for in showing us the consequence and effect of our actions in the present, does it not tell us what the future will be?"* In reasoning, your conclusion is always as strong — or weak — as the evidence that supports it, just as a table is only as stable as its legs.

Let's say that you are trying to take a position on a challenging issue, such as whether efforts at human cloning should be allowed to proceed. On the one hand, you recognize that there are reasons to support this genetic initiative, including the fact that it will permit certain couples incapable of producing sperm or ova to have children who share their genes. Also, you acknowledge that historically, there has always been resistance to scientific breakthroughs that have gone on to become commonplace, such as heart transplants or *in vitro* fertilization. Nevertheless, in reasoning through this issue, you conclude that efforts at human cloning should not be permitted, at least at this time. Your reasoning goes something like this.

- In the cloning of Dolly the sheep, there were 276 failures of the embryo to develop normally before a successful sheep was cloned. I consider the possibility of creating 276 failed *human* embryos to be unethical.
- With the case of Dolly, 25 percent of the embryos that were ultimately born were deformed and only lived a few days. Again, I don't think we have the moral right to play with human life in this way.
- If human cloning becomes commonplace, people who are reproductively healthy may choose to pursue cloning for the wrong reasons: the egotism of duplicating themselves; trying to create a Michael Jordan, Albert Einstein, or Princess Diana; or trying to eliminate the birth of anyone different from the social "norm."
- There are many other ways for infertile couples to have children besides cloning, both through new reproductive technology and through adoption.
- *Therefore, I have concluded that efforts at human cloning should be prohibited at this time.*

In this case, you have used your reasoning ability to analyze a complex issue and reach an informed conclusion. If you have reasoned well, then your conclusion will be intelligent, supported by cogent reasons that you will be able to discuss with other people. However, people often reason poorly about complex issues, or not at all, an unsettling state of affairs observed by Voltaire several centuries ago: "*Many are destined to reason wrongly; others, not to reason at all; and others to persecute those who do reason.*"

To make sense of complex issues, you need to have thought critically and reasoned analytically about them, before reaching a well-supported conclusion. All opinions are *not* equally valid. Some conclusions *do* make more sense than other conclusions because they provide a compelling analysis and are supported by persuasive reasons. We show the most respect for people (including ourselves) by holding them to intellectual standards of rigor and honesty, informed by knowledge and reflection. And in doing so, we encourage them to make the effort to elevate their understanding, instead of being satisfied with superficial and misguided ways of thinking. In order to puzzle out the complex and intricate world in which we live, we need to be equipped with a sophisticated view of knowledge and advanced reasoning abilities.

The central reasoning tool required to analyze complex issues is constructing and evaluating arguments. As we saw in the foregoing examples, arguments are a form of thinking we use to *decide, predict,* and *take a position.* Whenever we offer reasons to support a conclusion, we are considered to be presenting an *argument.*

Argument: A form of thinking in which *reasons* are offered in support of a *conclusion*

The definition of *argument* given here is somewhat different from the meaning of the concept in our ordinary language. In common speech, *argument* usually refers to a dispute or quarrel between people, often involving intense feelings. (For example: "I got into a terrible argument with the idiot who hit the back of my car.") Instead of this common usage, we use its more technical meaning, including the main ideas that make up an argument:

Reasons: Statements that support a *conclusion*, justify it, or make it more probable

Conclusion: A statement that explains, asserts, or predicts on the basis of *reasons* that are offered as evidence for it

The type of thinking that uses arguments — *reasons in support of conclusions* — is the key to the reasoning process, and it is the thinking you have been doing throughout your life to make decisions, make predictions, and take positions on various issues. But people's reasoning is not always correct. For example, the reasons someone offers may not really *support* his conclusion. Or the conclusion may not really *follow from* the reasons stated. Nevertheless, whenever you accept a conclusion as true based on certain reasons, or whenever you offer reasons to support a conclusion, you are using arguments to engage in reasoning (and vice versa) — even if your reasoning is weak or faulty and in need of improvement.

In addition to constructing and evaluating arguments, there are additional thinking skills needed in order to reason effectively, which you have been developing in previous sections of the book. Here is an outline of the reasoning model for analyzing complex issues that we will be using:

The Thinker's Way to Analyze Complex Issues

1. How can I clearly define the issue?
2. What are the different points of view on this issue?
3. Are the arguments sound?
   - 3A. Are the reasons true?
   - 3B. Do the reasons support the conclusion?
4. What are the consequences?
5. What is the conclusion?

ANALYZING AN ISSUE

Let's examine how this model works by reasoning through an example. Read the following article, and think about your position on the issue described. Do you believe it is ethically appropriate to destroy frozen human embryos? What reasons support your conclusion? How would you argue for the opposite point of view?

British Clinics, Obeying Law, End Embryos by Thousands

Breaking open glass tubes stored in freezing nitrogen, scientists at fertility clinics reluctantly destroyed several thousand abandoned human embryos today under a law limiting storage to five years. The Government rejected pleas from anti-abortion activists to intervene to save the embryos, products of in-vitro fertilization. Scientists complained about the waste of their work as they smashed glass tubes containing the embryos, four-cell dots the size of a grain of sand, which died within minutes and were then incinerated. Couples trying to have babies by in-vitro fertilization often are able to produce multiple embryos, some of which are frozen to keep for future attempts in case the first implantation is not successful. The couples had a total of 3,300 unclaimed embryos and their permission was needed to extend storage for up to five more years, or to donate the embryos to other women or to research programs.

— NEW YORK TIMES, August 2, 1996

1. *How Can I Clearly Define the Issue?* In order to analyze complex issues successfully, it's necessary to identify exactly what the issues are. The language that people use has multiple levels of meaning, and it is often not clear precisely what meaning(s) is being expressed. For example, you may enter a discussion believing that you share the same views with others, only to discover that you are in sharp disagreement once the issue is properly defined. Of course the opposite may happen as well: You may begin a discussion believing that you are on opposite sides of an issue, and end up finding that you are in basic agreement once the issue is clarified. To avoid misunderstandings and sharpen your own thinking, it is essential that you clarify the key concepts as early as possible.

Is it ethical to destroy frozen human embryos? The first step in answering this question involves defining the key terms involved. People morally opposed to destroying the embryos, like the protesting anti-abortion activists cited in the article, view such an action as mass murder because they view the frozen embryos as *human lives*. Beginning with this equation (frozen embryos = human lives), destroying the embryos is naturally viewed as "murder" — the taking of a human life.

But is a frozen embryo a "human life"? Certainly it has the *potential* to become a person. But is it a person in its current state as a "four-celled dot the size of a grain of sand"? Since the development of human life is a continuous process that begins with a fertilized egg and ends with a baby, deciding when the embryo — or fetus, for that matter — becomes a "person" depends on what point in the process of development you decide to draw the line. And this is exactly the point of contention upon which the entire issue rests. For if you view the four-celled embryos simply as potential (but not yet) human lives, then destroying them cannot be viewed as murder.

2. *What Are the Different Points of View on This Issue?* One of the hallmarks of critical thinkers is that they strive to view situations from perspectives other than their own, to "think empathetically" within other viewpoints, particularly those that disagree with them.

In this example of destroying frozen human embryos, there are at least two legitimate points of view:

- The four-celled embryos are *potential* (but not yet) human lives.
- The four-celled embryos *are* human lives.

An accomplished thinker works to get to the heart of the issue and fully appreciate the arguments on both sides — which is a much more productive approach than hurling out epithets like "murderer" or "fascist."

3. *Are the Arguments Sound?* In order to evaluate the *soundness* of the arguments that you and others construct, you need to determine how *true* and how *valid* the arguments are. The *truth* of an argument refers to how accurate the reasons are that are being offered in support of the conclusion. The *validity* of an argument means to what extent the reasons support the conclusion. These are the two criteria you should always use to evaluate arguments that are being presented to you, as well as arguments that you construct yourself.

Criteria for Evaluating Arguments

A. How *true* are the reasons being offered to support the conclusion?

B. How *valid* is the argument? (To what extent do the reasons *support* the conclusion, or to what extent does the conclusion *follow from* the reasons offered?)

For instance, consider the following argument *against* destroying the frozen embryos:

Reason	Murder is against the law.
Reason	Destroying frozen human embryos is murder.
Conclusion	Destroying frozen human embryos should be against the law.

3A. How True Are the Supporting Reasons? The first aspect of any argument you must evaluate is the *truth of the reasons* that are being used to support a conclusion. Does each reason *make sense?* What *evidence* is being offered as part of each reason? Do you know each reason to be true based on your own *experience?* Is each reason based on a *source* that can be trusted? You use these questions and others like them to analyze the reasons offered and to determine how true they are. As noted in Step 1: Think Critically, evaluating the sort of beliefs usually found as reasons in arguments is a complex and ongoing challenge.

Is the first reason — *Murder is against the law* — true? Although this statement is generally accurate, it still needs to be clarified. For example, killing someone in self-defense is not against the law. And killing someone in a war or in the process of apprehending a criminal is not only legal, it is considered commendable. Even permitting a terminally ill person to die by withholding medical treatment is permitted by law in some states. So in order for this reason to make a meaningful point, it would have to be much more specific about what type of murder you're talking about.

What about the truth of the second reason — *Destroying human embryos is murder?* As we saw in 1. How Can I Clearly Define the Issue?, the truth of this reason depends entirely on how you view the frozen embryos: if you see them as human lives, then the statement is true. But if you view them as *potential* (but not yet) human lives, then the statement is false.

Let's now examine an argument that *supports* the destruction of the embryos.

Reason	A frozen human embryo is not a human life; it is simply a fertilized egg that has the potential to become a human life.
Reason	Each frozen embryo belongs to the couple who paid to have it developed through a medical procedure (in vitro fertilization).
Conclusion	*Since these embryos remain unclaimed beyond the five-year limit, they should be destroyed.*

Is the first reason true? Well, again, answering this gets back to whether the embryo is viewed as a human life or a potential (but not yet) human life. What about the truth of the second reason? Answering this again depends on your basic definitions in this case. If the embryos are seen as merely fertilized eggs, then they clearly *do* belong to the couples who paid to have them created, frozen, and stored. *However*, if the embryos are seen as human lives, then the parents don't "own" them, in the same way that children aren't "owned" by their parents. When you own something, such as a piece of jewelry, you are free to do what you want with it, including destroying it. But if you're a parent, you don't have the right to "destroy" — or even abuse — your child. Their right to exist is protected by law. So if society were to conclude that these embryos are human lives, then the parents would not "own" them with the option of destroying them.

3B. *Do the Reasons Support the Conclusion?* In addition to determining whether the reasons are true, evaluating arguments involves investigating the *relationship between* the reasons and the conclusion. When the reasons support the conclusion, so that the conclusion follows logically from the reasons being offered, the argument is *valid.* If, however, the reasons do not support the conclusion so that the conclusion does *not* follow from the reasons being offered, the argument is *not valid.* Here's a simple test for determining the validity of an argument: Ask yourself, "*If* the reasons were true, would the conclusion logically follow?" If so, then the argument is valid.

In examining the arguments both against and in favor of destroying the embryos included above, it is clear that *if* you assume that the reasons are true, then you must believe that the conclusion *necessarily follows.* That is, if you believe that the frozen embryos are human lives and that destroying them is therefore murder, then it is logical to conclude that destroying the embryos should be considered against the law. However, if you believe that the frozen embryos are not yet human lives, then it is logical to conclude that destroying these embryos should be permissible, provided that the parents have not made arrangements to continue paying for their storage. The *structure* of both arguments is *valid:* The conclusion you agree with will depend on how you evaluate the truth of the reasons, which depends on whether you view the frozen embryos as human lives.

Soundness: *Are the Reasons True and the Argument Structure Valid?*
In terms of arguments, "truth" and "validity" are not the same concepts.

"Truth" relates to how accurate the reasons are, while "validity" relates to how logical the structure of the argument is. When an argument includes both *true reasons* and a *valid structure*, the argument is considered to be *sound*. When an argument has either false reasons or an invalid structure, however, the argument is considered *unsound*. The relationships among truth, validity, and soundness are illustrated in the following chart:

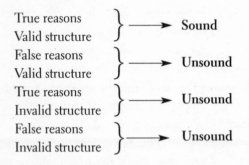

4. *What Are the Consequences?* The next step in the reasoning process of constructing and evaluating arguments is to determine the *consequences* of alternative conclusions, decisions, solutions, or predictions. The consequences refer to what is likely to happen if various conclusions are adopted. Looking ahead in this fashion is helpful not only for anticipating the future but also for evaluating the present. For instance, in the case of the frozen embryos, if they are judged to be human lives, what are the implications of this action? Does this mean that every couple who creates a number of fertilized eggs and then has the extras frozen as a back-up for the future is responsible for maintaining these fertilized eggs forever? And if they are not interested in using or maintaining them, does this mean that society has a responsibility to maintain them in a frozen state? Once such embryos are created, is there then a moral obligation to continue their development by implanting them in some woman's womb? If a couple creates twenty such embryos, should they be expected to turn all twenty into children? Should cou-

ples be permitted to create only the embryos that they intend actually to use?

On the other side of the issue, what are the consequences of destroying the frozen embryos? By condoning such an action, are we somehow devaluing human life? Will this encourage people to view procreation simply as a mechanical process that can be tinkered with any way they want? Will this encourage people to create "perfect" children by experimenting with embryos, callously getting rid of those deemed less worthy at later stages of development?

As is apparent, taking the consequences into consideration when analyzing issues has the potential of complicating these complex issues even more. But this is the only way to analyze issues properly. If we try to analyze issues with blinders on, ignoring the future implication of our actions, then we are ignoring the perceptive maxim *"Fools rush in where angels fear to tread."* For jumping to conclusions without trying to look into the future surely does qualify us as fools.

5. *What Is the Conclusion?* The ultimate purpose of reasoning by constructing and evaluating arguments is to reach an informed and successful conclusion. This is a complex process of analysis and synthesis in which you consider all points of view; evaluate the supporting reasons, evidence, and arguments; and then construct a perspective that you think makes the most sense. As a critical thinker, you should be aware that your perspective may change or be modified as you increase your understanding. Don't fall into the trap of thinking that there is only one "right" conclusion and that once you reach it you must defend it at all costs. You should feel confident in your point of view yet open-minded enough to welcome new insights and take them into consideration.

THINKING ACTIVITY

Analyzing Issues

Locate several articles describing controversial issues in current publications and analyze them by using The Thinker's Way to Analyze Complex Issues.

1. How can I clearly define the issue?
2. What are the different points of view on this issue?
3. Are the arguments sound?
   - Are the reasons true?
   - Do the reasons support the conclusion?
4. What are the consequences?
5. What is the conclusion?

Reasoning about Surveys and Polling

IN ADDITION to analyzing arguments, a critical thinker also needs to understand the reasoning involved in polls and surveys, an increasing — and often unwelcome — presence in modern life. Have you ever wondered how the major television and radio networks can accurately predict election results hours before the polls close? These predictions are made possible by the power of a form of reasoning known as *empirical generalization*: a form of reasoning in which a general statement is made about an entire group (the "target population") based on observing some members of the group (the "sample population").

Empirical generalizations are one of the most important reasoning tools used by both natural and social scientists, but it is a tool that is often misused by practitioners and misunderstood by the general population. Public opinion polls are ubiquitous in our lives. Consider how often you receive telephone calls from polling organizations and market researchers requesting "just a few minutes of your time to ask you a few questions," or the number of surveys you are asked to complete on the street, in restaurants, and in stores. Almost every electronic or mechanical product comes with a survey attached to the warranty card. Or think about the many times you are invited by a television show to call in and express your views on issues ranging from the guilt of O. J. Simpson to the state of our country. All of these requests for your opinions are designed to have you participate in empirical generalizations people are trying to form.

Network election predictions, as well as public opinion polls that occur throughout a political campaign, are based on interviews with a select number of people. Ideally, pollsters would interview everyone in the *target population* (in this case, voters), but this, of course, is hardly practical. Instead, they select a relatively small group of individuals from the target population, known as a *sample*, who they have determined will adequately represent the group as a whole. Pollsters believe that they can then generalize from the opinions of this smaller group to the target population. And with a few notable exceptions (such as in the 1948 presidential election, when New York governor Thomas Dewey went to bed believing he had been elected president and woke up a loser to Harry Truman), these results are highly accurate. (Polling techniques are much more sophisticated today than they were in 1948.)

There are three key criteria for evaluating the reasoning of empirical generalizations:

- Is the sample *known?*
- Is the sample *sufficient?*
- Is the sample *representative?*

Is the Sample Known? An empirical generalization is only as strong as the sample on which it is based. For example, sample populations described in vague and unclear terms — such as "highly placed sources" or "many young people interviewed" — provide a treacherously weak foundation for generalizing to larger populations. In order for an empirical generalization to be persuasive, the sample population should be explicitly *known* and clearly identified. Natural and social scientists take great care in selecting the members in the sample groups, and this is an important part of the data that is available to outside investigators who may wish to evaluate and verify the results.

Is the Sample Sufficient? The second criterion is to consider the *size* of the sample. It should be sufficiently large to give an accurate sense of the group as a whole. In the polling example discussed earlier, we would be concerned if only a few registered voters were interviewed and the results of these interviews were generalized to a much larger population. Overall, the larger the sample, the more reliable the inductive conclusions. Natural and social scientists have developed precise guidelines for determining the size of the sample needed to achieve reliable results. For example, poll results are often accompanied by a qualification such as "These results are subject to an error factor of ±3 percentage points." This means that if the sample reveals that 47 percent of those interviewed prefer candidate X, then we can reliably state that 44 to 50 percent of the target population prefer candidate X. Because a sample is usually a small portion of the target population, we can rarely state that the two groups match each other exactly — there must always be some room for variation. The exceptions to this are situations in which the target population is completely homogeneous. For example, tasting one cookie (the "sample") from a bag of cookies (the "target population") is usually enough to tell us whether or not the entire bag is stale.

Is the Sample Representative? The third crucial element in making effective empirical generalizations is the *representativeness* of the sample. If we are to generalize with confidence from the sample to the target population, then we have to be sure the sample is similar to the larger group from which it is drawn in all relevant aspects. For instance, in the polling example, the sample population should reflect the same percentage of men and women, of Democrats and Republicans, of young and old, and so on, as the target population. It is obvious that many characteristics, such as hair color, favorite food, and shoe size, are not relevant to the comparison. The better the sample reflects the target population in terms of *relevant* qualities, however, the better the accuracy of the generalizations. On the other hand, when the sample is *not* representative of the target population — for example, if the election pollsters interviewed only females between the ages of thirty and thirty-five — then the sample is termed *biased*, and any generalizations made about the target population will be highly suspect.

There are two significant problems with many of these surveys and polls. First, most of them are unscientific, not bothering to follow the guidelines we just examined (is the sample known? sufficient? representative?). For example, the people who are inclined to call in to voice an opinion are not *known* and probably not *representative* of the general population, making the results biased and unreliable. Second, many people are encouraged to voice opinions on subjects about which they don't know much, rendering their opinions next to worthless. In the case of the numerous polls about Louise Woodward (the British "nanny" accused of murdering a child in her care), most of those offering opinions had not watched the trial closely, day after day, and they did not possess an in-depth knowledge of the evidence. But with TV shows and pollsters encouraging them to offer their *uninformed* opinions, they were in effect being told that it didn't matter if they were ignorant of the facts — their opinions were still valuable. No wonder we live in an increasingly unthinking society — people are being encouraged to believe that all opinions are equal, both the informed and the uninformed, the intelligent and the ignorant. The journalist Michael Kinsley comments on this sorry state of affairs:

> The typical opinion poll about, say, foreign aid doesn't trouble to ask whether the respondent knows the first thing about the topic being opined upon, and no conventional poll disqualifies an answer on the ground of mere total ignorance. The premise of opinion polling is that people are, and of right ought to be, omni-opinionated — that they should have views on all subjects at all times — and that all such views are really valid. It's always remarkable how few people say they "aren't

sure" about or "don't know" the answer to some pollster's question. ("Never thought about it," "Couldn't care less," and "Let me get back to you on that after I've done some reading" aren't even options.) So, given the prominence of polls in our political culture, it's no surprise that people have come to believe that their opinions on the issues of the day need not be fettered by either facts or reflections.

THINKING ACTIVITY

Evaluating Empirical Generalizations

Review the following examples of empirical generalizations. In your Thinking Notebook, evaluate the quality of the reasoning in each case by answering the following questions:

- Is the sample known?
- Is the sample sufficient?
- Is the sample representative?
- Do you believe the conclusions are likely to be accurate? Why or why not?

"Where Have All the Lefties Gone?

A survey of 5000 people by Stanley Coren found that while 15 percent of the population at age 10 was left-handed, there was a pronounced drop-off as people grew older, leaving 5 percent among 50-year-olds and less than 1 percent for those aged 80 and above. Where have all the lefties gone? They seem to have died. Lefties have a shorter life expectancy than righties, by an average of 9 years in the general population, apparently due to the ills and accidents they are more likely to suffer by having to live in a "righthanded world."

— NEW YORK TIMES, January 23, 1992

Moral Compasses of Young People

One recent survey analyzed the ethical values 5,012 young people use to guide their decisions in moral situations. They were asked the question: "If you were unsure of what was right or wrong in a particular situation, how would you decide what to do?" According to the researchers, these were how the people interviewed responded:

- 3 percent: I would follow my conscience.
- 9 percent: I do not know what I would do.
- 10 percent: I would do whatever would improve my own situation.
- 16 percent: I would do what God or the Scriptures say is right.
- 18 percent: I would do whatever made me happy.
- 20 percent: I would follow the advice of an authority like a parent or religious leader.
- 23 percent: I would do what is best for everyone involved.

When these people were asked their beliefs about anything from lying, stealing, and using drugs to abortion or reasons for choosing a job, these rudimentary ethical systems or "moral compasses" turned out to be more important than the background factors that social scientists habitually favor in their search for explanations, like economic status, sex, race, and even religious practice.

Understanding Scientific Thinking

SCIENTIFIC THINKING is another prevalent form of thinking in our lives, based on the assumption that the world is constructed in a complex web of causal relationships that can be discovered through systematic investigation. Scientists have devised an organized approach for discovering causal relationships and testing the accuracy of conclusions — the *scientific method.* Causal reasoning is a type of reasoning in which an event is claimed to be the result of the occurrence of another event. It is the backbone of the natural and social sciences; it is responsible for the remarkable understanding of our world that has been achieved.

As we use our thinking abilities to try to understand the world we live in, we often ask the question "Why did that happen?" For example, if the engine of our car is running roughly, our natural question is "What's wrong?" Or if sales have been down at the company we work for, we wonder, "What has happened?" In each of these cases we assume that there is some factor responsible for what is occurring, some *cause* that results in the *effect* we are observing (the rough engine, the lower sales). Imagine how bewildered we would feel if a mechanic looked at our car and told us there was no explanation for our poorly running engine. Or if the CEO of our company asserted that there was no way to account for declining sales. In each case we would be understandably skeptical of the diagnosis and would probably seek another opinion.

The *scientific method* was developed to explain these and countless other events in our lives. The sequence of steps is as follows:

1. Identify an event or relationship between events to be investigated.
2. Gather information about the event (or events).
3. Develop an hypothesis or theory to explain what is happening.
4. Test the theory or hypothesis through experimentation.
5. Evaluate the theory or hypothesis.

Let's examine how this method works when applied to some of the issues that affect our lives.

Controlled Experiments (Cause-to-Effect)

Examples of causal reasoning in everyday life tend to focus on causal relationships between specific events (e.g., water in our car's gas tank is causing engine trouble). However, much of scientific research concerns causal factors influencing populations composed of many individuals. In these cases, the causal relationships tend to be much more complex than the simple formulation A causes B. For example, every package of cigarettes sold in the United States carries this cautionary notice: "*Surgeon General's Warning: Smoking Causes Lung Cancer, Heart Disease, Emphysema, And May Complicate Pregnancy.*" This does not mean that every cigarette smoked has a direct impact on one's health, nor does it mean that everyone who smokes moderately, or even heavily, will die prematurely of cancer, heart disease, or emphysema. Instead, the statement means that if you habitually smoke, your chances of developing one of the diseases normally associated with smoking are significantly higher than are those of someone who does not smoke or who smokes only occasionally. How were scientists able to arrive at this conclusion?

The reasoning strategy scientists use to reach conclusions like this one is the *controlled experiment,* and it is one of the most powerful reasoning strategies ever developed. This reasoning pattern is illustrated by the following article.

Hormone Use Helps Women, A Study Finds

Hormone replacement after menopause can significantly reduce a woman's risk of death as long as she continues it, a large study has found. In the first decade of hormone use, the chance of dying was 37 percent lower among women in the study who were using hormones than among women who did not, primarily because of fewer deaths from heart disease among the users. But the mortality benefit among those taking hormones dropped to 20 percent after 10 or more years of hormone use when the women's risk of death from breast cancer rose. Increased breast cancer risk is the major worry for women using hormone replacement, but the 16-year study of 60,000 postmenopausal women suggested that even women with breast cancer might benefit as a group, if they took hormones.

— NEW YORK TIMES, June 19, 1997

Do you think postmenopausal women should take hormone replacements based on this study? Can the results of studies like this be trusted? How do researchers develop their conclusions?

The first step in conducting reliable research is identifying a group of people who accurately represent all postmenopausal women in the United States, because testing all postmenopausal women simply isn't feasible. This involves following the guidelines for empirical generalizations we explored in the last section. It is important that the group you select to test be *representative* of all women in this category (known as the *target population*), in order for your results to provide reliable information. For example, if you selected only women of a certain race, geographical location, or socioeconomic status, your research could be generalized only to those specific populations. This representative group is known as a *sample*. Scientists have developed strategies for selecting sample groups to ensure that they mirror fairly the larger group from which they are drawn.

Once you have selected your sample of postmenopausal women — in this study it was 60,000, quite a large number — the next step is to divide the sample into two equal groups — here, each approximately 30,000. Each group should mirror the other in all relevant respects. The best way to ensure that the groups are essentially alike is through the technique we called *random selection*, which means that each individual selected has the same chance of being chosen as everyone else. You then designate one group as the *experimental group* and the other group as the *control group*. Next, you give the individuals in the experimental group hormone-replacement therapy, and you give either no treatment or a harmless placebo to the control group. At the conclusion of the testing period, you compare the experimental group with the control group to evaluate the effects of the hormone treatment.

Suppose that a number of individuals in the experimental group do indeed show evidence of health changes, as reported in this study over sixteen years. How can we be sure this is because of the hormone and not simply a chance occurrence? Scientists have developed a statistical formula based on the size of the sample and the frequency of the observed effects. For example, imagine that 3,900 of the 30,000 women in the experimental group show evidence of health changes, whereas no one in the control group shows any such evidence. Statisticians have determined that we can say with 95 percent certainty that the health changes were caused by the hormone treatment; that the results were not merely the result of chance. This type of experimental result is usually expressed by saying that the experimental results were significant at the 0.05 level, a standard criterion in experimental research.

Based on this information, you can see that you shouldn't automatically accept every research study that reports results, particularly if the research is not published in reputable scientific or medical journals that have a rigorous review process. Often newspapers, magazines, and news commentators will state with confident certainty, "A new study has found . . ." When this occurs, a healthy skepticism is in order. It's essential that the research be designed and conducted in a way that leads to reliable results. There have been many examples of faulty research that has led to conclusions and recommendations that have turned out to be inaccurate. For example, when our daughter was two years old, she had a seizure that lasted more than an hour. The accepted medical treatment for febrile (fever-related) seizures at that time was phenobarbital, which was universally prescribed in these situations. Twelve years later, a large and reliable research study found phenobarbital to have *absolutely no effect* in preventing seizures in children.

Even studies published in reputable scientific and medical journals can turn out to be inaccurate. For instance, a study sponsored by Tulane University Researchers published a paper in the highly respected journal *Science* (June 1996), which said that small amounts of ordinary pesticides, harmless by themselves, might be causing a devastating rise in estrogen hormones when mixed together, causing breast cancer, diminished sperm counts, and birth defects. The study made headlines in the United States and Europe, resulting in frantic research initiatives and special provisions in the Safe Water Act and the Food Safety Protection Act. However, other laboratories were unable to replicate the results and the authors of the paper quietly withdrew it a year later.

THINKING ACTIVITY

Evaluating Scientific Studies (Cause-to-Effect)

Carefully evaluate the following experimental research by answering these questions:

- What is the proposed causal relationship (the theory or hypothesis)?
- How representative is the sample?
- To what extent do the results support the proposed theory or hypothesis?

Nicotine Patch Found to Have Minimal Long Term Effect

The ads seem too good to be true: Slap a patch on the arm, change it every day, and two or three months later, you've kicked the habit. However, the truth is more elusive. Studies submitted to the F.D.A. indicated that smokers who used nicotine patches for 8 to 12 weeks were about twice as likely to have quit at the end of that period as were those who used dummy patches without nicotine. But as any smoker will testify, quitting is easy; the problem is that starting up again is even easier. So smokers wonder whether the patches will conquer their craving for nicotine and help them quit permanently or whether they will have to continue to purchase the patches at a cost of $300 for the 12 week supply. So far, research suggests that those who quit with the help of patches relapse at about the same rate as anyone else. In one series of follow-up studies, the share of individuals still smoke-free six months after they stopped using patches ranged from zero to 48 percent, as compared with a six-month success rate of zero to 40 percent for those who did not use them. Other studies indicate that success rates then continue to drop for at least a year, with patch users retaining some of their initial edge. Taken together, the figures suggest that the patches can help a small fraction of smokers. Each year 17 million Americans try to quit smoking, but only 1.3 million manage to do so.

— NEW YORK TIMES, April 8, 1992

CONTROLLED EXPERIMENTS (EFFECT-TO-CAUSE)

The research on the nicotine patch illustrates the first type of scientific reasoning with controlled experiments: *cause-to-effect*. With this type of reasoning, experimenters manipulate the possible cause (the nicotine patch) in order to determine if it is responsible for the effect (reduced incidence of smoking). A second form of scientific reasoning employing the controlled experimental design is known as *effect-to-cause*. In this case the experimenter works backward from an existing effect to a suspected cause. For example, imagine that you are investigating the claim by many Gulf War veterans that exposure to chemicals and nerve gases has resulted in significant health problems for them and for children born to them. Naturally, you would not want to expose people to a potentially harmful substance just to test the hypothesis, and people are no longer being exposed to these chemical and nerve agents as they were during the war. So investigating the claim involves beginning with the effect (health problems) and working back to the suspected cause (chemical and nerve gases). In this case the target population would be Gulf War veterans who were exposed to chemical/nerve gases, so you would draw a representative sample from this group. You would form a matching control group from the population of Gulf War veterans who were *not* exposed to chemical and nerve gases. Next, you would compare the incidence of illnesses claimed to have been caused by chemical and nerve agents in the two groups and evaluate the proposed causal relation.

Thinking Activity

Evaluating Scientific Studies (Effect-to-Cause)

Carefully evaluate the following research by answering these questions:

- What is the proposed causal relationship (the theory or hypothesis)?
- How representative is the sample?
- To what extent do the results support the proposed theory or hypothesis?

New Clues in Alzheimer's

Last week, a paper published in the *Journal of the American Medical Association* suggested that a person's cognitive style early in life is a good predictor of the chances of ending up with

Alzheimer's disease. In a study involving elderly nuns, the researchers wanted to see if nuns who had challenged their mental powers by earning college degrees and by spending their lives teaching would be less likely to get Alzheimer's than nuns who never got past high school and worked at menial tasks around the convent. They were startled to find that there was no significant difference — one group was about as likely to get the disease as the other. But what perplexed scientists even more was that they could guess, by looking at essays the nuns had written more than half a century before (when they were in their 20's), which would later develop Alzheimer's disease. Their guesses were 90 percent accurate. For reasons that no one pretends to understand, the nuns whose sentences were grammatically complex and packed with ideas were less likely to get the disease than those whose prose was simple and bare.

— NEW YORK TIMES, February 25, 1996

Reasoning about Court Cases

MANY SOCIAL ISSUES are explored, analyzed, reasoned about, and evaluated through our judicial system. High-profile trials have transfixed the nation and spawned countless, and often heated, discussions: O. J. Simpson (murdering his ex-wife), Timothy McVeigh (the Oklahoma City bombing), the Menendez brothers (murdering their parents), Alex Kelly (fleeing to Europe for seven years of jet-setting after being accused of rape), and Louise Woodward (killing an infant in her charge). Noteworthy court cases are typically complicated and require sophisticated critical thinking skills to reason through them. Often people can't understand why a jury reached a particular verdict, and the jurors themselves are often unable to articulate a coherent rationale for their verdicts. This has fueled suspicion that many of the people selected for jury duty simply have not developed the critical thinking abilities needed for a thoughtful and impartial consideration of the evidence, a concern expressed in the following article.

Must a Juror's Mind Be Empty to Be Open? I Think. Therefore I Am Not a Juror.

As jury selection in the Oklahoma City bombing case began in Denver last week, some unsolicited advice about the process of finding good jurors came from Philadelphia. In an old training videotape for young prosecutors, a man who is now running for district attorney urged his charges to avoid blacks from poor neighborhoods, and he had this additional tip: "You don't want smart people." Many Americans suspected as much. Some people wonder whether the nation's sales reps and bus drivers, however competent and sensible, are up to the task of deciding complex cases. Others aren't that generous. "The entire American legal system is upside down," the comedian Dennis Miller said a few years ago. "We have people's lives being determined by 12 people whose main goal in life is to wrap it up and get home in time to watch reruns." Even people who find beauty in the justice wrought by ordinary citizens acknowledge that recent high profile cases have been a public relations disaster for the jury system.

— NEW YORK TIMES, April 6, 1997

In this section, we will examine the reasoning abilities needed to analyze judicial issues successfully. If you are serving as a member of the jury, your role is to hear and weigh the evidence; evaluate the credibility of the witnesses and the relevance of their testimony; analyze the arguments presented by the prosecution and defense; determine whether the law applies specifically to this situation; and render a verdict on the guilt or innocence of the defendant. To perform these tasks with clarity and fairness, you have to use a variety of complex thinking abilities, which are summarized below:

The Thinker's Way to Analyze Court Cases

- What is the charge?
- What are my biases and how can I go beyond them in order to be impartial?
- What is the evidence? (Is the information relevant? Is the witness credible? Is the information accurate?)
- What are the explanatory theories?
- What are the arguments? (Are the reasons true? Are the arguments valid?)
- What is the verdict?

WHAT IS THE CHARGE?

Every criminal case begins with an alleged violation of the law that the prosecution is trying to prove the defendant is responsible for. Consider the case of Louise Woodward, a nineteen-year-old au pair from England who was hired to care for the two young children of Drs. Deborah and Sunil Eappen. On February 4, 1997, Ms. Woodward called 911 to report that the eight-month-old Matthew Eappen was having difficulty breathing. He was taken to a nearby hospital in a comatose state, suffering from swelling of the brain and bleeding in the head and interior linings of the eyes. He was also found to have a 2½-inch skull fracture. After spending five days in a coma, he died.

The district attorney's office concluded that Ms. Woodward was responsible for the death of Matthew Eappen, who had been in her sole care during the day in question. There were a variety of charges that could have been brought, ranging from first-degree murder to involuntary manslaughter. Your first task as a juror is to understand the specific conditions of the crime she is being charged with — not what *you* think she is guilty of, but what the prosecutors have decided is the most serious crime that they will be able to *prove* the defendant is guilty of. Ms. Woodward was charged with second-degree murder, which alleged that she was *aware* of the deadly consequences of her actions — she *intended* to cause harm — but she had not planned it in advance. A charge of involuntary manslaughter would have alleged that she was *unaware* of the damage she was causing; that although she exercised poor judgment and acted out of frustration and perhaps some anger, she did not *intend* for Matthew to be harmed in this way. Often prosecutors will bring more serious charges than the case warrants in an effort to encourage the defendant to plea-bargain down to an appropriate charge.

Can You Be Impartial?

As part of the jury selection process, you are asked by the prosecutor and defense attorney whether you will be able to set aside your initial reactions or preconceptions to render an impartial verdict. This means you should try to identify any ideas or feelings related to this case — your personal "lenses" — that might make it difficult for you to view it objectively, asking questions like: Are you a parent? Do you have a child who baby-sits? Have you ever had any experiences related to the issues in this case? Do you have any preconceived views concerning individual responsibility in situations like this? Having identified potential biases, you should then evaluate whether you will be able to go beyond your initial reactions to see the situation objectively.

There is some question regarding whether people can overcome deep-seated biases in order to view a case objectively. In Step 1: Think Critically, we saw that each of us views the world through our own unique "lenses" that shape and influence the way we view the world, process information, and make decisions. While it is impossible ever to completely take our lenses off, we can become aware of them and endeavor to compensate for their inherent bias. This process is aided by discussing issues with people who have different perspectives (because of their lenses) on a situation. So in theory, at least, people should be able to go beyond their inherent biases to weigh the evidence fairly and reach a just verdict. But the reality often falls short of this ideal.

Several years ago I served on a jury in which the defendant was accused of selling drugs outside a school. The evidence seemed overwhelming, and the defendant never took the stand to contradict the police testimony; it appeared to be an open-and-shut case on which we could quickly reach a verdict. When we entered the jury room, one juror immediately declared: "I never believe anything any policeman says." It took two days for the rest of us to put her preexisting opinions aside and view this case on its own merits.

The issue of bias was an important part of the O. J. Simpson case. A predominantly black jury found him innocent in the criminal trial, while a predominantly white jury found him guilty in the civil trial. These contrasting verdicts mirrored opinion polls, which found that a majority of blacks thought he was probably innocent, while a majority of whites thought he was probably guilty. In the case of Louise Woodward, the overwhelming majority of people in England were convinced that Ms. Woodward was completely innocent and was being victimized by a pernicious American legal system. In America, the opinion of people was more evenly divided.

Can people overcome their innate biases, formed over years of experience and often the result of powerful cultural and psychological forces? In many cases the answer is a qualified yes, but it requires a determined motivation to be fair-minded and enlightened about one's biases — qualities that are often in short supply, not just in the jury rooms but in the rest of life as well.

What Is the Evidence?

The evidence at judicial trials is presented through the testimony of witnesses called by the prosecution and the defense. As a juror, your job is to absorb the information being presented, evaluate its accuracy, and assess the reliability of the individuals giving the testimony. To be an effective critical thinker, you should not simply accept information as it is presented. You need to try to determine the accuracy of the information and evaluate the credibility of the people providing the information. You can use these questions to guide your evaluation:

- Is the information *relevant* to the charges?
- Is the witness *credible?* What *biases* might influence the witness's testimony?
- To what extent is the testimony *accurate?*

As a juror, performing these activities effectively involves using many of the higher-order thinking and language abilities explored in this book, and you need all of them because evaluating testimony is a very challenging task. Let's examine some of the testimony in the Louise Woodward case.

Police Testimony: When the police interviewed Ms. Woodward on the day of the incident, she admitted that she had "lightly shook" Matthew to wake him and that she might have "been a little rough" with him. According to police, she also said that she had "dropped" the baby on the bed and "dropped" him on some towels on the floor. Ms. Woodward later denied having said that she was "rough" with him and also claimed that she had said "popped" not "dropped."

- *Is the information relevant to the charges?* Clearly yes. The information is crucial in determining what role Ms. Woodward played in the child's injuries. Often people will confess or provide the most truthful account initially, and then later — after consulting with a lawyer and thinking about the implication of their statements — will recant or try to modify what they initially said. In some cases police have been accused of coercing confessions, but not in this case.
- *Is the witness credible? What biases might influence the witness's testimony?* In general, police testimony is considered credible, although there are certainly cases in which police lie to protect one another or to make a stronger case against someone they are

convinced is guilty. In the Woodward case, most people assumed they were telling the truth, and there was no apparent motive for them not to.

- *To what extent is the testimony accurate?* By combining the *relevance* of the testimony with the *credibility* of the witnesses, the accuracy of the information provided by the police scores high. However, the *significance* of the information is not as clear. What did Ms. Woodward mean when she described her behavior as a "little rough," that she had "lightly shook" him and "dropped" (or "popped") him onto the bed or the floor? One interpretation is that she was confessing her guilt, but trying to minimize her responsibility, as humans tend to do.

Parents' Testimony: According to Matthew Eappen's parents, Louise Woodward seemed to be doing a satisfactory job, but there were areas of conflict. They wanted Louise to observe a curfew while Louise wanted to be free to come and go at night. Initially, Louise had her way, and she went out almost every evening, often returning after midnight. She attended a production of the musical *Rent* more than twenty times. These late nights made it difficult for her to get out of bed in the morning. On January 30, matters came to a head and the Eappens threatened to fire her if she did not observe an 11:00 curfew. The incident with Matthew happened five days later.

- *Is the information relevant to the charges?* Clearly yes. On the one hand, the parents had not observed any evidence of abuse or neglect of Matthew or his two-year-old brother by Ms. Woodward, and as they were medical doctors, that was significant. On the other hand, Ms. Woodward was clearly unhappy and angry over the restrictions on her social life. She had not been trained as a "nanny," having undergone only a four-day orientation by the au pair agency that placed her. Her immaturity and resentment clearly created a potentially volatile situation. Since Louise was the sole caregiver of Matthew outside of themselves, the Eappens stated they believed that Ms. Woodward *must* be guilty of killing

Matthew. Their suspicions were strengthened by the fact that Ms. Woodward did not call or come to visit Matthew in the hospital before he died, and she never expressed explicit remorse.

- *Is the witness credible? What biases might influence the witness's testimony?* As articulate and caring parents, the Eappens seemed credible, although it would be natural to expect them to be biased against Ms. Woodward. The information regarding the conflict over a curfew was corroborated by the defendant, as was her lack of contact after Matthew was hospitalized.
- *To what extent is the testimony accurate?* Since the conflict over curfew was acknowledged by both parties, we can assume that it's true. The Eappens' belief that Ms. Woodward killed Matthew was flatly denied by her.

Louise Woodward: Ms. Woodward testified that she was absolutely innocent of all charges. "I didn't do anything!" she protested at the trial. Contradicting the police testimony of her initial statements, she contended that she had never admitted being "rough" with Matthew, and claimed that she had told police she had "popped" him on the bed and the floor, not "dropped." Ms. Woodward testified that she loved the two boys and would do nothing to hurt them. However, she was unable to provide an alternative explanation for how Matthew sustained his injuries. According to a friend of Ms. Woodward's, she (Ms. Woodward) had complained that she was not happy, that the Eappens were "demanding," that their children were "spoilt" and that Matthew was a "brat."

- *Is the information relevant to the charges?* Certainly yes. Ms. Woodford's protestation of innocence gets to the heart of the case.
- *Is the witness credible? What biases might influence the witness's testimony?* We would expect the defendant to paint herself in the best possible light, biased in her own favor, and she did.
- *To what extent is the testimony accurate?* Her claims were not directly verifiable. However, it is disturbing that her version of events conflicted in certain respects with that provided by the police and

her friend, and also that she was unable to provide any other explanation for Matthew's injuries.

Medical Experts: The only witness to Ms. Woodward's behavior was Matthew's two-year-old brother, Brandon, who did not express any indication that Ms. Woodward had injured his brother. In the absence of any other witnesses, the medical testimony became the fulcrum upon which the case turned. The medical witnesses for the prosecution, pediatricians who were experts in the field of child abuse, were certain in their diagnosis: This was a classic case of "shaken baby syndrome," the result of a violent shaking and slamming of a young child, which is believed to cause about three hundred deaths and hundreds more injuries each year among children under the age of two.

The defense presented medical testimony from several doctors who testified that the age of blood clots found in Matthew's brain appeared to be about three weeks old; that in postmortem photographs, the baby's skull fracture appeared to be knitting together, indicating it, too, was old; that the baby had no neck injuries or obvious bruising when he was taken into the hospital; and that a brain scan showed no swelling at the site of the skull fracture, meaning his head could not have been recently slammed against a hard surface. In essence, the defense claimed that a relatively mild impact on February 4 could have reaggravated an old injury and led to the baby's death.

The prosecution witnesses countered that everything known about children's injuries did not conform to such a picture. They testified that Matthew's symptoms — trouble breathing, bleeding in brain and eyes, a fractured skull — are the result of an extremely violent shaking and impact. Further, it was impossible that Matthew could have incurred a severe brain injury three weeks before February 4 and continued to function more or less normally. Matthew also had a broken arm, of which there was no previous indication. The defense contention that a relatively mild shaking caused rebleeding doesn't make sense, because it is not bleeding that kills a shaken baby, but rather the swelling of its brain tissue, which puts pressures on the part of the brain that controls vital functions. Finally, three weeks earlier, Ms. Woodward had *also* been the primary caregiver and so could have been responsible for any old injuries — child abuse is usually repetitive.

- *Is the information relevant to the charges?* Certainly yes. The medical testimony was central to this case.
- *Is the witness credible? What biases might influence the witness's testimony?* Naturally the prosecution and defense use expert witnesses who are sympathetic to their point of view. That's one of the jurors' dilemmas: whom to believe when experts disagree. However, there were some differences between the two sets of experts. The prosecution doctors were experts in the field of child abuse with in-depth and extensive familiarity with "shaken baby" cases like this. The defense doctors were not pediatricians; they had other specialties (one was a pathologist). Following the trial, forty-nine medical experts in child abuse released a letter which said in part: "The prosecution put forward well-established medical evidence that overwhelmingly supported a violent shaking/impact episode on the day in question, when Matthew Eappen was in the sole custody of Ms. Woodward."
- *To what extent is the testimony accurate?* It is up to the jurors to think critically about all of the information and witnesses, and decide what they believe is most accurate. This is a very challenging task, but one that accomplished critical thinkers are well equipped for. Uncritical thinkers, in contrast, are in a nearly hopeless situation.

WHAT ARE THE EXPLANATORY THEORIES?

Facts don't exist in isolation but are always part of a larger framework, and the way we view the facts is influenced by the framework we are using. Did Ms. Woodward become enraged with Matthew Eappen and intentionally shake him so violently and hit his head against a hard surface in order to cause him bodily harm? Or did Ms. Woodward, frustrated by her inability to quiet the crying child and angry with her situation, inadvertently cause his injuries by shaking him and perhaps accidentally striking his head against the wall or floor? Or was there another explanation? The defense tried, unsuccessfully, to prove that Matthew suffered from a genetic disorder that would have explained his injuries, and also suggested at one point that a "boisterous" Brandon, the two-year-old brother, might have caused the damage. Ultimately, the defense could not provide a viable alternative theory.

As a juror, the theory that you decide on will dramatically influence how you view the evidence as well as Ms. Woodford's ultimate guilt or innocence. This is the way people — and jurors — typically reason, but there are pitfalls to this approach. In an article by Daniel Goleman (author of the book *Emotional Intelligence*) entitled "Jurors Hear Evidence and Turn It into Stories," he cites research that explores the stories that jurors tell themselves to understand the mounds of disconnected evidence, often presented in a confusing order. The research suggests that jurors' unspoken assumptions about human nature play a powerful role in their verdicts. "People don't listen to all the evidence and then weigh it at the end," said Dr. Nancy Pennington, a psychologist at the University of Colorado. "They process it as they go along, composing a continuing story throughout the trial that makes sense of what they're hearing."

The danger is, naturally, that once people decide on the "story" to believe, this will influence how they interpret the evidence. They will tend to focus on evidence that supports their story and discount evidence that contradicts it. And people's backgrounds influence the stories that they are likely to tell, which accounts for the rapid development of the science of jury selection, an initiative designed to help identify the types of jurors who will be most inclined to agree with the "story" you are advocating, be it prosecution or defense.

WHAT ARE THE ARGUMENTS?

After the various witnesses present their testimony through examination and cross-examination, the prosecution and defense then present their final arguments and summation. The purpose of this phase of the trial is to tie together — or raise doubts about — the evidence that has been presented in order to persuade the jury that the defendant is guilty or innocent. Both the prosecution and the defense are attempting to persuade the jurors (and the public, in high-profile cases), that their "story" is the one to believe. In the Eappen case, the defense maintained that Ms. Woodward was an innocent victim, wrongly accused, or at the very least, that there was "reasonable doubt" as to her guilt. The prosecution, on the other hand, argued that Woodward was "an aspiring little actress" who had told "half-truths and half-lies" on the stand. Her real purpose in coming to the United States was not to take care of children, but to get a "visa to party," a party that had gone horribly wrong.

WHAT IS THE VERDICT?

Following the final arguments and summations, the judge will sometimes give specific instructions to clarify the issues to be considered. In this case the judge reminded the jury that they must focus on the boundaries of the law and determine whether this case falls within these boundaries or outside them. The jury then retires to deliberate the case and render a verdict. For a defendant to be found guilty of second-degree murder, the prosecution must prove that he or she intended to kill someone, made a conscious decision to do so at that moment (without premeditation), and was aware of the consequences of his or her actions. The jurors must determine whether the evidence indicates, *beyond a reasonable doubt*, that the defendant's conduct in this case meets these conditions. What does the qualification "beyond a reasonable doubt" mean? A principle like this is always difficult to define in specific terms, but in general the principle means that it would not make good sense for thoughtful men and women to conclude otherwise.

After deliberating for a number of days, the jury found her guilty of *second-degree murder*. In a controversial gamble, the attorneys for Woodward had earlier prevailed upon the judge to prevent the jury from considering the charge of *involuntary manslaughter*, a common charge in a case of this sort. The defense was apparently confident that the jury would reject the second-degree murder charge, and they wanted complete exoneration for their client. They lost the gamble, and interviews with the jurors later determined that they would likely have found her guilty of the lesser charge if they had had that option.

In a stunning reversal two weeks later, the judge in the case, Hiller Zobel, made the highly unusual move of reducing the conviction to involuntary manslaughter, explaining that he did not believe the facts of the case supported the more serious charge. Even more controversially, the judge set the defendant free, sentencing her to the 279 days that she had already served in prison, rather than the customary three to five years for a conviction of this sort. Both the defense and prosecution appealed the judge's ruling, and it was sustained by the state's Supreme Judicial Court in a 4–3 vote.

Although reasoning through this court case is an oversimplified version of what takes place during an actual trial, the underlying thinking principles are exactly the same. When you reason through court cases in the future, whether as a juror or simply in informal discussion with others, be sure to employ these reasoning skills. Other people may get sidetracked with irrelevant issues and illogical arguments, but you will find that when you think clearly about these complicated issues, you will help them think more clearly as well.

Reasoning about the Media

THINK ABOUT how you get your information about the world. If you're like most people, 70 percent of your information comes from television, the remaining 30 percent from newspapers and magazines. People typically accept the information they are receiving at face value, as if it were objective and factual, particularly when it comes from "reputable" sources. Although we caution each other "not to believe everything we hear or read," the fact is that many people read their favorite newspaper and watch their customary television news program without much critical questioning. We rarely stop to consider if the information we are getting is accurate, complete, and unbiased. But as we saw in Step 1:

Think Critically, this information is *never* completely objective and factual. It's always filtered through the lenses of the person or organization presenting it. In every instance, decisions have been made about what to include and what not to include; which elements of the story to emphasize and which to play down; and what interpretations to give to the people involved, their behavior, and the significance of the events.

This shaping and editing of the news is going on all of the time; it's just that we're usually unaware of it. We only experience the finished product, not all of the decisions and intentions that have gone into constructing it. We get lulled into a false sense of security by information sources that appear to be serious, professional, and objective. And in many cases they are: It's just that no individual or organization can ever fully remove the lenses through which they view the world, lenses that influence what they focus attention on and their interpretation of it. These lenses can't be removed like glasses; they are a permanent part of the way each person views the world. However, we do expect that, as professionals, the news providers will try to compensate for their inherent bias. That's why we trust the objectivity of reputable news sources more than sensationalistic tabloids or publications with a stated agenda. However, even in the case of reputable sources, there is an inescapable bias of which we often are not aware.

What can you do in order to achieve a clear and objective understanding of the world? You need to think critically about all of the information you encounter, utilizing all of the thinking abilities and intellectual standards that are included in *The Thinker's Way*, in order to evaluate the accuracy of the information and the credibility of the sources. There is also another very powerful strategy that you can use and which, as a critical thinker, you should always endeavor to apply: *comparative analysis*. In the same way that it's prudent to seek second and third opinions when it comes to medical or legal advice, we should do the same thing with information — seek a second or third perspective. It is by contrasting different perspectives on the same issue or event that people's lenses are made visible, like brushing powder on a surface to reveal previously unseen fingerprints. These mental fingerprints are always present, we just don't normally see them because we're not dusting for them.

Let's analyze an example. Consider the following accounts of a dramatic event in history: the assassination of Malcolm X. It's a provocative example of what happens all of the time regarding media reporting. The first account is taken from the *New York Times*, the second from *Life* magazine.

> Malcolm X, the 39-year-old leader of a militant Black Nationalist movement, was shot to death yesterday afternoon at a rally of his followers in a ballroom in Washington Heights. The bearded Negro extremist had said only a few words of greeting when a fusillade rang out. The bullets knocked him over backwards.
>
> A 22-year-old Negro, Thomas Hagan, was charged with the killing. The police rescued him from the ballroom crowd after he had been shot and beaten.
>
> Pandemonium broke out among the 400 Negroes in the Audubon Ballroom at 160th Street and Broadway. As men, women and children ducked under tables and flattened themselves on the floor, more shots were fired. The police said seven bullets struck Malcolm. Three other Negroes were shot. Witnesses reported that as many as 30 shots had been fired. About two hours later the police said the shooting had apparently been a result of a feud between followers of Malcolm and members of the extremist group he broke with last year, the Black Muslims.
>
> —NEW YORK TIMES, February 22, 1965

> His life oozing out through a half dozen or more gunshot wounds in his chest, Malcolm X, once the shrillest voice of black supremacy, lay dying on the stage of a Manhattan auditorium. Moments before, he had stepped up to the lectern and

400 of the faithful had settled down expectantly to hear the sort of speech for which he was famous — flaying the hated white man. Then a scuffle broke out in the hall and Malcolm's bodyguards bolted from his side to break it up — only to discover that they had been faked out. At least two men with pistols rose from the audience and pumped bullets into the speaker, while a third cut loose at close range with both barrels of a sawed-off shotgun. In the confusion the pistol man got away. The shotgunner lunged through the crowd and out the door, but not before the guards came to their wits and shot him in the leg. Outside he was swiftly overtaken by other supporters of Malcolm and very likely would have been stomped to death if the police hadn't saved him. Most shocking of all to the residents of Harlem was the fact that Malcolm had been killed not by "whitey" but by members of his own race.

— LIFE MAGAZINE, March 5, 1965

In reading accounts like this, which present similar perspectives, you would have no reason to doubt that you were being presented with accurate, objective descriptions of what actually occurred. Here are some of the key points:

- Malcolm X is a violent and dangerous racist hate-monger. He is a "bearded Negro extremist," the "leader of a militant Black Nationalist movement," "the shrillest voice of black supremacy" who was about to deliver a speech "flaying the hated white man."
- His followers are a violent, uncritical mob and his bodyguards are not too bright. The 400 "faithful" have come to hear his hate-filled speech; the police have to "rescue" and "save" the assassins from a savage beating; the shooting is the result of a feud between them and another "extremist group." His bodyguards are "faked out," have to "come to their wits," and several of the assassins escape.

- Importance of the assassination: Malcolm X was not an important figure. In both accounts he is described only minimally.
- Racist bias: "Negroes" was a socially acceptable term in 1965: an advance over "colored." What is unusual about the *New York Times* account is that every time the people are referred to, they are labeled as "Negroes." If you substitute "whites" or "Caucasians" for "Negroes," this overuse of the ethnic label becomes even more apparent. The final sentence of the second account is also racially charged: "Most shocking of all to the residents of Harlem was the fact that Malcolm had been killed not by 'whitey' but by members of his own race." Do all of the residents of Harlem think alike? How does the author know what the residents think? Is the use of the term "whitey" sarcastic?

The audience is portrayed as "faithful" followers expectantly anticipating a racist speech. However, at this stage of Malcolm X's career, he was *not* delivering these types of speeches: his trip to Mecca had been transformational, causing him to see racial problems as issues of good and evil, not black and white. This general portrait of the audience as violent (the police have to "rescue" and "save" the assassins), racist, slow-witted people is very unflattering and plays into traditional stereotypes.

But now consider the following account of the same event from the *New York Post* that presents a somewhat different perspective.

> They came early to the Audubon Ballroom, perhaps drawn by the expectation that Malcolm X would name the men who firebombed his home last Sunday. I sat at the left in the 12th row and, as we waited, the man next to me spoke of Malcolm and his followers: "Malcolm is our only hope. You can depend on him to tell it like it is." There was a prolonged ovation as Malcolm walked to the rostrum. Malcolm looked up and said "A salaam aleikum (Peace be unto you)" and the audience replied "You aleikum salaam (And unto you, peace)."

Bespectacled and dapper in a dark suit, sandy hair glinting in the light, Malcolm said: "Brothers and sisters . . ." He was interrupted by two men in the center of the ballroom, who rose and, arguing with each other, moved forward. Then there was a scuffle at the back of the room. I heard Malcolm X say his last words: "Now, brothers, break it up," he said softly. "Be cool, be calm."

Then all hell broke loose. There was a muffled sound of shots and Malcolm, blood on his face and chest, fell limply back over the chairs behind him. The two men who had approached him ran to the exit on my side of the room, shooting wildly behind them as they ran. I heard people screaming, "Don't let them kill him." At an exit I saw some of Malcolm's men beating with all their strength on two men. I saw a half dozen of Malcolm's followers bending over his inert body on the stage, their clothes stained with their leader's blood. Four policemen took the stretcher and carried Malcolm through the crowd and some of the women came out of their shock and one said: "I hope he doesn't die, but I don't think he's going to make it."

— NEW YORK POST, February 22, 1965

Let's contrast this perspective with the first two.

- Malcolm X is a man of peace and a revered leader. He is "bespectacled and dapper in a dark suit," greets his followers in peace, and moves without hesitation to calm the staged disturbance in the audience. He is an inspiration to many people and can be depended on to tell the truth.
- His followers are a peaceful, devoted group of caring individuals, devastated by his shooting.
- Importance of assassination: Malcolm X's assassination was a significant event; he is the subject of the entire account, and the

words and actions of his followers suggest his considerable stature in the community.

• Racial bias: There is no reference to race in this account.

Which account is telling the "truth?" Was Malcolm X a violent racist or a man of peace? Were his followers a savage mob or a respectful group of citizens? Was the assassination an incidental event or did it have real significance? To what extent did this event involve racial issues? As readers, we have a shared responsibility to determine the truth. We can't sit back and expect the media to deliver it to us. We need actively to seek knowledge by analyzing various accounts, becoming aware of our own biases, by thinking critically.

Which account is telling the "truth"? None of them, of course. Each author viewed the event through his or her own lenses, which shaped and influenced the information selected, the interpretations of the individuals involved, and the language used to describe it. Some of this shaping may have been intentional, reflecting the beliefs of the author or the philosophy of the publication. Other influences may have been unintentional, the product of learning or unconscious motivations. Despite the differences in these accounts, we know that an actual sequence of events occurred on that February day in 1965. The challenge for us is to try to figure out what actually happened by investigating different accounts, evaluating the reliability of the accounts, and putting together a coherent picture of what took place. This is the process of achieving knowledge and truth that occurs in every area of human inquiry — a process of exploration, critical analysis, and evolving understanding.

THINKING ACTIVITY

Thinking Critically about Information

Locate three or more different newspaper or magazine accounts of an important event — court decisions, crimes, political events, and sports events are possibilities. Think critically about each of the accounts by analyzing the "lenses" of each of the writers. Use these guidelines for your *comparative analysis:*

- Compare the details of the events each writer has *selected* to focus on and which they chose to leave out.
- Compare the way each writer *organizes* the details that they selected. Remember that most newspaper writers present what they consider the most important information first and the least important information last.
- Compare how each writer *interprets* the people involved and the event itself.
- Compare the way each writer uses *language* to express his/her perspective and to influence the thinking of the reader.

How Well Do I Analyze Complex Issues?

DESCRIBED BELOW are key thinking abilities and personal attributes that are correlated with analyzing complex issues. Evaluate your position regarding each of these abilities and attributes, and use this self-evaluation to guide your efforts to become a more effective reasoner.

Make Analytic Reasoning a Priority

I analyze complex issues in a thoughtful, well-reasoned way.	I usually make quick decisions on issues without careful analysis.

5   4   3   2   1

Becoming a sophisticated reasoner means developing certain habits of mind that you use on a daily basis. As a critical thinker, you need to resist the trend toward thoughtlessness, analyzing issues carefully and encouraging others to do the same.

Strategy: *Beginning today, make a special effort to analyze issues thoughtfully before reaching a conclusion. Avoid making quick decisions based on incomplete information. Instead, ask questions, think carefully, and develop well-supported conclusions. Encourage others to become more thoughtful by asking them why they think what they do and helping them to clarify their analyses.*

Construct Sound Arguments

I am skilled at constructing valid arguments with true reasons and logical conclusions.	I usually don't take time to use logical arguments to organize and support my thinking.

5   4   3   2   1

Constructing sound arguments is the heart of the reasoning process — that's why so many people are poor reasoners. By developing your skills at constructing and evaluating arguments, you will gain a powerful reasoning tool that you can use in every area of your life.

Strategy: *Develop the habit of analyzing the key arguments in articles that you read, information from television, and conversations with others. Use your Thinking Notebook to first outline the arguments: What are the reasons? What is the conclusion? Then evaluate the soundness of the argument. Are the reasons true? Is the reasoning valid? Is the conclusion supported by the premises? This may seem time-consuming at first, but it is an invaluable activity, and before long you will find yourself arguing in a much more accomplished fashion.*

Use the Thinker's Way to Analyze Complex Issues

I use a systematic approach to analyze complex issues.	My approach to analyzing complex issues is more disorganized than I'd like.

5   4   3   2   1

The Thinker's Way to Analyze Complex Issues provides you with a versatile and flexible approach for analyzing any complex issue, a skill that most people sorely need. By defining the issue clearly; examining different points of view; evaluating the arguments; assessing the consequences; and reaching an informed conclusion, you will impress both yourself and others with your insightful understanding.

Strategy: Select an article from a newspaper or magazine each day and use The Thinker's Way to Analyze Complex Issues to explore it, recording your results in your Thinking Notebook. Then bring the issue up in a conversation, using your written analysis to guide your discussion. You will immediately begin to notice significant improvement in your ability to discuss these issues with insight and understanding.

Think Critically about Opinion Surveys and Polls

I have a sophisticated understanding of surveys and opinion polls.

I rarely think critically about surveys and opinion polls.

5   4   3   2   1

People in our society are being besieged with surveys and polls on every imaginable topic. Yet the overwhelming majority of these polls and surveys are unscientific and unreliable: The questions are phrased ambiguously, the sample is usually biased, and the results are consistently misinterpreted. To be an informed citizen in today's world, it is essential to be able to evaluate critically the design and validity of these new cultural icons.

Strategy: Make a point of applying the knowledge and skills from this chapter to the surveys and opinion polls that you encounter. Determine whether the sample is known, sufficient, and representative. Also evaluate whether the questions are constructed in a way that is likely to lead to intelligent results, or whether the findings are destined to be oversimplified and misleading.

Think Critically about Scientific Studies

I have a sophisticated understanding of scientific studies.

I rarely think critically about the scientific studies I read and hear about.

5   4   3   2   1

Another influential form of cultural thinking is the "scientific studies" that are reported to us regularly with both disturbing and promising information affecting our lives. Many of the conclusions, if true, have direct implications for our lives.

Strategy: *Seek out the details of scientific studies that are reported in newspapers and magazines and critically evaluate them using the skills and knowledge you developed in this chapter. Since the results reported on television and in some newspapers are virtually useless because they are so brief, find more detailed descriptions in other publications including, if you have a special interest in the topic, the original scientific journal in which the study was published.*

Think Critically about Court Cases

I thoughtfully examine the important evidence in a court case before coming to a conclusion.	I often offer definitive opinions about court cases based on limited information.

5   4   3   2   1

Court cases are not only integral parts of the criminal justice system, they are also popular vehicles for people to discuss and think about important social and moral issues. Yet many people express uncritical opinions colored by their personal biases, lacking a thorough understanding of the evidence, and displaying illogical reasoning.

Strategy: *Make a special effort to apply your critical thinking abilities to the court cases that are currently in the news. Read a variety of accounts regarding the court proceedings in order to provide yourself with an adequate base of information, and then use the approach described in this chapter to compensate for your biases, evaluate the testimony, and reach informed, well-supported conclusions.*

Think Critically about Information

I think critically about media information by comparing different sources and asking analytical questions.	I usually depend on a limited number of sources for my information and rarely ask probing questions.

5   4   3   2   1

The glut of information that we are subjected to serves to discourage us from thinking critically about the truth and value of this information. But this is the only way we can transform this *information* into *knowledge* that can be used and applied in our lives. Rather than blame the media for their bias and manipulation, we should instead take responsibility for analyzing various perspectives and coming to our own informed conclusions.

Strategy: *When possible, develop the habit of comparing different sources: reading several news accounts and viewing various news shows. This comparative analysis is a powerful strategy for disclosing the inherent and inescapable bias of every presentation of information, no matter how reputable the source.*

SCORING GUIDE

Add up the numbers you circled for each of the self-evaluation items above and use the following Scoring Guide to evaluate your ability to reason analytically.

Point Total	Interpretation
28–35	very effective reasoner
21–27	moderately effective reasoner
14–26	somewhat effective reasoner
7–13	comparatively ineffective reasoner

In interpreting your results, be sure to keep in mind that:

- This evaluation is not an exact measure of your ability to reason analytically, but is rather intended as a general indicator of how analytically you approach your life.
- Your score indicates how analytically you are functioning at the present time, *not* your reasoning *potential*. If you scored lower than you would like, it means that you are underutilizing your reasoning abilities, and that you need to follow the suggestions in the chapter to fully realize your talents.

THINKING ACTIVITY

Becoming an Analytic Reasoner

Select areas of your life in which you would like to improve your abilities as an analytic reasoner. Keep a record in your Thinking Notebook detailing your efforts and their results. Be sure to allow yourself sufficient time to develop these complex abilities and attitudes, and don't get frustrated if you don't succeed at once or if you suffer setbacks. Cultivate the qualities of effective reasoning that we have explored in this chapter:

- Make analytic reasoning a priority.
- Construct sound arguments.
- Use The Thinker's Way to Analyze Complex Issues.
- Think critically about opinion surveys and polls.
- Think critically about scientific studies.
- Think critically about court cases.

STEP 7

DEVELOP ENLIGHTENED
VALUES

We live in a time of moral rootlessness in which idealism has given way to cynicism, altruism to self-interest, and charity to greed. This chapter will enable you to construct a clear and coherent system of values that will serve as a reliable moral compass. You will be able to approach moral dilemmas with penetrating insight and confident resolve. Becoming a morally enlightened person — a person of character, compassion, and integrity — is a hard-won accomplishment that can be achieved only through clarity of vision and determined commitment. Morally mature people live lives of purpose and principle, contributing to the happiness of others and receiving rich fulfillment in return.

"We Are Discussing No Small Matter, But How We Ought to Live."

WE ARE A SOCIETY that is morally adrift, lacking a clear system of values to guide our choices and provide an intelligible direction for our endeavors. Having abandoned traditional moral codes as being out-dated and irrelevant, we have entered a vast, chartless domain, and there is an increasing sense that we have lost our way. The evidence of this moral breakdown is impossible to miss:

- Movies, music lyrics, and television shows have become so sexually explicit, so violent, so "adult" that we are effectively robbing children of their childhoods, a protected time when they can mature into adulthood thoughtfully and progressively.
- We are so accustomed to public figures lying, dissembling, and "spinning" the truth that they have lost credibility. Rather than role models, politicians are often held in the lowest possible regard by a cynical public.
- Personal responsibility has vanished, as people blame everyone but themselves for their misfortunes, and everyone seeks to cash in on the legal lottery system by suing others for events caused by their own choices, their neglect, and their thoughtlessness.
- "Moral statistics" like crime and illegitimacy have soared to astronomical levels, particularly among the young. And in a bizarre twist, these social pathologies have been morally "neutralized" through the power of language: illegitimacy is "nonmarital child-bearing"; violent behavior is the "acting out" of uncontrollable impulses; drug addicts and alcoholics have been classified as "disabled" in order to be eligible for Social Security benefits.
- Deviant behavior has been "normalized" through the repeated and nonjudgmental exposure to aberrant people on daily talk shows. This has had the cumulative effect of numbing our sense of right and wrong. "Rather than being mortified, ashamed or trying to hide their stigma, guests willingly and eagerly discuss their child-molesting, sexual quirks and criminal records in an effort to seek 'understanding' for their particular disease" (*The Journal of Popular Culture*, Drs. Vicki Abt and Mel Seesholtz).
- To stem the tide of amorality and immorality, efforts are made to "teach values" and "sensitivity-train" people in schools and organizations. The U.S. Army announced plans recently to add a week of basic training devoted to values and morals, in a belated effort

to counteract the sexual harassment and abuse that has become endemic to the armed forces.

- There are startling crimes committed by children from "good" backgrounds: A young teenage couple, attending their first year of college, kill their newborn infant and place him in a Dumpster; a popular high school senior gives birth in a bathroom during her senior prom, strangles and disposes of the infant in the bathroom, and then returns to dance the night away.

- Women have increasingly become the targets of stalkings, assaults, and murder by disgruntled husbands, rejected boyfriends, as well as total strangers. Date rape has become a prevalent menace on college campuses.

- The Internet, that much-touted "information superhighway," has proved to be a potent vehicle for magnifying moral deficiencies. The infection of child pornography has spread alarmingly throughout the net, permitting convicted sex offenders to contact, track down, and meet with young children. People have been lured from the false security of chat rooms and the illusion of "cyber-relationships" to face-to-face meetings, with sometimes catastrophic results.

- In a recent survey of college freshmen, 80 percent chose being well off as an essential goal and 40 percent chose developing a philosophy of life. These results are nearly the exact reverse of a similar poll in 1968, when 40 percent of freshmen selected financial security and 82 percent cited the importance of developing a philosophy of life.

This is just a sampling of the pervasive moral rootlessness that is threatening to unravel the social fabric. Even among people striving energetically to be "good" and do the "right" thing, these social forces have shaped and invaded their moral awareness, creating a moral insecurity that is deep and profound. The philosopher Thomas I. White reviews this dismal moral devolution in *Right and Wrong*:

Somewhere over the last quarter century, America lost its "moral rudder." We have gone from a nation committed to moral idealism to being reluctant spectators of one scandal after another. We have seen so much wrong-doing in government, business, education, and even religion, that unethical behavior has simply become "business as usual" in some quarters of the society. And what's the most telling sign of how bad it's become? We aren't even shocked anymore. Idealism has given way to cynicism, altruism to self-interest, charity to greed, and kindness to meanness. Otherwise intelligent, capable, and responsible people have been either morally blind or totally contemptuous of the fact that what they're doing is wrong.

If you recreate in your mind what the world was like when you were growing up and compare this memory with the world of today, you are likely to find yourself agreeing with at least some of this author's conclusions. To many observers there *does* seem to have been a steady decline of moral behavior and moral expectations. Not that the world of ten, twenty, thirty, or even forty years ago was perfect; it wasn't. In fact, there has certainly been moral advancement in areas like civil rights, women's rights, and creating a social safety net with programs like Medicare and Medicaid over the last several decades. But the general moral conscience of people seems to have eroded, replaced with a self-serving cynicism. People simply don't talk or think in moral terms very much these days. We seem almost embarrassed to announce clearly and unequivocally that we believe something (or someone) is immoral, unethical, or just plain wrong. The prevailing social climate encourages people to "respect" ethical aberrations, "understand" moral deviance, and resist condemning the morally reprehensible behavior or attitudes for fear of "imposing" our values on others.

Morality is intensely personal. William Bennett, in his influential work *The Book of Virtues*, communicates the centrality of morality in human experience through the use of traditional stories and poems in which the characters illustrate moral virtues through their thinking and actions. He states:

> Most of the material in this book speaks without hesitation, without embarrassment, to the inner part of the individual, to the moral sense. Today we speak about values and how important it is to "have them" as if they were beads on a string or marbles in a pouch. But these stories speak to morality and virtues not as something to be possessed, but as the central part of human nature, not as something to have but as something to be, the most important thing to be. . . . It is thus a kind of antidote to some of the distortions of the age in which we live.

It is not too late to change direction and begin pursuing the best of our potentials instead of the worst of our fears, to become moral individuals of the highest order. Each person needs to create, both individually and collectively, a clear, confident moral framework. This thoughtfully constructed moral value system will enable you to combat the moral rootlessness you may be experiencing and to eradicate the distressing feeling of continually shifting ground beneath your feet. Such a framework will serve as a reliable moral compass. You will be able to approach moral dilemmas with penetrating insight and confident resolve, instead of having to start from scratch every time you encounter a perplexing moral decision. Though you may feel that constructing such a moral framework is beyond your capabilities, it most assuredly is not. Great thinkers have been working on these problems for several thousand years, and you can reap the fruits of their labors. The critical thinking abilities that you have been developing in this book are the conceptual tools you need to construct your own philosophy of morals that will serve to integrate the fragments of your life and act as a guiding light for the future.

What Is "Ethics"?

THE STUDY of ethics is derived from the ancient Greek word *ethos*, which refers to moral purpose or "character" — as in "a person of upstanding character." *Ethics* and *morals* are terms that refer to the principles that govern our relationships with other people: the ways we *ought* to behave, the rules and standards that we *should* employ in the choices we make. The ethical and moral concepts that we use to evaluate these behaviors include "right" and "wrong," "good" and "bad," "just" and "unjust," "fair" and "unfair," "responsible" and "irresponsible."

Ethical and *moral* are essentially equivalent terms that can be used interchangeably, though there may be shadings in meaning that influence which term is used. For example, we generally speak about medical or business "ethics" rather than "morality," though there is no significant difference in meaning. *Value* is the general term we use to characterize anything that possesses intrinsic worth, that we prize, esteem, and regard highly, based on clearly defined standards. Thus you may *value* your devoted pet, your favorite jacket, and a cherished friendship, each based on different standards that establish and define their worth to you. One of the most important value domains includes your *moral* or *ethical values*, those personal qualities and rules of conduct that distinguish a person (and group of people) of upstanding character. Philosophers have traditionally distinguished two different types of ethical or moral judgments that we will identify as the *Ethic of Care* and the *Ethic of Justice*.

The *Ethic of Care* involves judgments of *moral value*, those actions or qualities that display moral "goodness" or "evil." Who is a "good person" and what is a "good action"? What can we do to promote the happiness and well-being of others?

The *Ethic of Justice* involves judgments of *moral obligation*, those actions which are morally "right" or "wrong." What moral obligations do we have toward other people? When should we be held morally responsible? How do we determine which choice in a moral situation is "right" or "wrong," "just" or "unjust"?

Although we can distinguish between the Ethic of Care and the Ethic of Justice theoretically — and as we will see, it is a useful distinction — in the practical arena of daily living these two approaches to ethical thinking work together in a partnership. For example, we expect a morally "good" person to make the "right" choice when they are confronted with an ethical dilemma, and to have a clear vision of "justice" and "injustice."

Who is a moral person? In the same way that you were able to define the key qualities of a "critical thinker," you can describe the essential qualities of a "moral person."

THINKING ACTIVITY

Who Is a Moral Person?

Think of someone you know whom you consider to be a person of outstanding moral character. This person doesn't have to be perfect — he or she doubtless has flaws. Nevertheless, this is a person you admire, whom you would like to emulate. After fixing this person in your mind, write down in your Thinking Notebook the qualities that this person displays that, in your mind, qualifies him or her as a morally upright individual. For each quality, try to think of an example of when the person displayed it. For example:

Moral courage: *Charles is a person in my company who always takes the action he believes is morally "right," even though his point of view may be unpopular with many of the people present. Though he has endured criticism, he never flinches or backs down, but instead defends his point of view with compelling reasons and stirring passion.*

If you have the opportunity, ask some people you know to describe their idea of a "moral person," and compare their responses to your own.

For more than twenty-five hundred years, philosophers and religious thinkers have endeavored to develop ethical systems we can use to guide our conduct. But most people in our culture today have not been exposed to their teachings in depth. They have not challenged themselves to think deeply about ethical concepts, nor have they been guided to develop coherent, well-grounded ethical systems of their own. In many cases people attempt to navigate their passage through these turbulent and treacherous waters without accurate maps, relying on a tangled mélange of childhood teachings, popular wisdom, and unreliable intuitions. These home-grown and unreflective ethical systems are simply not up to the task of sorting out the moral complexities in our bewildering and fast-paced world, contributing to the moral crisis described in the following passage by M. Scott Peck:

> A century ago, the greatest dangers we faced arose from agents outside ourselves: microbes, flood and famine, wolves in the forest at night. Today the greatest dangers — war, pollution, starvation — have their source in our own motives and sentiments: greed and hostility, carelessness and arrogance, narcissism and nationalism. The study of values might once have been a matter of primarily individual concern and deliberation as to how best to lead the "good life." Today it is a matter of collective human survival. If we identify the study of values as a branch of philosophy, then the time has arrived for all women and men to become philosophers — or else.

How does one become a "philosopher of values"? By thinking deeply and clearly about these profound moral issues; profiting from the efforts of great thinkers through the ages who have wrestled with these timeless questions; discussing these concepts with others in a disciplined and open-minded way; constructing a coherent ethical approach that is grounded on the bedrock of sound reasons and commitment to the truth. In other words, you become a philosopher of values by expanding your role as a critical thinker and extending your sophisticated thinking abilities to the domain of moral experience.

This may be your most important personal quest. Your values constitute the core of who you are. If you are to live a life of purpose and meaning, rich in quality and satisfying in fulfillment, it is essential that you develop a vital and enlightened code of ethics to guide you. Your moral "health" is at least as important as your intellectual and physical health, and certainly more essential than many of the activities in which you now regularly engage. Becoming a truly moral individual should be your paramount goal in life, a compelling insight expressed by the following biblical question still relevant today: *"For what does it profit a man to gain the whole world, but lose his own soul?"*

THINKING ACTIVITY

Your Moral Values

You have many values — the guiding principles that you consider to be most important — that you have acquired over the course of your life. Your values deal with every aspect of your experience. The following questions are designed to elicit some of your values. Think carefully about each of the questions, and if time permits, record your responses in your Thinking Notebook along with the reasons you have adopted that value. For example:

I don't think that spanking should be used to discipline children because I don't believe that it's beneficial to hit other people. I think it sends the message that complex problems can be solved through physical aggression. Instead, I believe in the power of reason to help people gain insight into their problems, develop productive attitudes, and make informed choices.

After you have completed this activity, examine your responses as a whole. Do they express a general, coherent, well-supported value system, or do they seem more like an unrelated collection of beliefs of varying degrees of clarity? This activity is a valuable investment of your time because you are creating a record of beliefs that you can return to and refine as you deepen your understanding of moral values.

- Should children be spanked as a form of discipline?
- Is it wrong to divulge a secret someone has confided in you?
- Should we eat animal meat? Should we wear their skins on our body?
- Is it all right to tell a "white lie" in order to spare someone's feelings?

- Is it wrong to kill someone in self-defense?
- Should people be given equal opportunities, regardless of race, religion, or gender?
- Is it wrong to ridicule someone even if you believe it's in "good fun"?
- Should you "bend the rules" if it's the only way you can advance your career?
- Is it all right to manipulate people into doing what you want, if you believe it's for their own good?
- Is there anything wrong with pornographic magazines and XXX-rated movies?
- Should we always try to take other people's needs into consideration when we act, or should we first make sure that our own needs are taken care of?
- Should parents be held responsible for the misdeeds of their children?

What Are Your Moral Values?

DEVELOPING AN intelligent moral code that will be your general framework and practical guide is an ambitious project that is best begun with an inventory of your current moral values. The purpose of this informal self-evaluation is to illuminate your current moral code and initiate the process of critical reflection. Which of your moral values are clearly articulated and well-grounded? Which are ill-defined and tenuously rooted? Do your values form a coherent whole, consistent with one another, or do you detect fragmentation and inconsistency? Obviously, constructing a well-reasoned and clearly defined moral code is a challenging journey, but by following the signposts provided in this chapter you will find yourself making significant and rapid progress.

Your responses to these questions reveal values that you currently have. Where did these values come from? Parents, teachers, religious leaders, and other authority figures have sought to inculcate values in your thinking, but friends, acquaintances, and colleagues do as well. And in many cases they have undoubtedly been successful. While much of your value education was likely the result of thoughtful teaching and serious discussions, in many other instances people bullied, bribed, threatened, and manipulated you into accepting their way of thinking. It's no wonder that our value systems typically evolve into a confusing patchwork of conflicting beliefs.

In examining your values you probably also discovered that while you had a great deal of confidence in some of them ("I feel very strongly that animals should never be experimented on in ways that cause them pain because they are sentient creatures just like ourselves"), you felt less secure about other values ("I feel it's usually wrong to manipulate people, although I often try to influence their attitudes and behavior — I'm not sure of the difference"). These differences in confidence are likely related to how carefully you have examined and analyzed your values. For example, you may have been brought up in a family or religion with firmly fixed values that you have adopted but never really scrutinized or evaluated, wearing these values like a borrowed overcoat. When questioned, you might be at a loss to explain exactly *why* you believe what you do, other than "This is what I was taught." In contrast, you may have other values that are clearly etched and deeply rooted, the product of thoughtful reflection and the crucible of experience. For example, doing volunteer work with a disadvantaged group of people may have led to the conviction that "I believe we have a profound obligation to contribute to the welfare of people less fortunate than ourselves."

In short, most people's values are not "systems" at all: They are typically a collection of *general principles* ("Do unto others . . ."), *practical conclusions* ("Stealing is wrong because you might get caught"), and *emotional pronouncements* ("Interracial marriages are wrong because they seem unnatural"). This hodgepodge of values reflects the unsystematic and serendipitous way they were acquired over the course of your life, and these values comprise your current "moral compass" that you use to guide your decisions in moral situations, even though you may not be consciously aware of it. Your challenge is to create a more refined and accurate compass, an enlightened system of values that you can use to guide your moral decisions with confidence.

Let's begin by providing an opportunity for you to discover more about your own moral compass. Think carefully about how you would respond to the following moral dilemmas and in your Thinking Notebook describe the reasoning that led you to your conclusion. Finally, identify the moral value(s) upon which your decision is based.

1. *The Lifeboat:* In 1842 a ship struck an iceberg and sank. There were thirty survivors, crowded into a lifeboat designed to hold just seven. With the weather stormy and getting worse, it was obvious that many of the passengers would have to be thrown overboard or the boat would sink and everyone would drown. Imagine that you were the captain of the boat. Would you have people thrown over the side? If so, on what basis would you decide who would go? Age? Health? Strength? Gender? Size? Survival skills? Friendships? Family?

2. *The Whistle Blower:* Imagine that you are employed by a large corporation that manufactures baby formula. You suspect that a flaw in the manufacturing process results in contamination of the formula in a small number of cases, and that this contamination can result in serious illness and even death. You have been told by your supervisor that "everything is under control," and you have been warned that if you "blow the whistle" by going public, you will be putting the entire company in jeopardy from multimillion-dollar lawsuits. You will naturally be fired and blackballed in the industry, and as the sole provider in your household, your family is depending on you. What do you do?

3. *The Patient:* As a clinical psychologist, you are committed to protecting the privacy of your patients. One afternoon a patient tells you that her husband, a person who has been abusing her physically and mentally for years, has threatened to kill her, and she believes him. You try to convince her to leave him and seek professional help, but she tells you that she has decided to kill him.

She is certain that he will find her wherever she goes, and feels that she will be safe only when he is dead. What do you do?

4. *The Friend:* As the director of your department, you are in charge of filling an important vacancy. Many people have applied, including your best friend, who has been out of work for over a year and needs a job desperately. Although your friend would likely perform satisfactorily, there are several more experienced and talented candidates who would undoubtedly perform better. You have always prided yourself in hiring the best people, and you have earned a reputation as someone with high standards who will not compromise your striving for excellence. Whom do you hire?

As you think your way through these moral dilemmas, you will probably find yourself appealing to basic moral principles that you typically use to guide your actions. Of course, what makes these examples *moral* dilemmas is the fact that they involve a *conflict* of traditional moral principles.

The Lifeboat involves a conflict between these moral beliefs:
- It is wrong to take any innocent life.
- It is right to save *some* lives rather than threaten *all* the lives on board.

The Whistle Blower involves a conflict between these moral beliefs:
- It is wrong to knowingly jeopardize the health of children.
- It is right to protect the welfare of your family and your career.

The Patient involves a conflict between these moral beliefs:
- It is wrong to violate the confidentiality of a professional relationship.
- It is right to prevent someone from committing murder.

The Friend involves a conflict between these moral beliefs:
- It is wrong to hire someone who is not the best qualified candidate for the job.
- It is right to try to help and support your friends.

What makes each of these examples *dilemmas* is that both of the moral principles that you are appealing to seem ethically sound and appropriate; the problem is that they contradict each other. What should you do when this happens? How do you decide which principle is more "right"? There is no simple answer to this question, any more than there is to the question "What do you do when experts disagree?" In both cases, you need to think critically in order to arrive at intelligent and informed conclusions.

Naturally the moral dilemmas described above are specifically designed to provoke intense angst and vigorous debate, but the situations nevertheless contain elements found in our everyday moral deliberations. For example, though you are unlikely to find yourself in a similar *Lifeboat* situation, you might be faced with the decision of which employees to fire in order to keep your company afloat. And though the *Whistle Blowing* example may seem extreme, the fact is that employees working for companies that manufacture baby formula, contraceptives such as the Dalken Shield, and tobacco products have often found themselves in precisely this moral dilemma. You yourself have likely been in a job situation where telling the truth or objecting to an unethical practice would jeopardize your position or opportunity for advancement. Many therapists, clergy, lawyers, and doctors wrestle daily with issues of confidentiality, analogous to that described in *The Patient*, and we all have to deal with the question of under what circumstances is it morally appropriate to break our promises to avoid a greater evil or achieve a greater good. It requires little imagination to identify the issues of *The Friend*. There are countless instances in which we are forced to balance our feelings of personal obligation with our objective or professional analysis.

In addition to these kinds of ethical situations, you will also undoubtedly confront other types of moral dilemmas that are at least as problematic. It is probable that at some point in your life you will have to make a "right to die" decision regarding a loved one nearing the end of his or her life. You might also find yourself in a situation in which you are torn between ending a difficult marriage or remaining as a full-time parent of young children. Or you might be tempted to take advantage of an investment opportunity that, while not completely illegal, is clearly unethical. Dealing with complicated, ambiguous moral challenges is an inescapable part of the human condition. Since these situations can't be avoided, you need to develop the insight and conceptual tools to deal with them effectively.

The Thinker's Way to Moral Decision-Making

AFTER WRESTLING with the moral dilemmas considered in the previous section, you might be wondering how exactly we *do* develop a clear sense of right and wrong to guide us in complex moral situations. The answer is found in applying to moral issues the same critical thinking abilities you have been developing throughout this book to create The Thinker's Way to Moral Decision-Making. Consider this as a guide, a moral blueprint for constructing your own personal moral code. Using the concepts and principles provided by this guide you can create a moral philosophy to analyze successfully virtually any moral situation and make informed decisions that you can justify with confidence.

According to The Thinker's Way to Moral Decision-Making, when you encounter moral situations in your daily life, you should:

- Carefully examine all of the facts of the situation with an awareness of your perceiving "lenses" in order to set aside your inherent bias.
- Explore all sides of the moral issue or choices, identifying and evaluating the reasons that support each perspective, taking care to give full credence to opposing viewpoints.
- Consider both the intentions and the consequences of each possible alternative, evaluating them in terms of their moral worthiness.
- Apply the ethical principles that constitute your individually created moral code, drawn from the framework presented in this chapter.
- Commit yourself to a conclusion that you are willing to defend and act upon, for which you can present a clear rationale.

- Remain open to the lessons of experience, refining your ethical code and modifying your actions as you gain more knowledge and better insight.
- Embrace your freedom and accept full responsibility for your actions as you strive to create yourself as a unique, worthy, and morally enlightened individual.

Analyzing a Moral Example

IMAGINE YOURSELF in the following situation. You have volunteered to participate in a psychological experiment sponsored by a well-known university in your area. When you arrive at the testing laboratory, you are greeted by the experimenter in charge, who introduces you to another subject in the experiment, a pleasant middle-aged gentleman. The experiment is designed to study the effects of punishment on learning. You and the other participant draw lots to determine each role; you become the "teacher" while the other subject is designated as the "learner," who is strapped into a chair, with electrodes attached to his arm. While being strapped, the learner mentions that he has a heart condition, and the experimenter assures both of you that while the electric shocks that will be administered may be painful, they cause no permanent tissue damage.

As the "teacher," you are instructed to read to the "learner" a list of word pairs, to test him on the list, and to administer punishment — an electric shock — whenever the learner makes a mistake. Before beginning you are given a sample shock of 45 volts which is mildly unpleasant. You are instructed to increase the level of shock one step on the shock generator for each mistake. The generator has thirty levels labeled from 15 to 450 volts, and beneath the voltage readings are labels ranging from "SLIGHT SHOCK" to "DANGER: SEVERE SHOCK," and finally "xxx."

The experiment starts routinely, as you administer shocks at the lower levels for incorrect responses, and the learner shows no reaction. However, at the fifth level, the learner grunts in annoyance, and by the

eighth level, he shouts that the shocks are becoming painful. When the
tenth level (150 volts) is reached, the learner cries out, *"Experimenter,
get me out of here! I won't be in the experiment anymore! I refuse to go
on!"* Concerned, you protest to the experimenter that the learner should
be released and the experiment ended, but he responds, "You must continue. You have no other choice." At the 270-volt level, the learner's response becomes an agonized scream, and at 300 volts the learner refuses
to answer further. When the voltage is increased to 330 volts, the learner
shrieks in pain at each shock and gives no answer as the volts are increased further, up to the maximum 450 volts. You have no way of knowing whether the learner is still conscious or even alive.

The above experiment was in fact conducted by the psychologist
Stanley Milgram, and is described in his book *Obedience to Authority.*
Of course, the "experiment" was a sham: the purpose of the experiment
was not to determine the effects of punishment on learning, it was to assess how far people would go in obeying authority. The "learner" was
an actor, and the only shock administered was the initial 45-volt shock
to the "teacher." Milgram conducted the experiment with forty subjects, representing a cross-section of New Haven, Connecticut, residents. Astonishingly, *65 percent (twenty-six out of forty) of the subjects
obeyed to the end (administering 450 volts), while virtually all of the others stayed on well into the experiment.* In other words, nearly all of the
participants willingly committed actions that they would normally consider to be highly unethical. Why?

In their perceptive analysis of Milgram's experiment, John Sabini and
Maury Silver, in their article "Critical Thinking and Obedience to Authority," identify a number of factors that influence people to abandon
their moral code and commit actions that under other circumstances
they would consider to be sadistic and highly unethical. They point out
that, first, the experimental conditions involved *gradual entrapment,* beginning with an innocuous shock and increasing a modest 15 volts at a
time. Such gradualness clouds clear thinking as we slide down the slip-
pery slope from innocence to evil. This is a phenomenon most people
are very well familiar with, as the best intentions typically erode by one
vodka, one jelly donut, or one cigarette at a time. Though we may ex-

pect moral situations to involve clear-cut choices between good and evil, the reality is often more ambiguous.

The second factor was *embarrassment*. Though participants protested often, the experimenter insisted that they must go on. In order to escape successfully from the situation, the participants needed to confront the experimenter on moral grounds, condemning the entire experiment as unethical. Yet they were unwilling to do this, reluctant to level such a devastating charge against someone personally. This is not unlike situations in which we witness unethical behavior — a parent smacking a child, for example — and do not take action because we "don't want to become involved." On a larger scale, this is an attitude that contributes to social persecution and moral atrocities in societies in which "ordinary" citizens refuse to speak up or "get involved."

The third factor was the participants' *"flight from responsibility,"* as Jean-Paul Sartre would describe it. Although the participants were upset over the apparent suffering they were causing, they were able to convince themselves that they were not personally responsible: They were just "following orders." The experimenter seemed to be a reasonable and authoritative professional representing a prestigious institution, and rather than simply confronting and rejecting this authority, the participants found it easier to "transfer" to the experimenter their freedom of choice and personal responsibility for the torture. But, of course, it is impossible to "transfer" our moral responsibility: we can only pretend to transfer it as we run desperately from our freedom. Trying to escape from our freedom and responsibility is what Sartre terms "bad faith," the insidious corruption of the soul that Socrates warned against.

How do we avoid the sort of moral failure epitomized in the Milgram experiment? We need to have a clear ethical code that we are used to living by. Let's apply The Thinker's Way to Moral Decision-Making that we developed in this chapter.

- *Carefully examine all of the facts of the situation with an awareness of your perceiving "lenses" in order to set aside your inherent biases.* If participants had evaluated the facts of the "experiment" objectively at the outset, they would have condemned its basic design as being morally unacceptable: administering high-voltage shocks to someone tied to a chair. Insight into their "lenses" (misplaced respect for authority) would have helped them question this "authority" and overcome their embarrassment about confronting him directly.

- *Explore all sides of the moral issue or choices, identifying and evaluating the reasons that support each perspective.* The participants persisted in the torture because they didn't seriously consider the other point of view: that the entire experiment was unethical and they ought not to continue participating. Instead, they never really questioned the "official" position: that the experiment represented legitimate research. Because they did not seriously consider the contrary perspective, the participants became locked into their original point of view. And then, as their moral discomfort increased, they kept stretching their ethical boundaries.

- *Apply the ethical principles that constitute your individually created moral code.* In order to live a moral life, you need first to recognize moral situations and then reason in an organized fashion to an enlightened moral conclusion. The participants in the experiment failed to recognize that they were being confronted with the need to make a moral decision, and so they didn't use their customary moral reasoning process to reach an intelligent conclusion. Instead, they offered up mild protests which were swept away by the experimenter, they tried to help the victim by giving him hints, or they exhibited passive resistance by slowing their administering of the shocks. But they never identified and grappled with the central moral issues.

- *Consider both the intentions and the consequences of each possible alternative, evaluating them in terms of their moral worthiness.* The participants focused on their intentions and paid insufficient attention to the consequences of their actions. While they didn't intend any harm, the obvious fact was their actions appeared to be causing a great deal of harm. Had they kept this reality in the forefront of their minds, they likely would not have continued.

- *Commit yourself to a conclusion that you are willing to defend and act upon, for which you can present a clear rationale.* "Forewarned is forearmed." Moral resolve is strengthened by deciding in advance what your moral position is going to be, specifying where you are going to draw the line which you will not cross. At the beginning of the experiment, if the participants had committed themselves to not going beyond a certain point (e.g., 90 volts), they likely would not have gradually slipped into the quicksand of unethical behavior. Lacking a clear, well-reasoned line of moral demarcation, people become vulnerable to the progressive erosion of their moral sense and resolve. In addition, if they had tried to justify their behavior with persuasive reasons, they probably would have recognized its inappropriateness.

- *Remain open to the lessons of experience, refining your ethical code and modifying your actions as you gain more knowledge and better insight.* Too often people commit themselves to a situation and then resist revising their initial appraisal even in the face of mounting evidence to the contrary. In the Milgram experiment, once the participants administered the first shock, they were symbolically expressing their approval of and complicity in the experiment. But as their moral discomfort mounted, it was difficult for them to break the momentum of their initial commitment and revise their thinking. It would have been admitting that they had been wrong in their initial approval, and people are generally reluctant to acknowledge mistakes, even to themselves. In fact, they often take pride in having not changed their positions over many years, an inflexibility that they should probably be ashamed of. Ralph Waldo Emerson said it best: "*A foolish consistency is the hobgoblin of little minds.*"

- *Embrace your freedom and accept full responsibility for your actions as you strive to create yourself as a unique, worthy, and morally enlightened individual.* As previously noted, the Milgram participants attempted to transfer their freedom of choice and personal responsibility to the experimenter, a typical human reaction when life circumstances become difficult. But this effort is doomed to failure: People cannot transfer freedom, they can only flee from it, leaving weak and pitiful creatures behind. If the participants had fully accepted their freedom and responsibility, it would have made it impossible for them to continue to engage in behavior that so violated their basic human decency and ethical standards. By saying to themselves, "I am personally responsible for choosing to administer these shocks and inflicting great pain, and I know that this type of behavior is wrong," they would have been able to confront the experimenter and withdraw from the experiment.

Rationale for the Thinker's Way to Moral Decision-Making

ANY MORAL GUIDE is only as sound as the reasons that support its point of view. As we have seen, it's very easy for someone to make a moral judgment or recommend a moral principle, but it's much more difficult to provide a compelling rationale for the belief or principle. That is the purpose of the remainder of the chapter: to explore the philosophical foundation of The Thinker's Way to Moral Decision-Making. This will involve applying the principles of critical thinking that you have been developing throughout this book, as well as examining some ideas of the most prominent ethical thinkers from the past twenty-five hundred years. This exploration will help you develop an in-depth understanding of important ethical concepts and reasoning, conceptual tools that you will need to create your own informed moral code.

A CRITICAL THINKING APPROACH TO ETHICS IS BASED ON REASON: SOME ETHICAL VIEWPOINTS ARE "BETTER" — MORE ENLIGHTENED — THAN OTHER VIEWPOINTS, BASED ON THE SUPPORTING REASONS AND EVIDENCE

The logic of ethical statements demands that they be supported by reasons. Ethical viewpoints are not a matter of taste, like your preferred hairstyle or your favorite kind of pizza. Unlike moral judgments, it *does* make sense to say "I like pepperoni pizza, but I can't give you a reason why. I just like it!" But it would not make sense for someone to say "Your taste in pizza is wrong." Ethical judgments are very different from expressions of taste. They are independent of personal preferences, and are evaluated in the public arena. When someone says, "I think that child abuse is immoral," they are not expressing a personal preference that applies only to them. They are making a pronouncement that they believe applies to *everyone*: Child abuse is immoral for *all* people. And they should be prepared to justify their conclusion with a rationale that others can discuss and evaluate. Unlike matters of taste, it *does* make sense to disagree with someone's ethical judgment: "I don't agree that legalized gambling is immoral because . . ." Ethical statements are usually intended to be universally true.

As a result, ethical views are primarily statements of reason, *not* expressions of emotion. When you express your moral disapproval toward child abuse, you are communicating what you think about this issue, based presumably on a thoughtful analysis. If someone asks, "Why do you think this?" you should be able to provide persuasive reasons that support your conclusion. Of course, there may be strong feelings that accompany your moral belief about child abuse, but you are primarily making a statement based on reason. When you express feelings, you may be accurately describing your emotional state ("I feel angry when I hear stories about child abuse"), but you are not expressing a moral point of view that you believe applies to everyone.

A CRITICAL THINKING APPROACH TO ETHICS IS BASED ON THE ETHIC OF JUSTICE

We are all different, one from the other, and unless these differences pose some threat to other people, our individuality should be respected. A critical thinking approach to ethics is founded on the principle of *impartiality*: It is our moral obligation to treat everyone equally, with the same degree of consideration and respect, *unless there is some persuasive reason not to*. This is the basic principle of the Ethic of Justice. For example, differences among people based on race, religion, gender, or sexual orientation pose no threat to society, and so the people involved deserve to be treated with the same respect everyone is entitled to. However, if a person threatens the rights of others — assaulting, stealing, raping, killing — then that person is not entitled to be treated like everyone else. He needs to be segregated from the rest of society and possibly rehabilitated.

The Ethic of Justice emphasizes the *intentions* or *motivation* of an action, not the consequences. It expresses the conviction that you experience when, confronted by a moral decision, you respond: "I have to do my duty. It's the principle of the thing. Regardless of the consequences, it's important for me to do what's right." This emphasis on *moral duty through reason* was perhaps best articulated by the German philosopher Immanual Kant: Through reasoning, we can analyze moral situations, evaluate possible choices, and then choose the one we believe is best. Kant based his approach to ethics on a universal rational principle (the "Categorical Imperative") that every virtuous person should obey: "*Act only according to that maxim by which you can at the same time will that it should become a universal law.*" Should you spread unflattering gossip about an unpopular coworker, even if you think the person "deserves" it? Applying this principle, you should only do it if you believe that all people in all analogous situations should spread unflattering gossip. Yikes! Most people would be reluctant to sign on for this sort of universal rule.

But why should you go along with this Categorical Imperative in the first place? Because, as first and foremost a rational creature, you are necessarily committed to a belief in *logical consistency.* How could you defend doing something that you would condemn other people for doing? What qualities make you so unique, so superior to everyone else that you are not bound by the same rules and requirements? Objectively speaking, there are no such special qualities. Your intrinsic value is no greater and no less than that of any other rational person. Reason dictates that everyone's interests must be treated the same, without special consideration. We should be willing to make every personal choice a universal law.

Kant also formulated a second version of the Categorical Imperative in the following way: *"Act so that you treat humanity, whether in your own person or in that of another, always as an end and never as a means only."* Since all people possess the same *intrinsic value,* a value that is defined by an ability to understand their options and make free choices, we should always act in a way that respects their inherent dignity as rational agents. Imagine, for example, that you want to sell something: Is it all right to manipulate people's feelings so that they will buy? Or suppose that your child or friend is planning to do something that you don't think is in her best interests: Is it permissible to manipulate her thinking indirectly so that she will make a different choice? According to Kant, both of these actions are morally wrong because you are not treating the people involved as *"ends,"* rational agents who are entitled to make their own choices. Instead, you are treating them as a *"means" to an end,* even though you may believe that your manipulation is in their best interests. The morally right thing to do is to tell them exactly what you are thinking and then give them the opportunity to reason through the situation and make their own choices.

THINKING ACTIVITY

Evaluating Your Moral Beliefs with Reason

Apply Kant's two formulations of the Categorical Imperative to the ethical beliefs which you expressed in the Thinking Activity on page 314.

1. *Act only according to that maxim by which you can at the same time will that it should become a universal law.*
2. *Act so that you treat humanity, whether in your own person or in that of another, always as an end and never as a means only."*

How do your ethical beliefs measure up? Are they consistent with Kant's formulations? Think about a moral dilemma that you recently agonized over. Does either formulation of the Categorical Imperative point you in a clearer direction?

A CRITICAL THINKING APPROACH TO ETHICS IS BASED ON THE ETHIC OF CARE

The Ethic of Care is built on *empathy*, a critical thinking commitment to view issues and situations from multiple perspectives. According to an empathetic point of view, achieving happiness and fulfillment in life does not mean pursuing your own narrow desires; instead, it involves pursuing your aspirations in a context of genuine understanding of other people. When you actively work to transcend your own perspective and think within other points of view, particularly those with which you disagree, you are gaining a deeper and richer understanding. You need to listen carefully to people who disagree with you and try to appreciate what thinking brought them to their conclusion. Perspective-taking is the cornerstone of many of the world's ethical systems such as the Golden Rule: *"Do unto others as you would have others do unto you."* In other words, strive to place yourself in the position of the object of your moral judgment and see how that affects your evaluation. For instance, if you are trying to evaluate the morality of racism, imagine that *you* are the target of the evaluation. You didn't choose your racial heritage; it's just who you are. From this vantage point, do you think that you should be treated differently, discriminated against, condemned as being alien and inferior? *"Walking a mile in someone else's shoes"* can often have a dramatic impact on your understanding and evaluation. It's not easy to remain sanctimonious and self-righteous when you find yourself on the receiving end of the moral condemnation.

A CRITICAL THINKING APPROACH TO ETHICS IS BASED ON FREEDOM AND RESPONSIBILITY

From a critical thinking perspective, morality makes sense only if we assume that people are able to make free choices for which they are responsible. When people choose courses of action that we consider to be "right," we judge them as morally "good." On the other hand, when they choose courses of action that we consider to be "wrong," we condemn them as morally "evil." For example, when Princess Diana was the victim of a fatal car crash, it was widely reported that the photographers who were pursuing her (the "paparazzi") were preoccupied with taking photographs of the carnage rather than helping the victims. In France, not actively aiding a person in distress actually violates the law, while in most countries the photographers' actions would not be considered illegal. Nevertheless, most people would judge their failure to help and their efforts to profit from this tragedy to be "wrong": immoral, unethical, reprehensible. They were judged this way because they had a choice to make, they were aware of their options, their motivations, and the consequences of their actions. By choosing to take photographs rather than assist, they were motivated by greed and were diminishing the chances of survival for the occupants in the car. Had they put their cameras aside and devoted their energies to aiding the victims, they would have been motivated by compassion and empathy, and they would be enhancing the chance that the crash victims might be saved. From a critical thinking perspective, their actions were indeed evil, and they deserve to be condemned.

Now consider this situation. Imagine that you are driving down a street in your neighborhood, within the speed limit and stone sober, when a child darts out from between two parked cars. Though you brake instantly, you nevertheless hit the child. Is your action "wrong" — immoral, unethical? Most people would say no. This was an accident that was unavoidable, not the result of a free choice, and so you should not be held responsible for the tragedy. You were not faced with clear options from which to choose, you were not motivated by evil intentions, and you had no way of foreseeing the consequences of your action.

In order to be held morally accountable, for good or ill, your actions need to be the result of free choices. And in order to exercise your freedom, you need to have insight into your options, your motivations, and the consequences of your actions. This is the uniquely human gift; we have the intelligence, the imagination, and the reflective insight to consider a range of options and make choices. Sometimes we choose wisely, sometimes we choose poorly, but in all instances we are responsible for the choices that we make.

A CRITICAL THINKING APPROACH TO ETHICS SEEKS TO PROMOTE HUMAN HAPPINESS FOR ONESELF AND OTHERS

Evaluating moral choices involves examining both the *intent* or *motivation* behind the choice as well as the *consequences* of the action. In the case of the photographers at the scene of Princess Diana's fatal crash, their intent — to secure photographs that they could sell for a great deal of money rather than aid the victims — was certainly morally reprehensible. Their actions represented an inversion of common moral values, as they placed making money higher than preserving human life. But in addition to the immorality of their intent, the *consequences* of their actions were also catastrophic, as three of the four passengers died. We'll never know if their assistance could have made a difference to the victims. Had Princess Diana and the others survived the accident, the actions of the photographers, while still immoral in intent, might not have been judged so harshly. But with fatal consequences, their choices were evaluated even more gravely: They contributed to the accident by pursuing the car; they took photographs instead of helping the victims; and those who were able to went on to sell their photos for large sums of money. In the minds of many people, it doesn't get much worse than that.

Promoting human happiness and its corollary, diminishing human suffering, have been mainstays of many ethical systems through the ages. Most people are perfectly willing to pursue their own happiness: It's the way we're genetically programmed and taught as well. However, you don't receive moral accolades for pursuing solely your own interests. Moral recognition is typically earned by devoting your time and resources to enhancing the happiness of others, sometimes at the expense of your own interests. This moral value is founded on the principle of perspective-taking, which we explored earlier. Identifying with another's situation can generate the desire to assist the person that could just as easily have been you ("There but for the grace of God . . ."). This then is the wellspring of charitable acts toward others.

But this moral concept is relevant in our ordinary dealings with people also. All things being equal, it makes sense to promote the happiness of others through your words and actions. Being friendly, generous, supportive, understanding, sympathetic, helpful — these and other similar traits enhance the quality of others' lives, usually at a minimal cost to yourself. This is not to suggest that you should devote yourself to promoting the interests of others to the exclusion of your own. In fact, if you don't take care of your own interests, you probably won't be able to sustain the resources needed to help others. "Self-interest" and "selfishness" are not the same thing. Pursuing your self-interest is ethically appropriate and necessary for your own physical and emotional health. But if you are devoted *exclusively* to pursuing your own interests, then your life is morally empty. And if you are intent on pursuing your interests at the expense of other people, then you are being selfish. When you take more than your share of dessert, diminishing the portions of others, or you step on other people to advance your career, you are guilty of selfishness.

Promoting human happiness is the foundation of the ethical approach developed by Jeremy Bentham, a philosopher who was concerned with British social problems in the late eighteenth and early nineteenth centuries. From his perspective, "good" and "right" are defined in terms of what brings about the greatest pleasure for the greatest number of people, a moral theory which became known as *Utilitarianism*. Another British philosopher, John Stuart Mill, argued that we need to distinguish the "higher pleasures" (intellectual stimulation, aesthetic appreciation, education, healthfulness) from the "lower pleasures" (animal appetites, laziness, selfishness). Otherwise, he declared mischievously, it would seem preferable to be a contented pig rather than a discontented human, a conclusion that is surely absurd:

> It is better to be a human being dissatisfied than a pig satisfied; better to be Socrates dissatisfied than a fool satisfied. And if the fool, or the pig, are of a different opinion, it is because they only know their own side of the question. The other party to the comparison knows both sides.

But even this more refined notion of "higher pleasures" seems too limited. We need to expand the concept of "pleasure" to the more general idea of "human happiness" in a deep and rich sense. It *does* make sense for us to promote human happiness if this means helping other people secure shelter, food, and health care; providing education and creating opportunities for career success; protecting their freedom and supporting their quest for personal fulfillment. If we view human happiness within this larger framework, then helping the greatest number of people achieve it is surely a morally good and ethically right goal to pursue.

THINKING ACTIVITY

What Is Your Idea of Human Happiness?

Think about what you consider to be the ingredients of human happiness. What things do you believe most people need to achieve genuine happiness? Review the moral values that you identified on pages 314–315 and identify which ones promote human happiness as you have defined it. Can you think of other moral values that might contribute to the happiness of yourself and others?

A Critical Thinking Approach to Ethics Seeks to Develop Informed Intuition

When you find yourself in the throes of a moral decision, there may come a point when you have a clear "intuition" about what course of action you should take. Is this your conscience speaking to you? Is this your moral compass pointing you in the right direction? Can you trust your intuition?

To answer these questions, it's necessary to understand how the human mind operates. One dominant aspect of your thinking process is its *synthesizing* quality: It is continually trying to construct a "picture" of the world that is intelligible, and this picture is updated on an instantaneous basis as circumstances change. Your mind does this by taking into account all available information, utilizing appropriate concepts, and integrating all of this into a pattern that makes sense. When this pattern clicks into place, like fitting the final piece into a jigsaw puzzle, you experience an *intuition*. While some of these processes are conscious, others are unconscious, sometimes giving your intuition a mysterious aura. Many of your intuitions are commonplace: deciding on an ingredient when creating a new recipe or having the clear sense that someone you just met is not entirely trustworthy. Although these intuitions may seem to be coming out of the blue, they are generally the result of your accumulated experience, insight, and the information you are picking up at the moment. When you taste the sauce of your new dish, your accumulated expertise "tells" you what the recipe "needs." When you meet people for the first time, you are picking up a great deal of information about them on subtle and even subliminal levels communicated not just by their words and appearance, but by facial expressions, gestures, voice tone, eye contact, and so on. As you absorb this information at a dizzying rate, it is fed into your mental computer, programmed with lessons about people learned through years of experience. A pattern emerges, and . . . presto, an intuition!

These sorts of *informed* intuitions are often quite reliable because they are based on a great deal of experience, reflection, knowledge, insight, and expertise. But there are many *uninformed* intuitions as well, and these are *not reliable* — in fact, they can be catastrophic because they are not based on sufficient experience, reflection, knowledge, insight, and expertise. For example, imagine that you have just learned how to play chess, and suddenly you are struck with the intuitive certainty that you should sacrifice your queen. Since this intuition is not the product of accumulated knowledge and insight, it may very well lose you the game. If you think back on your own life, you can doubtless identify intuitions that seemed certain at the time but turned out to be tragically — or comically — wrong. You may have experienced the thunderbolt of "true love," and several months later wondered what you were thinking at the time. The point is that an intuition is only as sound as the foundation of experience, knowledge, insight, and expertise upon which it is based.

This is precisely the same situation with moral intuition. If your moral intuition is informed, the product of a great deal of thought and reflection, then it has a high degree of credibility. But if your moral intuition is uninformed, the product of inaccurate information or inadequate experience, then your intuition is not credible. People with depraved and underdeveloped moral sensibilities will have instincts and intuitions that reflect their diminished moral understanding. There is nothing magical or infallible about your conscience or moral intuition: If you have consciously worked at becoming a moral person, a person of character and integrity, then your intuitions will be largely trustworthy. But if you have not consciously striven to develop and refine your moral sensibilities, or if you have been raised in an environment saturated with destructive values like prejudice and violence, then you should be very suspicious of your moral intuitions.

While your intuitions may seem initially certain — "I *knew* immediately what the right thing to do was" — further reflection can plant seeds of doubt that eventually threaten that initial certainty. Moral judgments are not factual statements that we can easily prove or disprove through observation and experiment. In most moral situations, the facts are known — it's the *interpretation* of the facts and what to do about the situation that pose the moral problem. When a woman discovers, through amniocentesis, that the fetus developing inside her is severely malformed and disabled, the facts of the situation are fairly straightforward. What is not clear is what moral choice she and the father of the fetus should make, whether to have an abortion or confront the challenge of raising a severely retarded and physically disabled child. While it makes sense to gather as much accurate information as possible to anticipate what this child's life will be like and the impact it will have on the lives of the family, no amount of information will add up to making the moral decision. It's an entirely different category of reasoning, a deliberative process that often involves moral uncertainty and a profound sense of responsibility. Each one of us confronts this same anguish when we struggle with difficult moral questions for which there doesn't seem to be one clear, unambiguous answer. In these circumstances, appealing to one's "moral intuition" simply doesn't seem adequate.

THINKING ACTIVITY

Thinking About Your Moral Intuition

Think about the way you arrive at moral decisions. How do you "know" when you are doing the right thing? Where does your sense of moral certainty come from? Do you experience moral "intuitions" about good and evil, right and wrong? Consider the values which you identified in the Thinking Activity on pages

314–315, and other of your values as well. To what extent are they based on your moral intuition of right and wrong? How would you justify these values to a skeptical acquaintance? What does it *feel* like when you have a moral intuition?

DISCOVER THE "NATURAL LAW" OF HUMAN NATURE

There have been centuries of energetic efforts to provide a foundation for moral intuition, a grounding that will remove it from the grip of social conditioning and the shadowland of inscrutable mystery. Once again, it was the ancient Greeks who first elaborated this approach by making a distinction between Nature (*physis*) and Convention (*nomos*). The social conventions of a society are the man-made customs and beliefs, laws, and tastes that are peculiar to that society. That's why when you examine the numerous cultures in the world, past and present, you find a spectacular diversity in the social fabrics of each society: You are observing the *social conventions* that are relative to each individual society.

Nature, however, embodies the vast realm of truth that exists on a deeper level than social conventions, which exist on the surface. These "natural truths" are *not* relative to each society: They are constant from culture to culture, and from age to age. These truths are rooted in the fundamental *nature* of what it means to be human. According to this view, there is a *Natural Law*, which is based on man and woman's essential natures and which is universal and binding on all people. We can discover these natural moral truths through reason and reflection, and they have been articulated in the greatest legal and moral philosophies and theological systems of Western culture. The challenge for each individual and culture is to discover this immutable Natural Law that underlies the specific conventions of any society. It is an effort that the religious thinker St. Thomas Aquinas devoted his life to, and that America's founding fathers sought to articulate in the Declaration of Independence and the Constitution. "*We hold these truths to be self-*

evident; that all men are created equal; that they are endowed by their creator with certain unalienable rights. . . ."

In order to discover the specifics of the Natural Law, we need to develop an in-depth understanding of the essential nature of men and women, not simply as they currently are, but as they *could be* if they were fully morally developed. What are the basic requirements of human fulfillment? What are the most enlightened values that humans can aspire to? What are the norms of conduct that foster the most meaningful and productive society? What are the conditions that maximize the exercise of individual freedom and personal growth? What are the moral responsibilities that we have to each other as members of an interdependent human community?

To answer these difficult questions, many people turn to religion. After all, if we are indeed God's creations (whatever your religion's conception of God), designed in God's image, then it makes sense that by understanding our true nature we will be following the path of both moral *and* spiritual enlightenment. In fact, it would be shocking if there was *not* an essential identity between the ethics of our religion and our natural moral intuitions. By following what Thomas Aquinas described as the "dictates of reason," we are able to discover God's ethic encoded in our human nature, in the same way that we are able to display the mysteries of the physical universe through the study of science. In other words, we can use our critical thinking abilities to reveal the essential moral nature of people, the ideal image of fulfilled human potential — and then use this image to inform our moral choices and guide our personal development.

A CRITICAL THINKING APPROACH TO ETHICS MEANS CHOOSING TO BE A MORAL PERSON

An individual can possess a comprehensive understanding of moral concepts and approaches and *not* be a moral person. How is that possible? Just as people can possess an array of critical thinking abilities and yet choose not to use them, so people can be a walking compendium of moral theory and yet not choose to apply it to their lives. In order to achieve an enlightened moral existence in your own life, you need to *choose* to be a moral person struggling to live a moral life. You need to *value* morality, to aspire to an enhanced moral awareness, to exert the motivation and commitment required to reach this lofty but reachable goal.

Once you have developed a clear understanding of your moral code, the struggle has just begun. Becoming a morally enlightened person — a person of character, compassion, and integrity — is a hard-won series of accomplishments, not a one-time award like winning an Oscar. Every day confronts you with new choices and unexpected challenges, many of which you cannot possibly anticipate. With your moral code in hand to guide you, you need to commit yourself to making the choices that best express your moral philosophy of life. As a reflective critical thinker, you will be conscious of the choices you are making and the reasons you are making them, and you will "learn from experience," refining your code of ethics and improving your moral choices through self-exploration. Achieving moral enlightenment is an ongoing process, and it is a struggle that is not for the faint-hearted. But it is a struggle that cannot be avoided if you are to live a life of purpose and meaning, created by a self that is authentic and, as Aristotle would say, "great souled."

The psychologist Abraham Maslow conducted a comprehensive study of the qualities of what he considered to be self-actualized people, and found that people with healthy human personalities also had strong moral characters. Morally mature, psychologically healthy people think, decide, and act in accordance with thoughtfully developed moral standards; are open-minded about their moral beliefs; defend them with reasoned argument when they are challenged; and change or modify them when they are shown to be false or unjustified. Their conclusions are based on their own reflective analysis, rather than being unquestioning "children of their culture." And they are fully committed to *living their values*, recognizing that ethics is not an intellectual game: it's a light that guides their moral growth and personal evolution.

These considerations provide a convincing answer to the question *"Why be moral?"* As it turns out, becoming a moral person helps you become a psychologically healthy person; promoting the happiness of others frequently enhances your own happiness. Often adages are clichéd and empty of meaning, but in this case, *"Virtue is its own reward"* contains a substantial measure of truth, a point noted by Socrates in his observation that doing wrong *"will harm and corrupt that part of ourselves that is improved by just actions and destroyed by unjust actions."* As a free individual, you create yourself through the choices that you make much as a sculptor gradually forms a figure through countless cuts of the chisel. If you create yourself as a moral person, you create a person of character and worth, with an acute sense of right and wrong and the power to choose appropriately. But if you don't choose to create yourself as a moral person, you gradually become corrupted. You lose your moral sensitivity, developing a moral blindness that handicaps your ability to see yourself or the world clearly. It is no wonder that Socrates believed that *"It is better to suffer wickedness than to commit it."* You gain true power when you possess the unfettered and unrestrained ability to choose freely. Choosing immorality binds your hands, one loop of thread at a time, until your freedom of movement disappears. In the same way that substance abusers gradually surrender their freedom of choice to their destructive cravings, so immoral people have only the illusion of genuine freedom in their lives. While moral people enjoy healthy personalities and spiritual wholeness, immoral people are corrupted at their core, progressively ravaged by a disease of the spirit.

How Moral Am I?

DESCRIBED BELOW are key personal attributes that are correlated with having an enlightened sense of morality. Evaluate your position regarding each of these attributes, and use this self-evaluation to guide your choices as you shape the moral person that you want to become.

Make Morality a Priority

I am very aware of the moral
choices in my life.

I don't give much thought to
moral issues in my life.

5   4   3   2   1

In order to live a life that achieves your moral potential, you must work
to become aware of the moral issues that you face, and strive to make
choices that are grounded in thoughtful reflection and supported by
persuasive reasons. By living a morally enlightened life you are defining yourself as a person of substance, with a vision that embraces the
quality of your relationships with others.

Strategy: *During the next week, note in your Thinking Notebook moral
issues that you encounter in your daily life involving other people —
choices related to right and wrong, good and evil, just and unjust. Select
several of these moral choices and think about the approach you used in
your decision: What was the issue? What choices could you have made?
Why did you make the choice you did? If you had it to do over again,
would you make the same choice? Why or why not?*

Develop a Clear Moral Code

I have a clear moral code I use
to guide my choices.

I am often confused and
uncertain about my moral
choices.

5   4   3   2   1

The key to living a moral life is developing a clear, intelligent moral
code to guide your choices. Such a moral code should be *coherent* (your
values fit together with consistency), *comprehensive* (your code can be
applied effectively to many different kinds of moral situations), and *well
grounded* (your beliefs are supported by cogent reasons).

Strategy: *Using your responses to the Thinking Activities as a spring-
board, record in your Thinking Notebook the moral principles that you
use to guide your choices. After writing down your moral principles, eval-*

uate them for consistency and try to organize them into coherent patterns. *Keep developing and refining your moral code as you learn through experience and increase your moral maturity over time.*

Adopt the Ethic of Justice

The Ethic of Justice is an important part of my moral code.	The Ethic of Justice is not something I have consciously applied to my moral code.

5   4   3   2   1

The Ethic of Justice is built on the concept of *impartiality*, which is our moral obligation to treat everyone equally, with the same degree of consideration and respect we accord ourselves, unless there is some persuasive reason not to. It is both illogical and immoral to discriminate against other people.

Strategy: *Think about your own biases toward others, and begin working to treat these people with the respect they are due.*

Adopt the Ethic of Care

The Ethic of Care is an important part of my moral code.	The Ethic of Care is not an important part of my moral code.

5   4   3   2   1

The Ethic of Care expresses a moral responsibility to others, which is based on your ability to *empathize* — to imaginatively put yourself in other people's situations and view the world from their perspectives. This ability to empathize enables you to feel compassion and sympathy toward others, and serves as the foundation of all your healthy relationships.

Strategy: *Increase your ability to empathize by making a special effort to transcend your own perspective and place yourself in other people's "shoes." In your dealings with others, use your imagination to experience* *what you believe they are thinking and feeling, and observe whether this influences your attitudes and actions toward them.*

Universalize Your Moral Choices

I often "universalize" my choices in deciding what to do.	I rarely "universalize" my choices in making moral decisions.

5   4   3   2   1

A very effective strategy during your moral deliberations is to ask yourself if you would be willing for everyone, in situations similar to your own, to make the same choice that you are making.

Strategy: *As you deliberate the various moral choices in your life, both small ("Should I cut ahead in line?") and large ("Should I pursue my own self-interest at the risk of hurting someone else?"), make a conscious effort to universalize your anticipated action. Would you be willing for everyone to take this same action in similar circumstances? If not, evaluate whether the action is truly morally justified and consistent with other moral values you hold.*

Treat People as Ends, Not Means

I usually treat people with respect for their autonomy.	I often treat people as a means to achieving my own interests.

5   4   3   2   1

Although Kant's admonition to treat people *always* as "ends" and *never* as a "means" to our own ends may seem extreme, we should perhaps take his recommendation more seriously than we normally do. By respecting someone else's right to make free choices — even a child's — we are bringing out the best in them as we enhance our own moral stature.

Strategy: *Think about some recent instances in which you attempted to influence someone's thoughts, feelings, or behavior. Did you make a clear case for your recommendation, respecting his or her right to make a free choice? Or did you try to manipulate them by using techniques de-*

signed to influence them without their knowledge or coerce them against their wishes? If you discover examples of manipulation, try to imagine how things would have turned out if you had taken a more forthright approach, and record your reflections in your Thinking Notebook.

Accept Responsibility for Your Moral Choices

I usually accept responsibility for the moral choices I make.

I often avoid accepting responsibility for my moral choices.

$$5 \quad 4 \quad 3 \quad 2 \quad 1$$

It is impossible to achieve genuine moral stature without accepting responsibility for the choices that you make. If you are to create yourself as a person of moral integrity, you must have the courage to acknowledge moral failure as well as the humility to accept moral success.

Strategy: *Strengthen your moral integrity by actively seeking to acknowledge your moral failings, and then committing yourself to improve. Self-honesty will build your inner strength and moral fiber, and you will find that moral integrity of this sort is both rewarding and habit-forming.*

Seek to Promote Human Happiness

I actively strive to make other people happy.

I do not spend much time trying to make others happy.

$$5 \quad 4 \quad 3 \quad 2 \quad 1$$

Happiness breeds happiness, in the same way that aggression escalates aggression and negativity inspires negativity. When you actively work to help other people become happy, through your words and actions, their happiness reflects back onto you, creating a sense of satisfaction and fulfillment. Happiness and goodwill are not limited commodities. There are, in fact, inexhaustible supplies.

Strategy: *Think about specific ways in which you can increase the happiness of people in your life. It may involve bestowing a small kindness on someone you know casually, or making a more significant commit-*

ment to someone to whom you are very close. Create and implement a plan for the next few days and then evaluate the results of your efforts after a week in your Thinking Notebook. How did working with extra effort to make others happy make you feel? How did they respond? Doesn't it make sense to continue the effort and even increase it?

Develop an Informed Moral Intuition

I have a reliable moral intuition that I trust.

I don't feel confident about my moral intuition.

5   4   3   2   1

An informed moral intuition is the product of thoughtful exploration and reflection on moral issues throughout your life. Developing an informed, reliable moral intuition involves achieving insight into the essential nature of humans: What are the basic qualities that define who we ought to be as individuals and how we should treat others? Once you have developed an intuition in which you have confidence, you need to *use* it to help you think your way through moral dilemmas.

Strategy: *The idea of an informed intuition-based "natural law" provides a productive framework for you to conduct your moral investigations. Imagine an ideal, perfect human being: what personal qualities would such a person possess? How would such a person treat other people? What moral vision and specific moral values would such a person display? Using these explorations, construct a composite portrait of an ideal person that you can use to guide your moral intuitions.*

Choose to Be a Moral Person

I am determined to create myself as a moral person.

Becoming a moral person is not a conscious priority.

5   4   3   2   1

Becoming a morally enlightened person — a person of character, compassion, and integrity — is a daily struggle that requires true grit and determination. You must consciously choose to achieve your moral potential, reflecting on the moral choices you make and working to clarify and refine your moral code.

Strategy: *Develop the habit of conducting a regular appraisal of yourself and your life, written in your Thinking Notebook. Ask — and answer — questions like: Am I achieving my goals as a moral person? As a critical thinker? As a creative individual? Use this evaluation regularly to maintain a much-needed perspective on your life, reminding yourself of the "big picture," and guiding your evolution into the most worthy person you can become.*

SCORING GUIDE

Add up the numbers you circled for each of the self-evaluation items above and use the following Scoring Guide to evaluate your moral awareness.

Point Total	Interpretation
40–50	very morally aware
30–39	moderately morally aware
20–29	somewhat morally aware
10–19	comparatively morally unaware

In interpreting your results, be sure to keep in mind that:

- This evaluation is not a measure of your moral character, but is rather intended as a general indicator of how aware you are of your moral nature.
- Your score indicates how morally aware you are at the present time, *not* your *potential* to be morally aware. If you scored lower than you would like, it means that you need to follow the suggestions in this chapter to increase your moral awareness to the level of which you are capable.

THINKING ACTIVITY

Nurturing Your Moral Growth

No matter how highly evolved you are as a moral person, you can achieve a more enlightened state by *choosing* to pursue this aim. Your critical thinking abilities will give you the means to explore the moral dimension of your experience with insight, and your personal dedication to moral improvement will provide you with the ongoing motivation. Remember that becoming a moral person is both a daily and a lifetime project. Nurture your continued moral growth by cultivating the qualities that we explored in this section, and record your progress in your Thinking Notebook.

- Make morality a priority.
- Develop a clear moral code.
- Adopt the Ethic of Justice.
- Adopt the Ethic of Care.
- Universalize your moral choices.
- Treat people as ends, not means.
- Accept responsibility for your moral choices.
- Seek to promote human happiness.
- Develop an informed moral intuition.
- Discover the "natural law" of human nature.
- Choose to be a moral person.

THINK THROUGH
RELATIONSHIPS

Forming healthy relationships is at the center of a meaningful and re-
warding life, and these relationships pose the greatest challenge to our
thinking abilities. This chapter will show you how to build on the skills
and insights you have been developing, learning how to nurture produc-
tive and caring relationships with family, friends, colleagues, children,
and your intimate partner. Thinking critically, living creatively, solving
problems, communicating effectively, applying enlightened values—
these are the tools you can use to create deep and fulfilling relationships
based on genuine caring, empathy, and mutual respect.

RELATIONSHIPS. WHEN YOU think about the happiest, most fulfilling and meaningful experiences in your life, they can likely be
traced to relationships with others. Similarly, the saddest, most painful
and frustrating experiences are probably also the result of human relationships. Why are relationships so complicated? Why do they continually elude understanding? What can you do to build strong,
positive relationships in every area of your life, to make intelligent de-

cisions in the most confusing of circumstances, and to solve the most challenging interpersonal problems? These are the questions that this chapter will explore. Of course, it would be the height of hubris — and folly — to think that the mystery of relationships could be solved in one chapter, or one book. But you will come to see that the critical thinking abilities and insights that you have been developing will provide you with powerful tools for enhancing the relationships in your life, with family, friends, lovers, children, and, perhaps most important, your "self."

Since the moment of your birth — and even before as you floated in your amniotic sac — relationships with others formed the basis of your identity, the medium through which you experienced the world. The person that you are today is in large measure the product of the personal relationships that have shaped your development, beginning with the most dominant influences, your parents. These early relationships established cognitive and emotional patterns that form the core of your personality, creating both personal strengths and weaknesses, resources and vulnerabilities. Your personal growth was further molded by the parade of people moving through your life.

Yet despite all of your experiences with these many different people, it is likely that you still find personal relationships to be frequently messy, frustrating, infuriating, frightening, hurtful, and just generally bewildering. There's a good reason for this. Looked at individually, even the simplest person is extraordinarily complicated, a dynamic organism with countless dimensions and hidden depths that are often unknown even to the person herself. When you mix one person with another, both bringing their entire personal histories to the encounter, a dynamic reaction takes place as these two living identities commingle and interact. The chain reaction from this initial contact creates an evolving web of connections of such complexity that mapping the whole would take a lifetime. It is no wonder that the relationships in your life so often seem beyond your control and comprehension, ongoing dramas in which you are a lead actor who must improvise without benefit of a script or essential knowledge of the other key players.

The Logic of Relationships

YOUR THINKING abilities provide you with the power to untangle the complex mysteries of the relationships in your life. By thinking clearly about your social connections, you can avoid miscommunications and solve interpersonal problems when they arise. Many emotional difficulties — including insecurity, depression, anger, jealousy, selfishness, rigidity, insensitivity, narrow-mindedness, immaturity — are the product of confused thinking. Since it is these "negative" emotions that are responsible for the majority of relationship problems, transforming these "negatives" into "positives" — security, optimism, love, respect, support, generosity, flexibility, empathy, creativity, maturity — makes it possible for you to have a wide range of positive, healthy relationships. Clear thinking can't make you fall in love with someone you judge to be a good candidate. But clear thinking *will* make it possible for you to fall in love and have a sustained, nurturing, intimate relationship. Clear thinking *will* make it possible for others to appreciate your best qualities, for them to experience you as a thoughtful, caring, intellectually vital person.

In order to understand the enigma of the human mind and the mystery of human relationships, we need to employ a logic that captures the organic connections between people. Human relationships are dynamic encounters between living persons, and virtually every significant encounter changes all participants, for better or for worse, as Carl Jung observed, *"The meeting of two personalities is like the contact of two chemical substances: if there is any reaction, both are transformed."* This is particularly true with close, long-term relationships in which your life literally "grows" into another's, and his or her life into yours. That's why the breakup of such close relationships, through separation or death, causes such wrenching pain and despair. It is as if a closely knitted fabric is being torn apart, leaving jagged tears and loose threads along with a profound sense of loss and incompleteness. We often don't realize the extent to which our lives have intertwined with others until such a separation occurs, because the process of shared growth has been so natural, so gradual.

The transformational nature of human encounters occurs in less intimate relationships as well. For example, think of someone you have dealings with on a daily basis whom you are not personally close to — perhaps a coworker or supervisor at your workplace or the staff at the school where you donate your time. Even these relatively straightforward encounters typically involve complex communication, practical negotiations, emotional reactions, and all of the other basic elements of relationships. Over time, these encounters, and your reflections on them, change you as person, influencing your ongoing creation of who you are. Even momentary encounters with others affect you: the Good Samaritan who shows you an unexpected kindness; the enraged motorist who tailgates your bumper, flashing his lights and making obscene gestures. The Good Samaritan's kindness may stimulate you to think about your moral responsibilities to others, even strangers, and strengthen your resolve to act more charitably. The enraged motorist may get you thinking about the pressures of modern life that cause such hostile behavior in people, insights that may help you handle your own frustrations in more positive ways.

When you encounter someone different from yourself, the interaction of ideas, emotions, and attitudes creates a "relationship," a living social creation that is continually changing and evolving.

First Things First: Who Am I?

ONE OF LIFE'S paradoxes is that in order to develop positive, healthy relationships with other people, you first have to have a positive, healthy relationship *with yourself.* If you don't love and trust yourself, then it will not be possible for you to treat others with love and trust, emotions that are the lifeblood of healthy relationships. Many people have been taught that "self-love" and "love of others" are in competition with one another, and in fact this was the basis of Sigmund Freud's "theory of narcissism": The more love you turn toward the outside world, the less love is left for yourself — and vice versa. But this sort of thinking commits a logical fallacy. Self-love and love for others are not mutually exclusive; they are *synergistic*. The more you love yourself, the *more* you are able to love others; while the less you love yourself, the *less* you are able to love others.

"Selfishness" is not the same thing as "self-love" — in fact, selfishness is caused by a *lack* of self-love. If you despise your "self" and feel profoundly unworthy, then it is natural to try to compensate for these desperate personal feelings of emptiness and frustration by grasping and acquiring at the expense of others — the definition of selfish behavior. In contrast, if you honestly cherish and value your "self," your life is founded on an inner security that gives you the confidence to act self-*lessly*, cherishing and valuing others.

This insight is expressed in the biblical command "Love your neighbor as yourself," a point noted by the humanistic psychologist Erich Fromm. Respect for your own integrity and uniqueness, love of yourself, cannot be separated from love and respect for another individual. In this sense, love is indivisible: An active striving for the growth and happiness of the person you love enhances your capacity to love.

Why is it difficult to develop intimate relationships that are healthy and lasting? Why do so many people who spend time by themselves feel unbearably lonely? These are serious questions for people in today's world, a world in which technology and information are plentiful but intimate relationships and peaceful solitude are often in short supply, leading to lives of personal bleakness and desperation. Personal alienation is one of the persistent themes in twentieth-century literature, philosophy, and popular culture. When people are unaware of their deep, intense needs for intimacy and solitude, or when they conclude that these needs cannot be met, their sense of personal power is greatly diminished. And in a world that can easily seem overwhelming, uncaring, and out of control, not having the confidence that comes from a solid sense of self and stable intimate relationships can make life seem frightening and depressing. As the psychotherapist Stephanie Dowrick explains in her book *Intimacy and Solitude*, at the heart of many emotional difficulties is a lack of understanding that each of us needs closeness with others, and also a knowledgeable, nurturing relationship with our own self. *"How we experience ourselves is reflected in the way we can approach and experience other people: we cannot know and trust other people better than we know and trust our own selves."*

The challenge, then, is for you to develop a relationship with yourself that is trusting, loving, genuine, empathetic, respectful, secure, generous, flexible, optimistic, open, sensitive, and creative, because this is the only way for you to develop analogous relationships with others. By understanding *who you are* and *how you became* the person you are, you can then make intelligent choices to shape yourself into the kind of person you want to become.

THINKING ACTIVITY

Whom Do You Want to Become?

- In your Thinking Notebook, describe the emotional qualities that you would like to develop more fully in your relationship with *your self*, such as trusting, confident, loving. Be specific, and list as many qualities as you think are appropriate.
- Then describe the emotional qualities that you would like to develop more fully in your relationships with *other people*, such as empathetic, flexible, supportive.
- Finally, compare the two lists you have created. What qualities characterize both your feelings about your self and your feelings about others? Are there qualities on one list that, on reflection, you think should be placed on both lists? As a daily reminder to yourself regarding these personal and interpersonal goals, you might want to summarize your thoughts on a card that you can place in a prominent location (your refrigerator door or desk) where you will see it on a regular basis.

YOUR PERSONAL HISTORY

Your attitudes toward your self and the people in your life take shape immediately after your birth. If you began with the certainty that you were loved, that you were valued, and that nothing could threaten this intimate connection, you were well on your way to developing a secure sense of your self and your ability to form intimate relations with others. This sense of personal security is described eloquently by the psychoanalyst Marie-Louise von Franz: *"The experience of Self brings a feeling of standing on solid ground inside oneself, on a patch of eternity, which even physical death cannot touch."*

But suppose, as is the case for many — perhaps most — people, your initial experiences did not conform to this ideal scenario, or you suffered through emotionally disruptive events in your childhood. In this case, rather than building a solid sense of self, your "self" may feel shaky, your inner reality cloudy and uncertain. In these circumstances, self-love and self-trust are difficult to establish, and lacking this solid ground, it will be just as difficult for you to love and trust others. When you are in relationships, you may lack the certainty that the other people value you, or indeed that you deserve to be valued. There is likely always to be in the background the fear that the loved one is going to leave and not return, taking a part of yourself with him or her. In the absence of a secure and independent identity that can give and receive love with confidence, your relationships may be built on feelings of emotional dependence, vulnerable to the threat of loss and the coercion of others more powerful than yourself.

For most of us, our upbringing was less than the ideal of two parents showering us with unconditional love. But we can overcome a possibly troubled start and, if we choose, become the kind of parents to our children that we wish we had had.

EMPATHY

In all relationships, trust and intimacy are rooted in "empathy," the ability to infer, with your imagination, what others are feeling, and the confidence that your belief is (usually) accurate. It is a certainty that you *know* what someone is feeling and that you *share* the same emotion. This complex, subtle, reciprocal sharing of deeply felt emotions originates in the intimate communications of your earliest relationships.

When people have difficulty in experiencing this reciprocal empathy, it inhibits intimate, healthy relationships of every sort: romantic liaisons, friendships, even productive professional relationships. If you lack the ability truly to share what others are feeling, and to care about what they are experiencing, then forming meaningful relationships will be very difficult. Similarly, if you conclude that someone you care about is unable to empathize with what *you* are feeling, then you will likely have serious misgivings about continuing such a one-sided relationship.

Your "True Self" versus Your "False Self"

In addition to empathy, creating a sense of *personal independence* is also crucial in developing a stable and integrated sense of your self, one that is strengthened over a lifetime. Both qualities — empathy and independence — are essential ingredients in becoming a fully formed critical thinker. Children, as well as adults, are under enormous pressure to conform to the expectations of those around them, pressures that are applied continually in both explicit and subtle ways. The cost of not conforming is high: As a child you risk social rejection, withdrawal of love, stern disapproval, and outright punishment. As an adult, not conforming can threaten your career, create tension in your relationships, and subject you to social condemnation.

Yet the price of conforming is at least as high, particularly when conforming means acting in ways that conflict with your "true" self. You are forced to create a "false" self you present to the world, in the same way that an actor adopts a role that is at odds with his natural personality. Since children are in a more malleable stage of development, the consequences are more immediate and profound. In many cases adults don't sufficiently respect and value a child's evolving inner self. They believe that they "know best," and that it's in the child's best interests to accede to their superior knowledge. Despite protestations from the child, adults bully, cajole, and terrify children into being formed in the adult's image. But the "image" that is created is not a *real self*, it's a *pseudo-self*, reflecting outer demands, not the child's inner reality.

Torn between wanting to maintain a true, authentic self and conforming to the rigid demands from powerful people around them, children (and adults) respond in the only way they can — they divide themselves into two "selves" — an inner self and an outer self, a real self and a pseudo-self, a genuine self and an inauthentic self. Everyone does this to some extent, and you are no doubt extremely aware of the various "roles" that you are called upon to play with the diverse people in your life. We all sometimes choose to "bite our tongues" to avoid giving unnecessary offense, follow dress codes that don't reflect our preferred taste in fashion, and undertake tasks we would rather not do if we had the choice. In instances like these, if your inner self is strong, you are making pragmatic choices that do not compromise "who" you really are.

But if your inner self is weak and fragile, cowering in the face of external demands and pressures, then you run the very real risk of having your core self overwhelmed, submerged, even lost. In these instances, you are continually looking outside yourself for guidance and approval: "What do others want me to do?" "What will they think?" "Will they approve of my decision?" This type of "other-directed" thinking can become endemic, a situation in which the pseudo-self becomes preeminent and dominates your identity. The consequences of this are personally catastrophic. Because you are always looking outside yourself for cues on what to think, how to feel, and how to behave, you become chronically insecure. Without a solid sense of self to ground and orchestrate your actions, you are likely to become overly dependent on those around you, constantly looking for direction and seeking approval. You are likely to feel weak and fragile on the inside, the "self" that you present to the world a carefully constructed artifice lacking your authentic self, your "soul." And without a genuine inner self that originates choices and is grounded on the certainty of being loved, it is impossible for you to develop emotionally mature, empathetically rooted relationships. Relationships that are based on pseudo-selves cannot be anything but pseudo-relationships, superficial and unstable.

Of course, this is rarely an either/or situation: It's typically a continuum. We all place somewhere in between the extremes of a weak, insecure, fragmented, totally "false" self at the one end, and a strong, resilient, integrated "authentic" self at the other. And depending on the specific context and time in your life, you may find yourself at different places on the scale. But wherever you are on the continuum, the challenge remains the same: How can you move away from the "false" self toward the "authentic" self? In other words, how can you become a more secure, optimistic, loving, respectful, supportive, generous, flexible, empathetic, creative, mature person?

THINKING CRITICALLY, LIVING CREATIVELY, CHOOSING FREELY

Although you can't change the historical events that contributed to shaping who you are, by *thinking critically* about your life you can develop insight into how these formative experiences are continuing to affect you in the present. This knowledge — a deep, emotional knowledge — provides you with the power to alter the direction of your life. You can reshape who you are by making choices in line with the new plan for yourself.

By thinking critically about your childhood, for example, you might discover that you were affected by being raised in a family in which physical affection and emotional intimacy were discouraged. This is the past, and it cannot be changed. But what can be changed is your *attitude* toward these events. You can come to understand how an emotionally repressed upbringing undermined your trust in yourself and others, and made it difficult for you to express and receive love. This knowledge acts like a key in a lock, opening your awareness to dynamics in your personality that you can now reshape by changing your attitude and choices. The renowned psychologist Alfred Adler describes this process:

We are affected less by the events which happen in our lives (which we cannot always control) than by our attitudes to those events (which we have rather more chance of "choosing").

Living creatively is the second stage in reconceptualizing your self and redirecting your future. The key is your imagination, the unique human ability to conceive of a situation that is a transformed version of what currently exists. Your imagination gives you the ability to create a much different picture of your self: a self that is loving, secure, and spontaneous. You can also envision a much different life for yourself: an emotionally fulfilling life with warm friendships and intimate relationships. This creatively imagined self and life serve as a blueprint for your future, a life plan that you can use to guide your choices.

The third and final stage of your personal transformation is *choosing freely*. As we discovered in Step 3, genuine freedom of choice requires that you free yourself from internal and external constraints so that you can make choices that are unfettered. If the demons of your childhood are still operating on unconscious levels, for example, you will not be able to choose a new path for your life. This will be possible only if these demons are exorcised. That's why the first stage of this process, *thinking critically*, is so essential. Developing insight into your childhood history and the personality dynamics that were established (and are still operating) serves to illuminate influences of which you were previously unaware. This "truth" can indeed "set you free" from their power. Once liberated, you can, with an act of will, re-create the person you are and the life you are living, following the new plan you have created. The writer C. S. Lewis eloquently describes this:

> Every time you make a choice you are turning the central part of you, the part of you that chooses, into something a little different from what it was before. And taking your life as a whole, with all your innumerable choices, all your life you are slowly turning this central thing into either a heavenly creature or into a hellish creature.

THINKING ACTIVITY

Thinking about Your Childhood

Think about the family circumstances in which you were raised, and respond to the following questions in your Thinking Notebook:

- To what extent did the relationships between family members foster trust in your self and others, a belief in your personal value and the need to value others?
- To what extent did the relationships between family members encourage you to express and receive love and affection?
- Can you identify traumatic events in your family that may have inhibited you from trusting and loving your self and others?
- Can you describe how your childhood relationships with family members may have contributed to the person you are now? Can you detect patterns in your attitudes toward your self and others that reflect these early relationships, particularly in the areas of trust and love?

The questions in this Thinking Activity are enormously complicated. You can think of them as threads that lead to the very fabric of your self, which has been woven over the course of your life, a day at a time, a choice at a time. Pulling these threads can elicit troublesome and even painful memories, as well as cherished recollections. Because the answers to these questions may be deeply buried, your ability to comprehend their significance will not occur overnight. It is likely to take many nights and days to expose fully the dynamic structures of your self to which they are connected. Though time-consuming, there is no substitute for tracing your personal history, and it is a necessity if you want to understand fully who you are in the present.

Closely examining the past does not mean *remaining* in the past. In fact, staying rooted in past events, obsessively reliving them and their emotional content, typically inhibits you from leaving the past behind in order to create a healthier and happier present and future. If you were the victim of painful or depersonalizing experiences in your childhood years, it is important for you to acknowledge and understand them, *and then move on.* As with many things in life, the key is to strike an appropriate balance, using your insight into the past not as a sinkhole to get mired in, but as a point of reference to inform your understanding of the present and your plans for the future.

The Thinker's Way to Healthy Relationships

THOUGH YOU may not have realized it, you have been developing all of the abilities needed for healthy relationships as you worked through the various thinking Steps in the book. Here is an outline of the approach we will be using:

The Thinker's Way to Healthy Relationships

- Think critically.
- Communicate clearly.
- View all perspectives.
- Build trust through reason.
- Foster creativity.
- Value freedom and responsibility.
- Problem-solve.
- Balance dependence and independence.

THINK CRITICALLY ABOUT YOUR RELATIONSHIP

Every relationship is unique and mysterious in its own way, but it is possible to understand a great deal about what is going on and why it is happening, and to influence what will occur in the future — if you make an effort to think clearly. To begin, you should identify what *goals* you have for the relationship. There are general goals that apply to most relationships — being congenial, having clear communication — but there are also goals specific to the relationship in question, whether it is a relationship with a coworker, the doorman, your parent, a close friend, your supervisor, a client, your niece, the baby-sitter, your ex-spouse, a doctor, your latest romantic interest. Too often, however, people *don't* identify objectives or stick to a plan, and as a result they end up spending too much time with people they don't want to be with, and not enough time with those they do. Or they may wreck a potentially good relationship by piling on more expectations than one person can possibly fulfill: lover, best friend, therapist, roommate, tennis partner, drinking buddy, career counselor . . . and more! By defining the goals of the relationship more narrowly — and realistically — the relationship might function more successfully, while imposing excessive expectations might serve as the death warrant.

Another element of thinking critically about relationships is to *look beneath the surface* of what is happening in order to understand the underlying dynamics of what is taking place. Much of our behavior with other people is symbolic, symptomatic of deeper processes and subliminal messages. For example, children, adults, and even pets sometimes act obnoxiously in order to garner negative attention. One of the worst experiences for a person is to be ignored — any attention, even condemnation or reprimand, is preferable. Yet instead of recognizing what the behavior represents and responding to that reality, parents, teachers, supervisors, and virtually everybody else typically responds to the negative behavior with *more* condemnation and reprimands, simply perpetuating the vicious circle. When appropriate, bring these hidden motivations to the surface by asking, for example, "What's the *real* reason you're acting so disruptively or insensitively?"

COMMUNICATE CLEARLY WITH THE OTHER PERSON(S)

Faulty communication is responsible for more problems in relationships than any other factor. How often have you heard — or uttered — the lament "We just don't seem to communicate"? As we discovered in Step 5: Communicate Effectively, clear communication involves a complex blending of thinking, language, and social skills. For example, people often talk *at* each other, not really listening because they are concentrating on what they're going to say next. People can know each other for years and yet lack an in-depth understanding of what the other person is *really* thinking and feeling, all because they don't try to listen and understand.

In order to engage in a productive discussion, you have to articulate your viewpoint clearly, listen carefully to the response of the other person, and then *respond* to their response or *ask questions* to better understand what they are saying. When both people approach the dialogue in this fashion, within a context of mutual respect and caring, meaningful communication can take place. Also, people do have different communication styles that you need to understand in order to avoid misunderstanding, conflict, and fractured relationships.

Another essential dimension of communicating effectively is using language that is *clear* and *precise*. When language is vague or ambiguous, people tend to read into the vagueness their own personal meanings, assuming that other people are thinking exactly the same things that they are. They are often mistaken in this assumption, and trouble follows close behind as a result. A simple expression like "I love you" can express an astonishing number of different meanings, depending on the individual and the particular context. And if for one person, "I love you" means "I think you are an engaging person whom I am sexually attracted to," while the other person is thinking "You are the perfect mate for me, and I expect us to spend eternity together," then there's a Force 5 tornado on the horizon that's likely to hit the relationship sooner or later. Disciplining yourself to speak and behave in ways that are clear, precise, and unambiguous will work wonders in avoiding miscommunications that can begin small but then snowball into much larger problems.

VIEW ALL PERSPECTIVES IN YOUR RELATIONSHIPS

The success of most close relationships — romance, family, and friendships — is directly related to the extent to which you can imaginatively place yourself in the other person's situation and fully appreciate what he or she is experiencing. This in-depth empathy is what emotionally close relationships are all about. In contrast, when two people are excessively concerned with their own interests, with what the other person can do for *me*, then the relationship is in serious trouble. Healthy relationships are based on *shared* interest, not only *self*-interest. It is your ability to identify with the other person that acts as a catalyst for your love, compassion, and understanding — the emotions that form the heart of every vital relationship.

Think back on the last significant altercation you had with someone you are close to. You undoubtedly believed that you viewed the issue with a clarity that the other person didn't possess, and that while you were trying to be the soul of reason and restraint, the other person was trying to coerce you into viewing things his or her confused way. Naturally, the other person was likely experiencing the situation in *nearly the same way that you were*. Once two (or more) people establish these one-sided and self-serving postures, things generally deteriorate until a culminating crisis forces each person to become truly aware of the other.

There is an alternative to this unsatisfactory approach. As a critical thinker, you can make an extra effort to view things differently by asking the other person *why* he or she has arrived at his or her point of view, and then to place yourself in his or her position. And then you can ask the other person, "If you were in my position, how would you view the situation and what would you do?" Exchanging roles in this way, thinking and feeling empathetically within another's perspective, changes the entire tone of the discussion. Instead of exchanges becoming increasingly rancorous ("You don't understand anything"; "You are insensitive and blind"), there is an excellent chance that both of you will work together in a more harmonious and collaborative way to achieve mutual understanding.

BUILD TRUST THROUGH REASON IN YOUR RELATIONSHIPS

Of course, relationships cannot be fully understood by reason any more than reason can fully disclose the mysteries of an exquisite work of art, a moving musical passage, a transcendent spiritual experience, or the spontaneous eruption of delight occasioned by humor. Your reasoning ability is powerful, but it has limits as well, and it is important to appreciate those limits and respect them. People who try to reduce every dimension of the rich tapestry of human experience to logical categories and rational explanations are pursuing fool's gold. Still, reason helps you make sense of the contours and patterns of your emotional life, as well as many other of the elements that form the phenomenon of human relationships.

Suppose someone whom you feel close to does something that wounds you deeply. When you confront the friend and ask *why* he did what he did, further imagine that his response is "I can't give you any reason — I just did it." How would you feel? Probably bewildered and angry, and with good "reason." That's because we expect people — including ourselves — to try to understand why they do what they do, so that they can exert some control over their choices. People hurt other people who are close to them for many different reasons: They may have been acting thoughtlessly, selfishly, stupidly, callously, unconsciously, sadistically, or any number of other ways. There *are* reasons why people behave the way they do, and your confidence and trust in others depend on this conviction. If your friend says to you, "I hurt you and I'm very sorry — I was only thinking of myself during that moment and did not fully appreciate how it might affect you; it was a mistake, and I won't repeat it in the future," then you have a foundation upon which you can build the future of your relationship. But if your friend says to you, "I hurt you for no reason that I can identify, and I don't know if it will happen again," then that makes it very difficult for you to continue trusting him. Remaining in such a relationship is like playing Russian roulette — you don't know when another live round is going to end up behind the firing pin and tear into your heart.

Reason is the framework that makes relationships possible. The more intimate the relationship, the more important the role reason plays. In intimate relationships you are most vulnerable, your emotions laid bare. Reason is the safety net that gives you the courage to take those halting and dangerous steps on the high wire. You build trust in the other person because you believe their choices are governed or at least influenced by reason, and you depend on that assurance. Of course, even the best of intentions can be overwhelmed by mindless passion, unruly emotions, unexpected compulsions. But although emotions may erupt and temporarily swamp your rational faculties, your will and determination can once again set things right, reasserting the primacy of reason in directing your emotions so that your choices reflect your highest values. That's why thoughtful people continue to step onto the high wire again, even after they have fallen, because they have confidence in the rule of reason in well-intentioned people.

FOSTER CREATIVITY AND POSITIVE ATTITUDES IN YOUR RELATIONSHIPS

Think back on the last time you began a new relationship. Wanting to make a good impression, it is likely that you invested a great deal of creative energy in nurturing the budding romance or friendship. Handmade cards, surprise gifts, planning unique activities, making an extra effort to have engaging conversations. Now reflect on long-term relationships in which you are currently engaged: Do you find that a certain staleness has set in? That you have fallen into routine patterns of activity, doing the same things on a fixed schedule? Do your conversations revolve around the same few topics, with the same comments being made with predictable regularity? Have the handmade cards, spontaneous presents, and little surprises disappeared? If so, don't be too hard on yourself: This is a very common deterioration in relationships.

The expression *"Familiarity breeds contempt"* points to the chronic human trait to take for granted the people who are most important to us, letting habit and routine sap the vitality of our relationships. Since relationships are dynamic and alive, treating them as if they were machines running on past momentum will eventually cause them to become rusty and stop working altogether. In many cases, however, they can be revived by choosing to bring the same creative energy to them that you invested at the beginning of the relationship and by encouraging your partner to realize his or her creative potential. The result: a creative fusion between the two of you that will inspire you both with its power.

VALUE FREEDOM AND RESPONSIBILITY IN YOUR RELATIONSHIPS

Healthy relationships are ones in which the participants willingly take responsibility for themselves and value the freedom of others. As noted in Step 3: Choose Freely, responsibility is the logical consequence of freedom, and while people cherish their personal freedom, they tend to flee from responsibility when things don't go according to plan. Consider the following situations. You are working collaboratively with a number of other colleagues on an important project. When the client rejects the results of your group effort, the CEO wants to know who's to blame for the fiasco. With your career on the line, what do you say? Or imagine that you are the parent of a child with an approaching birthday. You promised tickets to a special concert, but you procrastinate, and by the time you get around to buying the tickets, they're sold out. What explanation do you give to your child? If you found yourself instinctively trying to minimize your personal responsibility in these situations (and maximize the responsibility of other people), it's not surprising. These are common human reactions. But healthy relationships are based on a willingness to *assume responsibility*, not evade it. By fully acknowledging your responsibility, you gain stature in the eyes of others, and encourage them to accept responsibility for their actions as well. However, if you chronically *avoid* responsibility for your mistakes and failings, you erode the trust and goodwill in relationships, and you shrink in stature.

Accepting responsibility means promoting freedom. Pursuing your own personal freedom is a natural and appropriate thing to do. But to foster healthy relationships with others it is equally important to promote and respect their freedom. For example, suppose that you are absolutely certain you know what is best for someone — your child should choose a certain college, your romantic partner should agree to marry you. Are you justified in subtly shaping and manipulating their thoughts and emotions so that they'll make the "right" decision? In the long run, this course of action would not be what's best for the relationship or perhaps for the other person. Healthy relationships value the autonomy of other people to make their own decisions, independent of our wishes. Once they discover, as they likely will, that you are trying to pressure or manipulate them, you run the risk of undermining the mutual trust that the relationship is based on.

PROBLEM-SOLVE IN YOUR RELATIONSHIP

Problems are a natural part of life, and they are an unavoidable reality in relationships as well. The only question is how you are going to deal with the problems that you will inevitably encounter. You can approach problems with fear and loathing, letting them intimidate you and contaminate your relationship. Or you can approach these same problems with the confidence of a critical thinker, viewing them as opportunities to clarify important issues and improve your relationship. Frederick Nietzsche's observation *"What doesn't kill you makes you stronger"* applies to relationships as well. The strongest, most resilient relationships are those that have been tested, have overcome adversity, and ultimately have triumphed through the efforts of all parties. The most vulnerable relationships are those that have *not* been tested, thus being denied the opportunity to develop coping skills and the confidence that the first serious wave won't capsize the boat. Repeated successes with problems both large and small breed confidence in your problem-solving abilities, and in the resilience of your most significant relationships.

For example, solving problems is one of the main activities of any relationship. Many of the problems are benign: The television is broken; there's nothing in the refrigerator for dinner; you've been invited to a wedding that neither of you wants to attend. Other problems are more serious: You or your partner has been offered an attractive job opportunity in a different city; you disagree over the religious faith in which your child should be raised. And finally, there are the most serious problems that strike at the heart of the relationship, problems that pose a threat to its very existence: There is no visible love between you and your partner; only one of you wants to have children; your relationship is dominated by acrimonious fighting.

Not all of these problems can be solved perfectly, but by taking an informed problem-solving approach such as that described in Step 4: Solve Problems Effectively, it is possible to identify clearly the central issues, generate and evaluate many possible alternatives, reach an intelligent solution, and implement your conclusion with determination and flexibility.

BALANCE DEPENDENCE AND INDEPENDENCE IN YOUR RELATIONSHIPS

Healthy relationships blend dependence and independence in a dynamic balance. Problems can occur when this balance is upset: that is, if one or more of the people involved become either too dependent or too independent. You have likely experienced both kinds of imbalances in your life. In some situations you may have leaned heavily on the relationship, while the other person seemed much less invested. In other relationships, you may have felt that the other person was excessively needy and "clingy" compared to the role of the relationship in your life.

You have probably played both of these roles with different people in your life, sometimes simultaneously. For example, you may be very emotionally dependent on a parent but relatively independent with your close friendships. Or you may find yourself excessively dependent on your boss for approval and direction, but reasonably independent with regard to your romantic partner. In addition, the same relationship can evolve through different stages. You may begin a romantic relationship feeling very independent, but gradually become increasingly dependent until you have lost control of your emotions. Or you may begin a friendship by leaning heavily on it for many personal needs, but as time goes by transform this into a more independent role. Dependence and independence are roles that can shift back and forth between the participants in a relationship, reflecting different stages of development. This is particularly true of the relationships between parents and children, as dependence and independence are often exchanged at different life stages.

If you find that a relationship is out of balance, that you are either too dependent or too independent, how do you go about setting things right? We saw earlier in the chapter that healthy relationships require a strong, secure sense of "self." When you feel too dependent in a relationship, this is a symptom that your sense of self is weak and that you are looking outside yourself for stability, strength, and completeness. Since you do not love yourself sufficiently, you are hoping that someone else can fill this void, and this unrealistic expectation fuels the anxiety and urgency that you feel when you say such things as "I don't know what I would do if you left me." But someone else's affection cannot compensate for your own lack of self-love, and since you do not believe yourself to be worthy of love, you won't be able fully to accept their affection anyway. Hence the insecurity in dependent relationships: "Do you really love me? Will you tell me again? Can you prove it to me?" The more desperate and demanding you become, the more likely that the other person in the relationship will back off from it. Overcoming dependency begins by developing a strong, vital sense of your self based on self-love and self-respect.

Interestingly, too much independence in relationships stems from the same personality dynamics as too much dependence: a weak sense of self, lacking sufficient self-love and respect. This inner fragility and low self-esteem make it difficult for you to develop close, intimate relationships because it feels very dangerous to risk the potential rejection and hurt that such emotional openness entails. Excessive independence is often a flight from intimacy, a profound fear of emotional closeness masquerading as cool detachment. The path to overcoming this alienated approach to relationships is the same as for excessive dependence: establishing a strong, vital sense of your self that is grounded on self-love and self-respect.

Thinking about Romantic Relationships

THE CONTEMPORARY romantic couple is a fragile life form that is evolving— or mutating, depending on your perspective — at an alarmingly rapid pace. For centuries the "couple" was a necessary social structure. People went through courtship rituals with a limited number of potential partners (often just one) and then directly into marriages that were expected to be lifetime commitments. Romantic love, while desirable, was not considered to be the only — or even most important — ingredient of these marriages, which were often arranged or influenced by the parents. More significant than love was the marriage's role as a building block for social stability: to raise children, pass on values, serve as an economic nucleus, and carry on the daily tasks of living.

The relationships between couples today are expected to serve all of these social functions and also attend to all of the emotional and sexual needs of the partners — and to do so in relative isolation. While in the past the family was tied closely to extended families and surrounding communities that provided a great deal of emotional and logistical support, couples today are often sailing on their own small boats, rather than sharing passage on a larger vessel. With both parents pursuing careers and entering the workforce, this has led to unprecedented complexities in child-rearing. And the truly brave new world of genetic technology means that "couples" are no longer needed to conceive a child.

Under barrage from all sides — burdensome expectations, increasing isolation, and inflated demands for personal happiness — the modern couple is a fragile and endangered species. Relationships fall apart as easily as they are formed, accelerated by the frantic pace and mobility of modern society. And yet — people *do* continue to seek love, form relationships, and have children. They *do* aspire to finding long-term intimacy and meaning in relationships born of optimism and personal commitment. Their intentions are typically honorable, their hopes and dreams understandable, and the successes that do occur serve as inspiration. There is a new trend: to preserve a marriage or long-term relationship, to persist and "work it out" despite the powerful currents of social evolution that are often beyond our control and comprehension. In many ways, the self-absorbed "me" decade of the 1980s is gradually being replaced by the "we" decade of the 1990s. But we're going to have to use all of our critical thinking abilities to insure that these admirable intentions are fulfilled in reality.

THINKING ACTIVITY

Your Real and Ideal Relationships

Think about your personal history with romantic relationships by responding to the following questions in your Thinking Notebook.

- Describe one or more of the most important intimate relationships you have had in your adult life. Identify both the positive and negative qualities of the relationship(s). If the relationship has continued successfully, analyze the qualities that have enabled it to endure. If the relationship ended, analyze the factors that accounted for its dissolution.
- Using the power of your imagination, conjure up a detailed image of an ideal romantic relationship for yourself. What qualities would it possess? What needs would it fulfill? What kind of person would your partner be? What are the best qualities of yourself that the relationship would bring out?
- Compare your ideal relationship with your actual relationship(s). In what ways has your real experience(s) matched your ideal? In what ways has it fallen short? Do you think your ideal relationship is attainable? Why or why not?

THE STAGES OF ROMANTIC RELATIONSHIPS

Think back to the beginning of an important romantic relationship in your life. It was probably a time of wonder, excitement, anticipation, and discovery, fueled by a primal energy that involved all aspects of your being. You felt intelligent, witty, engaging, sexually attractive — qualities that you viewed through the eyes of your enamored partner. You likely experienced a special connection with this person, the interlocking of two complex puzzles: At last, here was someone who appreciated your uniqueness, whom you could trust with your deepest emotions and innermost thoughts, someone whom you instinctively *responded to* in a very immediate and profound way. Here was your life partner, your missing half. Your coming together generated its own electricity, created its own aura.

Then time passed. And with the passage of time, the voltage ebbed, the aura dimmed. You began to discover some disappointing but very human traits in your partner. Worse than that, your formerly perfect partner began to discover some imperfections in you, *and began to point these failings out!* Routine set in, and the anticipation of unexpected discoveries gradually gave way to the humdrum of daily life. Minor differences of opinion progressively developed into roaring conflagrations, fueling raised voices, hurtful words, and contorted expressions in your former beloved. You asked yourself, "Was I blind? How could I have viewed this person as my life partner? What a fool I was to trust such a person."

Your relationship may have ended at this point, as you went off in search of another perfect partner, believing that, though wounded, you were wiser and would avoid making the same mistakes again. Or you might have decided that the relationship had enough potential to justify trying to resuscitate it. You and your partner persevered, working through the pain and disappointment, readjusting your expectations from the fantastical to the realistic. Though the initial shimmering beauty of the relationship was tarnished, you began to discover depths, talents, and resources in the other person you hadn't initially appreciated. Together, you and your partner discovered approaches for resolving disagreements that prevented destructive escalation, and you developed an empathetic appreciation for your partner's point of view. You learned that you could solve problems together, that you could learn from your painful experiences and create a future together that would be long-lasting and personally fulfilling. Which brought you back, on a deeper level, to your initial optimistic point of view.

In their book *Couples: Exploring and Understanding the Cycles of Intimate Relationships*, couple therapists Barry Dym and Michael L. Glenn identify recurring stages common to all enduring relationships and contend that by understanding how these stages function, you can learn how to navigate — and affirm — your own intimate relationships.

These stages are common to most relationships and generally recur many times: We are attracted, we drift away, and then we come together again. But each successive pass through the stages is both similar to and different from the previous passes, and each couple develops its own "character," created by its distinctive ways of negotiating each of the stages. If couples are able to learn to recognize their cycles of conflict and resolution and adapt to them, they develop the ability to survive the difficult times, grow closer together, and thrive. In time, they may reach a clarity of vision in which they see their partner fully and are able to accept and love without ambivalence or reservation.

People who are able to weather problems are people who think critically, who approach their relationships thoughtfully and courageously. Developing an enduring intimate relationship is an achievement of the highest order. It is a living badge of courage and commitment, symbolizing two people's determination to sustain their relationship in the face of long odds, hostile influences, unexpected tragedies, self-doubts, and recriminations. Many relationships never achieve this state of enduring intimacy, either because the match was wrong or because one or both of the partners lacked the desire or the capability to succeed over the long haul. Achieving enduring, intimate relationships involves learning to negotiate successfully their recurring stages, the crucible through which your relationships are formed and reformed.

The Thinker's Way to Healthy Relationships described previously provides a useful framework for guiding your journey through *all* relationships, but there are additional principles that are particularly relevant to intimate relationships.

UNDERSTAND THE CONTEXT OF YOUR RELATIONSHIP

Knowledge is power. By understanding the various forces at work on your relationship, you are better able to understand the issues clearly and exert meaningful influence. For example, no person approaches a new romantic relationship as a blank slate, and no intimate relationship exists in a vacuum. It's essential that you view your relationship within the context of what Barry Dym and Michael L. Glenn term the *Cultural Narrative* and your *Individual Narrative*. The Cultural Narrative is the vast social script that articulates society's views of how people should relate to one another, including how they should form and carry out romantic relationships. This "conventional wisdom" is expressed as contemporary parables in films, television, fiction, and popular psychology, as well as the stories and personal experiences related by important people in your life.

For better or for worse, the Cultural Narrative acts as a third presence in the relationship — supporting and criticizing, reassuring, and raising doubts. If a couple complies with the traditional roles and patterns, their relationship fits seamlessly into the cultural framework. But deviation from the norm creates dissonance and subtle condemnation: a "house-husband" whose wife is the primary breadwinner; a gay couple with children; an interracial couple; a couple who choose to be childless. To achieve reflective insight, a couple must be aware of how the themes of the Cultural Narrative are woven into their relationship and understand the influence these themes exert.

The couple is further defined by the Individual Narratives that each partner brings to the relationship. Your Individual Narrative is, quite literally, the "story of your life according to you." It is likely that other people would tell the story differently, but from your standpoint, your version is the one that counts. Your story weaves together your accumulated experiences and your concept of your "self" to form a living narrative. A significant part of this narrative encompasses your intimate relationships with others: what they have been; what you would like them to be. As you approach a new potential partner, you are bringing with you a host of assumptions, expectations, and aspirations — the "lenses" through which you view this person and the budding relationship. And of course, the other person is doing exactly the same thing. The underlying problem, as we found in Step 1: Think Critically, is that people are generally unaware of their lenses that are shaping their perceptions, and so they consistently make the mistake of believing that the "reality" they see is objectively true. This unconscious assumption lim-

its understanding and leads inevitably to conflict with other people's
"realities." You see your partner one way, while your partner sees himself differently. These potential confusions can be sorted out only by
both partners becoming aware of the Individual Narratives that they are
bringing to the relationship, enabling them to create a *Couple Narrative* that reflects their shared "reality."

UNDERSTAND THE DYNAMICS OF YOUR RELATIONSHIP

Reason gives us the power to understand the dynamic processes at
work in human relationships and adapt ourselves to them. "You can't
hurry love," one song advises, and this is true of many life processes, including the developmental stages that couples encounter. These stages
are beyond our control; like strong currents, they pick us up and carry
us along. But there are many things we can do to facilitate the process
if we are thinking clearly. For example, simply being aware of the stages
and their cyclical movement should provide you with a conceptual
framework that helps you understand what you are experiencing and
why you are experiencing it. While you are enjoying fully the passionate and idealistic initial stages of a relationship, you can at the same time
be aware that what you are experiencing is, to a certain extent, a mutually created infatuation that will be tested by harsh judgments during
subsequent stages. But forewarned is forearmed. With this understanding in mind, you won't have to panic when the bloom steals off the rose
and your shared fantasy is exposed to the light of reality. You will understand that you are simply following the typical developmental path
of romantic relationships, influenced by forces that you can become
aware of and explore with your partner. Similarly, when your relationship is mired in the depths of conflict and disaffection, you can be assured that things have not necessarily fallen completely apart, and that
if you and your partner persevere, you can build a stronger and wiser
intimacy.

THINKING ACTIVITY

Understanding Your Relationship

Work with your partner to answer and discuss the following issues.

- Using the idea of "relationship stages," map the path of the intimate relationship in which you are currently involved (or your most recent relationship). What stages have you passed through? In what stage do you think the relationship is currently situated? Based on your analysis, in what direction should you and your partner be moving to promote the vitality of your intimacy?
- Articulate the *Cultural Narrative* and the *Individual Narratives* that serve as the context for your relationship, and analyze the effects these potent narratives have on your dealings with each other.

FOSTER POSITIVE ENERGY IN YOUR RELATIONSHIPS

Creativity is a vitalizing force in every relationship, as well as in your life as a whole, but it is particularly important for maintaining the energy and freshness of your intimate, romantic relationships. In general, relationships benefit dramatically when the partners avoid negative judgment, emphasize curiosity, and instinctively assume the best, rather than the worst. Love, kindness, consideration, generosity, humor, playfulness — these are not fixed quantities that must be spent carefully. They represent inexhaustible funds that require only our willingness to draw on them, and our willingness is inspired by our partner's willingness.

AVOID BLAMING YOUR PARTNER IN THE RELATIONSHIP

Intimacy thrives on emotional honesty and generosity of spirit, but these can only occur when you respect the free autonomy of your partner while assuming full responsibility for your own thoughts, actions, and feelings. It is more the exception than the rule to find two emotionally mature people who take primary responsibility for their own happiness, even while being loved and supported by their partner. It is much more common for couples to accuse the *other* person of being responsible for their *lack* of happiness, with sentences like "If only you would ——, I could be happy," or "I am unhappy because you are ——." At the same time, we often (consciously and unconsciously) work to undermine the genuine freedom of our partners by attempting to manipulate, control, or influence their thinking using any means we can, rather than encouraging their autonomy and respecting their free choices. Stephanie Dowrick observes:

> You cannot *make* other people happy. If who you are increases someone else's happiness, that is a joy for you both. But it is impossible to accept the burden of someone else's happiness (or their unhappiness) without coming to resent it, and risking losing respect for the selfhood of that person.

Although it may boost your ego to have someone tell you, *"You make me so happy,"* it's a dangerous statement that can just as easily become *"You make me so unhappy."* It's essential for both partners to accept responsibility for themselves but not for the other person, just as both people must accept their own freedom and respect the freedom of others.

THINKING ACTIVITY

Enriching Your Relationship

Accentuating the "positive" and diminishing the "negative" will enrich and energize your relationship.

- Make a special effort to acknowledge and respond in kind to positive words and action from your partner. Identify negative intentions immediately and transform them into something positive.

- Identify the "blame" statements that occur in your intimate relationship and analyze them (with your partner, if possible). Where do these statements originate? What needs do they reflect? To what extent is it justifiable to hold the "blamed" person responsible?
- Work toward creating the "ideal love" by fostering a caring, open, trusting relationship in which both partners are both strong and loving.

Nurture Thinking Children

WE BEGAN this book with the provocative statement *"We are becoming a society of nonthinkers,"* and nowhere is this more evident than in our relationships with our children. In theory, adults recognize the importance of raising children who are thoughtful, independent, creative, and morally principled. "Children are the future" is a cliché that is frequently heard, always accompanied by nodding heads and murmured assent. In practice, however, adults often act in ways that prevent and inhibit the development of thoughtful, independent, creative, and morally principled children. This conflict between theory and practice in raising and educating children means that we are creating a world that is *less* thoughtful, *less* creative, and *less* moral than it ought to be. And we are squandering an incalculable fortune in human potential as a direct consequence of our actions.

THE POWER OF CRITICAL THINKING

As discouraging as the current trends regarding our children are, the process is reversible. The human mind is an extraordinary resource, boundless in its capabilities and inexhaustible in its energy. It needs only to be stimulated and directed in order to achieve extraordinary results. The challenge is not so much for the children as for the adults: Do *we* have the vision and the will to encourage children to become thoughtful, independent, creative, morally principled individuals? For many adults, the answer is not obvious. If we are to truly pursue these ideals for our children, we must as a consequence:

- encourage them to *think for themselves*, even when their conclusions disagree with ours;
- encourage them to *question and evaluate* what they are told, even when we are the authorities telling them;
- encourage them to *think and act creatively*, even though the results may run counter to established norms, accepted styles, or popular wisdom;
- encourage them to develop *well-reasoned moral beliefs* and an understanding of their *spiritual natures*, even though their point of view may deviate or even conflict with our convictions.

In other words, if we truly want children to become thoughtful, independent, creative, and morally principled, then we have to *respect* them as individuals and *trust* their abilities to think carefully and act with integrity. We have to surrender our innate desire to control them "for their own good," and we have to give up the idea that we "always know best." This doesn't mean that we shouldn't make every effort to guide children toward wisdom and enlightened values — but it does mean that we recognize that the only meaningful thinking that people do is thinking for themselves, and the only meaningful choices that people make are the choices they make themselves after thoughtful analysis.

WHEN DO YOU START TEACHING PEOPLE TO THINK?

I am always amused when "experts" declare that people cannot engage in formal operational thinking until their late teens, cannot think critically until their junior or senior year of college, and are not capable of fully abstract thinking until their twenties. Such theoretical pronouncements simply ignore the subtlety, sophistication, and power of children's thought processes.

"When do you start teaching people to think?" As soon as possible.

Recent studies have discovered that actively speaking to infants in the very first months of life shapes their abilities to think for the rest of their lives. The neurological foundations for rational thinking, problem-solving, and general reasoning are largely established by age one, and language spoken to them by attentive, engaged caregivers (television and radio do not work) has an astonishing impact on their brain development, creating more complex networks of neurons that enable them to be intelligent, creative, and adaptable in all the years that follow. Some of the research suggests a direct correlation between language and thinking: The number of words an infant hears each day is the single most important predictor of later intelligence, school success, and social competence.

Beyond speaking to infants, the advent of language in children provides the first opportunity to nurture their thinking processes directly. While our daughter Jessie displayed a remarkably calm, philosophical demeanor as an infant (which she has retained to this day!), our son Joshua was more than willing to express his displeasure when things didn't go his way. All of this changed when he acquired language. My wife and I could explain to him why it was time to go to bed, the dangers of walking down the stairs unassisted, the need to dress warmly when going outside on a cold day. In other words, we could *reason* with him, and in doing so, we were helping him develop his own reasoning abilities, tools he could use to understand what was going on and, more significantly, *why*. Armed with this insight and sense of control, his tantrums disappeared, replaced with a spirited analytical ability (that continues to this day!). The twin processes of thought and language evolve together, intertwining in such complex relationships that they are soon impossible to disentangle. And both of these processes begin at the earliest stages of human development.

CHILDREN ARE NATURAL PHILOSOPHERS

Young children are brimming over with intellectual energy, blending innate curiosity, passionate convictions, and imaginative speculation: not coincidentally, the essential ingredients required for thinking critically and developing a philosophical perspective on the world. "Why?" is perhaps the most penetrating question in human language and thought, and children use it liberally, sometimes driving adults to distraction. Asking "Why?" shakes up complacent attitudes, forcing us to expose hidden assumptions and to articulate the rationale for our conclusions.

But how do adults respond to children's spirited passion for exploring, reflecting, discussing, and understanding? The disappointing reality is that adults often respond poorly. They become irritated with "all these questions" and dismissive. Rather than treasuring and nurturing these budding intellects, adults often trample the buds in the name of "reality." Why? In large measure because they have lost their own abilities to wonder, to speculate, to think deeply. They are so caught in the demanding minutiae of daily existence that they have lost sight of their essential nature as a thinking, exploring, reflecting, living "self," engaged in the ongoing process of self-creation and re-creation. They have forsaken the pleasure of exploring the life of the mind, the courage to stray off the path of socially accepted explanations to confront both the terror and exhilaration of the unknown. Aristotle recognized that "*Philosophy begins in wonder.*" Losing the ability to "wonder" is perhaps the greatest price that many adults have paid in growing up, adapting to social expectations, and taking their place in the adult world with the burden of reality strapped to their backs.

When adults fail to respond to children's wonder and passion for understanding with openness and enthusiasm, the consequences are devastating. They impoverish their own intellectual lives, failing to seize the opportunity to reignite their own long-extinguished imaginations and love of intellectual exploration. They diminish their relationships with their children, undermining the children's belief in themselves and weakening the trust that is built on mutual respect and acceptance. And finally, they discourage in their children the spirit of independent intellectual inquiry, thus inhibiting their development into intelligent, productive, and fulfilled human beings. The cumulative effect of failing to nurture the minds of our children is a society that emphasizes superficiality over thoughtfulness, practicality over wonder, passive acceptance over active inquiry. It is a society that too often reflects our fears rather than our hopes, our anxieties rather than our dreams — a society that has ignored the insight expressed by Henry Ward Beecher: *"The imagination is the secret of civilization, / It is the very eye of faith."*

How to Think with Children

"Why did God create life?" "What is at the end of space?" "What happens after forever?" "Do people still love after they die?" "Suppose that animals could think just as well as we could, what would the world be like?" "Imagine that stuffed animals had feelings, how would you treat them?" These questions, and countless others like them, were served up to me by my children, Jessie and Joshua, during their early years of development. As they have matured, their challenging questions have continued unabated, reflecting their evolving intellects and increased knowledge. Their questions are more typical than unique, because for most children, philosophical thinking is as natural an activity as playing games or singing. So how do you respond to children's questions in order to nurture their thinking and expand their minds? Here are some guidelines:

Take Their Questions and Observations Seriously: This is probably the most important contribution you can make. By treating their questions and observations seriously, you are according them respect, validating the worth of their thinking, and creating a trusting relationship in which they can let their minds run free without fear of condemnation or ridicule. And their thinking *should* be taken seriously. Though you may not recognize it initially, you will often find very subtle and sophisticated reasoning at work as you explore ideas together. Well into my discussion of the hypothetical reality of stuffed animals with Jessie, she finally remarked: *"You probably don't think about my animals the same way that I do. I really think that they're real and have feelings. I feel so sad that I can't play with all of them. I wish I had 550 arms so I could hold them all at the same time."* At the age of six, when we had this discussion, Jessie "knew" on one level that her stuffed animals weren't "real" in a literal sense. But she also knew that they possessed an emotional reality for her that was extremely important. Had I responded to her initial query with an amused, condescending "But stuffed animals aren't real!" it is unlikely that we would have had a chance to explore the deeper processes at work.

Ask Questions Instead of Trying to Provide Answers: Although children are framing their thoughts as questions, they are really meant to be springboards for using their minds and engaging in lively discussions. Many adults (and too many teachers, unfortunately!) believe that they should have a ready answer for *any* question a child asks. This is a misguided illusion: Many of the most profound questions do not have simple answers, or perhaps any conclusive answer, echoing H. L. Mencken's challenging observation, *"To every complex question there's a simple answer — and it's wrong!"* What's even more harmful is the adult's attempt to appear omniscient. By pretending to know everything, you make the child feel inadequate and you run the very real risk of coming across as a hypocrite. What's worse, providing "the answer" stops the discussion in its tracks, short-circuiting explorations into unknown territories. Conversely, when you exhibit the confidence to say "I don't know the answer," your unembarrassed candor gains you stature in the eyes of children and adults alike. When Jessie surprised me with *"Why did God create life?"* as we were driving one day, I knew immediately that I was overmatched. *"Why do you think God created life?"* I asked gamely. She thought a minute, and then replied, *"So that He would feel useful. Otherwise, what use would He be?"* Bravo, Jessie!

Enter Your Child's World Instead of Imposing Your Own: As noted previously, it's an almost irresistible temptation for adults to view children as "imperfect adults," similar but less developed. This is a mistake. Children have their own way of organizing reality, guided by their own priorities and internal logic. What they lack in real-world knowledge, they more than compensate for in imagination and creativity. But you will never find out much about their world if you don't make the effort to leave your own world and enter theirs. This is precisely what great literature asks of us, to suspend our disbelief and enter a different universe governed by its own rules and logic. Entering worlds different from your own helps you develop flexibility in your thinking, can provoke new ideas and fresh perspectives, and can lead to emotional "truths." When, at the age of six, Joshua asked how weather balloons worked, I started to answer and then caught myself. "How do you think they work?" I asked. He replied, *"I think that there is just one big weather balloon and God, who is everywhere, whispers to it what the weather will be, and then puts it gently on the ground."* What such a response lacks in scientific accuracy, it more than makes up for in imagination and poetic beauty.

Encourage Perspective-Taking: As we have seen throughout our explorations together, striving to view issues and situations from different perspectives is one of the central abilities of thinking critically, and children are never too young to begin developing this mental flexibility. By adopting another's point of view, you are able to develop an empathetic understanding that broadens your vision and deepens your insight. This helps children transcend their natural egocentrism, and enhances your understanding as well. One evening when Joshua was giving me a particularly hard time about going to bed, inundating me with compelling arguments (*"If I stay up longer we can spend more time together"*) and endless distractions (*"Let's go see what the stars look like tonight"*), I finally said in exasperation: *"Okay. You be the dad and I'll be the son. It's your job to get me to bed."* We played these new roles for about ten minutes. After an energetic start, Joshua gradually lost enthusiasm for his new role. Finally, he said: *"It's hard being the dad. Let's go back to the way we were."* He went to bed without further incident (not that this was a lasting solution!). Several months later he assured me, *"There's one job you're never going to lose and that's being my father."*

This perspective-taking lesson came back to haunt me recently. I was rollerblading with Joshua on a path that runs along the Hudson River when I collided with a man rollerblading from the opposite direction. "That idiot — he should watch where he's going," I complained angrily. Joshua (now twelve) observed, *"It was partially your fault, Dad."* I did not appreciate his unsolicited opinion and told him so. He looked me in the eye and said, *"You're supposed to be the critical thinker. Put yourself in his position and see it from his point of view."*

Don't Be Afraid to Tackle the Tough Issues: Adults sometimes go out of their way to protect children from some of the unpleasant realities of life, but such caution is usually misplaced. Children think deeply about serious issues, and are acutely aware of the full range and nuances of human emotion. Death, for example, is the source of existential anguish for all of us, young and old, and our attempts to create euphemisms ("Grampa went away on a long trip"), or avoid the subject entirely often reflect our own fears as much as concern for our children. At the age of four, Joshua observed, *"The problem is, Dad, you grow and then you die. I don't want to die."* It would have been disingenuous of me to try to sugarcoat the reality of death. Joshua was already beyond that in his thinking. My role, I believed, was to acknowledge his fears and assure him that such feelings are universal.

Children appreciate a serious discussion of the issues. Shortly after the death of her maternal grandfather, Jessie, aged four, asked, *"Do people still love after they die?"* She wanted to know if the connections we have formed in life continue in some form after death. Since I believe in a continued spiritual existence after death, I was able to respond honestly that I thought they did, but that this was a question that was very serious and complicated. My father died last year, and on the evening of his death Joshua, then eleven, said in his bedtime prayer, *"Thank you for taking Grandpa so peacefully, without pain. Please welcome him into eternal happiness. Watch over him, because he is a great man."* At the funeral service Jessie, then seventeen, said in part, during her eulogy, *"I won't forget you. I won't forget our long walks together, and someday we'll walk down that road again. You've been the best grandfather I could ever imagine. I love you."*

Our children need us to help them confront and deal with the many difficult challenges life presents to them. We should actively endeavor to share with them, honestly and openly, the understanding that we have earned through our years of experience. They do not need protection from life's harsh realities, they need our love and support as they seek to discover their own answers to life's mysteries.

Foster Moral Intelligence: Some of the most difficult issues that children wrestle with are moral in nature: how they ought to behave, how they ought to treat other people. Once again, adults tend to underestimate the sophistication with which children think through the complexities of moral issues. *"Why are bad people bad?"* Jessie encapsulated the enigma of evil in this trenchant question at an early age. Are people born evil? Are they taught or conditioned through social circumstances to be evil? Or do they choose to be evil? After viewing the movie *Treasure Island* together, we had a number of discussions focused on the question of whether Long John Silver was a "good" man or a "bad" man. His moral ambiguity makes him a fitting character for exploring these issues. He is an unrepentant murderer and thief, but he also has a genuine affection for Jim Hawkins and protects him from harm. "Good" man or "bad" man? Our analysis concluded that these are not clear-cut categories, that each of us is capable of both good and evil.

In his insightful book *The Moral Intelligence of Children*, the psychiatrist and author Robert Coles provides a penetrating analysis of the nature of morality and how it develops — or fails to develop — in people.

> Children who are kind, who think about others, who are generous in their willingness to see the world as others see it, to experience the world through someone else's eyes, and to act on that knowledge with kindness — these are children who have developed an enlightened moral sense.

How did they develop this moral sense? By observing the people in their world and reflecting on their observations.

As adults, our responsibility to children is twofold. First, we need to recognize that we act as moral models for children, and that our character (or lack of character) is expressed through every choice we make, every action we take. Children are much too shrewd to be deceived by people who preach high moral values but who act in immoral ways. So our first obligation is to provide the best moral example that we can, by helping them understand that, despite our best intentions, we are imperfect creatures ourselves. We strive for the best, falter, try to learn from our mistakes, and become better through the process. And this is our second responsibility to children, to help provide them with the thinking abilities they will need to reason through moral dilemmas on their own. The principles and conclusions explored in Step 6: Develop Enlightened Values are as true for children as they are for adults, and we should help them profit from the moral wisdom that is available.

Encourage Self-Insight and Responsibility: After more than twenty years of teaching, I have come to believe that the successful development of young people is based on the twin pillars of *personal responsibility* and *respect* (for yourself and others). Accepting responsibility for yourself means that you acknowledge that you have the capacity to make free choices, and that the choices you make create the person that you are. As noted in Step 3: Choose Freely, there are many influences in our culture that are designed to restrict and erode our sense of personal freedom, and young people are particularly susceptible to these forms of mind-control and manipulation. When people — young or old — come to believe that their freedom is illusory or severely circumscribed, they feel powerless and depressed. So it is our responsibility, as adults, to help young people (of every age) see that personal freedom is real, but only if they seize it. Their destiny is in their hands, but they must *choose* to accept this control and not cede it to others.

Use a Problem-Solving Approach: Many young people are poor problem-solvers because they either don't recognize the nature of their problems, or they don't believe that they can do anything to affect their outcome. Young people can learn from Step 4: Solve Problems Effectively. They can learn to recognize and accept their problems, a breakthrough that depends on embracing their personal freedom and acknowledging their responsibility. They then need to develop a "deep" knowledge of an effective problem-solving method, similar to that described in Step 4, and the confidence (and support) needed to put this method into action. As I have witnessed over and over, when people see the power and success that accompanies such an approach, it is a process that becomes self-motivating and self-perpetuating. But adults need to teach young people to approach their problems in a thoughtful and organized way, and that means that the adults *themselves* need to be accomplished problem-solvers. We need to teach them by example, in the way we approach our own problems; and we need to teach them as teachers, with insight and patience. Children of very young ages are able to fully understand the basics of such an approach and their responsibility in implementing it.

Inspire Them to Believe in Themselves and Achieve Their Greatest Potential: We create reality at least as much as we discover it. In one famous research study, teachers were assigned two classes and were told that one class was a "bright" class, while the other was "average." In actual fact, both classes were of equal ability. Over the course of the term, the teachers created self-fulfilling prophecies: that is, they treated the "bright" classes as if they were exceptionally intelligent, and as a consequence the students *believed* that they were and performed superbly. In contrast, the same teachers treated the "average" classes as if they were average, and this is the conclusion that the students arrived at, performing at a much lower level than the "bright" group.

This same phenomenon occurs in adults' individual relationships with children; in fact, the consequences are even more pronounced. When adults treat children as if they are valuable, intelligent, and uniquely talented, this is the self-concept that they are likely to form of themselves, providing they have additional confirming experiences. However, when adults are consistently critical and belittling, always finding fault rather than giving *thoughtful* praise, then the children will tend to view themselves as inadequate and unworthy.

This is a tremendous power adults have over children, and it is often not fully recognized and as a result can be terribly misused. Adults are routinely tough on children "for their own good," and they are often critical of even stellar achievements in order to "bring out the best in them." Adults also permit their anger and frustrations over the day's events to spill over onto their children because they are the most readily available targets, or they simply ignore them and their achievements because they are so wrapped up in their own lives. The human consequences of these behaviors are devastating and long-lasting. It may take years of arduous effort for a person to construct a reasonably secure identity and positive self-esteem in the place of the ruins of his or her childhood.

But the opposite is also the case. When you believe in children, place your faith in them, support their efforts, encourage them through the rough times, and praise them for their successes — these same children will amaze you with their accomplishments. That is our solemn and moral responsibility to young people: to give them every opportunity to believe in themselves and realize their potentials, and to do everything we can to avoid doing harm. The writer Franz Kafka wrote, *"The arrows fit exactly into the holes that they have made."* When we abuse children — mentally, emotionally, or physically — we are creating wounds that they ultimately come to believe they deserve. But we can easily rework this potent metaphor to: *The hands of encouragement lift people up to the towering heights where they belong.*

How Well Do I Relate to Others?

DESCRIBED BELOW are key personal attributes that are correlated with engaging in successful relationships. Evaluate your position regarding each of these attributes, and use this self-evaluation to guide your choices as you shape the way you relate to other people.

Make Relationships a Priority

I strive to develop productive and caring relationships.	I don't give much thought to understanding relationships.

5   4   3   2   1

Fostering healthy and productive relationships requires that we make a concerted effort to understand the dynamics of relationships and the strategies we can use to improve them.

Strategy: *Make an inventory of the relationships in your life in your Thinking Notebook. For each relationship, develop a "plan of action" based on the strategies in this chapter, and then implement your plan in your daily interactions.*

Develop a Strong, Integrated Self

I am a secure, integrated person with a healthy sense of self-love and self-respect.	I often feel insecure and I have a low sense of self-esteem.

5   4   3   2   1

In order to develop positive, healthy relationships with other people, you first have to have a positive, healthy relationship with yourself. It is very difficult to love and trust others if you don't love and trust yourself.

Strategy: *Review the section "Who Am I?," and use this as a basis for developing a stronger and more integrated "self."*

Think Critically about Your Relationships

I establish clear goals for my relationships and seek to look beneath the surface.	I let my relationships evolve without trying to set goals or achieve deep insight.

5   4   3   2   1

Many relationships falter, crushed by the weight of too many expectations or losing their way because they lack a clear sense of direction. You can establish clear goals and in-depth understanding in relationships without sacrificing their natural mystery and spontaneous growth. In fact, constructing an intelligible framework for your relationships will enrich their development, in the same way that tending a healthy garden requires providing the conditions for optimal growth.

Strategy: *Identify your goals for each of the important relationships in your life and record them in your Thinking Notebook. Then evaluate to what extent the relationships are meeting the goals you would like them to, and what actions you can take to improve them.*

Communicate Clearly with the Other Person(s)

| I am able to communicate clearly and honestly in my relationships. | I often encounter difficulties in relationships because of communication breakdowns. |

5   4   3   2   1

Clear and honest communication is the lifeblood of healthy relationships. It enables both parties to express their thoughts and feelings and to be listened to. Honesty helps build mutual trust and contributes to a genuine caring and empathy.

Strategy: *Evaluate the communication — or lack of same — in your relationships by using the elements of successful communication described in Step 6: Communicate Clearly.*

View All Perspectives in Your Relationships

| I actively strive to view situations from the other person's perspective. | I have difficulty in seeing things from the other person's point of view. |

5   4   3   2   1

Successful relationships depend on identifying imaginatively with other people's situations and fully appreciating what they are experiencing. It is this ability to truly empathize with others that acts as a catalyst for love, compassion, and understanding — the central emotions in every vital relationship. Taking other perspectives also helps you clear up misunderstandings and become more flexible in your responses.

Strategy: *Write down a description of how you see your relationship: What are your aspirations for the two of you? What are the strengths and weaknesses of the relationship? What things can be changed, and what must be accepted? Then, imagine yourself as the other person and answer these same questions as you think he or she would. Finally, invite the other person to complete the same activity. Exchange your descriptions and discuss them — you should have a lot to talk about.*

Build Trust through Reason in Your Relationships

I usually strive to be reasonable and provide explanations for my actions.	Other people frequently say that I am unreasonable, and I often act without thinking.

5   4   3   2   1

Reason is the framework that makes relationships possible. You build trust in other people (and they in you) because you believe their choices are governed or at least influenced by reason, and you depend on that assurance.

Strategy: Communicate the reasons for your behavior with the other people in your relationships by developing the habit of saying "I did — or want to do — this because . . ." At the same time, you should feel comfortable in asking the other people in your relationships why they did what they did or plan to do. This accountability and openness will have the cumulative effect of both clarifying and enhancing your relationships.

Foster Creativity and Positive Attitudes in Your Relationships

I make a consistent effort to bring creativity and a positive attitude to relationships.	My relationships often end up unimaginative, and I have a tendency to be critical.

5   4   3   2   1

The secret of maintaining vital relationships is retaining the same positive, creative energy that you brought to the beginning of your relationship. You can reinvigorate your relationships by permitting your creative impulses to energize every aspect of your life.

Strategy: Whatever significant relationships you are involved in, make a concerted effort to think positively, act creatively, and assume the best of the other person — and ask him to do the same. You might initially have to grit your teeth a few times in order to let provocations and perceived insults go by you without making a response in kind. But acting and responding with kindness, respect, and understanding will encourage these same qualities in well-intentioned friends and partners.

Value Freedom and Responsibility in Your Relationships

I try to accept responsibility for my life and respect the autonomy of others.	I find myself blaming others when things go wrong and I often try to control others.

5   4   3   2   1

Healthy relationships are ones in which the participants willingly take responsibility for themselves and value the freedom of others. By fully acknowledging your responsibility and by avoiding attempts to control and manipulate, you build trust and mutual respect.

Strategy: *Resist the natural tendency to avoid responsibility when things go wrong in your relationships. Acknowledging your responsibility is likely to disarm other people and encourage them to acknowledge their responsibility. Embrace fully your freedom of choice in relationships, and respect the rights of others to make independent choices based on the best information available.*

Problem-Solve in Your Relationship

I approach problems in my relationships in an organized way.	I have difficulty in thinking clearly about problems in my relationships.

5   4   3   2   1

Many people suspend their thinking abilities in the face of relationship difficulties, responding emotionally and not thoughtfully. But emotions need the guidance of reason in order to be pointed in productive directions, and so bringing an intelligent approach to problems is an essential part of sustaining successful relationships.

Strategy: *Identify several of the more manageable problems in your close relationships and, working with the other people, use the problem-solving approach explained in Step 4 to reach satisfactory solutions. As you gain confidence and expertise, expand your efforts to the more complex and challenging problems.*

Balance Dependence and Independence in Your Relationships

Most of my relationships strike a healthy balance between dependence and independence.	I often find that my relationships are either too dependent or too independent.

5   4   3   2   1

In general, it is wise to aim for a balance between dependence and independence, a harmony that is based on a strong and stable self. When you feel too dependent in a relationship, this is a symptom that your sense of self feels weak and incomplete. Excessive independence also derives from inner fragility and low self-esteem, making it difficult for you to develop close intimate relationships because of the emotional risk. The path to successful and fulfilling relationships lies in establishing a strong, vital sense of yourself that is grounded on self-respect.

Strategy: *Evaluate the key relationships in your life in terms of dependence and independence. If you find that there is a pattern of excessive dependence or independence, give some serious thought to the issues raised earlier in the chapter.*

SCORING GUIDE

Add up the numbers you circled for each of the self-evaluation items above and use the following Scoring Guide to evaluate your moral awareness.

Point Total	Interpretation
40–50	relate very well to others
30–39	relate moderately well to others
20–29	relate somewhat well to others
10–19	relate comparatively poorly to others

In interpreting your results, be sure to keep in mind that your score indicates how well you relate to others at the present time, *not* your *potential* to develop healthy relationships. If you scored lower than you would like, it means that you need to follow the suggestions in this chapter to develop fully your ability to relate to others to the level of which you are capable.

THINKING ACTIVITY

Fostering Healthy Relationships

No matter how highly developed you are at relating to others, you can become even more successful by *choosing* to pursue this aim. Your critical thinking abilities will give you the means to explore the relationships in your experience with insight, and your personal dedication to promoting productive relationships will provide you with the ongoing motivation. Remember that fostering healthy relationships is both a daily and a lifetime project. Nurture your continued growth by cultivating the qualities that we explored in this section, and record your progress in your Thinking Notebook.

- Make relationships a priority.
- Create a strong, integrated self.
- Communicate clearly.
- View all perspectives.
- Build trust through reason.
- Foster creativity.
- Value freedom and responsibility.
- Problem-solve.
- Balance dependence and independence.

CREATE A LIFE
PHILOSOPHY

We shall not cease from exploration
And the end of all our exploring
Will be to arrive where we started
And know the place for the first time.
— T. S. ELIOT, *Four Quartets*

THE UNEXAMINED LIFE IS NOT WORTH LIVING. We began this book with Socrates' provocative challenge, and it is now time to come full circle, reflecting back on your personal journey through the previous 8 Steps. As someone who has chosen to read a book such as this, you are likely striving to live a meaningful life, to become a person who is intellectually accomplished and morally enlightened. And though you might not think of yourself as a philosopher, your personal quest to understand your life in a deep and profound way qualifies you as a "lover of wisdom" — the Greek definition of *philosophy*. Does this condemn you to be a "discontented Socrates" rather than a "contented pig," as John Stuart Mill posed? Clearly not: people who search for life's deeper meanings, who strive to reach their full potential, have a much greater chance of living a "contented" life than those who simply live out their days without reflection or wonder. And the contentment that springs from a philosophical approach to living is a richer, more fulfilling experience than the more limited pleasures of an unthinking life.

397

This book has provided you with the opportunity to act on Socrates' dictate, to explore thoughtfully every significant dimension of your life The Thinker's Way. If you have worked through the 8 Steps, you will have begun the process of transforming yourself into a more enlightened person by:

- strengthening your *critical thinking*;
- expanding your *creativity*;
- increasing your *freedom*;
- improving your *problem-solving*;
- enhancing your *communication*;
- sharpening your *issue-analysis*;
- developing your *values*;
- enriching your *relationships*.

The purpose of this final chapter is to help you weave all of these threads together into a coherent whole, into an intelligent life philosophy.

Over the several thousand years of recorded human ideas, there have been countless attempts to construct life philosophies: by philosophers, religious leaders, political theorists, psychologists, novelists, scientists, and others. Many of these people have insightful things to say, and you should become familiar with all of those that interest you. But in the final analysis you need to construct *your own* Philosophy of Life. You need a "custom tailored" philosophy, not one that you simply take "off the rack." After a great deal of reading, discussion, reflection, and critical analysis, you may consciously choose to adopt an existing philosophy, but even then you will be modifying, adapting, and tailoring this theory to fit your unique self and special circumstances. More likely, you will take elements of a number of different philosophies and create your own synthesis.

In the end, you are responsible for the Philosophy of Life that you adopt. The quality of your philosophy will in large measure determine your personal happiness and success. It will define the quality of the life you live. Are you a person of substance that others will admire? Is your life characterized by stellar accomplishments and lasting relationships that will distinguish you as a memorable individual both during and after your life? What will be your epitaph? These are difficult questions, but they must be faced if you are to truly lead a life of purpose and meaning.

You have been working on your Philosophy of Life for a long time, though you may not have been aware of it. If you have been reflecting on the Thinking Activities in this book and expressing your ideas in your Thinking Notebook, you have had many opportunities to articulate your most important beliefs and to evaluate critically their viability. This is precisely the process used to construct a Philosophy of Life: forming beliefs through a process of critical evaluation. But a philosophy is more than just a collection of random beliefs; it is a *coherent system* of beliefs built around central organizing beliefs and principles. At its root, every philosophy tries to answer the "Big Questions," including:

- Who am I?
- What is the meaning of my life?

As we will see, seeking to answer these fundamental questions leads to many other questions — and answers — that touch on the major themes of this book.

Who Am I?

WHO ARE YOU? You are a remarkable and unique individual, a dynamic life-force, capable of *thinking critically*, *living creatively*, and *choosing freely*. These three essential dimensions of your "self" exist optimally when they work together in harmonious and synergistic unity.

Think of what you aspire to: a life of purpose and meaning, the respect and devotion of those around you, success and fulfillment in your chosen endeavors, a secure sense of who you are with the courage and vision to accomplish great things — these aspirations are within your grasp, but only if you develop *all* of these fundamental dimensions of yourself to their fullest potential.

"I AM A CRITICAL THINKER"

Every day presents you with decisions, forks in the road, and the choices that you make progressively shape you as a creature who, in the words of C. S. Lewis, is "heavenly" or "hellish." The starting point for understanding "who" you are is your *thinking* ability, that extraordinary capacity to symbolize, organize, and give meaning to your experience. Although everyone "thinks" in some sense, not everyone thinks intelligently, insightfully, wisely. This is the first goal of *The Thinker's Way*: When asked, "Who are you?," you will be able to respond, confidently and accurately, *"I am a critical thinker."* But how do you go about shaping yourself as a critical thinker? You need to use the conceptual tools of critical thinking and apply these in an ongoing way in your daily life.

CRITICAL THINKING TOOLS

Become More Reflective: Becoming a critical thinker begins with the process of *reflection*, making a concerted effort to examine your thinking process, explore the underlying levels of your "self," and answer the "big" questions that life poses. Critical thinkers have a reflective attitude toward life, automatically examining, exploring, and questioning meanings in their experience. They think about *moral* questions ("What is the morally right thing to do?"); *spiritual* questions ("How can I best develop my spiritual nature?); *humanistic* questions ("How can I best achieve my human potential?"); *existential* questions ("What is the meaning of life?"), and many others as well.

Support Your Points of View: As a critical thinker, you should be committed to supporting your conclusions with intelligent reasons and persuasive evidence. Critical thinkers habitually ask themselves *"Why?"* whenever they are analyzing an issue or listening to someone else present an idea. Asking *"Why?"* trains your mind to always look beneath the surface for the reasons and evidence that may (or may not) support various points of view, and it enables you to discriminate between views that are knowledgeable, reasonable, and informed and those that aren't. Resist making snap decisions about complex issues — "I don't think that the Boston au pair looks capable of killing a baby" — and carefully examine the evidence on *both* sides of the issue before reaching an informed conclusion.

Strive to Be Open-minded: While it's essential to support your own points of view, it's equally important to think empathetically within *other* points of view, even if they contradict your initial conclusions. This is a critical thinking tool that is vital to fostering your mental flexibility and developing the fullest understanding of the world. No one perspective, no matter how informed, is adequate for making sense of any complex issue, situation, or person. You need to make that extra effort to view things from multiple perspectives, and seek to understand the reasons and evidence that support those different perspectives.

Become Aware of Your Personal "Lenses": All individuals view the world through their own unique "lenses," which shape and color what they perceive, how they process information, and how they decide to act. The "prescription" of your lenses reflects everything that makes you "you" — individual values, past experiences, interests, biases, predispositions. To think critically you must become aware of your "lenses" (and those of others) by examining various viewpoints on issues and situations. This enables you to overcome your natural biases by taking them into account and compensating for them, and it encourages others to become more objective by making them aware of their own biases.

Evaluate the Accuracy of Information and the Credibility of Sources: Don't believe everything you read — or hear, or see. *All* information is biased and incomplete, and it is presented by sources of varying credibility. This critical thinking tool encourages you to cultivate a healthy skepticism and apply intellectual standards to all information that you encounter. A story like "I gave birth to alien triplets" in a supermarket tabloid or a commercial that promises you "sexual allure in a bottle" may be easy to discount, but even information provided by "reputable" news sources and individuals is often slanted, biased, and manipulative. You need to bring all of your reasoning abilities to bear in evaluating the arguments and detecting the fallacies that bombard you constantly.

"I AM CREATIVE"

Using *The Thinker's Way* as a guide, your second response to the question "Who are you?" should be "*I am a creative individual who brings a unique and valuable perspective to life.*" While your ability to *think critically* brings order and understanding to your life, your *creative thinking* enriches your life with vitality and meaning — that is, if you *choose* to let it. Many people view creativity as a luxury, reserved for children and artists. But in denying their creativity, they are denying an essential aspect of *who* they are. How do you awaken your *creative potentials*, which for most people are "sleeping" and go unrealized? As we explored in Step 2: Live Creatively, the natural creative impulses of most people are progressively discouraged by the pressures to conform to accepted ways of thinking; by the humdrum details of everyday living; and by the fear of failure if they try out unique, untested ideas. These are intimidating anti-creativity forces, while on the other side of the scale, there are probably very few pro-creativity influences in your life. The fact is that most people, groups, and organizations do not want you to be an original, independent, creative individual. They prefer you to be passive, easily manipulated, anxious to conform to existing practices — and not *too* successful.

Your creative Essence is an essential part of who you are, and forsaking this creative center because of the pressure of conformity comes at an incalculable cost. When you commit yourself to living creatively, you will discover that you have the inexhaustible resources of your creative Essence at your disposal. Once released, your creative energies will suffuse every area of your life, enhancing their vitality and meaning for you. Lived creatively, your life will be one of daily adventure, as you eagerly engage the unexplored mysteries of each new experience. You will feel *alive* in the way you once did as a child, attuned to rich textures, symphonic sounds, and vibrant colors of your world.

CREATIVITY TOOLS

How can you achieve this creatively enlightened state of being? Step 2: Live Creatively explored practical strategies for unleashing your creative energies and discovering your creative Essence.

Learn to Understand and Trust the Creative Process: Although there is no recipe for creativity, there are attitudes and insights that nurture the growth of your creative self. These include:

- Explore the creative situation thoroughly.
- Work with absorption and cultivate mindfulness.
- Prime the creative pump with activities like brainstorming and mind-mapping.
- Allow time for ideas to incubate.
- Seize ideas when they emerge and follow them through.

As you learn to attune yourself to your creative process, it will gradually come to penetrate and infuse all dimensions of your life. You will find that you won't have to try consciously to "be creative"; instead, it will become habitual, you will naturally approach all aspects of your life in a creative fashion. You will learn to "expect the unexpected," rely on your creative intuitions, and guide your choices by the illumination provided by your creative insight.

Eliminate the "Voice of Judgment": Your "Voice of Judgment" (VOJ) embodies all of the negative inhibitions and destructive criticisms that you have internalized throughout your life. To live creatively, you must vanquish the VOJ, and though this is a challenging task, it is eminently achievable by using the strategies detailed in Step 2.

Establish a Creative Environment: Living creatively is best achieved by surrounding yourself with people who encourage these impulses in you, and in turn welcome your support of their creative natures. The synergy of creative people working together is an extraordinary natural event that produces optimal personal growth and stunning creative breakthroughs.

Choose to Become a More Creative Person: Achieving your creative potential means deciding that you want to become more creative and then *choosing* to implement this commitment in your daily life. You need to choose, on an ongoing basis, to make creativity a priority, take creative risks, cultivate your imagination, strive for independence, foster mindfulness, cultivate curiosity, and avoid negative judgments. The more you make these choices, the more this creative way of thinking, feeling and acting becomes naturally integrated into your life.

"I AM FREE"

Your third response to the question "Who are you?" should be, based on the approach of this book, *"I am a free individual who is responsible for creating myself."* Your capacities to think critically and live creatively are of little use to you unless you freely choose to exercise these abilities.

You are *"condemned"* to be free, in Sartre's words, because freedom is an intrinsic part of your nature. You were created with the capacity to create your self, guided by the insight of your intellect and the spontaneous intuitions of your creative Essence. But personal freedom is an achievement, and your capacity to make free choices only becomes genuine freedom when you seize it and the profound responsibility that comes with it. In many instances, people are not able to make genuinely free choices because their freedom is constrained by external threats or internal compulsions, *of which they are often unaware.* In addition, people often try to *escape* from their freedom because they don't want to assume the burden of responsibility that freedom entails.

In contrast, when you fully accept your freedom, you redefine your daily life and your future in a new light. By working to neutralize the constraints on your autonomy and guiding your life in positive directions, you see alternatives that were not previously visible, concealed by the limitations of your vision. Your future becomes open, a field of rich possibilities that you will be able to explore and choose among. A life that is free is a life that is vital and exciting, suffused with unexpected opportunities, success, and the personal fulfillment that comes from a life well lived.

FREEDOM TOOLS

Accept Your Freedom and Responsibility: In order to become fully free, you must *choose* to embrace your freedom and the responsibility that comes with it. Many people would like to have freedom without responsibility, but that's not possible. You need to have the strength of character to say, "I freely chose to be who I am; I am fully responsible for what I do; and I have the power to create myself as the person I want to be." To make these statements and *mean* them requires great personal courage, but they reflect a Philosophy of Life that is enlightened and inspiring. By liberating yourself from the habit of blaming others for things that go wrong in your life, you are committing yourself to be the author of your life, empowered to shape your destiny through your freely made choices.

Break Free from the Constraints on Your Freedom: When you make a free choice, it can only be considered genuinely free if it is not coerced by external forces or compelled by internal demons. This is a very challenging project, though it becomes progressively easier as you work toward the goal of liberating and strengthening your free will. You need to use your critical thinking abilities to become aware of outside influences, and then employ your willpower to liberate yourself from their power. Analogously, you are also victimized by many internal forces that do not represent your truest desires and deepest values. These internal constraints may have initially resulted from events in your life, but you have perpetuated them through the inner messages you use to talk to yourself. We are all vulnerable to this negative self-talk that, repeated over and over to ourselves, shapes our thinking and feelings in self-destructive ways: "I'm a failure," "I'll never amount to anything," "I'm unlovable." Once again, your *critical thinking* abilities provide you with the insight to become aware of these internal voices and devise a plan of action to replace them with positive, constructive voices. Your *freedom to choose* gives you the strength and determination to execute the plan, built around the model of Search, Challenge, Solve explained in Step 3.

Choose the "Good Life" for Yourself and Others: According to the psychologist Carl Rogers, *each individual's Good Life is the one selected when there is psychological freedom to move in any direction.* Having freed yourself from external and internal constraints, you are able to fulfill your true human potential and you are able to live fully in every moment. By achieving psychological freedom and heightened awareness, you can begin to trust your intuitions because they accurately reflect your deepest values, your genuine desires, your authentic self. The choices that emerge from this enlightened state will, in conjunction with your personal freedom, help you create a life that is enriching, exciting, challenging, stimulating, meaningful, and fulfilling. You will stretch and grow as you both discover and achieve your potential. Your personal quest is not an isolated project, as you are part of a complex web of social relationships. Achieving the Good Life for yourself inevitably involves working in concert with others to help them achieve their own Good Lives, as they help you to realize yours.

What Is the Meaning of My Life?

THE PURPOSE of this book has been to serve as a guide for your personal journey of self-discovery and self-transformation. Its intention has been *not* to provide you with answers, but rather to equip you with the thinking abilities, conceptual tools, and personal insights to *find your own answers*. Each "Step" has addressed an essential dimension of human experience, and the issues they raise form a comprehensive blueprint for your life, a life that you wish to be clear in purpose and rich in meaning.

In order for you to discover the meaning of your life, you need to seek meaning actively, commit yourself to meaningful projects, meet the challenges that life throws to you with courage and dignity. You will have little chance of achieving meaning in your life if you simply *wait* for meaning to present itself to you or if you persist in viewing yourself as a *victim* of life. If you squander your personal resources by dwelling on the "unfairness" of life and wallowing in self-pity, then there will be no room left in your life for genuine meaning. Reversing this negative orientation requires a radical shift of perspective, from complaining about what life "owes" you to accepting the responsibility of meeting life's expectations, whether rewarding or cruel. Even in the dire conditions of the concentration camp, there were men, like Victor Frankl, who chose to act heroically, devoting themselves to comforting others or giving away their last piece of bread. They were living testament to the truth that even though life may take away everything from a person, it cannot take away *"the last of the human freedoms — to choose one's attitude in any given set of circumstances, to choose one's own way."*

Though you may have to endure hardship and personal tragedy, you still have the opportunity to invest your life with meaning by the way that you choose to respond to your suffering: whether you let it defeat you, or whether you are able to rise above it triumphantly. In the words of the German philosopher Frederick Nietzsche, *"He who has a why to live can bear with almost any how."* Your ultimate and irreducible freedom to *choose* freely your responses to life's situations defines you as a person and determines the meaningfulness of your existence.

But how do you determine the "right" way to respond, the path that will infuse your life with meaning and fulfillment? You need to *think critically, live creatively, and choose freely* — all of the thinking abilities and life attitudes that you have been cultivating throughout this book. They will provide you with the clear vision and strength of character required for you to create yourself as a worthy individual living a life of purpose and meaning. Your explorations throughout this book have given you the opportunity to become acquainted with yourself and the potential that resides within you: your unique intellectual gifts, imaginative dreams, and creative talents. As the psychologist Abraham Maslow notes, you are so constructed that you naturally press toward fuller and fuller being, realizing your potentialities, becoming fully human, everything that you *can* become. But you alone can determine what choices you will make among all of the possibilities: which will be condemned to nonbeing and which will be actualized, creating your immortal portrait, the monument to your existence.

Clearly, the ultimate meaning of your life can never be fully realized within the confines of your own self. Meaning is encountered and created through your efforts to *go beyond* yourself, as Frankl explains:

> The true meaning of life is to be discovered in the world rather than within man or his own psyche. . . . Being human always points, and is directed, to something, or someone, other than oneself — be it a meaning to fulfill or another human being to encounter. The more one forgets himself — by giving himself to a cause to serve or another person to love — the more human he is and the more he actualizes himself.

In the same way that "happiness" and "success" are the outgrowths of purposeful and productive living rather than ends in themselves, so your life's meaning is a natural by-product of reaching beyond yourself to touch the lives of others. This self-transcendence may take the form of a creative work or a heroic action that you display to the human community. It may also be expressed through your loving and intimate relationships with other people, your contribution to individual members of your human community.

What is the meaning of your life? It is the truth that you will discover as you strive, through your daily choices, to create yourself as an authentic individual, committed to enhancing the lives of others, fulfilling your own unique potential, and attuning yourself to your spiritual nature and the mysteries of the universe. It is the reality you will find as you choose to respond to both the blessings and the suffering in your life with courage and dignity. Joy and suffering, fulfillment and angst, birth and death — these are the raw materials that life provides you. Your challenge and responsibility is to shape these experiences into a meaningful whole, guided by a Philosophy of Life that you have constructed with your abilities to think critically, live creatively, and choose freely. This is the path you must take in order to live a life that is rich with meaning lived by a person who is noble and heroic — a life led *The Thinker's Way*.

INDEX

ABOUT THE AUTHOR

John Chaffee, Ph.D., is a nationally recognized leader in the study of intellectual development. His books include the bestselling *Thinking Critically, The Thinker's Guide to College Success,* and *Critical Thinking, Thoughtful Writing.* He is Director of the New York Center for Critical Thinking and Language Learning and Professor of Philosophy at the City University of New York. He conducts Critical Thinking workshops and lectures throughout the country. He can be reached by e-mail at JCthink@aol.com.

Now in paperback

CONSCIOUSNESS EXPLAINED
by Daniel C. Dennett

Drawing a wealth of new information from the fields of neuroscience, psychology, and artificial intelligence, Daniel C. Dennett refutes the traditional, commonsense theory of consciousness and presents a startling new model.

"Nothing short of brilliant ... as audacious as its title."

— GEORGE JOHNSON,
New York Times Book Review

"A good-humored, imaginative, richly instructive book.... His sophisticated discourse is as savvy and articulate about good beer or the Boston Celtics as it is about parallel processing, modern cognitive experimentation, neuropathology, echolocation by bats, or Ludwig Wittgenstein."

— PHILIP MORRISON,
Scientific American

"A profound and important book that is also clear, exciting, and witty; *Consciousness Explained* represents philosophy at its best."

—DOUGLAS R. HOFSTADTER,
author of *Gödel, Escher, Bach*

Available wherever books are sold

Now in paperback

HOW TO MEDITATE
A Guide to Self-Discovery
by Lawrence LeShan

An unrivaled source of inspiration and practical instruction for anyone seeking inner peace, relief from stress, and increased self-knowledge.

"A practical guide to meditation. Drawing upon such disciplines as Zen, Sufism, yoga, Christian and Jewish mysticism, LeShan describes specific exercises and programs ranging from breath counting and simple mantras to group movement and sensory awareness."

— SAM LOVE,
Washington Post Book World

"One of the most sensible books on the subject.... LeShan's wide experience and sound scholarship are evident in each helpful chapter."

— *Library Journal*

Available wherever books are sold